THE COMPLETE
GEORGE BEST

EVERY GAME - EVERY GOAL

BY DARREN PHILLIPS

EMPIRE
PUBLICATIONS

First published in 2008

EMPIRE PUBLICATIONS
1 Newton Street, Manchester M1 1HW
© Darren Phillips 2008

ISBN 1 901 746 51 8

Cover design and layout: Ashley Shaw

Printed in Great Britain by: Digital Book Print Ltd, Milton Keynes, UK.

contents

Introduction

If Duncan Edwards epitomised the 1950s football hero, so George Best emerged as the suave playboy bestriding the game a decade later. A flawed genius with enough sex appeal to sell everything from haute couture to pork sausages, Best became Britain's first soccer superstar, transcending the football firmament and taking a starring role in national life.

As likely to feature on the front page as the back, his career on the pitch often became an irrelevance as gossip columnists speculated on his latest girlfriend, nightclub exploit or all-night bender.

The attention didn't do the once humble Belfast lad any favours. He was different alright, but sometime after his starring role in the 1968 European Cup, Best crossed the fine line dividing favouritism and lawlessness, confirming the belief of his team-mates that there was one rule for George and another for the rest of the squad. As a result team spirit and the player's own mental state suffered.

Following the retirement of his mentor Sir Matt Busby, George descended further into the celebrity abyss. As his mates settled down with marriage and kids, Best hit the bottle - a European champion at 22, he retired in 1972, before making a final failed comeback before leaving top level football for good in January 1974 following a New Years Day defeat at Queens Park Rangers.

It would be easy, from this brief summation of his career, to conclude that Best wasted his talent. Yet it is my belief that Best's achievements have never been fully appreciated by the British public. An unhealthy obsession with celebrity tends to cloud most issues and the football career of George Best was perhaps one of the first to suffer, for there is little doubt that George acheived more than most give him credit for.

Certainly George's celebrity might explain why, when he passed away in November 2005, the tributes were out of all proportion to those accorded a famous footballer. Best, the first superstar footballer, was accorded more reverance than fellow professionals such as Bobby Moore and Stanley Matthews.

From the minute-by-minute accounts of his final hours to the State

Funeral in his honour at Stormont in Northern Ireland via the floral tributes left by supporters of all persuasions outside Old Trafford, Britain hadn't seen anything like it since Princess Diana's death.

Yet among the tributes to his tricks on the pitch and his capacity for enjoyment off it, there was little concentration on Best the footballer. There were debates about how he threw it all away, how he could have gone on to bigger and better things if he had stopped drinking but I maintain his contribution to football in general and Manchester United in particular was greater than that.

For instance, commentators mentioned the brevity of George's career, how he retired from top class football at the age of just 28 (when most footballers are approaching their peak) and dismissed his football career after 1968 as a sad postscript to what had gone before. They often ignored the fact that George appeared 470 times for United - that's more appearances than Tom Finney made for Preston. Or that he scored 179 goals and was top scorer for United every season from between 1967-68 and 1971-72.

Alongside fantastic goals he also scored some fairly straightforward ones, perhaps sliding in at the far post to poke home a cross or beating the keeper from the edge of the area with a snapshot. Not only that but some of his finest performances came in a team that was clearly past its peak. He single-handedly took United to the top of the league in Christmas 1971 with a string of performances that took the breath away while his double-hat-trick at Northampton in 1970, following a month long suspension imposed by the FA, is a feat unlikely to be repeated in the modern era.

For some reason Best was always thought of as selfish, not least by colleagues such as Bobby Charlton and Denis Law who would scream for the ball before applauding the Irishman as he wheeled away in celebration at yet another improbable goal scored. Yet both Charlton and Law have been accused of selfishness themselves and one supposes that team-mates screamed at Pele, Cruyff and Maradona in the same way.

Best's ability to juggle the ball through some of the toughest defences British football has produced, over a mudheap that most modern footballers wouldn't deign to play on, was unparalleled. Yet just as astounding was his goals to game ratio. For a winger to score every two and a half games was almost unheard of. In an earlier era the great Stanley Matthews scored 71 goals in 690 club appearances - or just under a goal every 10 games.

Last season, Ronaldo shattered records as he finally surpassed a few of

George's scoring records - an astonishing feat. Yet even Cristiano will admit that compared to the conditions his predecessor played under, he leads a sheltered life largely protected by referees with laws that favour attacking football. Best, on the other hand, had none of these advantages - that he avoided serious injury was in itself a minor miracle.

Darren Phillips has compiled an excellent work that follows the intricacies of George's career - tracing every game he played for Manchester United and Northern Ireland with summaries of his career at Fulham, in the NASL and the various other guest appearances he made for teams as diverse as Hibernian and Bournemouth covering a 20 year playing career that took in more highs and lows than any other. It sheds fresh light on one of the stellar careers in British football.

Enjoy the book.

Ashley Shaw
Editor.

...in the making

A t the Belfast home of George Best's parents there stood a photograph of a baby boy controlling a toy ball with a poise that belied his tender age - these were the first steps of George Best - football genius. Yet as George took his first tentative steps with his toy ball, a quiet revolution was taking place across the Irish Sea.

Matt Busby's arrival at Manchester United wasn't top of the sporting agenda in 1945. The Red Devils had been the city's poor relations before the war and few would have had their name top of the list of challengers for the First Division title or FA Cup. Somehow Busby fashioned a unique spirit, taking the club to the runners-up spot in four out of five seasons after the war before clinching the First Division title in 1952.

More memorably United won the 1948 FA Cup playing an attacking brand of football at odds with the drab certainty of post-war life. In these years Busby transformed United from also-rans to glory boys – the club were back page news, everyone's second favourite team.

In the years that followed Busby switched tack and sought to recruit their own lads via a comprehensive youth system. This move was rushed through out of necessity as much as anything else for United were still playing home games at Manchester City's Maine Road and paying high rents for the privilege. Unlike the 'big' clubs of the day, United couldn't afford to buy the finished product so instead attempted to polish the rough diamonds hewn from youth football into the real thing.

By the mid-1950s Busby had fashioned a first eleven of youngsters that threatened to rule both domestic and European football for the next decade. They were christened the Busby Babes and, barring signings such as Tommy Taylor, they had all emerged from this new set-up.

The average age of the 1955-56 championship winning side was just 22 and when the same team retained the crown 12 months later and made a run to the last four of the European Cup - only losing to the great Real

Madrid - Manchester United's future at the top of the game seemed assured. Within 12 months however that hegemony was shattered. The Munich Air Disaster wiped out eight of that promising team, including the gargantuan Duncan Edwards, captain Roger Byrne and England's finest centre-forward Tommy Taylor among others. Busby was twice read the last rites but recovered from life threatening injuries.

The following five seasons were clouded by the fall-out from the crash. Assistant manager Jimmy Murphy had been chief trainer to the Babes and, with only Bobby Charlton and Bill Foulkes left in any kind of shape to continue, United struggled against a tide of well-meaning hysteria.

Busby's quest for European success was still not sated by the crash and he felt he owed it to the victims' families to continue the search for the Holy Grail - the European Cup. To win it Busby also recognised that he didn't have the time or the resources to develop players himself but was forced to sign players. Denis Law and Pat Crerand were purchased in 1962 and with Bobby Charlton developing into a world class midfielder the Scot felt sure that, following victory in the 1963 FA Cup Final, United were in a position to challenge for the top honours again. He just needed to find the the elusive final piece in the jigsaw…

Concurrently United's scouting operation had got wind of a genius from Belfast. When Northern Ireland scout Bob Bishop first clapped eyes on Best he could have been forgiven for thinking that the youngster's frail frame would never withstand the rigours of professional football. He was tiny, standing just over five feet tall and weighed in at a mere eight stones but appearances were deceptive. With the ball at his feet the teenager was electric and a telegram message sent to Old Trafford by Bishop recommending the then 15 year old for trials stating simply, "I think I've found you a genius".

It was a huge billing to live up to but Busby and his coaches quickly recognised that they did indeed have something very special. During training sessions at The Cliff, Best would repeatedly embarrass senior professionals - Northern Ireland goalkeeper Harry Gregg recalls all too vividly that George took great delight in waltzing round or nut-megging experienced professionals and goalies alike!

Yet George was shy and retiring. Within 24 hours of arriving at Old Trafford he returned to Belfast blaming homesickness. A fortnight later after long conversations between his father Dickie and the manager, George returned.

Best's father and his father figure in Manchester forged a cordial relationship over the years and spoke regularly. During one talk at a banquet to celebrate the club's 1963 FA Cup win, the United boss was asked for an honest assessment of his son's abilities by Mr Best. Dickie believed that if Busby felt his son had no chance of making the grade he could find young George a job at a printers back in Belfast but as the job could only be held for six months a final opinion was  needed. Dickie got his answer - within weeks George made his first team debut.

Though he could not sign professional forms until the age of 17, a job was found for him as a clerk with the Manchester Ship Canal Company and then as an electrician with a firm owned by a United fan. The jobs were nothing more than shams which allowed him to earn a living while training but they provided George with money to sample the delights of the city while he settled in at his Chorlton digs.

Meanwhile Busby ordered his coaches not to try and instil the disciplines most professionals were expected to learn for fear of coaching away the very thing that made George so different from a host of aspiring teens. The ball skills and the impudent flicks, tricks and mazy dribbles which often saw defenders flat on their backsides would not usually have been encouraged but this was a special case.

The George Best legend continued to grow, with his name mentioned in hushed tones by United supporters. Regulars at youth and reserve team games told of his exploits at that level and supporters were soon anxious to see the lad in the first team.

On Saturday 14th September 1963 they finally got their chance - they would not be disappointed...

1963-64
BOY BEST FLASHES
IN RED ATTACK

MANCHESTER UNITED 1 WEST BROMWICH ALBION 0
DIVISION ONE 14 SEPTEMBER 1963

THE CUSTOMARY GENTLE introduction began in the 'A' and 'B' teams though with rave reviews in his favour and having finally been able to shed his amateur status in May 1963 Best was selected for the reserves. He played just three times in the Central League before being handed a first team debut for a Division One game played at home against West Bromwich Albion in September.

The absence of Ian Moir created an opportunity for the pack to be reshuffled slightly with George coming in on the right side of midfield but as United boasted a number of versatile wingers there was little immediate indication that George would play. In fact the reverse was true. Matt Busby told the player he had been drafted in as cover should one of the other senior men be forced out. However, all along the manager had pencilled him into the starting XI but decided to allay any nerves by springing a last minute surprise and informing his charge that he would be starting just an hour before kick off.

Albion's Welsh international Graham Williams, a dogged left back who would eventually captain the side to an FA Cup win, had little knowledge of the young man who would face him that afternoon but must have fancied his chances against the slight looking winger. He had no such luxury. Precocious and with little respect for reputations one of Best's first moves on receiving the ball was to poke it in front of Williams and then perform an audacious nutmeg. Other vastly experienced opponents were similarly embarrassed.

Somewhat angered by his treatment from the upstart Williams weighed in with a number of heavy tackles intended to intimidate the young debutant. Best had a member of his own coaching staff Jimmy Murphy to thank for the bruises he would be nursing as a result. The United coach was in charge of the Welsh national side and advised his full-backs to hammer wingers who tried it on, reasoning that most flair players were cowards.

Murphy's theory was a good one for the most part though Best refused to stop running or attempting to use his skills. However, he was switched to the opposite flank after half-time when he saw much more of the ball and enjoyed an easier time. Many years later the defender was said to have stopped George at a function and asked to look at his face. When a puzzled George asked why Williams replied 'all I've ever seen was your arse disappearing up the touchline'.

United took the spoils with the only goal of the game scored by David Sadler who shared lodgings with George in his early days at Old Trafford and had made his breakthrough the previous month. Sadler's progress was a source of inspiration but it was a return to the second string for Best who had to be content with life on the fringes for the next three months before getting another chance.

Within hours of the final whistle the *Manchester Evening News* headline, 'Boy Best Flashes in Red Attack' neatly summed up the contribution of the winger but George himself was slightly disappointed with his debut feeling he didn't do himself justice. Matt Busby's decision to place him straight back into the second string and not include him in first team squads for a number of weeks could have been taken as an indication that he agreed but nothing was further from the truth.

Whether the player knew it or not his career to that point had been carefully developed by the man at the top who knew he had a rare if precocious talent which he needed to bring through steadily.

MANCHESTER UNITED 5 BURNLEY 1
DIVISION ONE 28 DECEMBER 1963

MOIR RETURNED TO the side a couple of days after the West Brom game and shared the position with David Herd to accommodate various reshuffles over the next dozen games. Results were mixed throughout this period and included a 6-1 hammering at Burnley's Turf Moor ground on Boxing Day. The sides were due to meet at Old Trafford 48 hours later and Best, who had learnt of the reverse while in Belfast having been given time off for the festive period, was asked to report for duty ahead of schedule. His spell of home leave curtailed and reckoning that his recall could attract a premium price, he agreed on condition that he was flown to Manchester and then back to Ulster soon after the game.

The club agreed and were rewarded for the indulgence with a 5-1 win and a debut goal for

Best who opened the scoring with a right footed shot from the edge of the area. With all the confidence of an experienced professional, rather than a raw teen who had only recently ended his apprenticeship, George gave a complete exhibition of his talents and experienced left back Eric Alder - a regular with Northern Ireland - had a torrid afternoon. He also switched flanks to give right back John Angus an occasional roasting too.

Balls were put through legs, into space either side of the defender and when George wasn't looking to use his pace, his quick feet mesmerised anyone brave enough to mount a challenge. Best

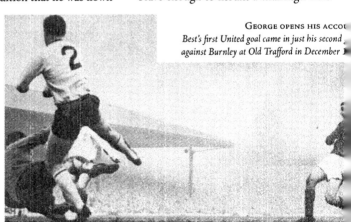

GEORGE OPENS HIS ACCOU
Best's first United goal came in just his second
against Burnley at Old Trafford in December 1

thought he would not actually get a game until the defence of the FA Cup began the following week with a tie against Second Division Southampton. Best did indeed feature in that match and retained his place until the end of the season.

Shay Brennan and Albert Quixall, who had played on the flanks until that point, were dispensed with and replaced by Best and 16 year-old Liverpudlian Willie Anderson. The Boxing Day humiliation proved to be Quixall's last contribution to the club before a transfer to Oldham Athletic. Brennan, a full back comfortable on either flank, had been asked to play further up as he had in youth football and did return to make many more appearances for United over the next

seven years but mostly at full-back.

Graham Moore and David Herd scored two goals a piece to complete the rout. There had been no attempt to man mark Best who, having featured just once in the senior side three months earlier, had apparently disappeared without trace. No one from the Turf Moor coaching staff was likely to have seen him on scouting missions and even if they had it's debatable whether they would have been able to work out a way to contain him. His abundant energy, effervescent ball skills and electric pace made him almost impossible to defend legally. Already defenders up and down the land were taking note.

SOUTHAMPTON 2 MANCHESTER UNITED 3
FA Cup 3rd Rd 4 January 1964

Though Southampton were a Second Division side and unfancied in this tie they were challenging for promotion having won eight of their last nine games so could not be taken lightly. Their confidence looked well-founded as they strolled into a 2-0 half-time lead after Terry Paine and Martin Chivers scored within a minute of each other.

Publicly Matt Busby refused to be drawn on his selection saying he would not make up his mind until the eve of the game but most attention was heaped on the teenage wingers who had done so

well against Burnley and surely played themselves into the team as a result. They enhanced their reputation as United mounted a recovery which Best and his partner on the opposite flank, the similarly raw Anderson, played no small part in.

Graham Moore scored his third goal in two games courtesy of a fine cross five minutes after the interval. David Herd and Paddy Crerand also got on to the scoresheet to see United through by the odd goal in five.

MANCHESTER UNITED 1 BIRMINGHAM CITY 2
Division One 11 January 1964

Denis Law returned to the side after suspension to link up with Best at

inside left but Bobby Charlton dropped out of the reckoning to be replaced by

David Sadler. Willie Anderson, who had originally been named as twelfth man, would have come in had he not been suffering from a bout of 'flu. David Herd was shoved over to outside-right.

Former City forward Alex Harley gave Birmingham a deserved lead when he beat covering defenders and rounded keeper David Gaskell to slip the ball into an unguarded net.

United had the lion's share of possession at most other times but couldn't gel as too many big players had quiet games and they paid the penalty for some slapdash play and an inability to hit the target. When they did Colin Withers was in excellent form.

Untidy passing provided plenty of possession for the visitors and Best often linked well with Law. However, the team's overall performance was mediocre and these passages of play ultimately allowed Birmingham to score both their goals.

WEST BROMWICH ALBION 1 MANCHESTER UNITED 4
DIVISION ONE 18 JANUARY 1964

BEST, WHO HAD been omitted from an under-21 team to play England youth at Old Trafford in midweek, finally made the same starting line-up as Bobby Charlton and Denis Law in the return league fixture with West Bromwich Albion. The three would eventually become known as the 'Holy Trinity' and the performance of each was nothing short of heavenly for the entire 90 minutes.

The last few clashes with Midlands opposition had seen United well beaten by Wolves, Aston Villa and Birmingham. Charlton's return was a boost but Best made a real difference. Experienced right back Don Howe was charged with keeping as close as he could to George but found his many seasons as a professional did him little good. The West Brom skipper was wearing gloves on a cold winter afternoon which drew some derision from the United players. Most of the first team had caused a stir a few weeks earlier by wearing tracksuit bottoms.

Tricky conditions required Best to adjust his usual style and take a touch more than normal but he adapted quickly and was outstanding at both ends. Energised for the entire 90 minutes he gave Baggies' outside-right Clive Clark a torrid time by constantly chasing back and refusing to give the midfielder an inch. Clark snapped at shots and crosses as a result which affected his accuracy.

Busby's men left the Hawthorns as comfortable 4-1 winners. Each of the trio scored with Law claiming two but George's goal was the most stylish. Taking a pass from the Scottish international he seemed heavily out-numbered but a drop of the shoulders and a burst of pace took him clear. Al though the angle was acute, geometry mattered little as Best slid the ball in with little difficulty.

Afterwards there were complaints about the pitch. Most players thought it was a 'glue pot' which saw many players wear baseball shoes rather than boots to retain their balance.

MANCHESTER UNITED 4 BRISTOL ROVERS 1
FA Cup 4th Rd 25 January 1964

BRISTOL ROVERS HAD upset the form book on their last meeting with United eight years previously, winning 4-0. Even though The Pirates had dropped a division and were now a middle-ranking club in the third tier of English football, nothing was left to chance. Just days after beating West Brom, the United squad began preparations with a few days in Llandudno, North Wales.

Switching Bobby Charlton to central midfield was a major boost for the club and it gave Best a left-wing niche from which he could shine - vital if he was to retain his place. But it threatened to be a poisoned chalice for the England man at international level as Alf Ramsay already had a settled central midfield and many believed that playing in that position week-in, week-out would prove a bar to selection at International level.

Another youngster, Phil Chisnall, a star for England's under-23 team and United's youth side, came in for Graham Moore. The forward had been given a few chances but couldn't resist Moore permanently and only gained temporary recalls. Rovers had a few early chances but otherwise United were in total command with Best a constant thorn in the side of Doug Hillard who had to resort to unfair means in order to halt him.

Law opened the scoring, grabbing the first of his hat-trick. David Herd also netted in what turned out to be a comfortable win even though United didn't play that well for long periods. An injury to Noel Cantwell was responsible in some part. The skipper took a knock early on and was pushed to outside-left. The switch was a necessity in the days before substitutes but it affected The Reds rhythm as they soldiered on with ten fit men.

MANCHESTER UNITED 3 ARSENAL 1
Division One 2 February 1964

AN EARLY GOAL from David Herd, who followed up his own effort when Jim Furnell only half-saved, prompted United to drop back for a spell. McCulloch equalised on 16 minutes and the Gunners pressed hard to get ahead but United's backline held firm. Maurice Setters then Law gave the score a lop sided look when Arsenal seemed good value for at least a point.

LEICESTER CITY 3 MANCHESTER UNITED 2
Division One 8 February 1964

DENIS LAW OPENED the scoring within two minutes against the side United had defeated in last season's cup final but through no real fault of his own was responsible for his side leaving Filbert Street without a point to show for their efforts. Mike Stringfellow equalised then Billy Hodgson made the most of

Leicester's domination of the second half to make it 3-1.

David Herd narrowed the gap and United would have gained a share of the spoils had Law's late equaliser not been judged offside. A Best header looked easy enough for Gordon Banks until he spotted the onrushing Scot in his line of vision. Rather than concentrate totally on the save Banks was distracted and uncharacteristically allowed the effort through his hands. Law was almost on the line when the ball hit the net.

The linesman reasoned that he must have been offside to reach that position so quickly but failed to account for Denis's speed. When the ball was struck toward goal he was in a ruck of players. Anticipating an error he had rushed towards the keeper in order to pick up the scraps, most obervers reckoned he was onside.

BARNSLEY 0 MANCHESTER UNITED 4
FA Cup 5th Rd 15 February 1964

Lowly Barnsley may only have been a Third Division outfit but they were immensely proud to host one of England's biggest clubs and earn a chance of an upset. As a result they came out fighting, though they were lucky to see an early Bobby Charlton effort ruled offside.

As the visitors, United were not expected to press. Then again Matt Busby's men were not the type of side to look for the odd chance then sit on an advantage. Best established a lead midway through the first half when a clever flick from Law played him in. His forward play

had been impeccable while his defending was appreciated by his team-mates as he ably supported Noel Cantwell at left back. Law made it 2-0 just after the break and Herd added a third two minutes later. Best returned the compliment for the first goal providing a chance for Law who yet again gambled on a colleague's effort only being half saved.

This time he beat the offside flag when Best's shot dribbled through the keeper's hands. It may well have gone in but Denis took no chances and poked it over the line.

MANCHESTER UNITED 5 BOLTON WANDERERS 0
Division One 19 February 1964

Bolton were struggling to avoid the drop and a sound hammering by United failed to help their cause. Best was magnificent and made light of Roy Hartle's fearsome reputation, embarrassing The Trotters' skipper throughout and beating him on the inside for the first goal. George let fly a shot which may well have been accurate enough to beat the keeper but a

deflection from Dave Lennard certainly helped. A clean strike and excellent finish in the 71st minute wrapped up the game.

Denis Law had missed a penalty earned after a cynical foul by Hartley on Best when he was about to pull the trigger just moments earlier. David Herd with a couple and Bobby Charlton completed the scoring.

BLACKBURN ROVERS 1 MANCHESTER UNITED 3
DIVISION ONE 22 FEBRUARY 1964

THOUGH PHIL CHISNALL grabbed a lead for United Blackburn, who had won just once win since Boxing Day and exited the cup to Fourth Division Oxford United, were by far the better team until the break and deservedly equalised soon after the restart.

Best had passed a fitness test on his ankle and gave defender John Bray the run-a-round all afternoon helping United into a deserved lead, before they pulled further away courtesy of Law's top class performance. Strangely Best rarely strayed from the touchline but did test Fred Else with a high shot that the keeper did well to deal with.

Victory marked the start of a huge week in the club's bid for treble glory.

MANCHESTER UNITED 4 SPORTING LISBON 1
EUROPEAN CUP WINNERS' CUP QF 1ST LEG 25 FEBRUARY 1964

WINNING THE FA CUP against Leicester City the previous May had seen United return to European competition for the first time since Munich. There had been an invitation to contest the European Cup in 1958/59 at the behest of Uefa but this was withdrawn at the Football League's insistence following a complaint from then champions Wolves.

Prior to George's emergence in the first team, Tilburg Willem II of Holland had been well beaten in the first round. Then came holders Tottenham Hotspur who won the first leg 2-0 but had their advantage overturned at Old Trafford as United came through 4-3 on aggregate.

Portuguese side Sporting Lisbon, who had been drawn to meet United in the last eight, knocked out the Italians Atalanta after a replay. Earlier they had thrashed Cypriot Cup holders Apoel Nicosia 16-1 in the opening leg of the first round but limited the damage to just two goals without reply when hosting the return.

Lisbon were heavily defeated here and, with a three-goal cushion built after the opening leg at Old Trafford, it seemed United had one foot in the last four. Denis Law hit a hat-trick including two penalties while Bobby Charlton grabbed the other United goal.

However, it should be noted that Lisbon came to attack and gave keeper Dave Gaskell plenty to do. Gaskell was in magnificent form, denying a host of Sporting's players with superb saves. It was enough to suggest that the return leg would be no formality, though United had to feel confident that a three goal lead could be successfully defended. However Portuguese football was formidable in this period with Sporting's city rivals Benfica one of the leading teams on the continent.

MANCHESTER UNITED 3 SUNDERLAND 3
FA Cup 6th Rd 29 February 1964

WITH JUST FOUR minutes of this game remaining, United looked like bowing out. Second Division Sunderland had established a 3-1 lead and the Mackems, who were heavily tipped for promotion to the top flight and had beaten league leaders Everton in the last round, looked handily placed to continue their giant-killing run.

Costly defensive errors were the cause of United's predicament but they never gave up the fight even when it looked hopeless. George Best typified the spirit. On occasion he had been guilty of holding the ball too long and failing to notice colleagues in better positions. He also shot weakly a couple of times but his resolve couldn't be faulted. Minutes after a poor finish was delivered he sent a devilish ball across the six-yard area. Unfortunately nobody was there to meet it but Bobby Charlton benefited from the resulting corner and smashed home.

There was still work to do if the rescue mission was to be completed and the visitors threw all their resources into defence. Eleven men guarded the Sunderland box but no one had an answer to Best who raced through the cover to shoot low and hard through a forest of legs and past the keeper, the ball creeping just inside the post with seconds remaining.

SUNDERLAND 2 MANCHESTER UNITED 2
FA Cup 6th Rd Replay 4 March 1964

OVER 68,000 FANS attended this replay, 5,000 more than had witnessed the first game at Old Trafford and the capacity Roker Park crowd urged Sunderland on, raising the roof when they took the lead before half-time. Yet United responded once more, Denis Law equalising midway through the second half and the score remained that way until the final whistle.

Extra-time was no more than 30 seconds old when Sunderland made it 2-1 and just as had happened in the first game, they held the lead to the very last. Law, Maurice Setters and Shay Brennan were all struggling with injuries during the additional half hour.

The tension ratcheted up as the minutes ticked by before, with time almost up, Bobby Charlton stooped to nod a low cross past Jim Montgomery. Once again there was barely time to take another kick of the ball before the referee signalled full-time.

For a second time in a week United had clawed a deficit back in the final seconds and the nature of each come back made many wonder whether United's name was on the cup.

MANCHESTER UNITED 5 SUNDERLAND 1
FA Cup 6th Rd 2nd Replay 9 March 1964

A NEUTRAL VENUE equidistant between the two clubs was needed for the second replay and the FA hit upon Huddersfield Town's Leeds Road ground. While United had done little better than cling on throughout the two previous ties, their refusal to accept defeat was rewarded here as they finally underlined their class with a sumptuous performance from beginning to end.

Sunderland opened the game well but their fizz soon evaporated as United finally got a grip on the tie. The Makems opened the scoring against the run of play, making the most of United's slow start to the second half. Denis Law levelled affairs after latching on to a David Herd shot which had fallen into his path after rebounding off a couple of defenders.

There may have been an element of fortune in the equaliser but from that point on The Reds were anything but lucky. Phil Chisnall quickly made it 2-1 and by the 51st minute Law had provided a two goal cushion from the penalty spot. Just past the hour mark the Scot had a hat-trick - his seventh of the season. A quarter of the game still remained when Herd rounded off the scoring and set up a semi-final with West Ham United.

Best had been given a night off for the trip to West Ham earlier in the week and was one of six changes. The rest seemed to do him the power of good as Martin Harvey, a centre back who had been deployed to do a specific marking job on the teenager, testified after the game.

WEST HAM UNITED 3 MANCHESTER UNITED 1
FA Cup Semi-Final 14 March 1964

THE TRIALS OF three gruelling cup games finally caught up with United who were well beaten by the Hammers.

Heavy rain made the Hillsborough pitch a quagmire, limiting the contribution skilled players could make. United's forwards in particular put in a lethargic performance. Law and Best, who could only be tested by the most extreme conditions, were the only exceptions. Phil Chisnall managed to square a ball for Law to convert but Bobby Moore was in commanding form, marshalling a five-man defence so effectively that it proved the perfect basis for West Ham's midfield

and attack to build on.

The extra body was certainly a boost for right back John Bond who, though beaten almost every time he challenged Best, had the any damage limited by the spare defender. George still managed to create chances but some of his colleagues' finishing left a lot to be desired.

West Ham reached Wembley for the first time since contesting the inaugural Empire Stadium final in 1923 and went on to claim the cup after beating Preston North End.

SPORTING LISBON 5 MANCHESTER UNITED 0 (AGG 4-6)
European Cup Winners Cup QF 2nd leg 18 March 1964

GOING OUT OF the FA Cup was a bitter pill to swallow but four days later United players and fans also had to digest an even greater humiliation at the hands of Sporting Lisbon in the second leg of the European Cup Winners' Cup quarter-final.

Lisbon were rumoured to be on a £300-a-man bonus to overturn a three-goal deficit and no doubt found the money an incentive of equal measure to rescuing their pride. Meanwhile United's pre-match preparations had been marred by disputes over bonus payments should The Reds reach the final or win the cups or league title.

The slog of competing in the latter stages of all three competitions was exhausting and United, who had already lost their best shot at silverware on Saturday, quickly lost their next best chance 4 days later. Within an hour of this game starting any hope of a first piece of European silverware were dashed. Sporting were 5-0 up and in complete control. Osvaldo Silva proved as devastating in front of goal as Law had three weeks earlier and the warnings posted at Old Trafford were rammed home with real consequence.

Just two minutes in a penalty was conceded which Osvaldo dispatched without much ceremony. Then Denis Law almost got a toe to a centre from David Herd and these two moments signalled the beginning of a turnaround. Osvaldo struck again beating Gaskell comprehensively with a shot on the right side of the area. Mascarenas had one cancelled out for handball but United failed to capitalise on their fortune.

Best played Law in during the final minutes of the first half with a deft header but the striker hit a post. Eco levelled on aggregate soon after the restart but once Momas scored then Osvaldo completed the hat-trick United looked beaten. They had recovered impossible looking positions more than once that season but this time were without an answer.

After the game Matt Busby acknowledged that his troops were tired after a long season but privately bawled his players out for their display. He told his tired troops that they'd have to pick themselves up by the boot straps quickly in the league. Despite United's tiredness Sporting had to be congratulated for their daring approach and for sticking to it throughout the game. It could only be hoped that lessons would be learned for future campaigns on the continent but the players could barely bring themselves to look each other in the eye.

Sporting went on to lift the cup after replayed victories over Lyon and then MTK Hungaria. This may at least have offered some compensation for United but having had the tie under control this defeat would stay long in the memory of the players, officials and fans.

Matt Busby had been offered a reported £200 a week to coach Sporting Lisbon just days prior to the FA Cup semi-final.

The deal was said to have been formally put to the United board on the day of this clash. Busby rejected the offer before it was even tendered stating "Manchester has been my life, is my life and I hope will stay my life."

The club was only too happy to hear the news and rejected any overtures.

TOTTENHAM HOTSPUR 2 MANCHESTER UNITED 3
DIVISION ONE 21 MARCH 1964

FURIOUS AT THE attitude of some players, Matt Busby rang the changes for the trip to White Hart Lane, most significantly Maurice Setters was finally replaced by Nobby Stiles on a permanent basis. Despite hitting a couple of goals in the previous year's cup final David Herd was suffering from a crisis of confidence which wasn't helped by his scapegoating by sections of United's support, he made way for David Sadler. Phil Chisnall also made way for Graham Moore.

Tottenham made a good start to the game during which United struggled to cope and Spurs opened the scoring but three goals in ten minutes boosted United's title hopes and severely dented Spurs'. The home side pulled one back through a hotly disputed penalty but United were well worth the victory.

MANCHESTER UNITED 1 CHELSEA 1
DIVISION ONE 23 MARCH 1964

DESPITE GOOD APPROACH play by Best, there was too little end product for United's forwards to capitalise on and, as George became more anxious, he tried the more spectacular when the basics would have sufficed.

Law's pace and clever running got United in for a goal but Chelsea quickly levelled and kept it that way until the whistle.

A 1-1 draw meant victories over Easter were vital if United were to catch up with both Merseyside clubs who had established a useful gap at the top. Each of the top two now had to make slip ups if United were to win the title.

FULHAM 2 MANCHESTER UNITED 2
DIVISION ONE 27 MARCH 1964

UNITED WERE DENIED a precious point when Bill Foulkes hit the bar. The stalwart defender had been ushered upfield for a set piece but seemed destined not to double his career tally.

Goals from Denis Law and David Herd gleaned a share of the spoils but the title dream was disappearing fast. Everton had drawn at home with West Brom but still led the table while Liverpool, who had fewer games to play, eased through the gears beating Spurs 3-1 at White Hart Lane.

MANCHESTER UNITED 2 WOLVES 2
DIVISION ONE 28 MARCH 1964

GEORGE BEST FINALLY signalled defeat in his battle to maintain his impressive start to life in the first team, looking particularly off the pace in a match United would have fancied themselves to win handsomely.

Frailties in front of goal ranked among the main reasons for Wolves leaving Old Trafford with a draw. Denis Law was sorely missed. In fairness, most United players looked tired but George struggled to get into a game he started alongside fellow Northern Ireland man Harry Gregg for the first time. The keeper had been out for almost a year after breaking his collar bone the previous season in a challenge with Liverpool captain Ron Yeats.

LIVERPOOL 3 MANCHESTER UNITED 0
DIVISION ONE 4 APRIL 1964

WITH EVERTON HAVING rediscovered the winning habit during the week before losing at Blackpool, both sides had a huge incentive to win. In fact Liverpool had managed to retake pole position from their Mersey neighbours after that slip. A win would put United in second just a point behind the day's hosts should Everton be defeated again.

Best took over at outside right from Ian Moir for this key game. An early surge by Liverpool put The Kop in good voice and seemed to unnerve Gregg who dropped the ball allowing Ian Callaghan to slip in for the opener. The memory of that injury may have been a factor and Yeats was not shy at challenging the keeper. Liverpool cruised to their win from that point on to all but make certain of the championship. A demoralised United were rarely in the game as an attacking force with even Denis Law clearing the ball off his own line at one stage.

Everton lost on the same afternoon by the odd goal in five at Stoke which did at least mean no ground had been lost in the challenge for runners-up spot.

MANCHESTER UNITED 1 ASTON VILLA 0
DIVISION ONE 6 APRIL 1964

VILLA FRUSTRATED UNITED with an offside trap executed to such perfection that it seemed they must have worked exclusively on it during training sessions. Nobody seemed able to adjust their game accordingly and when the trap was sprung Charlton and Stiles wasted chances. Fortunately Denis Law didn't prove as profligate and his goal finally put United clear in second place.

MANCHESTER UNITED 4 MANCHESTER CITY 1
FA YOUTH CUP SF 1ST LEG 8 APRIL 1964

THOUGH NOW ACCEPTED AS a first team regular, Best was still young enough to play in the FA Youth Cup and was drafted in for the latter stages of the competition including a clash with Manchester City in a two-legged semi-final witnessed by more than 50,000 spectators. There had been a clamour to get him involved far earlier in the competition as United struggled during some games and were drawn against a number of very promising sides. Having won the trophy five successive times since its inception in 1953, the tournament had a special resonance to United fans. However, the club had failed to reach the final since Munich when many of that year's vintage were called up prematurely for the first team.

Fortunes at Maine Road and Old Trafford had dipped the previous season. United had won the FA Cup but in the true test of a side - the league - neither had fared well. The Sky Blues had slipped into the Second Division finishing next to bottom. United had finished two places and three points better off though just one ahead of the third relegated side Birmingham City. United had drawn at City in the penultimate game of the season with a late penalty guaranteeing survival. The point was not enough for the hosts who were soundly beaten 6-1 at West Ham the following week.

However, both the city's professional clubs were bringing through a promising crop of youngsters. Like Best, many on either side had already made a breakthrough, albeit with a more limited impact. The youngsters - minus George - had beaten Barrow, Blackpool, Sheffield United and Wolves in order to reach this stage so they had progressed well without their first team graduates but with civic pride at stake, a number of prominent players were drafted back in to the set up.

A notable feature over recent weeks was Matt Busby's experiment with Best on the right hand side of the field and when he stepped into the youth side it was in his old position of inside right as a direct replacement for John Pearson.

Albert Kinsey opened the scoring for United with an effort from close range and The Reds continued to make the running throughout most of the first half. It wasn't until seconds before the break that Glyn Pardoe made a George Best style surge through the midfield beating three players before setting himself up for a chance on the left hand side of the area. He cracked a shot past Jimmy Rimmer which hit the underside of the crossbar on its way to goal but had such venom that it rebounded back into play after hitting the net.

Kinsey rather than Best was the star of the night completing a hat-trick after the break but the game, coming as it did on top of the Easter period, meant George had played three matches in four days.

It was a tall order for a young player but one which George relished, even if he looked a little tired at various stages. That was good news for left-half Phil Burrows, a trainee quantity surveyor who got the bus to the ground after finishing his day's work only to be told he would be marking Best. He must have made an impression as he was invited to sign professional forms that very evening on his 18th birthday.

George's fellow first-teamer David Sadler hit the only other goal of the night to make it 4-1 and send United into the return with a real expectation of bringing the youth cup back to its spiritual home.

Starved of a derby game that term and knowing that outside any cup draws there would be no prospect of a clash the following season, almost 30,000 watched this match.

MANCHESTER UNITED 2 SHEFFIELD UNITED 1
DIVISION ONE 13 APRIL 1964

GEORGE WAS BACK in the senior team at the first opportunity for the visit of Sheffield United. Ian Moir, who began on the left, was so disappointing that Busby switched him to the other flank from where he scored a 72nd minute winner. United had started well and could have had a couple within the first 10 minutes but one lapse midway through the opening period allowed the Blades a chance. Denis Law equalised just before the break, feeding off the scraps after a Bobby Charlton shot had rebounded off a post before Moir's strike.

WALES 2 NORTHERN IRELAND 3
HOME INTERNATIONAL 15 APRIL 1964

DESPITE MAKING A name for himself with Cregagh Boys Club and drawing scouts from many clubs and the Northern Ireland youth set-up, George had been passed over for schoolboy and youth squads a number of times. Those who watched him admired the skills but felt he was far too small and his build too slight to withstand the demands at that level. That was until he arrived at Old Trafford and was invited to join the under-18 set up. Even then he failed to make every team selected.

However, just 21 games into his United career and around a month before he turned 18, the international selectors redeemed themselves. Northern Ireland manager Bertie Peacock decided to call the teenager up for the home international with Wales alongside promising Watford keeper Pat Jennings who also made his debut at Swansea. Jennings replaced United's Harry Gregg who had been omitted following an 8-3 hammering by England the previous November.

International recognition capped a remarkable season for Best who became one of his country's youngest ever full internationals at just 17 years and 328 days.

Sunderland's defensive stalwart Martin Harvey, Jimmy McLaughlin of Swansea Town and Falkirk's Sammy Wilson scored the goals in a 3-2 win.

STOKE CITY 3 MANCHESTER UNITED 1
DIVISION ONE 18 APRIL 1964

A SORE THROAT forced Denis Law out and the Scot was replaced by David Sadler. David Herd moved over to fill the gap left by Law at inside-left. The Scot's absence robbed United of their usual zing and Stoke were good value for their win. Best was constantly probing and the finest United man going forward but had no cutting edge and made uncharacteristic errors. in front of goal.

MANCHESTER CITY 3 MANCHESTER UNITED 4
FA YOUTH CUP SF 2ND LEG 20 APRIL 1964

THOUGH CITY HAD their skipper Alf Wood back, the forward line really needed to excel if they were to overturn the lead United had established in the first leg. The task was further hampered when Mike Doyle managed to put through his own goal early on. Glyn Pardoe equalised close to half time to provide some hope and City were the better side for most of the game but just after play resumed United more or less wrapped up the tie.

David Sadler, who scored in the opening leg and had the freedom of the penalty area, picked his spot. Best, who was completely devastating when he received the ball, hit the third soon after.

Pardoe and Belfast born Bobby McAlinden levelled on the night but Sadler ensured United recorded an impressive 8-4 aggregate win to reach the final.

NOTTINGHAM FOREST 1 MANCHESTER UNITED 3
DIVISION ONE 25 APRIL 1964

A GOOD WIN ensured United's participation in the next season's Fairs Cup. Denis Law finished the season with a double and scored the second despite being placed out on the left wing when he was reduced to walking pace with an injury. Graham Moore, who had set up the opener, grabbed the other goal.

George Best made light of his busy schedule with a huge contribution and thrilling runs which had supporters of both sides enthralled.

MANCHESTER UNITED 1 SWINDON TOWN 1
FA YOUTH CUP FINAL 1ST LEG 27 APRIL 1964

THE REDS FACED Swindon Town in the final with an unchanged team from the clash with City. Most of the youth squad had been rested but with the push to claim a passport back into Europe there was no such luxury for George who loved the game so much that he revelled in the chance to play as often as possible. The opening leg was tightly contested with a Best goal on 70 minutes capping a good all round display and earning a 1-1 draw at The County Ground. United failed to capitalise on all the chances made but a well placed shot from Peter McBride's pass had Tony Hicks well beaten and all but dashed any hopes The Robins may have had of holding on to their slender advantage when battle recommenced 72 hours later.

Don Rogers, Swindon's answer to Best, had put his side ahead after half an hour shooting low past Jimmy Rimmer but Rogers and his colleagues could only watch as Best turned the tide. That United only scored once after the dominance exerted was the real shock of the evening.

NORTHERN IRELAND 3 URUGUAY 0
FRIENDLY INTERNATIONAL 29 APRIL 1964

JUST A FORTNIGHT after winning his first international cap George doubled his tally in a prestige friendly against former World Cup holders Uruguay. Many fancied this would be the second cap of a long and distinguished international career which could see Northern Ireland qualify for the final stages of tournaments for the first time in many decades.

An immediate return to Manchester was arranged after the game and a car picked Best up at Ringway Airport to ensure he got as much rest as possible before the next day's vital game and a chance to finish the season in style. It would round off a six-day period in which he had played four very important games.

MANCHESTER UNITED 4 SWINDON TOWN 1
FA YOUTH CUP FINAL 1ST LEG 30 APRIL 1964

THOUGH THE OPENING leg in Wiltshire had been a close affair - at least in terms of the score - the return at Old Trafford was more one sided. If George felt slightly jaded it was not apparent from any of his performances.

Swindon were clearly worried about the damage Best could do if encouraged. As such they went into the game with a defensive strategy which involved inside forward Dennis Peapell playing as a sweeper.

The extra man mattered little to George who was as outstanding in this game as he had been in any other that term. John Aston Junior found the net with David Sadler claiming a hat-trick but readily admitting that each of his three goals owed something to the devastation wreaked down the right hand side of the pitch by Best whose name was repeatedly chanted during the presentation ceremony.

It was a scene which looked certain to be repeated for some years to come with the trophies getting bigger in stature and more plentiful in number.

1963-64

Unitled had finished the season empty handed but there was still plenty to feel positive about. Midway through the season Bobby Charlton had moved from left wing to central midfield - a position he had coveted for some time and from which Matt Busby felt he would be much more of a threat. This left the flanks in a state of flux for the early part of the campaign. Many players were tried as wide men with Johnny Giles, Ian Moir, Albert Quixall and David Herd all asked to fill in on the right.

Given that most were not natural wingers but forwards or midfielders none had much success and results reflected this. Switching Charlton also required another winger to be found and at first the decision seemed to make no sense at all, that was until Busby plunged two of his young but promising players into first team action.

George was asked to play on the right for his debut but more often than not took the left hand berth with a license to roam once his performances demonstrated he not only had the talent but maturity to cope. Defences struggled to contain his scampering runs and dribbles and with a roving brief to contend with opposing defenders didn't always know who had responsibility for him.

A rare quality evident at this early stage was that Best rarely wasted possession. He may have been a little greedy but had the skills to justify his insatiable appetite for the ball and would never pass to a colleague in a poor position just to get out of a hole knowing that he had the ability to not only dig himself out but create an opportunity once he emerged.

United's run to the last four of the FA Cup provided some of Best's brightest moments. After beating The Saints Busby's side threatened to go all the way registering huge margins of victory over Bristol Rovers, Barnsley and, after a marathon tussle, Sunderland. George contributed creatively to many superb goals and bagged a couple in half a dozen appearances. Finally losing the chance to defend the cup and going out of Europe in quick succession had a minimal effect on league form but not enough to prevent Liverpool from easing to top spot.

Though there was no silverware for the trophy cabinet from the seniors, United's youth side captured the national knock-out competition and a number of fresh faces made their way into the first team. Without much doubt the most celebrated was George who even at that stage distinguished himself against not only those of his own generation but a range of his elders.

While George may have been the find of the year, Denis Law was without doubt Player of the Year. An accolade he scooped at domestic and European level after hitting seven hat-tricks including two in the Cup Winners' Cup which went some way to him becoming the first British player to lift Le Ballon D'or since Stanley Matthews in 1956.

However, Matt Busby knew he had to bring some more quality in if United were to go the extra yard and regain the championship which would bring another crack at the European Cup. That quest had almost claimed his life but the same tragedy also served as his motivation. The purchase of experienced winger John Connelly from Burnley towards the end of the season demonstrated that he had already formed plans for the season to come.

Off the field George seemed to be looking towards the future and made investments in various businesses, opening the first of half-a-dozen clothes boutiques, in Sale, Cheshire. He would go on to take a share in a travel agency, a bar and two nightclubs as financial partners queued up to be associated with the emerging star. George was becoming a face in Manchester society.

DATE	OPPONENT	VENUE	SCORE	ATTD	1	2	3	4	5	6	7	8	9	10	11
14 September	WBA	Old Trafford	1-0	50,453	Gregg	Dunne(A)	Cantwell	Crerand	Foulkes	Setters	Best	Stiles	Sadler[1]	Chisnall	Charlton
28 December	Burnley	Old Trafford	5-1	47,834	Gaskell	Dunne(A)	Cantwell	Crerand	Foulkes	Setters	Anderson	Moore[2]	Charlton	Herd[2]	Best[1]
11 January	Birmingham City	Old Trafford	1-1	44,695	Gaskell	Dunne(A)	Cantwell	Crerand	Foulkes	Setters	Herd	Moore	Sadler[1]	Law	Best
18 January	WBA	The Hawthorns	2-1	25,624	Gaskell	Dunne(A)	Cantwell	Crerand	Foulkes	Setters	Herd	Moore	Charlton[1]	Law[2]	Best[1]
1 February	Arsenal	Old Trafford	3-1	48,340	Gaskell	Brennan	Dunne(A)	Stiles	Foulkes	Setters[1]	Herd[1]	Moore	Charlton	Law[1]	Best
8 February	Leicester City	Filbert Street	2-3	35,538	Gaskell	Brennan	Dunne(A)	Crerand	Foulkes	Setters	Herd[1]	Moore	Charlton	Law[1]	Best
19 February	Bolton Wanderers	Old Trafford	5-0	33,926	Gaskell	Brennan	Dunne(A)	Crerand	Foulkes	Setters	Herd[2]	Stiles	Charlton[1]	Law	Best[2]
22 February	Blackburn Rovers	Ewood Park	3-1	36,726	Gaskell	Brennan	Dunne(A)	Crerand	Foulkes	Setters	Herd	Chisnall[1]	Charlton	Law[2]	Best
21 March	Tottenham Hotspur	White Hart Lane	3-2	56,392	Gaskell	Brennan	Dunne(A)	Crerand	Foulkes	Stiles	Best	Moore[1]	Sadler	Law[1]	Charlton[1]
23 March	Chelsea	Old Trafford	1-1	42,931	Gaskell	Brennan	Dunne(A)	Crerand	Foulkes	Stiles	Best	Moore	Sadler	Law[1]	Charlton
27 March	Fulham	Craven Cottage	2-2	41,769	Gaskell	Brennan	Dunne(A)	Crerand	Foulkes	Stiles	Best	Moore	Herd[1]	Law[1]	Charlton
28 March	Wolves	Old Trafford	2-2	44,470	Gregg	Brennan	Cantwell	Crerand	Foulkes	Setters	Best	Chisnall	Herd[1]	Setters	Charlton[1]
4 April	Liverpool	Anfield	0-3	52,559	Gregg	Brennan	Dunne(A)	Crerand	Foulkes	Setters	Best	Stiles	Herd	Law	Charlton
6 April	Aston Villa	Old Trafford	1-0	25,848	Gregg	Brennan	Dunne(A)	Crerand	Foulkes	Stiles	Best	Charlton	Herd	Law[1]	Moir
13 April	Sheffield United	Old Trafford	2-1	27,587	Gregg	Brennan	Cantwell	Crerand	Foulkes	Stiles	Best	Charlton	Herd	Law[1]	Moir[1]
18 April	Stoke City	Victoria Ground	1-3	45,670	Gregg	Brennan	Dunne(A)	Crerand	Foulkes	Stiles	Best	Charlton[1]	Sadler	Setters	Moir
25 April	Nottingham Forest	Old Trafford	3-1	31,671	Gaskell	Brennan	Dunne(A)	Crerand	Foulkes	Setters	Best	Moore[1]	Herd	Law[2]	Charlton

FA Cup

DATE	OPPONENT	VENUE	SCORE	ATTD	1	2	3	4	5	6	7	8	9	10	11
4 January	Southampton	The Dell	3-2	29,164	Gaskell	Dunne(A)	Cantwell	Crerand[1]	Foulkes	Setters	Anderson	Moore[1]	Charlton	Herd[1]	Best
25 January	Bristol Rovers	Old Trafford	4-1	55,772	Gaskell	Dunne(A)	Cantwell	Crerand	Foulkes	Setters	Herd[1]	Chisnall	Charlton	Law[3]	Best
15 February	Barnsley	Oakwell	4-0	38,076	Gaskell	Brennan	Cantwell	Crerand	Foulkes	Setters	Herd[1]	Stiles	Charlton	Law[2]	Best[1]
29 February	Sunderland	Old Trafford	3-3	63,700	Gaskell	Brennan	Cantwell	Crerand	Foulkes	Setters	Herd	Stiles	Charlton[1]	Law	Best[1]
4 March	Sunderland	Roker Park	2-2	68,000	Gaskell	Brennan	Cantwell	Crerand	Foulkes	Setters	Herd[1]	Chisnall	Charlton[1]	Law[1]	Best
9 March	Sunderland	Leeds Road	5-1	54,952	Gaskell	Brennan	Cantwell	Crerand	Foulkes	Setters	Herd[1]	Chisnall[1]	Charlton[1]	Law[1]	Best[1]
14 March	West Ham United	Hillsborough	1-3	65,000	Gaskell	Brennan	Cantwell	Crerand	Foulkes	Setters	Herd	Chisnall	Charlton	Herd	Best

European Cup Winners' Cup

DATE	OPPONENT	VENUE	SCORE	ATTD	1	2	3	4	5	6	7	8	9	10	11
25 February	Sporting Lisbon	Old Trafford	4-1	60,000	Gaskell	Brennan	Cantwell	Crerand	Foulkes	Setters	Herd	Stiles	Charlton[1]	Law[3]	Best
15 March	Sporting Lisbon	Jose Alvalade	0-5	40,000	Gaskell	Brennan	Dunne(A)	Crerand	Foulkes	Setters	Herd	Chisnall	Charlton	Law	Best

1964-65
HARD MEN TARGET BEST

MANCHESTER UNITED 2 WEST BROMWICH ALBION 2
DIVISION ONE 22 AUGUST 1964

JOHN CONNELLY MADE his United debut while Paddy Crerand, who had looked off the pace in pre-season, was dropped for the first time since joining the club. Matt Busby was heartened by Denis Law passing a late fitness test. A groin strain had threatened to delay his start to the season but the forward was declared ready and skippered the side.

United proved their defence was porous during the latter part of the summer friendlies and it remained so against The Baggies. Tony Brown took full advantage to score before a quarter of an hour had elapsed while Graham Williams, embarrassed more often than

he would like at the same venue a season earlier when George Best made his bow, kept a tight rein on another right sided debutant - Connelly. As an attacking force United were sluggish and made few clear cut chances early on as a result. Those created were squandered. David Herd proved particularly wasteful but was by no means the only offender.

As the game wore on The Reds made more of the running but continued to let openings slip. Albion hit another and it took superbly taken goals from Law and Bobby Charlton to earn a point in a game United could and should have won.

WEST HAM UNITED 3 MANCHESTER UNITED 1
DIVISION ONE 24 AUGUST 1964

MATT BUSBY'S SIDE was making life far harder than it needed to be and cup holders West Ham took full advantage of their continued disarray. The Upton Park crowd exuberantly cheered the famous trophy as it was paraded around the ground in the first home fixture since their Wembley triumph over Preston North End.

With victory over United in the semi-final stage still fresh in their memories and buoyant at their pre-match reception, the home side set about their task with gusto. John Byrne scored after four minutes and before the match was 25 minutes old their lead had doubled.

It seemed United, too, had a recall of

the FA Cup game at Hillsborough and couldn't shake the hangover. Maurice Setters limped out of the fray on the hour, coming off worst in a bone crunching tackle which ruptured a vein in his foot.

Nobby Stiles and George Best went close before Denis Law headed in on 80 minutes but as United pushed forward in the time remaining The Hammers restored their two-goal cushion.

LEICESTER CITY 2 MANCHESTER UNITED 2
DIVISION ONE 29 AUGUST 1964

FILBERT STREET HAD earned a reputation as a bogey ground for United who were without a victory there since 1957. At Old Trafford, or a neutral venue, the Foxes were easy prey but with United still searching for a first win of the season this was the last place many wanted to venture. The Reds were struggling to stem a tide of goals and Leicester had already hit three in each of their opening games.

David Herd paid for a tough early season with his replacement by David Sadler but Crerand returned for the crocked Setters. Remarkably nine of the Leicester team that lost the 1963 cup final to United were on duty. Tom Sweeney at inside-right would have been the only alteration but left-back Ritchie Norman pulled out minutes before kick-off.

Despite a promising start from wingers Connelly and Best, United were quickly tamed by Leicester who were unlucky not to score prior to Ken Keyworth opening his account on ten minutes. From this point on Best was at his worst. The ball skills and dribbling were as good as ever but as a team player he left a lot to be desired, often holding on to the ball for longer than necessary and allowing cover to make its way back when a quick pass would probably have been more profitable.

Despite this, David Sadler headed one back and Law levelled from close range with two minutes remaining to earn a barely deserved point.

MANCHESTER UNITED 3 WEST HAM UNITED 1
DIVISION ONE 2 SEPTEMBER 1964

UNITED RESPONDED WELL to a poor start and took the opportunity provided by this swift rematch against West Ham to earn their first win of the new season. At the same time doubts about the side's potential to build on last season's runners-up spot were cast aside. John Connelly fired home in the opening minute and United remained on top until the final whistle.

Both wingers were key to the victory. Connelly and Best barely let up all evening and combined well with each other and colleagues in the middle. Just how the goal tally was kept at three is a mystery. The Hammers rode their luck but couldn't resist Law and Best who scored his first goal of the season. West Ham's sole strike was nothing more than a consolation with the game already over as a contest.

FULHAM 2 MANCHESTER UNITED 1
Division One 5 September 1964

Despite controlling the game from beginning to end, United left Craven Cottage with at least a point less than their endeavour deserved. Fulham only held possession for sporadic periods during the course of 90 minutes but somehow managed to score two goals.

Fulham stopper Tony Macedo played a blinder to ensure that that first away win of the season remained elusive. John Connelly hit his second in as many games just before the break but Fulham's brace shocked the visitors who grew frustrated and allowed it to show. United simply ran out of attacking ideas.

EVERTON 3 MANCHESTER UNITED 3
Division One 8 September 1964

Action was taken by Matt Busby, who was determined to ensure United kept amongst the pack of early title chasers, if not the leading bunch. David Gaskell was dropped for reserve Pat Dunne who had signed the previous summer from Shamrock Rovers. David Herd was back after a good show in the reserves where he found his form and more importantly the net.

This was a bruising encounter which left many United players nursing injuries. Law and Connelly were on the casualty list but George Best was also visibly struggling towards the end. United, heavily beaten on their last visit to Goodison, took the lead through Denis Law and then John Connelly continued his scoring spree but Everton equalised during a superb 20-minute second half spell that few teams could have ridden out.

Herd brought his form in the second string to the first XI at last, hitting the net in a league game for the first time since March. However, Alex Young made it 3-3 late on to cap a sensational game which neither team deserved to lose.

MANCHESTER UNITED 3 NOTTINGHAM FOREST 0
Division One 12 September 1964

The physical battle with Everton left Denis Law and John Connelly struggling for the visit of Nottingham Forest. Nobby Stiles and George Best were also slight doubts but only Law failed to make the cut on the eve of the game. Stiles switched to inside left as a result.

Within 24 minutes United made enough chances to win any game, managing to convert three. David Herd grabbed two well taken goals with John Connelly notching the other. Best was in great form - on hand whenever needed - putting in penetrating runs and supplying a forward line which was on fire.

MANCHESTER UNITED 2 EVERTON 1
DIVISION ONE 16 SEPTEMBER 1964

MATT BUSBY FENDED off interest from Southampton regarding Maurice Setters and Ian Moir. The latter had been the main casualty of George Best's emergence and candidly admitted that his time at Old Trafford was probably nearing a close as a result. However, at this stage with Denis Law out for an unknown spell Matt Busby was loathe to sanction any deal.

Despite an open if keenly contested first half, the game almost descended into anarchy after the restart. Tempers boiled over as players on both sides decided cynical fouls should win out over skill. Only one player remained cool enough to not only tolerate the hacking but ride the challenges - the exceptional George Best.

Weaving his way around furious challenges he was a sight to behold and proved just as valuable in defence as The Toffees pushed for an equaliser. His tackles didn't lack ferocity but were fair and raised no objection from the referee.

He had scored a superb opener and was shortly joined on the scoresheet by Law. United were putting on the same class of performance that had put paid to high flying Nottingham Forest though Pat Dunne gifted Everton a way back into the game when dropping a corner at the feet of Fred Pickering who made no mistake.

Two players from each side found their way into the referee's book and the official warned both teams about their conduct.

STOKE CITY 1 MANCHESTER UNITED 2
DIVISION ONE 19 SEPTEMBER 1964

DENIS LAW CAME off the worst after the casualties were counted and the troops regrouped in the Old Trafford dressing room following the Everton game. So much so that he was already rumoured to be a doubt for the league clash with Stoke and the Fairs Cup tie in Stockholm.

A welcome return to form for David Herd had already proved a huge factor in United finally managing to string a run of wins together after a poor start. Best was a huge contributor to the resurgence of both club and player, providing the forward with quality service - well weighted passes which evaded covering defences that allowed Herd to charge into

space and unleash a shot. Maurice Setters came back with Nobby Stiles pushed forward to replace Law.

The same XI had beaten Forest comfortably but with former Busby Babe Dennis Viollet in their ranks, The Potters could not be taken lightly.

United were without a win away from home all season but secured both points and finally made good for the many pundits who had tipped them to go one better than last season.

Paddy Crerand marshalled the side at both ends of the field and had a creative hand in goals by Herd and John Connelly. Stoke pulled one back but were hindered by an injury to full back Tony Allen early on which United exploited well. The pivotal Jimmy McIlroy was also reduced to little more than walking pace before the close.

DJURGAARDEN 1 MANCHESTER UNITED 1
FAIRS CUP 1ST ROUND 1ST LEG 23 SEPTEMBER 1964

UNITED'S FIRST EUROPEAN opponents since crashing out of the European Cup Winners' Cup to Sporting Lisbon the previous season did not have the same reputation as the Portuguese, though Matt Busby cautioned against a gung-ho attitude in the opening phases of the game against Swedish side Djurgaarden.

United rarely threatened their part-time opponents in the first half and were guilty of woeful finishing when the forwards finally did get their act together. For their part Djurgaarden could have put the result of the first leg beyond doubt during the opening period but only managed to convert one of a handful of chances.

They may still have been favourites to lose at Old Trafford but any kind of win would have been a huge embarrassment for United. David Herd spared any blushes with three minutes remaining linking up with John Connelly. George Best could not solely be blamed for the team's malaise and at times was as incisive as any of his colleagues but he still saw good opportunities he had carved out go begging. Arne Arvidsson in goal for the Swedes was in great form.

MANCHESTER UNITED 4 TOTTENHAM HOTSPUR 1
DIVISION ONE 26 SEPTEMBER 1964

IAN MOIR HAD been spoiling for a move after being omitted from the first XI since April. He had played just less than half the league and cup games the previous term and decided it was time to go public with his fears for the future in the hours before Tottenham came to Manchester.

Denis Law returned, scored a couple and looked sharp despite his lay off in a very open beginning to the game during which both sides threatened to make a breakthrough. United had a fair degree of luck in a game which, though won comfortably, they could so easily have drawn or even lost against an excellent Spurs side spearheaded by Jimmy Greaves.

Paddy Crerand hit an excellent drive from 20 yards and saw another effort dribble through Pat Jennings' legs. Stiles eventually shackled Greaves whose threat receded as the game wore on.

Best was superb going forward and tracked back to dispossess his opposite number Cyril Knowles countless times. Outside right Jimmy Robertson notched for Spurs.

CHELSEA 0 MANCHESTER UNITED 2
DIVISION ONE 30 SEPTEMBER 1964

EVEN AT SUCH an early stage of the campaign there was a definite order to the top of the Division One with United, Chelsea and newly promoted Leeds looking most likely to contest the title. The Yorkshire club had already beaten reigning champions Liverpool although they lost the return. They had also been beaten by Chelsea which effectively made the Londoners the strongest challengers to a United side which had finally begun to find some consistency after disappointing early reverses.

As may be expected The Blues made the early running, directed by the central midfield duo of John Hollins and Terry Venables. However, over time Bobby Charlton and Pat Crerand managed to reassert some authority, pushing Chelsea back and forcing them to defend closer to their own area.

It took a counter attack when a Chelsea corner failed to beat the first defender to provide United with the lead. Crerand emerged with possession, finding Denis Law who flicked the ball into space. Eddie McCreadie came in from the left and attempted to clear the danger by tapping the ball back to Peter Bonetti but Best read the pass and had closed the keeper down, stealing possession with just one man to beat there was only going to be one result.

United kept their lead until the break despite some severe tests. Gradually the visitors began to assert themselves and could have doubled their advantage on a

number of occasions. Chelsea had coped so far but Ken Shellito, who had been capped by England, albeit as a deputy for Blackpool's Jimmy Armfield, and was said to be one of the strongest and most fearless defenders in the game, had his life made a misery whenever Best received the ball. He was forced one way then the other as he tried to thwart the winger, Paddy Crerand later quipped that Ken was substituted because he was suffering from 'twisted blood'.

On occasions George did give him a break, preferring to switch flanks and taunt McCreadie, who had already been hugely embarrassed for the goal, from time to time. Both full-backs were pleased to leave the pitch by the end, knowing they would not face an opponent so dangerous for at least a few months - when Best lined up in the Old Trafford return. They, along with many other Chelsea players and fans, applauded George off the pitch.

Bobby Charlton had a header rebound back off the bar and somehow David Herd managed to miss from less than six yards out but the game was made safe during the latter stages when Best took possession closer to the halfway line than the goal. Shellito was beaten yet again and others held off before a cross found Denis Law who headed powerfully home. Bonetti got a finger tip to the ball but could only deflect it on to the underside of the bar.

NORTHERN IRELAND 3 ENGLAND 4
HOME INTERNATIONAL 3 OCTOBER 1964

A FLIGHT FROM London the morning after the Chelsea game took Best to Belfast for a first ever clash with England. It was his third successive call up since his international debut and once again he was played on the right but this time made little impact. With the game no more than a quarter old England were 4-0 up and rampant. Fred Pickering had opened the scoring with Jimmy Greaves of Spurs completing a hat-trick within 12 minutes. It seemed that the match was over and it was merely a matter of how many England could rack up.

Sam Wilson pulled one back after 52 minutes then James McLaughlin hit a couple meaning that with just under half an hour still to play Northern Ireland had closed the gap to a single goal. A come back to earn a point or even win was on the cards.

The majority of 58,000 fans were delirious but had no further goals to celebrate. Bobby Charlton was the only United representative on duty for England.

BURNLEY 0 MANCHESTER UNITED 0
DIVISION ONE 6 OCTOBER 1964

FORMER BURNLEY WINGER John Connelly skippered United for the visit to Turf Moor and along with Best put in some pacy and thrilling runs. Unfortunately neither flanker yielded an end product and due to some superb play from The Clarets few raids were mounted. Burnley were always looking to push forward and remained in that mind-set throughout the evening, keeping the backline permanently busy and starving dangerous players of the ball - United had little opportunity to attack.

Hull City threw their hat into the ring for Ian Moir's services but Matt Busby resisted the idea.

MANCHESTER UNITED 1 SUNDERLAND 0
DIVISION ONE 10 OCTOBER 1964

BRITAIN BEGAN AN election week but the back pages were filled with talk of Bobby Charlton being dropped from the England squad for the first time in the six years since he had established himself in the national side. It was a blow to Charlton but would prove to be to United's advantage in the long term.

United fluffed a host of chances here. Best had an early shot blocked close to the line after cutting in from the wing but other chances were missed at point blank range as early as the third minute. Thankfully United still took both points when David Herd converted a John Connelly corner.

Now that Matt Busby's strongest side was beginning to assert itself week in, week out a number of clubs set about trying to pick off fringe players. Swansea were the latest hoping to be successful in an enquiry for the much wanted Ian Moir.

NORTHERN IRELAND 1 SWITZERLAND 0
WORLD CUP QUALIFIER 14 OCTOBER 1964

A VERY STAGNANT game in which neither side looked likely to score was settled by a penalty just after the break awarded for a body check on Best who had run through and hoped to crack a shot away.

Johnny Crossan converted to provide Northern Ireland with two precious points against strong rivals for qualification.

WOLVES 2 MANCHESTER UNITED 4
DIVISION ONE 17 OCTOBER 1964

STAN CULLIS HAD been dismissed as manager of The Old Gold a month earlier, despite 16 years service and a decent level of success. But with Wolves now bottom of the table no mercy was shown by the Molineux board or for that matter Manchester United who cruised to a 4-0 lead before half-time.

Best and others proved support acts to not only the scorers but other forwards. Maurice Setters had turned down a switch to the Black Country club in the days leading up to the game - the second time he had rejected a move in recent weeks. He had been impressed by the club and the offer but decided against it after some thought.

MANCHESTER UNITED 7 ASTON VILLA 0
DIVISION ONE 24 OCTOBER 1964

ASTON VILLA HAD enjoyed a good start to the season and lay second in the table as a result but were blown away by a performance of sheer quality from a team that now looked favourite to take the title even though over six months of the season still remained.

Best was superb on the left and led the Villa right back a merry dance. His feet bamboozled opponents and the combination of the full array of his dazzling skills and shuttles down the touchline made him impossible to dispossess.

Even United fans, who thought they had seen his full range of flicks and tricks, gasped at times and the Villa back line let go a relieved sigh at the final whistle.

Denis Law had grabbed four, David Herd a brace and John Connelly, though less spectacular then Best, patrolled his flank well and deserved his goal after playing a part in many of the other six converted. Remarkably Villa had begun well and looked the most likely to score during the opening exchanges.

MANCHESTER UNITED 6 DJURGAARDENS 1
FAIRS CUP 1ST ROUND 2ND LEG 27 OCTOBER 1964

TORSTEN LINDBERG, WHO combined club duties with managing Sweden, had guided Djurgaarden to a seventh domestic title the weekend prior to the club's journey to Old Trafford and ensured his charges were difficult to break down. So much so that United had only scored one before the interval.

However, the containment exercise broke down miserably during the second half as relentless pressure finally broke Swedish resistance and United hit four goals in eight minutes.

Bobby Charlton, a doubt before the game, grabbed a brace - his first goals since the opening day of the season. Denis Law's hat-trick included a penalty after George Best was felled in the area.

Best himself scored the final goal of the half dozen, sliding his effort in off a post. The full back marking George, Jan Karlsson, had played him well until the final quarter of the game though the Irishman was guilty once again of holding the ball for far too long at times. Paddy Crerand was the real creative force and Arvidsson, again in great form, stopped the goal count reaching double figures.

LIVERPOOL 0 MANCHESTER UNITED 2
DIVISION ONE 31 OCTOBER 1964

LIVERPOOL'S 3-0 WIN at Anfield the previous season had ended United's chances of overhauling the Merseyside club at the top of Division One. Now a win and a reverse for Chelsea put Matt Busby's side top of the pile.

Phase one was completed with United coasting to a win despite Best missing a

THE COMPLETE GEORGE BEST

gilt edged opportunity after two minutes. John Connelly crossed for Herd who laid the ball off for George who took one touch too many in steadying himself when he may have been better advised to meet it first time.

United, in their new blue change strip, eventually overpowered Liverpool who had failed to live up to their status as champions so far that term and languished in the bottom half of the table. Despite their low position the Anfielders gave it their all but their defences were breached on 35 minutes when David Herd scored.

Liverpool pushed hard for an equaliser prior to the interval and remained on the front foot for some time after the restart but United resisted and hit Bill Shankly's side on the counter finally breaking their resolve.

There was a price to pay as Nobby Stiles was knocked unconscious during a valiant attempt to keep Liverpool at bay. At Stamford Bridge Burnley scored the only goal of the game allowing United to draw a point clear.

MANCHESTER UNITED 1 SHEFFIELD WEDNESDAY 0
Division One 7 November 1964

As THIS MATCH entered the final quarter a robust Wednesday side decided their best chance of rattling United was to adopt a 'hard but fair' approach. The Reds had started well, underlining their authority with a David Herd goal on 15 minutes.

The Owls probed and caused many attack minded players to track back. But for the best part of an hour United had everything their own way.

Best made some running while the game was open enough to give him the chance and he may have scored after combining with Charlton and Law to fashion a shot at goal. However, a last ditch challenge by Fred Hill meant he failed to test the keeper.

BORUSSIA DORTMUND 1 MANCHESTER UNITED 6
Fairs Cup 2nd Rd 11 November 1964

One of Europe's top sides were swept aside on their own turf as United built a commanding 6-1 advantage with the Fairs Cup tie still at its midway point.

Like United, Borussia Dortmund were challenging for their domestic title but recent results had seen them drop from first to sixth place in the league. They were also missing some important players which will have given United confidence but the margin of victory must have been beyond even their wildest dreams.

The Holy Trinity of Best, Law and Charlton were imperious despite a rigid and determined man-to-man marking system on each of the trio.

Charlton hit a hat-trick to bring him up to five goals in the competition. Law and Best also found the net as did David Herd. British and German newspapers raved about the quality of the team performance but each singled out Law, Charlton and Best for special praise.

42

NORTHERN IRELAND 1 SWITZERLAND 2
WORLD CUP QUALIFIER 14 NOVEMBER 1964

AT A TIME when other First Division managers looked set to deny Northern Ireland access to their players, a pragmatic Matt Busby, keen to maintain a good working relationship in Belfast, announced that he would be releasing George Best for the World Cup qualifier with Switzerland as soon as the squad was announced.

The match clashed with a full league programme meaning United would travel to Blackpool without their winger who had possibly run into the greatest form of his albeit short first team career. Best opened the scoring on 18 minutes but The Swiss soon equalised then went 2-1 ahead by the break. Though there were plenty of chances for both sides in the second period the score remained the same. At Bloomfield Road that score was repeated with United triumphing by the odd goal in three.

MANCHESTER UNITED 3 BLACKBURN ROVERS 0
DIVISION ONE 21 NOVEMBER 1964

IAN MOIR, WHO had seemed destined for Aberdeen, came in for what turned out to be his farewell appearance against Blackpool but made way for the visit of Blackburn and eventually joined the Seasiders in February. However, another long running transfer saga ended this week with Maurice Setters joining Stoke despite turning them down a month earlier.

The dropping of Bobby Charlton from the England team may have been a disappointment for the player but he hadn't let Alf Ramsey's snub affect his performances for United. Blackburn were a solid defensive unit but proved susceptible from the wings. Connelly and Best saw more of the ball as a result and each scored after cutting inside to unleash shots. David Herd hit the net for the seventh successive game.

Though competent in attack, Rovers lacked United's thrust in the final third and the momentary lapses which allowed the home forwards in were not repeated at the other end.

SCOTLAND 3 NORTHERN IRELAND 2
HOME INTERNATIONAL 25 NOVEMBER 1964

A HIGHLY ACCOMPLISHED Scotland side were favoured to emerge victorious but were shocked when Best opened the scoring on 10 minutes after a jinking run down the wing and a low shot past Campbell Forsyth. Davie Wilson equalised within a minute and Dundee's Alan Gilzean, the subject of recent bids from Tottenham Hotspur, put the Scots ahead with little more than quarter of an hour gone.

Ireland refused to lie down and

quickly recovered. Their superiority was underlined when Billy Irvine nodded in from right back Jimmy Magill's cross.

Wilson, partnering George's United teammate Denis Law in attack, made it 3-2 just before the break. For some reason the second half failed to reach the same dizzy heights and saw no further goals as the game petered out.

ARSENAL 2 MANCHESTER UNITED 3
DIVISION ONE 28 NOVEMBER 1964

UNITED'S LEAD AT the top grew to three points after a fine win at Highbury. The final score may have been tight but early on the game looked all but over as The Reds stormed into a comfortable lead.

Denis Law struck within four minutes. Soon after Connelly stretched the advantage and Law grabbed a second. David Herd looked dangerous against his old employers who hit back to reduce the gap to a single goal. However, failure to find a third meant United stretched their winning run to 17 games.

MANCHESTER UNITED 4 BORUSSIA DORTMUND 0 (AGG 10-1)
FAIRS CUP 2ND ROUND 2ND LEG 2 DECEMBER 1964

DESPITE THE HUGE lead established in Germany, there was no question of United taking things easy. Borussia had run into a bit of form since the last meeting and had some key players back.

Dortmund pooled much of their resources into defence in a bid not to be totally humiliated but succumbed to a first minute Bobby Charlton goal which stretched United's advantage to six. The same player hit another soon after. This kind of form and goalscoring had seen Charlton earn an England recall. Law and Connelly rounded off the scoring.

MANCHESTER UNITED 0 LEEDS UNITED 1
DIVISION ONE 5 DECEMBER 1964

LEEDS HAD BEEN promoted as Second Division Champions the previous season and were fancied to do well in the top flight, although few experts anticipated a title challenge. Just a few years earlier Leeds looked likely to drop into Division Three. A winning start had been marred by four defeats over the next seven games but now, as form became more consistent, the Yorkshire side rose to third, four points behind United at the top.

Prior to kick-off, as the players lined up in the tunnel, George felt the unmistakable rake of studs against his right calf. Leeds skipper Bobby Collins, who played at inside-left, a position with no real reputation for overtly aggressive play, stood grinning and warned George this was just for starters. With George on the right flank the two would obviously come into contact at various stages of the game and Collins wanted to ensure Best knew there would be a price if he came too close or made too much of a fool out of him.

Nobby Stiles, who acted as the midfield enforcer on the pitch and had the protection of Best almost written into his job description, slammed the snarling Scotsman into the wall promising to hit him harder every time he touched George.

Collins was rattled and his all-out assault never occurred, though Leeds remained physical in their approach with various players only too happy for George to know they were there. Worse still, Collins managed to grab the game's only goal, picking up the pieces after Pat

Dunne could only parry a Terry Cooper shot.

However, Leeds' Paul Reaney was the real star of the game. He had been detailed to man mark Best who rarely got much change out of matches with Leeds as a direct result. Don Revie relied heavily on maintaining a strong defence and instructed his wingers to drop deep whenever they didn't have the ball.

United still had a fair number of opportunities and should have kept the unbeaten league run going but found Gary Sprake in inspired form. It was The Peacock's first Old Trafford victory in 33 years and United's first league defeat in 16 games.

WEST BROMWICH ALBION 1 MANCHESTER UNITED 1
DIVISION ONE 12 DECEMBER 1964

JUST DAYS PRIOR to this journey to The Hawthorns, Denis Law had appeared at a FA disciplinary hearing on charges of swearing and making threatening gestures to referee Peter Rhodes of York. He had been sent off for the offences at Blackpool just under a month earlier but the severity of his transgressions meant the game's authorities needed to hold their own hearing. 24 hours before kick-off judgement was handed down.

A 28-day ban due to commence on the following Monday and a £50 fine with costs meant he could play this weekend but otherwise would remain out until United met Nottingham Forest on 16 January 1965 or a total of six games.

Law signed off in style with a goal on 15 minutes. A disputed John Kaye effort,

which seemed not to have crossed the line, equalised for The Baggies before the break and the score remained the same until the close.

Best came through this game although he still had badly bruised ribs suffered against Leeds - he had a quiet one as a result. United were in control of the match for all but brief periods and only had themselves to blame for missing out on the extra point after spurning a host of chances. John Connelly in particular missed a sitter. Albion came into the game during the final stages but good defence ensured United rode out the storm.

MANCHESTER UNITED 1 BIRMINGHAM CITY 1
DIVISION ONE 16 DECEMBER 1964

DAVID SADLER CAME in for the suspended Law with David Herd shuffled over to inside-left as a direct replacement for the absent striker. On an icy pitch Birmingham rarely ventured forward and massed behind the ball. An indication of the visitor's intent was to play inside forward Brian Sharples behind the centre-halfs for the entire 90 minutes.

United still created a host of chances.

However, for the third game in a row they were thwarted by poor finishing. Bobby Charlton hit a post and, but for a lucky save from John Schofield, would have gone one better before actually scoring from the spot. A Dennis Thwaites equaliser meant United dropped points against Midland opposition for the second time in four days.

SHEFFIELD UNITED 0 MANCHESTER UNITED 1
DIVISION ONE 26 DECEMBER 1964

A FROZEN OLD Trafford pitch had seen the game with Leicester City scheduled for the previous Saturday called off. With United through to the next phase in Europe, a decent bet to progress in the FA Cup due to the kindness of the draw and the league run in due to commence soon there were already concerns about fixture congestion.

Best scored the game's only goal but was forced to play second fiddle to Bobby

Charlton on the afternoon who was magnificent and covered all areas of the pitch. It was a rare occasion when an on song George was outshone by anyone but managers, players and fans eulogised about Charlton. Best had struggled with the hard ground early on but eventually began to cause problems shooting narrowly wide and forcing a good save from a header amongst plenty of other chances.

MANCHESTER UNITED 1 SHEFFIELD UNITED 1
DIVISION ONE 28 DECEMBER 1964

AFTER JOURNEYING BACK from Bramall Lane with a win bonus secured, United would have backed themselves to repeat the trick at home but a better Blades performance left them frustrated.

While Best had been excellent on Boxing day, he rarely touched the same heights here. His reduced input was the crucial difference between a home win and a share of the points though David

Herd wasted a good early chance after slipping at the crucial moment. Not long after John Connelly contrived to miss after taking a superb ball from Charlton which left him with most of the goal to aim at. The Blades keeper Hodgkinson was called into action to deny headers from Connelly and then Best. The latter save gave Sheffield great heart but seemed to nag at Best who appeared caught in two minds soon after when the ball ran into his path. The result was a shot which soared over the bar.

United upped the pressure after the break and Hodgkinson denied Charlton spectacularly before, on 53 minutes, Stiles sent a high ball into the area which the otherwise flawless keeper misjudged. Failing to read the bounce may have been his only error of the game but it was one

cruelly punished by David Herd who nodded into an empty net.

The Blades composed themselves quickly. Jones almost levelled before the visitors equalised on the hour, Dunne mishandling a Graham Shaw drive under pressure from the hardworking Jones. Alan Woodward's tap-in was no less than they deserved.

MANCHESTER UNITED 2 CHESTER 1
FA Cup 3rd Rd 9 January 1965

CHESTER OF THE Fourth Division landed draw's plum tie after an impressive 5-2 win over Barnsley in Round Two. These sides had never met in the league or cup before, though a team from Old Trafford had been dispatched to Sealand Road for a friendly to inaugurate the floodlights.

David Sadler was dropped after recent goal shy performances. Without Law, United were struggling for a hit man as, despite some great approach play. there was nobody to convert the chances. Liverpool born Albert Kinsey, who still lived on Merseyside, was brought in to link with Best on the left taking the inside forward position which he was likely to relinquish the following weekend when Law returned. Though he would have

played against Fulham seven days earlier but for a postponement.

The first few minutes were probably more open than Matt Busby would have preferred and Chester drew first blood through outside right Jimmy Humes. It took United almost an hour to get level despite taking control of the game from the point they fell behind.

However, once on terms Chester's spirit drained and the game was over within minutes of Best taking Charlton's pass to score. Kinsey, who could have had a debut goal prior to actually scoring, was relieved to find the net after seeing other chances saved by an inspired Dennis Reeves.

NOTTINGHAM FOREST 2 MANCHESTER UNITED 2
Division One 16 January 1965

DESPITE A CREDITABLE performance in the cup, Albert Kinsey was omitted as expected to make way for the return of Denis Law. Thanks to the weather he had missed fewer games than expected and his first touch was a pass to Best on

the wing. With each knowing what their colleague would do Law attacked the six yard box while the winger centred for his skipper. The ball was cleanly met after a slide through the mud but rolled inches wide. It was enough to convince everyone that United were back as goal threat.

Best cut in during the next attack though with the ball at his feet and delayed the shot which was cleared. A foul on George outside the area led to the opener. Law shaped to be involved in the set piece but then jogged away seemingly to an innocuous position but a reverse pass found the Scot who had been left in space and exploited the gift by rounding the keeper then firing in from close range with just three minutes gone.

Alan Hinton equalised after a quarter of an hour and Peter Hindley at right back kept Best on a tight leash after the opening exchanges but the United man got enough of the ball to create a fair proportion of chances. Law made it 2-1 and though Hinton levelled again with a goal which looked well offside there was some relief that United finally seemed able to turn territorial advantage into goals.

MANCHESTER UNITED 1 EVERTON 1
Fairs Cup 3rd Rd 1st leg 20 January 1965

Everton had a number of long and short term injuries. and, though their team was likely to be unsettled as a result, The Toffees seemed to get the better of this all-English European encounter with a 1-1 draw. It wasn't a bad result for an away leg during which United had dominated play but were loose in front of

goal again. Even Law struggled to hit the target.

John Connelly grabbed United's only goal. Everton snatched their chance. The ball broke off Bill Foulkes, who was trying to tidy up an attack, but inadvertently set up a chance.

MANCHESTER UNITED 1 STOKE CITY 1
Division One 23 January 1965

Maurice Setters made a swift return to Old Trafford following his transfer to The Victoria Ground and, though old favourite Dennis Viollet was a doubt, he made the starting line-up. Neither side established a psychological advantage for the cup clash to be played the following week. Stanley Matthews was rumoured to be ready for a return to the first team but in the end played for Stoke's reserves against United's second string.

Alan Bloor put Stoke into an early lead but Law equalised in a game which

followed a similar pattern to so many over recent months in that United dominated only to be frustrated by either the opposition or their own finishing. Setters, amongst other visiting backs, was exceptional, using his years of experience and inside knowledge to resist his old side.

STOKE CITY 0 MANCHESTER UNITED 0
FA Cup 4th Rd 30 January 1965

Matt Busby took his squad to Blackpool for most of the week to prepare for this game. Stanley Matthews was named in a 13-man squad for the home side which whetted many appetites towards the prospect of seeing the young and upcoming George Best and the near 50 year-old maestro on the same pitch. However, Tony Waddington omitted Matthews due to the tricky conditions underfoot. He didn't want to lose the winger for another spell during his last season in the Football League. A minutes silence was held after the recent death of Winston Churchill.

Best was involved in the first move of the game - zig-zagging across the field before sending in a cross which David Herd put over. Good approach play from the wings was let down by the limited amount of penetration United were able to make down the middle and a little wastefulness. Though once again Stoke's backline was superb.

MANCHESTER UNITED 1 STOKE CITY 0
FA Cup 4th Rd Replay 3 February 1965

United's needs ensured Matt Busby took a different approach to releasing George Best for international duty with Northern Ireland though this time, with the game being an under-23 international in Cardiff, the country's request was deemed a minor priority. It would have meant George playing two games within 24 hours as there was little chance he would not be selected for the crunch Fairs Cup tie with Everton.

David Herd notched a late winner. It seemed Stoke were content to defend and look for a third game if they could not nick something at Old Trafford. The onus was on United as the home side but the Potters barely had a chance of note.

TOTTENHAM HOTSPUR 1 MANCHESTER UNITED 0
Division One 6 February 1965

Both sets of forwards wallowed in an open game but were kept in check by superb defending. Nobby Stiles kept a vice like grip on Jimmy Greaves but full back Ron Henry hit a long range winner. It was the first goal of his career in a ten year stay at White Hart Lane.

Law and Best combined well at stages though United only really forced last gasp saves in the final quarter but an expensively assembled Spurs side held out.

EVERTON 1 MANCHESTER UNITED 2 (AGG 2-3)
FAIRS CUP 3RD ROUND 2ND LEG 9 FEBRUARY 1965

IN CONTRAST TO recent games which United had bossed but let themselves down in front of goal, Everton were the stronger side here but fell to a couple of sucker punches. The first of these was a quick break six minutes in when John Connelly fired home from close range forcing the ball through Gordon West's arms. A parried shot from Connelly picked up by David Herd all but sealed the win before half-time.

Everton cut off supply to the left wing forcing Best into less dangerous areas of the pitch and managed to keep Bobby Charlton starved of the ball too. A very competent defence saw United through with few alarms.

MANCHESTER UNITED 3 BURNLEY 2
DIVISION ONE 13 FEBRUARY 1965

UNITED SCORED THREE in a game for the first time in ten weeks and each of the players who scored needed the goals. Bobby Charlton had only hit two in the league this season but added a third here while David Herd and George Best scored their first goals of 1965.

George's goal came after ten minutes and set him up for a fine match. Superb ball play from Best was a highlight of the afternoon though he did deny an unmarked Nobby Stiles the chance to score by holding on to the ball for an inordinate amount of time while Stiles signalled frantically in the middle.

United led 3-1 for a long time but Burnley pulled one back before the close. Bill Foulkes would no doubt have preferred to keep a clean sheet in his 450th league game for the club.

MANCHESTER UNITED 2 BURNLEY 1
FA CUP 5TH RD 20 FEBRUARY 1965

UNITED DREW a team against which they had played a league fixture the previous week for the second round in a row. They looked likely to be exiting the cup as time ran out - Burnley held an interval lead through Andy Lochhead and were very good value for it, although Best had drawn a good save early on.

United were far better in the second half and controlled the game but couldn't force the ball over the line. It took 80 minutes for the equaliser to arrive when Best played Denis Law in. The pass had been completed without a boot on the Scot's foot. It had flown off during a typically committed tackle and the action was so frenetic that he had no chance to replace it and carried his footwear until full time. This period included the moment he took advantage of a Fred Smith injury to get round the back of the defence, passing for Paddy Crerand to net the winner.

SUNDERLAND 1 MANCHESTER UNITED 0
DIVISION ONE 24 FEBRUARY 1965

THE HEROICS OF midweek were replaced by a rather meek performance from a seemingly jaded and battered United side who had been similarly outclassed by Sunderland in the FA Cup two years earlier. A cannonball shot from Harry Hood gave Pat Dunne no chance and hit the net before he knew it. The Rokerites also had one disallowed and hit the post.

United, who created few opportunities, now lay three points behind Leeds United and Chelsea having wasted their game in hand over the top two. Few players were able to hold their heads up as Sunderland belied their status as relegation candidates. One of those walking tall was 18 year-old debutant John Fitzpatrick who came in for Nobby Stiles but a few players were doubts for the following week. Paddy Crerand required three stitches in a head wound while Best was limping throughout the final stages with a bruised thigh.

MANCHESTER UNITED 3 WOLVES 0
DIVISION ONE 27 FEBRUARY 1965

BEST PASSED A fitness test on the morning of the game and moved to inside forward replacing Bobby Charlton who switched to George's more accustomed outside left berth and scored two goals to justify Busby's reshuffle. The manager had gambled that Best could do untold damage from a more involved 'schemers' position rather than out on the flanks and so it proved.

Quick dividends had already been reaped from the tactical changes as after four minutes John Connelly scored converting a Charlton cross from close in. From then on the result was in little doubt. Charlton had seemed somewhat flat recent weeks but revelled in his new position.

WOLVES 3 MANCHESTER UNITED 5
FA CUP 6TH RD 10 MARCH 1965

DENIS LAW WAS a doubt before the game after receiving an accidental head butt from Bill Foukles in a goalmouth scramble. Surprisingly this was the third successive time United had been pitted against a side in the cup that they had just faced in the league immediately prior to a cup clash. Foulkes had broken his nose but also played.

Hugh McIlmoyle gave Wolves the lead after just three minutes, then hit another to make it 2-0 with less than a quarter of an hour gone. Both goals seemed unjust. The first appeared to involve a handball and the second a clear foul in the build-up. In those circumstances anyone could have been forgiven for wondering whether this would be Wolves' day but United drew on their reserves, experience and confidence in the ability of each other to turn things around, although Wolves almost hit a third before the tide finally turned.

Denis Law, leading a continuous assault, scored twice. Herd, Crerand and Best also found the net to complete a great comeback. Best's goal came direct from a corner kick which Law, the Wolves keeper and David Herd missed completely. The ball floating in.

United reached the semi-final for the fourth successive year, a record only Newcastle in the early 1900s could match.

MANCHESTER UNITED 4 CHELSEA 0
DIVISION ONE 13 MARCH 1965

CHELSEA WERE LOOKING to mount a serious title challenge and this fixture was a big opportunity for them to reinforce their credentials at the top of the table. Yet their hopes took a hammering at Old Trafford.

Manager Tommy Docherty had made a number of changes to the side beaten at Stamford Bridge earlier in the season. Ken Shellito was missing replaced by Ron Harris who had been deployed in a central position back in September. Chopper stood at 5' 7", roughly the same height as George Best but the Irishman was a giant on the day, giving the Chelsea rearguard a roasting.

A well-deserved goal was conjured up from nowhere after George had one of his hunches and attacked Eddie McCreadie's clearance. The defender panicked tried to readjust his plans but no more than feathered at a back-pass. He was left on his knees as Best latched on to the ball, accelerated forward and then chipped Peter Bonetti from an acute angle, the ball nestling in the far corner of the net.

The win over Chelsea meant United were back within striking distance of the top giving the club a boost and posting notice that George and the team were back to their best for the title run-in.

MANCHESTER UNITED 4 FULHAM 1
DIVISION ONE 15 MARCH 1965

UNITED WERE FINALLY hitting their stride again and at no more opportune time than the final six weeks of the campaign with three trophies still up for grabs. Rodney Marsh scored for Fulham four minutes in but United quickly equalised through a mistake by keeper Tony Macedo who made great saves before and after his lapse but found football a cruel fate.

Herd scored another with John Connelly's brace completing the scoring.

NORTHERN IRELAND 2 HOLLAND 1
WORLD CUP QUALIFIER 17 MARCH 1965

UNFANCIED HOLLAND SHOCKED the Irish when they took the lead after seven minutes - striker Hennie Van Nee letting fly from outside the area. Yet by the close they had been totally outclassed by the home side who deserved to win by more than one goal - the Dutch had only two shots all game (including that goal) and victory was more comfortable than the scoreline suggests.

Terry Neill may not have been a regular member of the Arsenal side but kept himself sharp with reserve team games and plenty of hard work in training. The national captain was an anchor in defence and won the tie with a header from George Best's dipping corner with an hour gone.

Earlier, inside-right Johnny Crossan had drawn Ireland level within four minutes of falling behind after rounding the keeper then rolling the ball into an empty net. He went close on three occasions seeing his efforts cleared by last gasp saves or clearances off the line but a shaky looking defence on the end of so much pressure will always find it tricky to hold out.

Best had almost directed an earlier corner which curled wickedly straight into goal and in the next attack he was released by Crossan and had a shot nudged over the bar by keeper Pieters Graafland.

SHEFFIELD WEDNESDAY 1 MANCHESTER UNITED 0
DIVISION ONE 20 MARCH 1965

AN INTERNATIONAL WEEK plus a league programme meant a busy time for George and his colleagues who were in the middle of a run of five games in 10 days.

A muddy Hillsborough pitch didn't help in this regard, pushing tired limbs to their limit. It became harder to move and United's attack was nullified by this as much as Wednesday's defence.

United created chances but didn't carry enough threat up front, before John Fantham scored a late winner for The Owls.

MANCHESTER UNITED 2 BLACKPOOL 0
DIVISION ONE 22 MARCH 1965

TIRELESS WORK IN midfield by Bobby Charlton and others saw United through. Denis Law scored both goals late on but the strikes would only have earned a draw had Blackpool not hit the bar twice in the last few minutes. Best, Herd and Law combined well but this was a game more suited to toughing things out than flair football.

MANCHESTER UNITED 0 LEEDS UNITED 0
FA CUP SF 27 MARCH 1965

LEEDS UNITED HAD rarely ventured beyond the opening rounds of the cup, between 1953 and 1962 they failed to win a single cup game. During this same period United had reached Wembley three times winning the coveted trophy in 1963. However with just one point between the two sides, who sat second and third in the table, this looked likely to be a close contest.

With memories of the clash at Old Trafford last December still fresh in his mind, plus capers between Leeds and other clubs well reported, George seemed reluctant to get involved in the pre-match hype. Matt Busby, on the other hand, was less appreciative of his opposite number, Don Revie, who, he felt, sent out his sides with the wrong agenda. He summed this up in his team talks when he went through the likely line-up labelling each a dirty bastard of one type or another. Even Bobby Charlton's brother Jack was summed up in the same dismissive terms. Only Billy Bremner, who Busby regarded as 'a good Scottish lad', was spared his wrath.

65,000 fans packed Hillsborough for this eagerly awaited semi-final. The game was no more than a minute old when Bremner sent Bobby Charlton nose first into the ground. The pitch had not improved since United's defeat to Wednesday a week earlier. The game inevitably became bogged down in the South Yorkshire quagmire with the more defensive-minded players holding sway.

Denis Law was also harshly dealt with by Bremner in the opening phases but the Leeds central midfielder was repaid with a bloody nose after one or two stiff challenges and almost put through his own goal in trying to divert a John Connelly centre forcing Sprake into a save.

Otherwise there was little constructive play throughout the game and more than half a dozen on either side seemed focussed on fighting rather than football as battles raged across the pitch. 24 free-kicks were given against United with 10 conceded by Leeds. As if to sum up the trench warfare of this contest, Denis Law trudged away at the end with his jersey ripped around the neck courtesy of a tussle with Jack Charlton.

LEEDS UNITED 1 MANCHESTER UNITED 0
FA CUP SF REPLAY 31 MARCH 1965

FOUR DAYS LATER United and Leeds reconvened at Nottingham Forest's City Ground. The game still had an edge to it with the free-kick count remaining high but this time, on a better surface, there was some football to admire.

Leeds dominated the opening quarter as their midfield stifled Pat Crerand. Terry Cooper, who had missed out on the first tie, was little short of superb never letting Crerand more than a couple of yards out of his sight.

Without a creative spark United toiled to get the ball forward meaning that Best, Law and Charlton were stranded upfield and only gained possession from long balls in innocuous areas where the damage they could do was limited. Any loose balls were easily dealt with by a well-drilled Leeds backline.

Best, roaming in a more central position, did get a header on target early in the second half but the ball was turned aside by Sprake who made good ground to the angle of crossbar and post. David Herd wasted a golden chance to square the ball to George when forced wider than he would have liked before shooting into the side netting.

These opportunities proved to be rare yet despite being on top Leeds couldn't breakthrough until the last minute - Billy Bremner made the most of the space Leeds created by nodding the ball home after a late run into a congested penalty area, to send Leeds to Wembley.

BLACKBURN ROVERS 0 MANCHESTER UNITED 5
DIVISION ONE 3 APRIL 1965

AFTER THE CUP HEARTACHE of midweek, this looked like a tough fixture against local rivals. Leeds still held a one point lead over United with Chelsea another point better off at the top.

Understandably United were under the cosh for long periods of the first half and had their back line to thank for keeping them in the game until the attack rediscovered the their form.

Bobby Charlton was the star of what turned out to be an Ewood stroll - hitting his first domestic hat-trick since the turn of the decade.

John Connelly and David Herd rounded off the afternoon with one apiece as United recorded their heaviest away win of the season.

HOLLAND 0 NORTHERN IRELAND 0
WORLD CUP QUALIFIER 7 APRIL 1965

THE RETURN GAME with Holland in Rotterdam was a complete contrast to events in Belfast five months earlier but Northern Ireland still emerged with a creditable draw and World Cup qualification remained firmly in their own hands.

Bertie Peacock's side gave their all for 90 minutes mostly packing 11 men behind the ball and even when a break was on only Billy Irvine would usually be far enough upfield to take advantage.

Best's ability to take the ball for long, time consuming periods was exploited to the full. Holland still had plenty of possession in the opposing half but were resisted with surprising ease and eventually ran out of ideas to break Northern Ireland down.

MANCHESTER UNITED 1 LEICESTER CITY 0
DIVISION ONE 12 APRIL 1965

The gap to Leeds was reduced to two points with this vital home win, meaning the clash at Elland Road that weekend, already perceived as a crunch clash in deciding the championship's destination, took on even more significance.

United were not as fluent as they had been at Blackburn but were always good enough to edge out Leicester. Bobby Charlton, who had starred for club and country in recent weeks, was devastating - creating opportunities which his fellow forwards failed to finish but a well worked David Herd goal proved enough.

John Aston Junior, son of former United defender and coach Johnny Aston, made his debut on the left wing lining up with George Best who had been pushed to inside left as a replacement for Denis Law.

Aston showed some decent touches but George had one of his rare off days which eventually showed in the play of his partner during the second half.

LEEDS UNITED 0 MANCHESTER UNITED 1
DIVISION ONE 17 APRIL 1965

THIS WAS THE fourth and most important encounter between United and Leeds in 1964-65. United had yet to score in 270 minutes against Revie's team and this title decider was expected to follow that form. The Tykes held all the aces going into this game, a win would send them 4 points ahead of United and, with Chelsea's title challenge fading fast, this was a great opportunity for Bremner et al to tie-up the title.

Understandably the intense atmosphere of a title decider transmitted itself to the players and the 52,000 fans packed into Elland Road watched football often wracked by anxiety.

Both sides looked set to a miss a key player until Denis Law, whose knee injury had flared up again, passed a late fitness test while Billy Bremner was forced to sit it out in the stands through suspension. Leeds certainly felt the Scot's absence.

Gary Sprake was kept busy from the first whistle before he was beaten by John Connelly with just a quarter of an hour gone. The right sided midfielder had just been recalled to the England side on the back of a good run of scoring form. This was the ex-Burnley man's 14th of the campaign and perhaps his most vital in a United shirt.

Best had helped create the goal after a cross had pulled Jack Charlton out of position. Full-back Tony Dunne went forward, fed Law who flicked on for Connelly who made no mistake in beating Sprake.

It was another mixed game for George, despite a return to the wing. Once again Bobby Charlton excelled but United's attacking thrust was blunted by knocks to Law and Herd. Both had succumbed to various setbacks over recent months and were limping around the field before the close. Thankfully a well drilled defence was able to hold off Leeds' late assault and Busby was now in pole position to land his first league title since Munich and earn a place in the European Cup to boot.

BIRMINGHAM CITY 2 MANCHESTER UNITED 4
DIVISION ONE 19 APRIL 1965

FULL-BACK NOEL CANTWELL was drafted in as a replacement for David Herd at centre forward. The 33 year-old had not played for just over 12 months and he was pressed into duty here as a striker as he had done the job on countless occasions for the Republic of Ireland.

United were now level with Leeds although the psychological advantage of winning at Elland Road made them favourites. Nevertheless, United looked edgy during the opening phases until Best notched to relieve the tension. Birmingham continued to look dangerous and took a deserved 2-1 lead. Best levelled before Charlton and Cantwell netted to give the final score a lop-sided appearance.

Sheffield Wednesday did The Reds a huge favour, winning a white rose battle with Leeds by a significant margin the same day while Chelsea were suddenly rocked by a scandal in Blackpool which saw eight players suspended by manager Tommy Docherty after they were discovered breaking a club curfew.

The breakdown in relations between players and management had a detrimental effect on The Pensioners' form following their 4-0 destruction of Liverpool the previous weekend - they quickly slipped out of the title picture.

MANCHESTER UNITED 3 LIVERPOOL 0
DIVISION ONE 24 APRIL 1965

WITH BILL SHANKLY reluctant to risk key players just seven days before their first FA Cup final in 15 years, Liverpool were represented by a team of fringe players. But as a number of their squad had a chance to state their case for a berth at Wembley, United could take nothing for granted.

Phil Chisnall made his first return to Old Trafford since his transfer to Anfield but his welcome was less than hospitable on the pitch as United made all the early play. Best was only just denied by a Ron Yeats challenge after a defence splitting ball had fooled everyone but Liverpool's dreadnought captain.

The visitors rallied then faded as Bobby Charlton exercised total control of the engine room - he hit the post twice but United were able to rely on Denis Law's instincts as a poacher to bag a couple. Connelly completed a comprehensive win leaving United a win short of the title.

MANCHESTER UNITED 3 ARSENAL 1
DIVISION ONE 26 APRIL 1965

UNITED ENTERED THE penultimate game of the season a point behind Leeds but with a game in hand. As this was effectively the last day of The Tykes' league season, United could win the league if they won and Leeds didn't.

Leeds travelled to St Andrews to face rock bottom Birmingham City, who were already relegated following United's 4-2 win at St Andrews the previous week, and had claimed just seven wins all term. The Blues were not fancied to take anything from the game. Remarkably they took the lead just four minutes in through Dennis Thwaites. However Birmingham's influential winger Alex Jackson was forced off the field with a dislocated shoulder after a robust clash with Terry Cooper meaning that the Midlanders would be a man down for the remaining 80 minutes or so.

At one stage the numerical advantage for Leeds increased to two as Malcolm Beard was forced out for a short spell but Birmingham maintained their lead until the break. It was an open game and either side could have added to the scoring but the Midland side had the better of the earlier exchanges after the break going 3-0 up within six minutes of the restart. Beard and Geoff Bowden with the goals.

Back at Old Trafford George Best netted for United after six minutes with a wondrous strike. Denis Law, all but limping due to a knee injury, still managed to get in advanced positions and doubled United's lead with little less than an hour

gone just as Arsenal were beginning to test United's back line.

Meanwhile Leeds, with an FA Cup final appearance looming that Saturday, refused to sit back. Billy Bremner moved up to act as an auxiliary centre forward as he had on a handful of occasions when necessity demanded. A foul on the Scot allowed Giles to pull one back from the spot but the title still looked all but over.

Meanwhile George Eastham pulled one back from the spot for Arsenal. It made things a little more interesting but Leeds still had to earn something from their game then hope that United were either pegged back or Arsenal completed an unlikely comeback to claim both points in the twenty minutes remaining.

Leeds poured everything into attack and right back Paul Reaney, who had never scored in over a century of league appearances, made it 2-3 before Jack Charlton, who had also been pressed into service as an emergency striker, thumped home an equaliser with two minutes on the clock.

In the seconds that remained Leeds camped in the Birmingham half but the hosts held on. Their only hope was that The Gunners could equalise at Old Trafford but with Law blasting in from a few yards out in the dying seconds United topped the league on goal average.

Only a heavy defeat in the final game at Villa Park could deny The Reds the title. This was Matt Busby's first league title since the Busby Babes era and, perhaps understandably, there was a great deal of emotion attached to United qualifying for the European Cup again.

ASTON VILLA 2 MANCHESTER UNITED 1
DIVISION ONE 28 APRIL 1965

UNITED WERE BROUGHt back to earth with a jolt but, as the title was all but secure, there was little harm done and Villa were good value for their win. The simple maths were that Villa needed to beat United by 19 goals in order to hand Leeds the crown but there was no question of anything other than a full strength side seeing out the campaign. Paddy Crerand, who was replaced by John Fitzpatrick, being the only change.

United seemed in poor form during a disjointed first hour and a slip by keeper

Pat Dunne gifted a comic goal to the home side when a shot went clean through his legs. Thinking he would turn round to see the ball in his net Dunne was slow to react. Only then did he realise it had not crossed the line due to heavy conditions. This allowed Villa's strikers the time to swoop and score one of the easiest goals of the season. Conversely Bobby Charlton's lone reply was possibly the finest goal of the campaign, beating several defenders with a blistering run before slamming the ball home.

NORTHERN IRELAND 4 ALBANIA 1
WORLD CUP QUALIFIER 7 MAY 1965

A CONVINCING HOME win over Albania took Northern Ireland to the top of their qualifying group with seven points from five games. John Crossan scored a hat-trick but any number of players could have run him close for that feat based on chances created.

He bagged the first after 16 minutes taking a flick on from Jimmy Nicholson's free-kick. On the half hour a move which began with Best sprinting down the left saw him notch a second.

Jashari, Albania's outside left, pulled one back to make it 2-1 soon after the break. The third came after Billy Irvine had been fouled in the area 20 minutes from time. George should have won a spot kick five minutes earlier when he was wrestled to the floor by keeper Joanku. However, he had the last laugh close to the end scoring directly from a corner. He had threatened to do this in a couple of games and the thought was that it had been deliberate on each occasion.

MANCHESTER UNITED 5 RACING STRASBOURG 0
FAIRS CUP QUARTER-FINAL 1ST LEG 12 MAY 1965

BY THIS STAGE of Fairs Cup history, the competition had become a shambles. Keen to ensure the competition prospered

UEFA had accepted 48 entries but with no preliminary round the initial stages had dragged on until mid-April. Replays had been required in a number of games and other commitments for clubs in different countries made progress impossible. Teams such as United who qualified for the last eight back in February had a further three months to wait before they could play their next game.

The absurdity of the situation was underlined by the fact that Strasbourg had been scouted as early as mid-March but that report may as well have been torn up given the time which had elapsed. In addition Ferencvaros, who lay in wait for the victors, had reached the last four a month previously.

United and Strasbourg had started disagreeing over dates during early spring. United wanted to relieve their fixture congestion but Strasbourg were keen to go ahead as soon as possible. This date was agreed despite disgruntlment within Old Trafford as a lucrative end of season trip was cancelled.

UEFA had previous form in failing to think through their decisions at the initial stages of this same trophy. The inaugural competition in 1955 took three years to complete just 23 games. Now there were too many clubs to narrow down the quarter-finalists meaning a couple of teams had been given byes but as United were not one of them the season had to be artificially extended.

With 55 games gone across all competitions the players had been given a well deserved rest but reported back for training in good time to prepare. Strasbourg had eliminated Barcelona on the toss of a coin after three games failed to break the deadlock but were no match for United who followed the parading of the championship trophy with a 5 star performance.

Goals from John Connelly, Bobby Charlton, David Herd and a couple from Denis Law, who combined effectively with Best, made the newly crowned English champions an irresistible force.

STRASBOURG 0 MANCHESTER UNITED 0 (AGG 0-5)
FAIRS CUP QUARTER-FINAL 2ND LEG 19 MAY 1965

UNITED COMPLETED THE job set-up so superbly in the first leg with a professional performance in the Stade de la Meinau. They should have added to the aggregate scoreline as a host of chances went begging but Strasbourg exited the competition with their pride intact as United preserved themselves for the task of taking on Ferencvaros in the semi-finals.

MANCHESTER UNITED 3 FERENCVAROS 2
FAIRS CUP SEMI-FINAL 1ST LEG 31 MAY 1965

CRACK HUNGARIAN SIDE Ferencvaros, who had already started their new season, and as reigning national champions would go into next term's European Cup, were acknowledged to be United's toughest test in the Fairs Cup to date. However, neither side got to play their football in a bad tempered affair which set the standard for most of this fraught encounter. Paddy Crerand, for one, was spoken to by the referee who struggled to maintain control.

A prolonged season looked like it was becoming too much for a young professional like Best who seemed in need of a break but could not be afforded the opportunity to take a holiday until the Fairs Cup campaign ended. David Herd scored twice with Denis Law adding another to give United a precarious lead.

FERENCVAROS 1 MANCHESTER UNITED 0 (AGG 3-3)
FAIRS CUP SEMI-FINAL 2ND LEG 6 JUNE 1965

DEFEAT BY THE odd goal left the semi-final level at 3-3 after 210 minutes of play or to be more accurate combat. Both sides had to take responsibility for the depths the match eventually descended to. It had already been a scrappy encounter with little to distinguish either club's pretensions to lift the trophy. Paddy Crerand was dismissed and could have few complaints.

FERENCVAROS 2 MANCHESTER UNITED 1
FAIRS CUP SEMI-FINAL REPLAY 16 JUNE 1965

THE SEASON FINALLY ended more than ten months after it had begun and although there would be no European final for United they at least bowed out on a positive note after taking part in the type of game this encounter should have been noted for.

Best missed a good chance to get United away to a perfect start but wasn't the only one to pull an effort off target. When Ferencvaros keeper Jeczi did manage to keep accurate shots out it was often down to luck. John Connelly scored in the 85th minute but with Ferencvaros already 2-0 up at that stage it was to no avail. Their comfortable margin had been established soon after the interval and each strike was down to superb wing-play.

The Hungarians finally went on to lift the trophy the following week though, rather than stage the tie at a neutral venue, finalists Juventus were invited to play hosts. Mate Fenyvesi scored the only goal of the game 16 minutes from time as Ferencvaros became the first club from the Eastern Bloc to win a European trophy.

1964-65

The 1964-65 season represented a turning point for Manchester United. Unlucky hitherto in their quest for the league their eventual triumph over Leeds and the nature of their victory at Elland Road told of a team developing the happy knack of winning important matches. Matt Busby's quest to build a third great team had already succeeded to some extent but the campaign for which this team was built, namely the securing of the European Cup, was now eagerly anticipated by a club denied the opportunity of European domination.

The foundation of the new look United was a solid defence led by Munich survivor Bill Foulkes and raw recruit Nobby Stiles. Yet it was the vibrant attack led by Denis Law, top scorer for the third successive season, that thrilled crowds home and away. Ably assisted by David Herd, John Connelly, Charlton and Best, who reached double figures and missed just one game in his first full season, United had one of the finest forward lines to ever grace English football.

Individually, George became the target for the league's boot boys. From Ron Harris at Chelsea to Leeds' Bobby Collins, opponents served warning that the humiliations endured by the likes of West Bromwich Albion's Graham Williams in George's debut match were not likely to be repeated against more ruthless opponents.

As a result of the attentions of the 'hard men' and an ardous 61-game season, George occasionally fired blanks, particularly around the middle of the term - when he failed to find the net for almost two months. Yet he continued to lay on chances for others and his reputation as a unique talent continued to grow. A flurry towards the close of the campaign, when George rediscovered his shooting boots, was vital in capturing the title on goal average from First Division new boys Leeds.

Meanwhile Best's fame grew. When later asked to pinpoint the moment he became a national celebrity, George would often refer back to the game against Chelsea at Stamford Bridge in late September 1964. With the lead football writers based in London, the press pack had been anticipating a virtuoso performance from the Irish wonderkid and he didn't disappoint. Turning in a display remembered fondly by Blues supporters, he single-handedly demolished a very good Chelsea side. Paddy Crerand famously claimed that Chelsea full-back Ken Shellito had been turned inside out so much that night that he had finished the game with 'twisted blood'.

Needless to say the former England international was never the same player again but then again neither was George. Applauded from the pitch by the home supporters, the capital was now his oyster as Best's looks and talent took his achievements beyond football as his army of admirers grew.

Football League Division One

DATE	OPPONENT	VENUE	SCORE	ATTD	1	2	3	4	5	6	7	8	9	10	11
22 August	WBA	Old Trafford	2-2	52,007	Gaskell	Brennan	Dunne(A)	Setters	Foulkes	Stiles	Connelly	Charlton[1]	Herd	Law[1]	Best
24 August	West Ham United	Upton Park	1-3	37,070	Gaskell	Brennan	Dunne(A)	Setters	Foulkes	Stiles	Connelly	Charlton	Herd	Law[1]	Best
29 August	Leicester City	Filbert Street	2-2	32,373	Gaskell	Brennan	Dunne(A)	Crerand	Foulkes	Stiles	Connelly	Charlton	Sadler[1]	Law[1]	Best[1]
2 September	West Ham United	Old Trafford	3-1	45,123	Gaskell	Brennan	Dunne(A)	Crerand	Foulkes	Stiles	Connelly[1]	Charlton	Sadler	Law[1]	Best
5 September	Fulham	Craven Cottage	1-2	36,291	Gaskell	Brennan	Dunne(A)	Crerand	Foulkes	Stiles	Connelly[1]	Charlton	Sadler	Law	Best
8 September	Everton	Goodison Park	3-3	63,024	Dunne(P)	Brennan	Dunne(A)	Crerand	Foulkes	Stiles	Connelly[1]	Charlton	Herd[1]	Law[1]	Best
12 September	Nott'm Forest	Old Trafford	3-0	45,012	Dunne(P)	Brennan	Dunne(A)	Crerand	Foulkes	Setters	Connelly[1]	Charlton	Herd[2]	Stiles	Best
16 September	Everton	Old Trafford	2-1	49,968	Dunne(P)	Brennan	Dunne(A)	Crerand	Foulkes	Stiles	Connelly[1]	Charlton	Herd	Law[1]	Best[1]
19 September	Stoke City	Victoria Ground	2-1	40,031	Dunne(P)	Brennan	Dunne(A)	Crerand	Foulkes	Setters	Connelly[1]	Charlton	Herd[1]	Stiles	Best
26 September	Tottenham H.	Old Trafford	4-1	53,058	Dunne(P)	Brennan	Dunne(A)	Crerand[2]	Foulkes	Stiles	Connelly	Charlton	Herd	Law[2]	Best
30 September	Chelsea	Stamford Bridge	2-0	60,769	Dunne(P)	Brennan	Dunne(A)	Crerand	Foulkes	Stiles	Connelly	Charlton	Herd	Law[1]	Best[1]
6 October	Burnley	Turf Moor	0-0	30,761	Dunne(P)	Brennan	Dunne(A)	Crerand	Foulkes	Stiles	Connelly	Charlton	Herd	Law	Best
10 October	Sunderland	Old Trafford	1-0	48,577	Dunne(P)	Brennan	Dunne(A)	Crerand	Foulkes	Stiles	Connelly	Charlton	Herd[1]	Law	Best
17 October	Wolves	Molineux	4-2	26,763	Dunne(P)	Brennan	Dunne(A)	Crerand	Foulkes	Stiles	Connelly	Charlton	Herd[1]	Law[2]	Best
24 October	Aston Villa	Old Trafford	7-0	35,807	Dunne(P)	Brennan	Dunne(A)	Crerand	Foulkes	Setters	Connelly[1]	Charlton	Herd[2]	Law[4]	Best
31 October	Liverpool	Anfield	2-0	52,402	Dunne(P)	Brennan	Dunne(A)	Crerand[1]	Foulkes	Stiles	Connelly[1]	Stiles	Herd[1]	Law	Best
7 November	Sheffield Wed	Old Trafford	1-0	50,178	Dunne(P)	Brennan	Dunne(A)	Crerand	Foulkes	Stiles	Connelly	Charlton	Herd[1]	Law	Best
21 November	Blackburn Rovers	Old Trafford	3-0	49,633	Dunne(P)	Brennan	Dunne(A)	Crerand	Foulkes	Stiles	Connelly[1]	Charlton	Herd[1]	Law	Best[1]
28 November	Arsenal	Highbury	3-2	59,627	Dunne(P)	Brennan	Dunne(A)	Crerand	Foulkes	Stiles	Connelly[1]	Charlton	Herd	Law[2]	Best
5 December	Leeds United	Old Trafford	0-1	53,374	Dunne(P)	Brennan	Dunne(A)	Crerand	Foulkes	Stiles	Connelly	Charlton	Herd	Law	Best
12 December	WBA	The Hawthorns	1-1	28,126	Dunne(P)	Brennan	Dunne(A)	Crerand	Foulkes	Stiles	Connelly	Charlton	Herd	Law[1]	Best
16 December	Birmingham City	Old Trafford	1-1	25,721	Dunne(P)	Brennan	Dunne(A)	Crerand	Foulkes	Stiles	Connelly	Charlton[1]	Sadler	Herd	Best[1]
26 December	Sheffield United	Bramall Lane	1-0	37,295	Dunne(P)	Brennan	Dunne(A)	Crerand	Foulkes	Stiles	Connelly	Charlton	Sadler	Herd	Best[1]
28 December	Sheffield United	Old Trafford	1-1	42,219	Dunne(P)	Brennan	Dunne(A)	Crerand	Foulkes	Stiles	Connelly	Charlton	Sadler	Herd[1]	Best
16 January	Nott'm Forest	City Ground	2-2	43,009	Dunne(P)	Brennan	Dunne(A)	Crerand	Foulkes	Stiles	Connelly	Charlton	Herd	Law[2]	Best
23 January	Stoke City	Old Trafford	1-1	50,392	Dunne(P)	Brennan	Dunne(A)	Crerand	Foulkes	Stiles	Connelly	Charlton	Herd	Law[1]	Best
6 February	Tottenham H.	White Hart Lane	0-1	58,639	Dunne(P)	Brennan	Dunne(A)	Crerand	Foulkes	Stiles	Connelly	Charlton	Herd	Law	Best
13 February	Burnley	Old Trafford	3-2	38,865	Dunne(P)	Brennan	Dunne(A)	Crerand	Foulkes	Stiles	Connelly	Charlton[1]	Herd[1]	Law	Best[1]
24 February	Sunderland	Roker Park	0-1	51,336	Dunne(P)	Brennan	Dunne(A)	Crerand	Foulkes	Fitzpatrick	Connelly	Charlton	Herd	Law	Best

Date	Opponents	Venue	Score	Att.	1	2	3	4	5	6	7	8	9	10	11
27 February	Wolves	Old Trafford	3-0	37,018	Dunne(P)	Brennan	Dunne(A)	Crerand	Foulkes	Stiles	**Connelly[1]**	**Charlton[2]**	Herd	Law	Best
13 March	Chelsea	Old Trafford	4-0	56,261	Dunne(P)	Brennan	Dunne(A)	Crerand	Foulkes	Stiles	Connelly	Charlton	**Herd[2]**	**Law[2]**	**Best[1]**
15 March	Fulham	Old Trafford	4-1	45,402	Dunne(P)	Brennan	Dunne(A)	Crerand	Foulkes	Stiles	**Connelly[2]**	Charlton	**Herd[2]**	Law	Best
20 March	Sheffield Wed	Hillsborough	0-1	33,549	Dunne(P)	Brennan	Dunne(A)	Crerand	Foulkes	Stiles	Connelly	Charlton	Herd	Law	Best
22 March	Blackpool	Old Trafford	2-0	42,318	Dunne(P)	Brennan	Dunne(A)	Crerand	Foulkes	Stiles	Connelly	Charlton	Herd	**Law[2]**	Best
3 April	Blackburn Rovers	Ewood Park	5-0	29,363	Dunne(P)	Brennan	Dunne(A)	Crerand	Foulkes	Stiles	**Connelly[1]**	**Charlton[3]**	**Herd[1]**	Law	Best
12 April	Leicester City	Old Trafford	1-0	34,114	Dunne(P)	Brennan	Dunne(A)	Crerand	Foulkes	Stiles	**Connelly[1]**	Charlton	**Herd[1]**	Best	Aston
17 April	Leeds United	Elland Road	1-0	52,368	Dunne(P)	Brennan	Dunne(A)	Crerand	Foulkes	Stiles	**Connelly[1]**	Charlton	Herd	Law	Aston
19 April	Birmingham City	St Andrews	4-2	28,907	Dunne(P)	Brennan	Dunne(A)	Crerand	Foulkes	Stiles	Connelly	**Charlton[1]**	**Cantwell[1]**	Law	**Best[2]**
24 April	Liverpool	Old Trafford	3-0	55,772	Dunne(P)	Brennan	Dunne(A)	Crerand	Foulkes	Stiles	**Connelly[1]**	Charlton	Cantwell	**Law[2]**	Best
26 April	Arsenal	Old Trafford	3-1	51,625	Dunne(P)	Brennan	Dunne(A)	Crerand	Foulkes	Stiles	Connelly	Charlton	Herd	**Law[2]**	**Best[1]**
28 April	Aston Villa	Villa Park	1-2	36,081	Dunne(P)	Brennan	Dunne(A)	Fitzpatrick	Foulkes	Stiles	Connelly	Charlton	Herd	Law	Best

FA Cup

Date	Opponents	Venue	Score	Att.	1	2	3	4	5	6	7	8	9	10	11
9 January	Chester	Old Trafford	2-1	40,000	Dunne(P)	Brennan	Dunne(A)	Crerand	Foulkes	Stiles	Connelly	Charlton	Herd	**Kinsey[1]**	**Best[1]**
30 January	Stoke City	Victoria Ground	0-0	53,009	Dunne(P)	Brennan	Dunne(A)	Crerand	Foulkes	Stiles	Connelly	Charlton	Herd	Law	Best
3 February	Stoke City	Old Trafford	1-0	50,814	Dunne(P)	Brennan	Dunne(A)	Crerand	Foulkes	Stiles	**Connelly[1]**	Charlton	**Herd[1]**	Law	Best
20 February	Burnley	Old Trafford	2-1	54,000	Dunne(P)	Brennan	Dunne(A)	**Crerand[1]**	Foulkes	Stiles	Connelly	Charlton	Herd	**Law[1]**	Best
10 March	Wolves	Molineux	5-3	53,581	Dunne(P)	Brennan	Dunne(A)	**Crerand[1]**	Foulkes	Stiles	Connelly	Charlton	**Herd[1]**	**Law[2]**	**Best[1]**
27 March	Leeds United	Hillsborough	0-0	65,000	Dunne(P)	Brennan	Dunne(A)	Crerand	Foulkes	Stiles	Connelly	Charlton	Herd	Law	Best
31 March	Leeds United	City Ground	0-1	46,300	Dunne(P)	Brennan	Dunne(A)	Crerand	Foulkes	Stiles	Connelly	Charlton	Herd	Law	Best

UEFA Fairs Cup

Date	Opponents	Venue	Score	Att.	1	2	3	4	5	6	7	8	9	10	11
23 September	Djurgaarden	Rasunda Stadion	1-1	6,537	Dunne(P)	Brennan	Dunne(A)	Crerand	Foulkes	Stiles	Connelly	Charlton	**Herd[1]**	Setters	Best
27 October	Djurgaarden	Old Trafford	6-1	38,437	Dunne(P)	Brennan	Dunne(A)	Crerand	Foulkes	Stiles	Connelly	**Charlton[2]**	Herd	**Law[3]**	**Best[1]**
11 November	Borussia Dortmund	Rote Erde Stadion	6-1	25,000	Dunne(P)	Brennan	Dunne(A)	Crerand	Foulkes	Stiles	**Connelly[1]**	**Charlton[3]**	**Herd[1]**	**Law[1]**	**Best[1]**
2 December	Borussia Dortmund	Old Trafford	4-0	31,896	Dunne(P)	Brennan	Dunne(A)	Crerand	Foulkes	Stiles	**Connelly[1]**	**Charlton[2]**	Herd	**Law[1]**	Best
20 January	Everton	Old Trafford	1-1	50,000	Dunne(P)	Brennan	Dunne(A)	Crerand	Foulkes	Stiles	**Connelly[1]**	Charlton	Herd	Law	Best
9 February	Everton	Goodison Park	2-1	54,397	Dunne(P)	Brennan	Dunne(A)	Crerand	Foulkes	Stiles	**Connelly[1]**	**Charlton[1]**	**Herd[1]**	**Law[2]**	**Best[1]**
12 May	Strasbourg	Stade de la Meinau	5-0	30,000	Dunne(P)	Brennan	Dunne(A)	Crerand	Foulkes	Stiles	**Connelly[1]**	**Charlton[1]**	**Herd[1]**	Law	Best
19 May	Strasbourg	Old Trafford	0-0	34,188	Dunne(P)	Brennan	Dunne(A)	Crerand	Foulkes	Stiles	Connelly	Charlton	Herd	Law	Best
31 May	Ferencvaros	Old Trafford	3-2	39,902	Dunne(P)	Brennan	Dunne(A)	Crerand	Foulkes	Stiles	Connelly	Charlton	**Herd[2]**	**Law[1]**	Best
6 June	Ferencvaros	Nep Stadion	0-1	50,000	Dunne(P)	Brennan	Dunne(A)	Crerand	Foulkes	Stiles	Connelly	Charlton	Herd	Law	Best
16 June	Ferencvaros	Nep Stadion	1-2	60,000	Dunne(P)	Brennan	Dunne(A)	Crerand	Foulkes	Stiles	**Connelly[1]**	Charlton	Herd	Law	Best

1965-66

EL BEATLE

MANCHESTER UNITED 2 LIVERPOOL 2
CHARITY SHIELD 14 AUGUST 1965

PREPARATIONS FOR THE World Cup had begun at Old Trafford which saw new cantilevered stands on the Scoreboard and United Road sides of the ground. 8,000 patrons were accomodated in the new stands which were opened for the first time in the Charity Shield game against FA Cup holders Liverpool.

A number of injuries picked up during the pre-season tour of Germany saw United field several players carrying knocks including Denis Law who was forced to limp off after aggravating a hip problem.

George Best and David Herd scored for United. Willie Stevenson hit the target for Liverpool but it only seemed likely to be a consolation until Ron Yeats equalised with four minutes remaining. John Aston was the star of the day occupying the experienced Chris Lawler so much that he rarely got the chance to support the attack. Best worked the opposite flank and had a good opening to the game forcing Tommy Lawrence to come for a teasing cross and narrowly missing the goal before finally getting his sights right.

Bobby Charlton drifted to the wing for a spell releasing George to stroll across the freshly prepared turf and give Liverpool's backs, who thought they had mastered the central positions when Law went off, plenty to think about.

MANCHESTER UNITED 1 SHEFFIELD WEDNESDAY 0
DIVISION ONE 21 AUGUST 1965

MATT BUSBY HAD demonstrated his intent should Law be forced out for a spell by pushing George Best over to the inside forward position against Liverpool and retained the formation for the opening league game of the season. This gave Willie Anderson his first chance to string a few games together since a memorable debut against Burnley almost two years previously.

While Best had retained his place in the side from that match on, Anderson had only made the subsequent FA Cup tie with Southampton and other than The Charity Shield game seven days earlier, had been afforded just one more chance late in the 1963-64 season.

It was clear that a summer's rest had done George a power of good as the Irishman was a constant threat which Wednesday struggled to deal with. If he could have been persuaded to part with the ball earlier or shoot rather than try and make certain United could have eased towards a comfortable lead.

It was the only feature of his game which distinguished him from a clinical finisher such as Law or David Herd who remained dangerous throughout and scored the only goal of the game. However, as a creative force when a shot on goal would not be expected Best was a potent force.

NOTTINGHAM FOREST 4 MANCHESTER UNITED 2
DIVISION ONE 24 AUGUST 1965

UNITED ENJOYED LENGTHY spells of possession and plenty of pressure in and around the Forest penalty area but failed to turn superiority into goals. In contrast to the attacking frailties which had beset United's start to the campaign, it was at the other end of the field which caused The Reds most problems and lost all the points on offer this evening.

In mitigation, Nobby Stiles and Bill Foulkes were visibly struggling with injuries but a lack of concentration, a sin at the top level of the game, allowed Forest to create chances at will. The home side looked a threat to many teams on the basis of this performance and certainly didn't need their chances gift wrapped.

John Aston was the sole highlight for United. He scored with a header and created a goal for Best with a weaving run of which George himself would have been proud.

NORTHAMPTON TOWN 1 MANCHESTER UNITED 1
DIVISION ONE 28 AUGUST 1965

PAT DUNNE PAID the ultimate price for the midweek defeat in Nottingham and was dropped allowing David Gaskell his first opportunity in almost a year. A fit again Denis Law made a welcome return and Best, who was placed out on the right, seemed keen to get the Scotsman back into the goals as quickly as possible.

His persistence won a corner before a minute had been played which The Cobblers were content to clear. When United did go ahead through John Connelly all seemed set for an away win and most anticipated that Northampton would be swamped. However, the United forward line was in the middle of a drought which even Law could not break and when in desperation The Reds resorted to a very basic style. The natural flair which should had seen them through against pre-season candidates for relegation was lost. Northampton battled away to earn a deserved equaliser and an unexpected point.

MANCHESTER UNITED 0 NOTTINGHAM FOREST 0
DIVISION ONE 1 SEPTEMBER 1965

A CAGEY GAME usually leads to a goalless draw and this score-line was on the cards from the opening exchanges. United had the recent defeat at The City Ground weighing heavily on their minds. No defender needed reminding of their lapses on that occasion and ensured that both teams appeared content with a point from the outset.

United created more direct chances during the second period but could not beat Peter Grummitt who thwarted Connelly three times. Denis Law still looked troubled, his plight worsened by the lack of an obvious goalscorer to cover his continued rustiness.

MANCHESTER UNITED 1 STOKE CITY 1
DIVISION ONE 4 SEPTEMBER 1965

UNITED PUT IN a performance of some worth but still couldn't make the game safe thanks to woeful finishing and most of the forward minded players were guilty in varying degrees. An Old Trafford crowd usually drew the best out of keepers of both sides and when he was required Stoke's Lawrie Leslie was brave

and resourceful in everything he did.

Leslie refused to buckle as he continued to do the simple things well: fielding crosses with ease and getting into the right position to make saves extremely well. United were thankful for David Herd's equaliser.

NEWCASTLE UNITED 1 MANCHESTER UNITED 2
DIVISION ONE 8 SEPTEMBER 1965

PUNDITS OFTEN OPINE that great teams are like an orchestra - various sections working together in order to create a harmony. Yet here George Best gave a virtuoso performance and worried Newcastle every time he received the ball yet proved too much of a soloist on occasions for the entire team to function effectively. It was Best's only fault in this game but an expensive one for the team which failed to build a deserved lead as a result.United still claimed full points but the final minutes of the game were nervier than anyone in red thought possible.

Best had inadvertently been the source of David Herd's opening goal when Gordon Marshall dropped his corner and another error allowed the scorer to turn provider, presenting Denis Law with a gilt-edged opportunity to open his account for the season.

Newcastle pulled one back with five minutes remaining which led to some anxiety. However, it seemed that once Best hit the same tune as his colleagues everything would click and some unlucky team would be in for a drubbing.

BURNLEY 3 MANCHESTER UNITED 0
DIVISION ONE 11 SEPTEMBER 1965

SCOUTING REPORTS MUST have suggested that Matt Busby's side had little response to high pressure in the latter third of the field as Burnley took the battle to United from the kick-off. A Gordon Harris goal on six minutes was richly deserved for The Clarets' endeavour. Even in such a short period of time the home side had done enough to justify their lead, though

a huge deflection certainly helped Harris's shot.

The Reds finally came into the game as a dominant force during the final stages of the first half and should have scored, though for the third game out of four they were forced to contend with a keeper in exceptional form. Harry Thomson refused to be beaten and was exceptional at distributing the ball which in turn took the pressure off his side and provided adequate time to repair their shape.

United's forwards were often left high up the field and saw little of the ball unless they dropped back. The sheer number of defenders tracking back often meant they could do little with possession. At any stage Best found himself swamped by defenders and, though he usually had a measure of the first couple, he rarely got the better of the third or fourth man in attendance.

MANCHESTER UNITED 1 NEWCASTLE UNITED 1
DIVISION ONE 15 SEPTEMBER 1965

ONCE MORE AN opposition keeper played a blinder. This time The Magpies' Gordon Marshall was exceptional and he had to be. There again United often made life difficult for themselves by wasting good positions. It was a great shame as their approach play deserved more but there was a pattern forming that had characterised United's slow start to the season.

United trailed for most of this match until a last-gasp goal by Nobby Stiles saved a point. It was redemption for Stiles as he had conceeded the penalty which looked likely to cost United dear.

Crowd trouble in the Stretford End during the home game led to eight fans being banned for the remainder of the campaign.

NORTHERN IRELAND 3 SCOTLAND 2
BRITISH CHAMPIONSHIPS 2 OCTOBER 1965

UNITED HAD MADE an emotional return to the European Cup for the first time since Munich but Best had missed the opening leg of the First round tie with Helsinki due to an ankle injury. When he was ready to return Matt Busby decided not to change his line-up. He had an embarrassment of riches but there seems little doubt that the defences of Arsenal, Chelsea and Finish club HJK Helsinki breathed a sigh of relief upon realising that they did not have to contend with the Irishman. United beat Chelsea and the Finns but lost at Highbury.

There was no respite at international level and despite being out of club action for the past three games George slotted in well for Northern Ireland.

MANCHESTER UNITED 6 HJK HELSINKI 0 (AGG 9-2)
EUROPEAN CUP PREMLIMINARY RD 2ND LEG 6 OCTOBER 1965

THOUGH OUT OF the side, Best had travelled to Helsinki as a standby should Denis Law be forced out again but a reluctance to change a winning side meant there would be no European Cup debut until at the return leg at Old Trafford.

United had continued to struggle without George, as evidenced by a heavy defeat at Highbury and a near embarrassment in Scandinavia, although

Chelsea had been well beaten at Old Trafford. In fairness the entire team seemed somewhat stagnant with just three wins in nine league games. United held a narrower than expected 3-2 advantage over HJK from the first leg.

John Aston, who had been preferred in Finland, retained his left-wing berth with George asked to play at inside-right while Bobby Charlton moved to centre forward. It was a fine tactical decision as George was keen to get back and whirled around at a furious pace. The malaise that had been so obvious domestically was forgotten as George seemed inspired by the greatest stage in club football.

His two goals on the evening were his first in eight games and a huge relief the entire team. The brace included a trademark surge past a number of defenders before an unstoppable shot was unleashed.

John Connelly hit a deserved hat-trick and Bobby Charlton notched the other to see United through to the next phase courtesy of the type of performance they were keen to turn in against fellow Division One sides. If they did, similar scoring feats would undoubtedly follow.

MANCHESTER UNITED 2 LIVERPOOL 0
DIVISION ONE 9 OCTOBER 1965

GEORGE BEST BEGAN where he left off at Old Trafford, linking well with Connelly on the right and the two almost created a goal for Bobby Charlton early on. Best danced through the Liverpool defence to play a clever ball for Law who almost converted then got himself in for an 18th minute strike - richly deserved after his contribution to that point. Defensive errors had presented the opportunity: keeper Tommy Lawrence lost the ball before Ron Yeats and Tommy Smith got involved in a mix up with their keeper which left Law to tap into an empty net.

The 'Holy Trinity' were irresistible and with Paddy Crerand in control of the engine room the stage seemed set for a memorable win after Charlton played a defence-splitting ball which Law accelerated on to before firing under Lawrence. Liverpool came back into the game as a force during the final half hour and could have sneaked at least a draw in the last ten minutes after creating a number of chances but this defeat was a severe dent to Shankly's title ambitions.

UP AND AT 'EM GEORGE
George Best rises high to head past Liverpool's Tommy Lawrence. George's heading ability is often forgotten but, as this header shows, Best was more than proficient in the air.

TOTTENHAM HOTSPUR 5 MANCHESTER UNITED 1
DIVISION ONE 16 OCTOBER 1965

UNITED'S PLAYERS MARKED the 20th anniversary of Matt Busby taking the hotseat at Old Trafford with a pre-match presentation. A specially commissioned crystal vase, standing almost two feet high and costing a few hundred pounds, had been bought by the squad who deputised Bill Foulkes to oversee the ceremony. United wanted to ensure their manager received another offering by full-time but Spurs, unbeaten at White Hart Lane since March 1964 in a run of 31 games, were too tough a proposition.

Bobby Charlton acted as a central striker while Best was kept at inside forward. The early running came from the home side who raided through Jimmy Greaves and Alan Gilzean. Either could have opened the scoring a couple of times before Gilzean finally found the net.

United refused to accept their fate and pelted Pat Jennings with decent efforts. John Connelly launched the sternest test of Best's international colleague but these chances became fewer as the first half wore on. Tottenham's influential midfielder Dave Mackay ran the game and created a white maelstrom which helped Spurs overpower United's defence.

The margin of victory was handsome but it could have been heavier. On the balance of play more or less double. Rather than George Best scoring the goal of the game, that honour was left to Jimmy Greaves who took the ball in the centre circle and weaved his way past five tacklers to the edge of the box before sliding the ball home.

MANCHESTER UNITED 4 FULHAM 1
DIVISION ONE 23 OCTOBER 1965

PADDY CRERAND SURVIVED an injury scare but Denis Law was not so lucky and was forced out again, David Herd coming into the XI. Fulham could and should have scored early on but were left to rue their misfortune by the final whistle. Rodney Marsh took possession just outside the area, did all the hard work, but took so long to shoot that Nobby Stiles got back and put a foot in. Then Johnny Key had one ruled out for offside.

United were finally jolted into action. Herd and Best combined to breakthrough. However, George was slightly out with his

aim once the chance had been fashioned. He then had one blocked by Mark Pearson. Results had shown that United were a different team at home and cruised to victory despite never looking that much better than Fulham who also hit a post. It was just that Busby's men had players such as Best and Bobby Charlton who, even when below their own high standards, had the edge over teams like The Cottagers. Both were instrumental in setting Herd up for a hat-trick with Charlton snatching the other.

BLACKPOOL 1 MANCHESTER UNITED 2
Division One 30 October 1965

DESPITE LOOKING LIKELY to return Denis Law remained on the sidelines. However, Harry Gregg made a welcome comeback in the only change to the previous weekend. Ian Moir was in the Blackpool side and as expected had a decent game. George Best, who had hastened Moir's departure from Old Trafford, was in and out of the match.

He wasted a decent chance which a player of his ability should have done more with after an excellent set-up by Charlton who got to the by-line then pulled the ball back at pace to an unmarked Best occupying the inside right position.

However, rather than attempt to connect with a first time effort George got the ball from out of his feet before shooting. Those precious moments allowed Tony Waiters to block.

The wastefulness continued as Best, Aston and Connelly allowed further chances to go begging. United, still shaky at the back, could have paid the price but a hotly disputed goal from David Herd in the final minute proved to be the winner. Blackpool's defenders claimed the striker was offside but an inexperienced right back covering for skipper Jimmy Armfield appeared to play the striker on.

MANCHESTER UNITED 2 BLACKBURN ROVERS 2
Division One 6 November 1965

PUBLIC OPINION WAS said to favour the dropping of Denis Law who had struggled to find the net and had been plagued by injuries which seemed to have robbed him of sharpness. David Herd had entered a decent run of goalscoring form in the meantime which heightened apprehension about a striker who would seem a natural casualty. However, it was John Connelly who made way and judging by the adulation at his emergence on to the pitch, rumours about Law's popularity amongst the fans was scotched.

Best switched to the right wing to replace Connelly, who was five days away from representing England against Northern Ireland so didn't need to be dropped. Law, on the other hand, was

visibly cheered to be back but blazed an early chance, created after a penetrating run and cross from Best, over the bar. He was also set up by Aston and Charlton but continued to find accuracy a problem. Though he was at least getting in the right positions which was a good sign.

Blackburn, often with eight men behind the ball, were hard to break down but United seemed to be easing towards a comfortable win after Bobby Charlton struck a thunderbolt prior to the break and Law gave a sample of what the team had been missing by ghosting past three men before slotting home. But the picture changed less than ten minutes from time when Harry Gregg was sent off for fouling Mike England. The striker seemed just as shocked at the decision but Rovers were deadly from set-pieces pulling one back from the resulting penalty before converting a free-kick deep in injury time.

ENGLAND 2 NORTHERN IRELAND 1
HOME INTERNATIONAL 10 NOVEMBER 1965

ON HIS WEMBLEY debut, George Best and Northern Ireland graced the grand old stadium by matching their hosts in every department. In many ways England were actually bettered and Alf Ramsey's side had to work hard to edge the game in the second half. Joe Baker of Arsenal provided an early lead for the hosts when he scored following a mazy run, hitting a low shot to give the hosts the lead. It took time for Ireland to adjust to his pace and skills.

Despite some average performances for his country over recent times, Nobby Stiles was outstanding at the back and in midfield Bobby Charlton excelled.

Soon after their goal it became England's turn to struggle to contain flair players. Best, making his Wembley debut, was a particular thorn in their side moving up and down with blistering pace then using his skills to glide inside but Billy Irvine was also faultless and with Derek Dougan a battering ram down the middle problems were caused.

Irvine equalised within 60 seconds of Baker's opener when a rare slip by Bobby Moore, who lost his footing when attempting to collect a through ball, left the Burnley man free to advance on Gordon Banks. Cheekily he shot through the keeper's legs.

Both teams went toe-to-toe after half-time as each looked for victory. England would have taken it on points had it been a boxing match. Nobby Stiles almost scored after linking with Baker who remained the most dangerous member of the Three Lions side and set up the winner 18 minutes from time when another Stiles shot was blocked by a defender. Even though the ball fell kindly for Baker there was little room in the area so he flicked the ball out to Alan Peacock who rammed it home.

LEICESTER CITY 0 MANCHESTER UNITED 5
DIVISION ONE 13 NOVEMBER 1965

GEORGE BEST LINED up against Gordon Banks for the second time in three days. Noel Cantwell, who bagged a treble for the reserves as an inside left, came in at left-back in place of Shay Brennan.

United finally hit their groove in the league at an unlikely venue given the club's recent record at Filbert Street.

Though Connelly scored a well crafted goal early on this was a hard working display which saw everything go right for the strikers. Denis Law was the only forward not amongst the goals but he was often the play-maker that set up the chances.

ASK VORWAERTS 0 MANCHESTER UNITED 2
EUROPEAN CUP 1ST RD 1ST LEG 17 NOVEMBER 1965

A TRIP BEHIND the Iron Curtain was always going to prove tricky. The atmosphere was intimidating and the temperatures freezing but United prevailed after a cautious start. Matt Busby's men were cagey in their play for well over an hour. Even United's star attackers, who hated to operate in that vein, refused to chance their arm unless a clear possibility arose.

It took three quarters of the game before Best got an opportunity to break free down the right and send in a cross which Law calmly directed into the goal. Within minutes the East Germans were broken again. This time it was Law who set up Connelly to net from close range.

The same combination for the opener had almost brought an early goal via a similar method but keeper Weiss, though way out of his ground when Law headed towards an empty net, somehow scrambled back. Best had always looked the most likely to get through a very sold ASK side and took some punishment for his efforts.

ALBANIA 1 NORTHERN IRELAND 1
WORLD CUP QUALIFIER 24 NOVEMBER 1965

VICTORY WOULD QUALIFY Northern Ireland for at least a play off against Switzerland as they would also finish on nine points having beaten Holland in Berne over a week earlier. As both sides had won their home ties it seemed sure to be a tight affair but the possibility of not only a first World Cup finals appearance since 1958 but one in England would prove a massive spur for any home nation.

Albania's international record only suggested one outcome. However, a late goal in Tirana not only gained the host's their first ever point in any qualification tie but dashed Irish hopes.

It was a stop start game with 46 free-kicks yet barely a bad foul. Rain and a poor pitch made play difficult and Northern Ireland rarely strung more than a couple of passes together during moves. With Albania one of the weakest teams in Europe it seemed unlikely that they could hold out as they had never kept a clean sheet in any competitive game.

The Irish led when a corner was cleared to Alex Elder on the left of the area. He sent the ball straight back in and it was converted by Irvine from a tight angle.

However, 12 minutes from time a free-kick for the home side was lumped into the area. There was no real direction to the pass but the ball was not dealt with properly. Rudi returned it into the box for Haxhiu to stoop with a diving header past Jennings for the equaliser.

MANCHESTER UNITED 3 SHEFFIELD UNITED 1
DIVISION ONE 20 NOVEMBER 1965

DAVID SADLER, WHO came through the ranks as a highly rated forward, was asked to fill in as a deputy for Bill Foulkes at centre-half despite never having played there at the top level and not appearing for the first team for almost a year. Foulkes was one of many players waging a fitness battle after the trip to Vorwaerts but the only one to lose out.

Sheffield United were keen to test The Reds and looked to cash in on any weariness shown by their hosts. United were pushed back for long periods; Denis Law made a spectacular scissor-kick clearance at one stage to relieve the pressure, George Best anticipated the clearance, he counter-attacked and centred for David Herd and although the Scot shot over, United had made their point and dominated from then on.

A quick exchange of passes between Crerand and Law created the opener. Law flicked the ball out to the on-rushing Best after drawing the defenders in. One touch and a yard or so later he smashed an effort past Bob Widdowson. George grabbed another and helped fashion a Law goal to build a 3-1 lead by half-time.

MANCHESTER UNITED 3 ASK VORWAERTS 1 (AGG 5-1)
EUROPEAN CUP 1ST RD 2ND LEG 1 DECEMBER 1965

ALFRED ZULKOWSKI TOOK over from Weiss in goal for little reason other than the match would be played under floodlights. Kicking off in the dusk under huge pylons was something many fans across the continent looked forward to but in East Germany almost all games took place in daylight - floodlit matches were rare.

The international 'keeper was one of few players with experience under artificial lights and was reckoned to have the perfect vision for such conditions.

However it took just 12 minutes for United to extend their lead through David Herd who went on to hit his second hat-trick in seven games. His predatory instincts were to the fore and though ASK managed to grab a goal the victory was smoothly executed and well-deserved with a great display from front to back.

MANCHESTER UNITED 0 WEST HAM UNITED 0
DIVISION ONE 4 DECEMBER 1965

WEST HAM HAD also enjoyed a good result in Europe during the week drawing with Greek side Olympiakos to progress in their defence of the Cup Winners' Cup. Meanwhile, Noel Cantwell's 100th league outing came against the side he had joined United from five years previously.

The Hammers were noted for their defensive capabilities so Busby instructed his team to regularly switch positions to confuse their rearguard. Best often interchanged with David Herd which really unsettled the visitors and gave United the upper hand. But superb organisation by Hammers' skipper Bobby Moore ensured the West Ham backline held out before the Londoners rallied.

For all their dominance United had little to show for it. The final ball and shooting were often short of the standard required. Johnny Byrne almost inflicted a first home defeat in the calendar year but hit a post after The Reds were caught on the break late on.

SUNDERLAND 2 MANCHESTER UNITED 3
DIVISION ONE 11 DECEMBER 1965

DENIS LAW HAD missed Scotland's crunch World Cup qualifier with Italy earlier in the week though he was fit enough for the visit to Roker Park despite his calf being covered in a heavy strapping. Charlton could have scored when Martin Harvey inadvertently played the ball to his feet on the edge of the area but his shot was blocked before Neil Martin scored against the run of play.

Best had a number of good chances down the right flank though he earned nothing more than a corner for his efforts until he hit the equaliser on 15 minutes.

His mazy run culminated with a low shot and soon he combined with Bobby Charlton to make it 2-1 with another well taken goal.

Sunderland played the last half hour a man down after injury to Gary Moore. With the substitute already used, there was little choice once it became clear the forward could not carry on. David Herd took advantage to complete the scoring as The Rokerites felt the pinch.

Under manned and over worked Sunderland never looked likely to come back despite a plucky effort.

MANCHESTER UNITED 3 EVERTON 0
DIVISION ONE 15 DECEMBER 1965

CITY AND UNITED met in the youth cup for the first time since that noted semi-final clash in April 1964 earlier in the week. This time George was not drafted in as another promising crop completed a 5-0 win at Maine Road. Meanwhile 33 year-old Harry Gregg returned to the first team, his 14-day suspension now over.

Best had his finest match for some time and toyed with an Everton side which came looking for an open game. Approaching their task with some confidence the visitors set about United in a creditable

manner but George twisted and turned past half of the Merseyside team to obtain a more central position before unleashing an unstoppable shot.

He almost repeated the feat a few minutes later but Ray Wilson cleared off the line with Geoff Barnett beaten. George's magnificent performance was maintained throughout and Best set up both Herd and Charlton for the other goals.

MANCHESTER UNITED 5 TOTTENHAM HOTSPUR 1
DIVISION ONE 18 DECEMBER 1965

THE DAY AFTER trouncing Everton so convincingly United drew Benfica in the last eight of the European Cup. It was a tall order, especially with the second leg in Portugal, but one to be optimistic about given the previous evening's display.

As they had proved just months earlier Spurs could be more than a match for any team on their day but regardless of the huge defeat suffered in North London, The Reds were confident and with good reason. United fans were looking forward to seeing George Best in the electric form of recent weeks - not only in setting up chances but scoring sublime goals.

As may be expected from two of England's better attacking sides the initial stages saw displays of open football despite conditions which would have suited mudlarks rather than highly skilled footballers.

Spurs cut through with most menace early on. Dave Mackay, making his first return to Old Trafford since breaking his leg in a typically robust challenge two years previously, was pulling the strings but Paddy Crerand gradually wrestled control and was a key figure in a superb United display that neatly reversed the score from the White Hart Lane encounter earlier that season.

Spurs' dominance lasted roughly twenty minutes until Bobby Charlton showed great technique to thrash in a half-volley. The shot from a headed clearance thundered past Pat Jennings and into the roof of the net. 90 seconds later Law doubled the lead and Spurs were finally overwhelmed with further goals from Law and Herd.

Though not as devastating as he had been of late, Best was still one of the classiest players on view and his form, as much as anyone's, had brought United right back into the title picture.

MANCHESTER UNITED 1 WEST BROMWICH ALBION 1
DIVISION ONE 27 DECEMBER 1965

A BONE HARD pitch stifled all but one United player - George Best - who never seemed to falter and created chances for himself and others while colleagues often resembled Bambi, so regularly did they lose their footing. West Bromwich Albion had no player in the same league as Best and were predictably direct in their attempts to ensure the ice didn't beat them.

Denis Law scored a penalty 20 minutes from the end for a foul perpetrated on him by Stan Jones but a mistake allowed the Baggies a late equaliser. No matter how basic their intent, Albion's performance deserved something for effort alone.

LIVERPOOL 2 MANCHESTER UNITED 1
DIVISION ONE 1 JANUARY 1966

AN ALREADY HIGHLY anticipated game drew a huge turn out from both sides in United's first New Year's Day encounter with Liverpool in 46 years. The Anfield side topped the table by five points but United had a couple of games in hand so the title race was still anything but over.

The Koppites were stunned when Denis Law snatched an early lead which Liverpool took time to retrieve. Best, who had been injured against West Bromwich Albion but passed a late fitness test, proved he was in shape by getting an early advantage over Liverpool left back Gerry Byrne.

Winning their first tussle George outmuscled the rugged Scouser but was stopped from unleashing an effort after making his way infield by Ron Yeats. However, the home side's giant skipper was unusually flustered just seconds later and had no answer to his international colleague Denis Law. No one was close enough to stop him rounding Tommy Lawrence for an easy goal just two minutes in.

United attempted to get the ball out to Best and Connelly on the flanks as often as possible. The tactic yielded dividends as Liverpool's central pairing were struggling and now had accurate centres to deal with.

As the first half wore on the home side became more of a threat and by the time an equaliser was found Liverpool had been the dominant force in the match for some time. Tommy Smith's effort minutes before the break levelled the score following a series of chances that included Ian St John hitting the bar twice in the same attack.

However, it seemed that United would hold out for a draw as the final whistle drew closer. That was until Gerry Byrne, who had finally mastered Best, hit a ball from 25 yards out which Gordon Milne flicked in with his head. It was a late win but deserved for the manner in which Liverpool fought back against the reigning champions and established themselves as favourites for the title. After a modest start United remained in contention but were now unquestionably outsiders to retain their crown.

MANCHESTER UNITED 1 SUNDERLAND 1
DIVISION ONE 8 JANUARY 1966

AS THEY HAD been at Roker Park a month previously, Sunderland were given a severe examination by Best but this time managed to limit the damage. Herd and Law had almost ripped through their cover before Best netted after seven minutes. The dominance continued throughout the opening period but breaks in play stalled United's momentum and The Rokerites gradually clawed their way back into the match.

Best remained dangerous as did Law and Charlton but the interval allowed the visitors to regroup and isolate each of the danger men. Later, Denis Law had a goal ruled out for offside despite a defender playing the ball into his path to compound United's frustration.

LEEDS UNITED 1 MANCHESTER UNITED 1
DIVISION ONE 12 JANUARY 1966

A LAX SECOND HALF against Sunderland was not ideal preparation for any game with Leeds and defeat would all but ensure United's concentration on the cups. George had recovered from a bruised knee which affected his play towards the close of the previous game but given recent encounters with the Yorkshire side, he realised the problem may flare up again.

Until coming up against full back Paul Reaney, George had never worn shin guards but experience changed all that.

Leeds were the better side here and unlucky to be pegged back on the hour but could only blame themselves for squandering a hatful of chances.

Don Revie claimed to have identified a weakness on high balls in United's rearguard and Leeds concentrated on that tactic for much of the game - United struggled as a result and were content to come away with a point.

FULHAM 0 MANCHESTER UNITED 1
DIVISION ONE 15 JANUARY 1966

FULHAM WERE JOINT bottom of the league but no one would have known that during the early stages as they adapted better to a frozen pitch.

The Reds struggled apart from George Best who didn't allow his flair to be blunted and got the better of many

defenders but either finished poorly or saw colleagues prove just as profligate. Bobby Robson had a shot pushed on to the bar before Law and Best combined to finally breakthrough and create a chance for Charlton to lash home.

DERBY COUNTY 2 MANCHESTER UNITED 5
FA CUP 3ᴿᴰ RD 22 JANUARY 1966

FRANK UPTON'S AVAILABILITY was a crucial boost for Derby. Their skipper was detailed to mark Denis Law when the ball was in the Derby half and did a superb job until the 13th minute when the Scot gave United the lead. Soon after, with County visibly rattled, George Best got onto the scoresheet twice in quick succession.

At half-time United looked likely to

run up a cricket score but Derby, who had barely threatened for most of the game, hit back twice to narrow the gap, even if one was as a result of a debatable penalty. The Reds simply flexed their muscles and hit a couple more with Law, Best and Charlton proving their class.

SHEFFIELD WEDNESDAY 0 MANCHESTER UNITED 0
Division One 29 January 1966

Despite being the away side United had plenty of possession and created a huge number of chances but nothing which really cut through Wednesday. Best was looking to use the unusual as well as his basic skills in order to give his side an edge and though he provided a heartbeat the team was without rhythm. Even Best, Charlton and Law struggled to link together and all fluffed chances.

Gradually Wednesday started to enjoy the better of the match and but

for Harry Gregg would have won at a canter as United's finishing continued to be wretched.

With such a key week approaching The Reds needed to hit the high notes. It was thought that while Rotherham would pose few problems in the FA Cup, Benfica would be a stiff test and United dared not throw away any chance of silverware with a successful defence of the league championship now a distant dream.

MANCHESTER UNITED 3 BENFICA 2
European Cup Quarter-Final 1st leg 2 February 1966

John Connelly replaced Aston for his first appearance since facing Liverpool on New Years Day. From the evidence of the first half display in this game there was little clue that United were struggling domestically. Even Eusebio was outclassed and no one performed better than Bobby Charlton. At the other end the Portuguese were shackled by Nobby Stiles and Bill Foulkes. Full backs Tony Dunne and Noel Cantwell were also particularly resilient.

Foulkes grabbed an early goal but Benfica were in no mood to fall too far

behind and equalised soon after. Even when Denis Law made it 2-1 following a goalmouth scramble and John Connelly added another The Eagles of Lisbon were still in the tie with the second leg in Portugal to look forward to.

United held their two goal lead well into the second half when Eusebio proved there was more than one genius on the pitch in setting up José Torres to score. With the advantage down to one goal Benfica were favourites to progress, especially as they had never lost on their own ground in any European competition.

MANCHESTER UNITED 6 NORTHAMPTON TOWN 2
Division One 5 February 1966

Grateful for a second chance, John Connelly grasped an opportunity to make himself indispensable and ran flat out at Northampton almost winning a penalty before Denis Law scored on six minutes.

Connelly himself found the net a few minutes later. The Cobblers' willingness to take the game to United had to be admired but ultimately proved to be their downfall. Bobby Charlton took full advantage to score a hat-trick and a goal for George Best was just reward for a tremendous performance.

In contrast to The Cobblers, who were enjoying their first season in the top flight, United were the most successful and consistent side since the war as proved by becoming the first club to register 1000 league points courtesy of the win.

MANCHESTER UNITED 0 ROTHERHAM UNITED 0
FA CUP 4TH RD 12 FEBRUARY 1966

A YOUNG ROTHERHAM side seemed to have little chance on paper but despite their lowly status were a real match for United over long spells and dealt with threats to their own goal well. Though United missed a number of decent chances, Old Trafford had rarely witnessed a lower league side so well organised that they were well worth the draw and a money-spinning replay at Millmoor.

ROTHERHAM UNITED 0 MANCHESTER UNITED 1
FA CUP 4TH RD REPLAY 15 FEBRUARY 1966

WOLVES AWAITED THE winners of this replay for which United made one change as Shay Brennan came in for Noel Cantwell. The season-long theme of missing good chances continued as David Herd, George Best and Denis Law saw opportunities go begging. The match should have been safe by half time.

It took a John Connelly goal in the closing minutes of extra-time to finally decide the tie after Rotherham had enjoyed a period of dominance during the third quarter of the game.

STOKE CITY 2 MANCHESTER UNITED 2
DIVISION ONE 19 FEBRUARY 1966

BEST AND LAW were doubts through a heavy cold and a knee injury respectively. Only George made it and started at inside-right partnering John Connelly on the wing. The game was eventually given the go ahead after two pitch inspections. The first at 2pm initially saw the game called off but 10 minutes later the referee decided to take another look and gave the go ahead.

Huge parts of the pitch were covered in mud which proved to be a huge factor in spoiling what promised to be an end-to-end contest given the attacking intentions of both sides who did well to get on top of the conditions.

Connelly and David Herd gave United a 2-0 lead but John Ritchie and Roy Vernon equalised. The Reds could have little complaint and may have come back home with nothing but for Harry Gregg.

MANCHESTER UNITED 4 BURNLEY 2
DIVISION ONE 26 FEBRUARY 1966

SECOND PLACE BURNLEY arrived at Old Trafford in confident mood knowing that a win would see them move three points clear of United. Law's return saw Best move to outside right. John Connelly patrolled the left hand side while John Aston was the unlucky twelfth man.

Courtesy of the 'Holy Trinity' United raced into a lead. Each of the trio were on top of their respective games and linked well.

A typical combination paved the way for Bobby Charlton's opener. Burnley twice came back from a goal deficit and fancied themselves to go on for the winner until falling behind once again to finally broke their resolve.

A draw may have been a fair result but United put the matter well beyond doubt before the end.

WOLVES 2 MANCHESTER UNITED 4
FA CUP 5TH RD 5 MARCH 1966

THERE COULD BE no worse start than conceding a penalty after 90 seconds. At least that was until United gave away another before ten minutes had elapsed. Few players had touched the ball before Terry Wharton struck the first spot kick firmly into the net. That number included Harry Gregg who got nowhere near the penalty.

Paddy Crerand's foul on Manchester-born Dave Wagstaffe had presented Wharton with his first chance and a hand ball by Bill Foulkes presented Wagstaffe with a further opportunity to show his expertise from the spot - The Reds were two down and heading out of the cup.

United's response was to remain patient. There was still plenty of time in which the lower division side could be broken down and the task was undertaken with contemplative football rather than panic.

Crerand atoned for his early error by playing a huge part in the comeback. He was one of the first to caution against a blood and glory approach. His shining example was followed by each of his colleagues and eventually reaped rich dividends.

Two headed goals from Denis Law underlined the Scot's return to form. The striker attacked space and gave defenders no chance of tracking him. George Best's runs created plenty of breathless moments for Wolves and a 50 yard dash over the half-way line and into the area during which he took on and beat a number of defenders - some twice - culminated in a text book goal. David Herd grabbed the fourth to give the score a lop-sided look.

BENFICA 1 MANCHESTER UNITED 5 (AGG 8-3)
EUROPEAN CUP QUARTER-FINAL, 2ND-LEG 9 MARCH 1966

THOUGH GEORGE HAD been a star on the English stage for more than a full season he had still to turn in the same calibre of performance in European competition. The slender 3-2 lead held from the first leg at Old Trafford was a precarious one and expectations were that Matt Busby would send his side out in the Stadium of Light with orders to play on the counter-attack and hope for the best. Famously Busby told his team to keep it quiet for the first twenty minutes but Best failed to heed the old man's advice. Busby later quipped that he must have had cotton wool in his ears.

Benfica were undefeated in 19 European Cup ties staged at their impressive Estadio De Luz which had wildly applauded the presentation of the European Footballer of the Year award to Eusebio minutes prior to kick-off. It seemed that all was set for a glorious night for The Eagles and a lengthening of that unbeaten run.

It was United's first return to Lisbon since that horrific defeat to Sporting and with memories still fresh in most minds nobody wanted to take the risk of a similar humbling. Around the same time the home side's star was receiving his accolade, Paddy Crerand broke a mirror in the changing rooms prior to kick-off. The more superstitious feared the portents but they reckoned without the skill of the Irish. Or at least one particular Irishman.

Within 12 minutes United were 2-0 up with both goals scored by Best - the first was a regulation header

from a Tony Dunne free-kick but the second was nothing short of sublime. A clearance from keeper Harry Gregg was flicked on by David Herd and found its way to George's feet. Haring on to it at breakneck speed Best's first touch beat one man, his second beat another and his third found the corner of the Benfica net. By the midway point of the first half, John Connelly had also netted and George was given even more scope to toy with the Benfica defence.

Clearly shellshocked the two times European champions took sometime to gather their wits and, though a number of set pieces prior to the break proved tough, Gregg was in superb form ensuring the ball kept his side of the line.

In possession the home side did little more than look for Eusebio who was so well marshalled by Nobby Stiles that any pass was effectively a wasted ball. On the flanks things were kept equally tight denying the dangerous Torres any opportunity in the air or the chance to cause confusion in the penalty area.

Benfica did pull one back through a Shay Brennan own goal and Pinto went close from distance but otherwise United were more than assured. Late goals from Bobby Charlton and Pat Crerand completed the scoring as United stunned Europe with a sublime display.

Even the Portuguese warmed to Best's display. If his first goal had led to silence around the stadium his second was greeted with sustained applause not unlike the stunned reaction and then applause that greeted Ronaldo's hat-trick for Real Madrid at Old Trafford in 2003. From then on the generous and knowledgeable crowd hailed his every touch as the Portuguese christened Best 'El Beatle'.

If Best left England a well-known footballer he returned a world star; a local paper featured a picture of the mop haired player in a sombrero boarding the plane home. The defeat was the largest ever inflicted at the Estadio De Luz but each of the 75,000 fans present, were enraptured by the performance of the United number 7. So much so that one fan attempted to take a lock of his hair and made it all the way to the centre of the pitch brandisihing a knife at the final whistle.

CHELSEA 2 MANCHESTER UNITED 0
DIVISION ONE 12 MARCH 1966

IT WAS A CASE of 'After the Lord Mayor's Show' as the demanding nature of the game against Benfica led to a number of injury doubts and though a few looked more than likely to miss the visit to Chelsea everyone was passed fit.

Yet the heroes of Lisbon suffered an immediate set-back when Bobby Tambling scored within a minute and another goal soon followed. Despite playing away from Old Trafford, the adulation for United's achievement in midweek was total.

The Chelsea fans were sporting enough to extend their praise throughout the pre-match warm up and early phases of the game. Whether this had its effect or not is questionable but Chelsea were in no mood to accomodate Best and co.

Yet somewhat remarkably the midfield battle was won by United. Charlton, Best and Crerand were excellent. Best in particular had good creative spells but couldn't break the Pensioners' resistance as United slipped to another league defeat.

MANCHESTER UNITED 2 ARSENAL 1
DIVISION ONE 19 MARCH 1966

DESPITE A TIGHT scoreline, victory was far easier than could have been expected. It was only United's unwillingness to humiliate The Gunners after establishing an early two-goal lead which gave the visitors a chance to keep the score down.

Arsenal clearly improved as the game wore on but in no way had enough to bypass the tough spine of the United team who were happy to retain their slight edge and close out the game.

PRESTON NORTH END 1 MANCHESTER UNITED 1
FA Cup 6ᵀᴴ Rd 16 March 1966

HAVING ACCOUNTED FOR Tottenham Hotspur in the previous round there was great anticipation at Deepdale for the visit of Manchester United. The Second Division side had beaten Charlton Athletic and Bolton Wanderers from their own league but the last two stages had seen the numbers reduce and the glamour ties increase.

A wall collapsed at the Kop End of the ground delaying kick-off by seven minutes though thankfully no serious injuries were suffered. The Lancashire weather had been inclement with heavy rain falling prior to kick-off. Though if North End expected this to be a levelling factor they were sadly mistaken.

United were by far the better side with Best uncharacteristically wasting a great chance to put United ahead after 13 minutes. A smart ball inside from Law found his colleague with nobody but keeper Tony Kelly to beat. However, the experienced stopper advanced and blocked with his legs.

As so often happens the lower league team hit back. North End's team included Busby Babe Alex Dawson, whose boots George Best used to clean as an apprentice. During his time at United Dawson had won two FA Youth Cups and netted an FA Cup semi-final hat-trick against Fulham just weeks after the Munich air disaster.

The former United frontman now threatened his former club's place in the cup missing two good chances: hitting a shot at Harry Gregg before smashing a header against the base of a post.

Ernie Hannigan may have opened the scoring had it not been for the sticky conditions but it was only a brief stay of execution for The Reds who fell foul of the 'law of the ex' five minutes before the break. This time Dawson, who boasted a great goals to games ratio with North End and thus far had notched in every round, linked with Alan Spavin to steer Proud Preston into the lead.

United set about redressing the situation as soon as the match restarted and within three minutes were level. Best beat his man and fed David Herd yards from goal who had the simple task of rolling the ball in. Just five more minutes elapsed before it seemed the same combination had seized the lead. George had weaved his way in field and past the defenders but Herd was standing offside.

Best remained an inspiration and at the heart of some dazzling moves but after 75 minutes was forced off until the last minutes after jarring his knee in a challenge. X-Rays and medical opinion advised that at least 10 days rest should follow.

MANCHESTER UNITED 1 LEICESTER CITY 2
DIVISION ONE 9 APRIL 1966

Best missed the replayed tie with Preston which United won 3-1 and a league game at Aston Villa in order to ensure his knee was given every chance of recovery. The joint was bandaged for the visit of Leicester City and the player was cleared to play in order that he had a match under his belt before the trip to Belgrade in midweek. It would also prove whether he was likely to last the 90 minutes.

Bobby Charlton, Nobby Stiles, Harry Gregg and David Herd, who had all missed out in midweek, also returned. However, Denis Law, Bill Foulkes and Tony Dunne were omitted to give them the greatest possible chance of being fit for the trip to the Balkans. Bobby Noble, the youth team skipper when Best won the FA Youth Cup two years earlier, made his senior bow.

George did see out the match but looked off the pace as did several other United players who may have had their mind focussed on the European Cup semi-final with Partizan. This was of little concern to The Foxes who caused disarray in the re-jigged backline. Shay Brennan symbolised their uncertainty by hitting his own post with a clearance.

Leicester re-asserted their status as a bogey team, only this time at Old Trafford where they ended United's 28-game unbeaten run in the league. Including all games the sequence stretched back 16 months and 40 matches. Mike Stringfellow hit two in a minute with only John Connelly replying. Had it not been for Gordon Banks United's record would have gone on for at least one more game. Pressure built up throughout the second half but the England keeper was equal to everything.

FK PARTIZAN BELGRADE 2 MANCHESTER UNITED 0
EUROPEAN CUP SEMI-FINAL 1ST LEG 13 APRIL 1966

MOST UNITED PLAYERS found the going tough in the Yugoslav capital but none more so than George Best. The cartilage injury sustained in the FA Cup tie with Preston had failed to heal sufficiently despite three weeks on the sidelines and the game with Leicester seemed to do him little good. Despite the odd flash of genius George was well below his best though possibly still the most potent member of the forward line as United suffered a bitter 2-0 reversal.

With the exception of the first ten minutes, after which the home team finally hit their stride, no player seemed to have the necessary spark and even Denis Law, by now rated as one of the finest goal scorers in Europe, bungled a good opportunity early on losing his footing at the vital moment. David Herd hit the crossbar during the opening exchanges with Law following suit early in the second period after a lobbed cross from George Best which travelled perfectly along the six yard line. The ball bounced back awkwardly with Herd tackled before he could get a shot in.

Velibor Vasovic received the Yugoslav Player of the Year Award prior to kick off but forward Mustafa Hasanagic was the star of the night scoring a goal soon after the restart.

On the balance of play United had throughout the game, few would have known that Best was injured. He seemed to cover every blade of grass as he went looking for the ball. Partizan struggled to contain the Irishman but somehow managed to shut him out. But for an excellent tackle he would have been in with just the keeper to beat once or twice. Another teasing run ended with an attempt at goal during the final moments of the first half which drew a fine save.

Just seconds later Best had another chance - latching on to a Paddy Crerand header. Disappointingly he fired at the keeper.

It proved to be George's last match of the campaign. The already sore knee was damaged beyond the repair simple rest could provide after 75 minutes when taking a pass from Denis Law and attempting to flick the ball past keeper Milutin Soskic.

Had United reached the final of the European Cup there was no question of the surgery being delayed or Best playing however an own goal from Soskic who fluffed a cross from Nobby Stiles failed to disrupt Belgrade's mission to protect what they had in the return as United's quest for European glory ended in frustration.

1965-66

The victory over Benfica excepted, this was a disappointing season for Matt Busby. Distraught at another failure in the European Cup, Busby even contemplated retirement. Yet his consistency in the competition, United would never go out before the semi-final stage under his management, was remarkable and he was eventually persuaded that the team would get another shot at the big prize soon.

For all that, one of the main factors attributed to United's poor finish to the season was the absence of Best for the crucial last month. George had demonstrated his genius to the whole of Europe in Lisbon but picked up an injury against Preston and was never fit enough to do his talent, or his team's ambitions, full justice.

United eventually won the tempestuos home leg with Partizan 1-0 (losing the tie 1-2 on aggregate) but the game ended in farce with Paddy Crerand dismissed following a free-for-all in front of the main stand. Three days later they lost 0-1 to eventual FA Cup winners Everton at Burnden Park, Bolton - George listened to the only goal from his hospital bed. Having finished fourth in the league there would to be no continental opposition to face the following season.

George Best's season (it could be said his career) was turned on its head by those 90 minutes in Lisbon. If the British press knew all about Best, there were few in Europe who anticipated his genius. In an era of defensive football dominated by Hellenio Herrera's ruthless Inter Milan team, Best's performance was a breath of fresh air. Unlike some of United's other opponents in Europe that season, Benfica were undoubtedly a great side, having reached four of the previous five European Cup Finals (winning the cup twice) while their reputation in the Stadium of Light ammounted to invincibility. Yet Best, perhaps ignorant of their fearsome reputation, blew them away inside 12 minutes and spent much of the rest of the game receiving the rapt adulation of the home fans.

The match is widely regarded as Best's greatest-ever performance, indeed it is reckoned by many to be the finest team performance by a British side in Europe. The manner of their 5-1 demolition of Benfica was proof that Busby had the side to fulfil his long-held ambition and it was this realisation that made defeat to a mediocre Partizan side so hard to take. Busby's gem of team had a febrile nature all its own - Manchester United could delight one minute and frustrate the next - 'twas ever thus.

DATE	OPPONENT	VENUE	SCORE	ATT'D	1	2	3	4	5	6	7	8	9	10	11
21 August	Sheffield Wed	Old Trafford	1-0	37,524	Dunne(P)	Brennan	Dunne(A)	Crerand	Foulkes	Stiles	Anderson(W)	Charlton	Herd[1]	Best	Aston
24 August	Nottingham Forest	City Ground	2-4	33,744	Dunne(P)	Brennan	Dunne(A)	Crerand	Foulkes	Stiles	Connelly	Charlton	Herd	Best[1]	Aston[1]
28 August	Northampton Town	County Ground	1-1	21,140	Gaskell	Dunne(A)	Cantwell	Crerand	Foulkes	Stiles	Connelly[1]	Charlton	Herd	Law	Best
1 September	Nottingham Forest	Old Trafford	0-0	38,777	Gaskell	Brennan	Dunne(A)	Crerand	Foulkes	Stiles	Connelly	Charlton	Herd[1]	Law	Best
4 September	Stoke City	Old Trafford	1-1	37,603	Gaskell	Brennan	Dunne(A)	Crerand	Foulkes	Stiles	Connelly	Charlton	Herd[1]	Law	Best
8 September	Newcastle United	St James' Park	2-1	57,380	Gaskell	Brennan	Dunne(A)	Crerand	Foulkes	Stiles	Connelly	Charlton	Herd[1]	Law[1]	Best
11 September	Burnley	Turf Moor	0-3	30,235	Gaskell	Brennan	Dunne(A)	Crerand	Foulkes	Stiles	Connelly	Charlton	Herd	Law	Best
15 September	Newcastle United	Old Trafford	1-1	30,401	Dunne(P)	Brennan	Dunne(A)	Crerand	Foulkes	Stiles[1]	Connelly	Charlton	Herd	Law	Best
9 October	Liverpool	Old Trafford	2-0	58,161	Dunne(P)	Brennan	Dunne(A)	Crerand	Foulkes	Stiles	Connelly	Best[1]	Charlton[1]	Law[1]	Aston
16 October	Tottenham Hotspur	White Hart Lane	1-5	58,051	Dunne(P)	Brennan	Dunne(A)	Crerand	Foulkes	Stiles	Connelly	Best	Charlton[1]	Law	Aston
23 October	Fulham	Old Trafford	4-1	32,716	Dunne(P)	Brennan	Dunne(A)	Crerand	Foulkes	Stiles	Connelly	Best	Charlton[1]	Herd[3]	Aston
30 October	Blackpool	Bloomfield Road	2-1	24,703	Gregg	Brennan	Dunne(A)	Crerand	Foulkes	Stiles	Connelly	Best	Charlton	Herd[2]	Aston
6 November	Blackburn Rovers	Old Trafford	2-2	38,823	Gregg	Brennan	Dunne(A)	Crerand	Foulkes	Stiles	Best	Law	Charlton[1]	Herd	Aston
13 November	Leicester City	Filbert Street	5-0	34,551	Gregg	Dunne(A)	Cantwell	Crerand	Sadler	Stiles	Best[1]	Law	Charlton[1]	Herd[2]	Connelly[1]
20 November	Sheffield United	Old Trafford	3-1	37,922	Gregg	Dunne(A)	Cantwell	Crerand	Foulkes	Stiles	Best[2]	Law[1]	Charlton	Herd	Connelly
4 December	West Ham United	Old Trafford	0-0	32,924	Dunne(P)	Dunne(A)	Cantwell	Crerand	Foulkes	Stiles	Best	Law	Charlton	Herd	Connelly
11 December	Sunderland	Roker Park	3-2	37,417	Dunne(P)	Dunne(A)	Cantwell	Crerand	Foulkes	Stiles	Best[2]	Law	Charlton	Herd[1]	Connelly
15 December	Everton	Old Trafford	3-0	32,624	Gregg	Dunne(A)	Cantwell	Crerand	Foulkes	Stiles	Best[1]	Law	Charlton[1]	Herd[1]	Connelly
18 December	Tottenham Hotspur	Old Trafford	5-1+	39,270	Gregg	Dunne(A)	Cantwell	Crerand	Foulkes	Stiles	Best	Law[2]	Charlton[1]	Herd[1]	Connelly
27 December	WBA	Old Trafford	1-1	54,102	Gregg	Dunne(A)	Cantwell	Crerand	Foulkes	Stiles	Best	Law[1]	Charlton	Herd[1]	Connelly
1 January	Liverpool	Anfield	1-2	53,790	Gregg	Dunne(A)	Cantwell	Crerand	Foulkes	Stiles	Best	Law[1]	Charlton	Herd	Connelly
8 January	Sunderland	Old Trafford	1-1	39,162	Gregg	Dunne(A)	Cantwell	Crerand	Foulkes	Stiles	Best[1]	Law	Charlton	Herd	Connelly
12 January	Leeds United	Elland Road	1-1	49,672	Gregg	Dunne(A)	Cantwell	Crerand	Foulkes	Stiles	Best	Law	Charlton[1]	Herd[1]	Aston
15 January	Fulham	Craven Cottage	1-0	33,018	Gregg	Dunne(A)	Cantwell	Crerand	Foulkes	Stiles	Best	Law	Charlton	Herd	Aston
29 January	Sheffield Wed	Hillsborough	0-0	39,281	Gregg	Dunne(A)	Cantwell	Crerand	Foulkes	Stiles	Best	Law	Charlton	Herd	Aston
5 February	Northampton Town	Old Trafford	6-2	34,986	Gregg	Brennan	Cantwell	Crerand	Foulkes	Stiles	Best	Law[2]	Charlton[3]	Herd	Connelly[1]
19 February	Stoke City	Victoria Ground	2-2	36,667	Gregg	Brennan	Dunne(A)	Crerand	Foulkes	Stiles	Connelly[1]	Best	Charlton[1]	Herd[1]	Aston

Date	Opponent	Venue	Score	Att.	1	2	3	4	5	6	7	8	9	10	11
26 February	Burnley	Old Trafford	4-2	49,892	Gregg	Brennan	Dunne(A)	Crerand	Foulkes	Stiles	Best	Law	Charlton[1]	Herd[3]	Connelly
12 March	Chelsea	Stamford Bridge	0-2	60,269	Gregg	Brennan	Dunne(A)	Crerand	Foulkes	Stiles	Best	Law	Charlton	Herd	Connelly
19 March	Arsenal	Old Trafford	2-1	47,246	Gregg	Brennan	Dunne(A)	Crerand	Foulkes	Stiles[1]	Best	Law[1]	Charlton	Herd	Connelly[1]
9 April	Leicester City	Old Trafford	1-2	42,593	Gregg	Brennan	Noble	Crerand	Sadler	Stiles	Best	Anderson(W)	Charlton	Herd	Connelly[1]

Charity Shield

Date	Opponent	Venue	Score	Att.	1	2	3	4	5	6	7	8	9	10	11
14 August	Liverpool	Old Trafford	2-2	48,502	Dunne(P)	Brennan	Dunne(A)	Crerand	Cantwell	Stiles	Best[1]	Charlton	Herd[1]	Law	Aston

FA Cup

Date	Opponent	Venue	Score	Att.	1	2	3	4	5	6	7	8	9	10	11
22 January	Derby County	Baseball Ground	5-2	33,827	Gregg	Dunne(A)	Cantwell	Crerand	Foulkes	Stiles	Best[2]	Law[2]	Charlton	Herd[1]	Aston
12 February	Rotherham United	Old Trafford	0-0	54,263	Gregg	Dunne(A)	Cantwell	Crerand	Foulkes	Stiles	Best	Law	Charlton	Herd	Connelly
15 February	Rotherham United	Millmoor	1-0	23,500	Gregg	Brennan	Dunne(A)	Crerand	Foulkes	Stiles	Best	Law	Charlton	Herd	Connelly[1]
5 March	Wolves	Molineux	4-2	53,500	Gregg	Brennan	Dunne(A)	Crerand	Foulkes	Stiles	Best[1]	Law[2]	Charlton	Herd[1]	Connelly
26 March	Preston North End	Deepdale	1-1	37,876	Gregg	Brennan	Dunne(A)	Crerand	Foulkes	Stiles	Best	Law	Charlton	Herd[1]	Connelly

European Cup

Date	Opponent	Venue	Score	Att.	1	2	3	4	5	6	7	8	9	10	11
6 October	HJK Helsinki	Old Trafford	6-0	30,388	Dunne(P)	Brennan	Dunne(A)	Crerand	Foulkes	Stiles	Connelly[3]	Best[2]	Charlton[1]	Law	Aston
17 November	ASK Vorwaerts	Walter Ulbricht	2-0	40,000	Gregg	Dunne(A)	Cantwell	Crerand	Foulkes	Stiles	Best	Law[1]	Charlton	Herd	Connelly[1]
1 December	ASK Vorwaerts	Old Trafford	3-1	30,082	Dunne(P)	Dunne(A)	Cantwell	Crerand	Foulkes	Stiles	Best	Law	Charlton	Herd[3]	Connelly
2 February	Benfica	Old Trafford	3-2	64,035	Gregg	Dunne(A)	Cantwell	Crerand	Foulkes[1]	Stiles	Best	Law[1]	Charlton	Herd[1]	Connelly
9 March	Benfica	Estadio da Luz	5-1	75,000	Gregg	Brennan	Dunne(A)	Crerand[1]	Foulkes	Stiles	Best[2]	Law	Charlton[1]	Herd	Connelly[1]
13 April	Partizan Belgrade	Stadion JNA	0-2	60,000	Gregg	Brennan	Dunne(A)	Crerand	Foulkes	Stiles	Best	Law	Charlton	Herd	Connelly

1966-67
CHAMPIONS AGAIN

MANCHESTER UNITED 5 WEST BROMWICH ALBION 3
DIVISION ONE 20 AUGUST 1966

EVERYONE WONDERED HOW George Best would fare in the cut and thrust of Division One after a summer out and virtually no match practice during the close season.

With little reason to replace John Aston, Matt Busby placed George on the right flank. Positions meant little to a player with Best's attributes including a great touch and control on either foot. It wasn't a skill that had come easily though and took years to develop during his junior days as he sought advantages which outweighed the slight frame that many coaches felt made him unsuited to the professional game. He would often wear just one plimsoll as a youngster to ensure he had to control the ball on his weaker foot and as a result ensured it became as strong as the other.

But with his knee now healed and full rehabilitation completed Best seemed better than ever and continued to haunt West Brom, scoring in the first minute of the season's opening game. Denis Law attempted to meet a cross from the left after John Connelly and Bobby Charlton combined but narrowly missed. David Herd spotted George easing in to the area on the right and allowed the ball to travel through, the Ulsterman made no mistake and slammed the ball home.

Despite the change in role Best was still allowed to roam the field but usually kept close to the touchline where he made goals for others. United were virtually untouchable early on and hit five goals within 20 minutes. Denis Law opened his account for the season with a double. David Herd and Nobby Stiles also scored while Bobby Hope pulled one back.

An easing up after the break was understandable given the hot sun combined with the early stage of the season. Though it allowed Albion to hit back twice the lead never looked under any real threat.

United's World Cup heroes Bobby Charlton, Nobby Stiles and squad member John Connelly were clapped on to the field while all the other players formed a guard of honour.

EVERTON 1 MANCHESTER UNITED 2
DIVISION ONE 23 AUGUST 1966

UNITED STOLE THE points at Goodison with a late winner. The Blues were the better side throughout but finished empty handed due to United's resistance in defence.

With the exception of Derek Temple's goal Everton were kept at arm's length. When United did get the ball forward the flair poured out of George Best who was booked for dissent to the referee after one too many stiff challenges came flying his way. Despite this he never hid and actively looked for the ball when he didn't have it playing a huge part in both Denis Law goals.

LEEDS UNITED 3 MANCHESTER UNITED 1
DIVISION ONE 27 AUGUST 1966

PRIDE SO OFTEN comes before a fall and if any United player believed a game against Leeds United would ever be easy they were brought down to earth with a huge bump. A jolt which was handed down by a number of youngsters and reserves brought in as the Yorkshire side were missing a host of established first teamers. Quite simply The Reds were outclassed.

A David Gaskell mistake led to the opener on five minutes when Johnny Giles lobbed in. With big players such as Law and Bobby Charlton anonymous there was little chance of United getting level. Paul Madeley scored with a header which should have been saved.

Best was well policed by Paul Reaney, only slipping his guard once in order to score but even then he still contributed most to United's cause.

MANCHESTER UNITED 3 EVERTON 0
DIVISION ONE 31 AUGUST 1966

UNITED REDRESSED THE problems of the weekend welcoming Everton to Old Trafford. The Toffees had been beaten at Goodison Park in a match United had been fortunate to win, yet this evening Matt Busby's side dominated from beginning to end and cruised to victory with goals from Bill Foulkes, John Connelly and Denis Law. It was a mild evening with the pitch ideal for skilful play with Best was an irresistible force.

MANCHESTER UNITED 3 NEWCASTLE UNITED 2
DIVISION ONE 3 SEPTEMBER 1966

UNITED TORE AT Newcastle from the first whistle, mounting raids down the flanks with John Connelly in particular looking to get involved at every opportunity going down both his own flank and through the middle. He linked with Best particularly well as did Crerand who almost played the winger through. Unfortunately his jinking run came to nothing and this proved to be the hallmark of the game until David Herd netted on the hour.

George was guilty of over-egging the pudding, delaying final balls too long and, when he should have shot, deciding to keep hold of possession until the angle or keeper and defenders obscured his effort. However, he remained one of United's most penetrating players and helped create the Herd goal before Ron McGarry made it 1-1.

Best carved out the second with one of those seemingly pointless yet beautiful runs which looked to have run out of steam until a ball was whipped across the face of goal for Connelly to convert before Denis Law added a third.

A David Craig goal four minutes from time ensured a grandstand finish but The Reds held firm.

STOKE CITY 3 MANCHESTER UNITED 0
DIVISION ONE 7 SEPTEMBER 1966

WITH DAVID GASKELL's confidence at rock bottom after that rough game at Leeds, Harry Gregg was brought back but with the twilight of his career approaching another keeper was sought. Not long before this game Chelsea rejected a £50,000 bid for Alex Stepney. Matt Busby was also said to be looking at Ron Springett and Stepney's club colleague Peter Bonetti. The boss was not one to be put off lightly and prepared for a long courtship with his intended targets.

Unsurprisingly, United hadn't looked particularly solid in defence thus far and little improvement seemed likely on the evidence of this performance. United were prised open far too easily at the Victoria Ground with Harry Gregg slipping up for the first when he dropped a Calvin Palmer shot, John Ritchie picking up the pieces to net. Palmer headed in a few minutes later and Ritchie made it 3-0 in the second half. At the other end John Farmer had barely a shot to save.

Losing John Fitzpatrick, who had kept Paddy Crerand away from the starting XI after an injury at Leeds, was undoubtedly a factor in United leaking so many goals. He would remain out for some time after a cartilage operation.

TOTTENHAM HOTSPUR 2 MANCHESTER UNITED 1
DIVISION ONE 10 SEPTEMBER 1966

JUST UNDER THREE months after becoming a football immortal as part of the World Cup winning squad, John Connelly was axed as Matt Busby tried to breathe life into an ailing side. In truth Connelly had performed no worse than others who had survived the shake up but his omission was the only way the manager felt he could get more out of his team. Charlton was moved to outside left in Connelly's place with George Best remaining on the right. David Sadler made a return to the side in a deep lying midfield role protecting a back four which included Bill Foulkes playing in his 500th league game for the club.

Foulkes was one of many defenders who struggled to hold Jimmy Greaves at bay. The England man had tested Gaskell a number of times and United were uncharacteristically hemmed in with only wayward shots from Bobby Charlton and George Best to show for their endeavours.

United's goal saw Best and Law combine in spectacular fashion when a corner was over-hit, flicked off Denis and sped towards the touch line. It seemed an innocuous situation until George fished it back into the area with an overhead kick which the Scottish forward headed powerfully home.

Prior to the season Law had demanded a wage rise plus a signing on fee if he was to renew his soon to expire contract, Matt Busby had responded by placing the Scot on the transfer list. Eventually the player backed down but not before h assured that he was the top earner at the club.

Meanwhile the chances of United regaining entry to the continent's premier club competition seemed bleak. Second half goals from Alan Gilzean and Greaves saw Spurs through. David Gaskell picked up an ankle injury making the transfer of Alex Stepney for a record £55,000 fee soon after the game all the more vital.

BLACKPOOL 5 MANCHESTER UNITED 1
LEAGUE CUP 14 SEPTEMBER 1966

UNITED MADE A return to the much maligned League Cup for the first time in six years. In common with most top clubs they had entered the inaugural competition but after a defeat to Bradford City of Division Three sat out subsequent seasons. United's League Cup record remained dismal after this hammering at Blackpool who, though a fellow top flight side, would not have been expected to have won so handsomely after collecting just one point out of a possible 14.

They had conceded 18 goals and could barely find the net with a map and compass having hit just four all season yet somehow managed to run out deserved 5-1 winners at Bloomfield Road.

Alex Stepney watched from the stands ready to come in for a baptism of fire in the following weekend's Manchester Derby. Amidst the heavy rain and mud Ray Charnley hit a hat-trick which included a penalty. Bobby Waddell at inside right was a class apart on the night and deserved his goal. The scoring was completed by Les Lea.

Too few players looked interested for United though despite the impossible situation faced George Best emerged with distinction as did John Connelly who had plenty to prove - David Herd scored a consolation for The Reds.

MANCHESTER UNITED 1 MANCHESTER CITY 0
DIVISION ONE 17 SEPTEMBER 1966

ALEX STEPNEY MADE a club debut on his 24th birthday as United and City squared up for the first time in three years. John Aston made his first league appearance of the season meaning George remained on the right. His partnership with David Sadler, who reverted to his old role as a striker with Herd injured, worked well though Dave Connor, a no-nonsense full-back charged with the task of marking Best, was not afraid to let

CRUNCH!
George gets an early taste of Manchester Derby action in this robust challenge with City full-back Tony Book

everyone in Old Trafford know the level of his intent to stop the winger early on.

The strong arm tactics continued throughout the first quarter until Best gained a measure of the task at hand and began to master the defender. City lacked adventure and United deserved a narrow win. Denis Law settled this game against his former club with a superbly timed over-head kick which gave Harry Dowd no chance. Alex Stepney had little to do but performed well enough to suggest he was worth the fee.

MANCHESTER UNITED 4 BURNLEY 1
DIVISION ONE 24 SEPTEMBER 1966

UNBEATEN BURNLEY JOURNEYED to Old Trafford looking to maintain their record but had to contend with George Best who overcame a knee injury and remained at outside left with Herd moving to the right wing.

Paddy Crerand won the midfield battle stifling playmaker Gordon Harris and then began the job of ensuring forward motion. Best was in excellent form, even though he still couldn't bear to part with the ball when others were better placed. However, his contribution to possibly the goal of the season was something few players could match. Surrounded and seemingly without an option he beat all defenders in attendance and teed up Denis Law for his second successive goal from an overhead kick.

It was a spectacular effort which, though equalised by perennial United bogeyman Andy Lochhead, failed to disrupt United's momentum. David Herd hit his 100th goal for the club to edge a lead with Crerand and Sadler making sure.

NOTTINGHAM FOREST 4 MANCHESTER UNITED 1
DIVISION ONE 1 OCTOBER 1966

BEST'S ALREADY WEAKENED knee was bruised further against Burnley but healed sufficiently for George to line up at outside right against Nottingham Forest. Denis Law failed a fitness test allowing John Aston to take over on the left. Forest had been a bogey side over recent times and exposed a defensive frailty evident away from Old Trafford.

Forward Joe Baker was exceptional during the opening stages and took a corner after 30 seconds which Chris Crowe converted. Baker then induced a comical error which saw Alex Stepney and Tony Dunne collide allowing Frank Wignall to roll the ball into an empty net. An injury to the keeper resulted weakened United's capacity to deal with the onslaught and a poor punch led to a third without United causing so much as a ripple in attack.

One player earning his corn was Best who proved tricky but with very little support the chances he could provide were wasted. The only exception being Bobby Charlton's consolation.

BLACKPOOL 1 MANCHESTER UNITED 2
DIVISION ONE 8 OCTOBER 1966

AN ESTIMATED 500 United fans were said to have broken into Bloomfield Road hours before kick-off for an impromptu game between themselves but as they were only discovered as the turnstiles opened they could only be chased back to the terraces. Conditions were heavy underfoot but that didn't affect United who looked dangerous from the outset and finally put an end to an away day curse that had lasted five games.

The League Cup humiliation was another spur but the afternoon started badly. An error of judgement by Noel Cantwell after a cross from the right gave Ray Charnley plenty of time and space to bring the ball down and fire in after three minutes. The same player seemed on a mission to put the game beyond United before the break, shooting at every opportunity though missing near enough everything created.

However, an injury to Glyn James saw the scorer pushed back to centre half blunting The Seasider's attack which in turn gave United less to worry about and allowed confidence to grow. Law hit an equaliser and then a penalty two minutes from the end.

MANCHESTER UNITED 1 CHELSEA 1
DIVISION ONE 15 OCTOBER 1966

DENIS LAW'S RETURN saw George shift to the left wing with David Herd at outside right and Bobby Charlton operating as an inside-left. Chelsea were unbeaten away while United were similarly impressive at home. It was the first time Alex Stepney had faced his old team since heading north and he contributed richly to an entertaining opening.

The sides went away with a point each though United could have snatched the lot had David Sadler not hit a post after rounding Peter Bonetti and missing an empty net. Law had opened the scoring reacting quickest to a rebound before Sadler saw a great shot spectacularly saved. A shaky defence withstood a stern test before Chelsea's fortunate equaliser from a deflection.

NORTHERN IRELAND 0 ENGLAND 2
EUROPEAN CHAMPIONSHIP QUALIFIER 22 OCTOBER 1966

A TOUGH ASSIGNMENT awaited Best and his international colleagues in the first England v Northern Ireland clash since the World Cup. The Irish had last beaten the English at Belfast in 1927.

The Jules Rimet Trophy was paraded prior to kick off and the afternoon was one most Irish fans would want to forget. It appeared the hosts could be in for a memorable start after George intercepted a pass from Alan Ball. He ran clear and into the path of Nobby Stiles, taking the opportunity to go past his United teammate in true George Best style. However, a slip at the vital moment allowed the England man to recover the situation.

For the most part Northern Ireland were outclassed and the England defence too tough to break down. A number of players, including Best, allowed their frustrations to show and niggly fouls were meted out.

Bill Ferguson became the first Irish player to be dismissed in an international and the first to see a red card in any match between the home nations since the British Championships began. Roger Hunt and Martin Peters ensured the World Champions secured an easy 2-0 win.

MANCHESTER UNITED 1 ARSENAL 0
DIVISION ONE 29 OCTOBER 1966

ARSENAL WERE AN expensively assembled and useful side which the United defence had to work hard to overcome. Strikers John Radford and George Graham were always likely to pose a threat but The Gunners rarely caused too much panic in the home defence while at the other end of the field it was a different matter.

Still, the final ball was a huge problem. Best and Charlton were the chief culprits as good moves foundered on the edge of the Arsenal box. Denis Law's tirelessness eventually proved the difference as he capped a fine display by setting up David Sadler for the first half winner.

CHELSEA 1 MANCHESTER UNITED 3
DIVISION ONE 5 NOVEMBER 1966

A NUMBER OF positional changes were required with Denis Law, Noel Cantwell and Tony Dunne ruled out. Bill Foulkes and John Aston were among the names welcomed back. Chelsea had the better of the early chances but Alex Stepney remained sturdy and organised his defence well against his former employers.

United came back into it and as the sides slugged it out for long periods and the play ebbed and flowed, Stepney and Peter Bonetti had to be faultless as a result. Chelsea's new £100,000 striker Tony Hateley was handled well by Foulkes.

John Aston scored two minutes before the break. Chelsea soon equalised but Aston restored the lead after the restart. A superb goal by Best stretched the advantage which was preserved until the end with few problems.

MANCHESTER UNITED 2 SHEFFIELD WEDNESDAY 0
DIVISION ONE 12 NOVEMBER 1966

JOHN RITCHIE, WHO had scored twice against United earlier in the season during his time with Stoke, had been signed by Sheffield Wednesday a little more than 24 hours before kick off for £70,000. The Owls had put early pressure on United and unusual slip-ups aided their cause. Ritchie and his colleagues resisted until Bobby Charlton found the net after 12 minutes. David Herd hit his first goal in seven matches with a header to complete an easy win.

SOUTHAMPTON 1 MANCHESTER UNITED 2
DIVISION ONE 19 NOVEMBER 1966

WITH DAVID HERD operating on the right George took the left flank and had a hand in creating a fine goal for Bobby Charlton in the first minute. Taking the ball past a handful of defenders with a cocksure reliance on his ball skills, he shimmied into a central position before releasing Charlton who was covering on the wing. A low shot caught Dave MacClaren unawares from 25 yards and sneaked in via the near post.

Southampton tried to redress the balance but Law and Best took centre stage at the other end. However, though United strung pretty passes together there was little cutting edge. Ron Davies scored a deserved equaliser before Charlton grabbed another. A miss by Terry Paine from just six yards out after the ball rebounded into his path and Alex Stepney's brilliance between the posts secured the points.

MANCHESTER UNITED 5 SUNDERLAND 0
DIVISION ONE 26 NOVEMBER 1966

SADLER CONTINUED AT centre half with Best switching from left to right wing as John Aston came in. Bill Foulkes was missing after being withdrawn at The Dell with hamstring trouble. David Herd operated at inside left with Charlton at centre forward.

Sunderland had hit a run of form in recent weeks with four wins out of five. However, with George Best up for this one from the start The Rokerites were forced to succumb. A combination of dazzling skills and footwork created a good chance for Aston before Herd opened his account with a typical thunderbolt.

The striker had re-discovered his scoring touch following a spell on the wing and demonstrated his new found confidence by hitting three more. Sunderland keeper Jim Montgomery was forced off with concussion after half an hour, yet none of Herd's goals were gimmes.

Neither could United be blamed for their killer instinct once a replacement had been found. The resultant 5-0 romp was United's biggest home win of the season.

LEICESTER CITY 1 MANCHESTER UNITED 2
DIVISION ONE 30 NOVEMBER 1966

WITH PADDY CRERAND and Bobby Charlton struggling and Noel Cantwell and Bill Foulkes also doubts, coach Wilf McGuinness was named in the 13 for the trip to Leicester.

McGuinness was 29 but had not played for the first team since November 1959 after breaking a leg at Nottingham Forest. He broke the same leg in the same place the following month in a reserve game with Stoke and had made nothing more than a partial return to the second string in recent weeks almost seven years after the injury.

In the end McGuinness wasn't required and Charlton, who comfortably made the game, underlined his form with a fine performance. The England international was key in directing the forward line and prompted colleagues masterfully. Law took advantage of Gordon Banks finding himself stuck in the mud to notch the opening goal and a George Best scorcher from distance wrapped up the points with a shot on the turn which flew into the roof of the net.

Victory fired United to the top of the table two points clear of Chelsea with Stoke a further two points behind ahead of champions Liverpool in fourth place on goal average.

ASTON VILLA 2 MANCHESTER UNITED 1
DIVISION ONE 3 DECEMBER 1966

GEORGE BEST'S FORM seemed to be improving with every game and he had already been identified as a man who could be amongst the greatest players the world had ever seen. The man currently occupying the role as the planet's finest, Pele, was sent off for the first time in his career during the opening leg of the Brazilian Cup final. Neither Pele or his team Santos had enjoyed a good game and as so often happened when a player gets frustrated, he lashed out with a bad foul. Cruzeiro won 6-2 but were already well ahead when the game's biggest talking point occurred.

George had to endure his own disappointments as United dominated at Villa Park but failed to win. An outstanding effort from the home defence thwarted The Reds as The Villains found all manner of unorthodox ways to keep the ball out until the 75th minute when David Herd hit the best goal of the game.

Unfortunately, when Villa couldn't help themselves, luck and poor finishing did and just to round off a terrible day Nobby Stiles received a late booking - his third of the season - which triggered a suspension.

The tone for the entire game was established early. John Aston missed an open goal after Denis Law drew Colin Withers out of his ground just a few minutes in. Having worked hard to get to the top of the pile United had now surrendered a precious advantage.

MANCHESTER UNITED 2 LIVERPOOL 2
DIVISION ONE 10 DECEMBER 1966

REIGNING CHAMPIONS LIVERPOOL approached a trip to Old Trafford with trepidation following a bad result in the European Cup. Dutch side Ajax had given the Merseysiders a lesson on the finer points of the continental game winning 5-1 at home with four goals being scored in the first half.

Shankly's side were struggling to adapt to the slower tempo of the game in Europe yet Ajax's display came as something of a shock - Dutch football was still an amateur game and few in England rated the team from Amsterdam.

For all that, Matt Busby knew his old friend would be champing at the bit to ensure his troops gave a good account of themselves just days after that rout, especially as both sides had real title aspirations.

Tony Dunne covered at left half for Nobby Stiles but was forced off before the end and with him went United's chances of victory. David Herd had been working effectively with George Best and posed a significant threat scoring the goal which equalised Ian St John's opener and then scored another before deputising at centre-forward.

In spite of some useful possession

United's attack seemed lightweight without Best. Once George had assumed Herd's striking role he worked tirelessly but lacked the killer finish.

Meanwhile Best was booked for reacting to what the entire United team held to be play acting by Ron Yeats. George pushed the Scotsman when he returned to his feet after a tackle. Had it been a punch he would have been dismissed. Later Yeats admitted that he had remained prone for longer than necessary claiming that he would have sought his own justice for the foul on him.

Despite the excitement surrounding his skipper Liverpool manager Bill Shankly was a huge fan of Best and usually ready with a sage word or seven. Though never one for inflating the egos of anyone outside Anfield Shankly made an exception for George who he took to one side after the game saying, "George, son, some advice: don't be too demanding, because it's a sad fact of life that genius is born and not paid."

It may have been a warning not to ask for too much during contract negotiations from a Scot who knew just how frugal his old friend Matt Busby might be at the negotiation table.

WEST BROMWICH ALBION 3 MANCHESTER UNITED 4
DIVISION ONE 17 DECEMBER 1966

A DEFENCE MISSING some key performers was grateful to have their protector-in-chief Nobby Stiles back in the fold but still allowed three headed goals to pass

through, making them even more grateful for some remarkable forward play with Best inspirational.

The Baggies had been comprehensively

beaten by Manchester City 3-0 the previous week and made wholesale changes in defence bringing in keeper Ray Potter and axing George's old foe, club captain Graham Williams.

Unusually it was Best's unselfishness that prompted United's first half goal fest - his play being on a par with anything produced by the game's greats.

His link-up with John Aston was crucial during the early part of the match as he created two goals for David Herd who notched a hat-trick before half time.

From the kick-off George was up for it as he launched attack after attack.

Few had answers to his twinkling feet on occasions like this and his stern tackling robbed West Brom's left-sided midfielder Ian Collard on many occasions throughout the game, only his shooting let him down.

A Denis Law strike made it 4-3 at the break and a cricket score looked likely once play resumed. United were better defensively after the break and needed to be as Albion attacked with far more menace. David Sadler, who looked anything but competent in the first half, settled down to command his area well.

SHEFFIELD UNITED 2 MANCHESTER UNITED 1
DIVISION ONE 26 DECEMBER 1966

TWO GAMES WITHIN 24 hours against Sheffield United would do much to shape the destination of the championship. The busy Christmas and New Year period often did and the compliments of the

season were extended to The Blades who, despite an average performance, took both points. David Herd was United's only scorer as chance after chance went begging.

MANCHESTER UNITED 2 SHEFFIELD UNITED 0
DIVISION ONE 27 DECEMBER 1966

UNITED WERE ONCE more disappointing and their performance lacked fluency. Fortunately the Yorkshire side were worse and a win returned The Reds to top spot. If Sheffield had believed in themselves a little more they could well have beaten United at a canter.

Paddy Crerand scored the finest goal of his career with a 30 yard drive to provide a half time lead. By comparison to his recent form David Herd's finishing was

woeful, though he did take one chance extremely well after a Bobby Charlton through ball. Best was as wasteful as anyone when more would have been expected. It was generally the same for Law and Charlton. John Aston provided one brief glimpse of elegance running free down the left and hitting a crisp shot past Alan Hodgkinson. Unfortunately it was ruled out for a foul he had committed in the build up.

MANCHESTER UNITED 0 LEEDS UNITED 0
Division One 31 December 1966

David Sadler started his third game in a row as cover for the suspended Nobby Stiles. Leeds were outstanding in the opening minutes and Tony Dunne in his 200th league game helped repel them with some excellent interventions. The match was good in parts with plenty of fine defending but poor finishing helped the game remain scoreless.

MANCHESTER UNITED 1 TOTTENHAM HOTSPUR 0
Division One 14 January 1967

The postponement of the Newcastle game and Liverpool's win over West Ham saw the Merseyider's snatch first place back from The Reds but with Denis Law missing courtesy of a twisted knee, the job of regaining the summit looked bleak.

Jimmy Greaves, the scourge of many English sides, had United's defenders at sixes and sevens. This included those such as George who had been detailed to track back. He misjudged a back-pass. and only Stepney's alertness prevented Greaves or or Saul from scoring.

The match was an excellent end -to- end tussle for the most part which was decided by a scrambled David Herd goal in the latter stages. The manner of the strike didn't befit a game of this standard but drew few complaints from jubilant Reds.

Best was well handled and though given room at various stages would be swamped with attention as soon as danger seemed to loom. It was a risky strategy but paid handsome dividends for Spurs. A similarly narrow victory at Sheffield Wednesday saw Liverpool remain top.

MANCHESTER CITY 1 MANCHESTER UNITED 1
Division One 21 January 1967

With young players such as Bobby Noble shining, the question was whether Nobby Stiles would be welcomed back at the first opportunity following his enforced lay-off. Had United been at full strength there is no knowing but with Law and Aston out, the door opened and made Matt Busby's decision easier. David Sadler was pushed forward and deserved to stay in the team for some excellent performances albeit in a different capacity.

Predictably Nobby was booed by the City fans. At Maine Road he would probably expect little else but the cat calls seemed to inspire him. The left half excelled, helping to hold a rampant home side who belied their league position.

United led until the final minutes of the game through a rare Bill Foulkes goal and seemed to have gained two more vital points in the battle to become league champions. However Stiles, who had grown up looking forward to derby days during his youth, put through his own net in the final minutes and was inconsolable for some time.

His frustrations were taken out on a wall in the visitor's dressing room after the game. Though the equaliser itself may have been deserved on the balance of play, the manner of the goal most certainly was not.

MANCHESTER UNITED 2 STOKE CITY 0
FA CUP 3ᴿᴰ RD 28 JANUARY 1967

THE CLASH OF the round saw high flying Stoke City come to Old Trafford. With Law back, Best switched from left to right wing though John Aston was overlooked for his vacant position in favour of Bobby Charlton.

The returning Law maintained his goal a game ratio in the competition, although Stoke were the better side until a period just before the interval. However, they fell to a cross from Best to the far post converted by the Scot who steamed in to net his 31ˢᵗ FA Cup strike - a post war record. With the goal United became more settled and skilful players such as Best showed the full range of their skills. Herd hammered in a thuderbolt to complete the scoring.

BURNLEY 1 MANCHESTER UNITED 1
DIVISION ONE 4 FEBRUARY 1967

THERE WERE DAYS when George Best fancied it and this was one such occasion. Often, just as today, the winger went looking for early involvement and his first touch would not be a flick or pass but the the start of a twisting run towards the penalty area. Sometimes he would look for the chance himself or seek to play somebody else in. More usually the former and had Harry Thomson not dived at his feet United would probably have taken the lead just a few minutes in.

As it turned out the first goal went to United, although it took some time for David Sadler to grab one of the many chances created. Unfortunately the versatile forward-cum-centre-half, in the form of his United career, turned from hero to villain giving away a penalty with just 30 seconds remaining.

The ball hit Sadler's arm as he attempted to clear a deceptive pass. In trying to bring the ball down on his chest rather than his head he seemed in two minds and ended up handling.

It was another occasion where United's opponents arguably deserved a point but the equaliser was conceded in an unfortunate manner.

MANCHESTER UNITED 1 NOTTINGHAM FOREST 0
DIVISION ONE 11 FEBRUARY 1967

BEST WAS AN initial doubt for this top-of-the-table clash with an ankle injury. Denis Law and Bobby Noble were also struggling but each made it and had terrific games. None more so than George who, in a playful mood, tied up not only the opposing full back but the inside left and the Forest winger throughout the game. With just one side of the field operable for the Midland side as a result, and the centre well patrolled by Paddy Crerand, the visitors struggled to maintain their periods of dominance and lost the initiative.

The match was a battle for second place as both sides vied to hold on to Liverpool's coattails. Peter Grummit was exceptional at Old Trafford yet again but with Alex Stepney just as safe in his handling it seemed a goalless draw would ensue - that was until Law plundered a late effort from a corner.

Bill Foulkes succumbed to injury but the blow failed to break United's stride as Sadler dropped back. Injuries often haunted teams during the late winter and spring but if the worst happened it seemed that The Reds, with such a rich pool of talent at their disposal, were able to resist the worst of it.

MANCHESTER UNITED 1 NORWICH CITY 2
FA CUP 4TH RD 18 FEBRUARY 1967

DESPITE STRUGGLING AT the foot of Division Two, Norwich City came to Old Trafford determined to give a good account of themselves with any result they gleaned a bonus. As expected they were well worked by United who could have snatched an early lead at various times.

However, The Reds fell into a listless phase which seemed to last until the close by which time those early misses were regretted. Stunned by Don Heath's goal midway through the first half United pulled themselves back and equalised through Denis Law following a swirling Jim Ryan cross. Yet despite the wake-up call, the malaise continued. George Best looked aimless but he was not the only one. A Tony Dunne backpass intercepted by Gordon Bolland gave The Canaries their winner and their greatest FA Cup success since beating Spurs in 1959 as United were forced to concentrate on the league for the remainder of the season.

MANCHESTER UNITED 4 BLACKPOOL 0
DIVISION ONE 25 FEBRUARY 1967

FIVE CHANGES WERE made to the side humiliated by Norwich, though some were caused by injury as Matt Busby stood by most of the under-performing stars.

Relegation-threatened Blackpool provided a good opportunity to bounce back with most newspapers calling for

George Best to be axed. Such a thought made most United fans scoff at the very thought. The journalist's opinions were rammed down their throats as Best laid on a superb pass for Bobby Charlton to notch the fourth and final goal of the game.

For the most part the Irishman was quiet but his colleagues were in no mood to open themselves up to more criticism. Blackpool were stoic in defence but once they were beaten by Denis Law's header from a John Aston cross, they capitulated.

ARSENAL 1 MANCHESTER UNITED 1
DIVISION ONE 3 MARCH 1967

SUCH WAS THE clamour amongst the United faithful to see this pivotal match during the title run-in that this Friday night game was relayed to Old Trafford by close circuit television with 28,423 fans in attendance. The numbers ensured a financial loss but demonstrated the popularity of the side and underlined just how many more tickets could have been sold at a capacity Highbury.

Arsenal made the early running and maintained their advantage for most of the first half. Denis Law gifted The Gunners a lead while lending a hand in defence when he hauled John Samuels to the ground conceding a penalty which the forward himself converted.

United equalised when Jim Furnell lost control of a tricky cross from Best, allowing Aston to net. George had actually hit the onion bag from a set piece prior to this but as the referee had already signalled for an indirect free-kick his superb shot was disallowed. Bobby Charlton was starved of the ball in his central position and his isolation restricted the number of chances The Reds created.

With Liverpool playing 24 hours later the clubs swapped positions but at this stage the Anfielders were more consistent and maintained their lead at the top with a win.

NEWCASTLE UNITED 0 MANCHESTER UNITED 0
DIVISION ONE 11 MARCH 1967

BEST WAS DETERMINED to silence the critics by underpinning his great skills with discernable results and creating chances for his colleagues or himself.

Unfortunately the other forward players were less effective than in recent weeks and no flashes of genius could spark off a move to create the vital goal that would

secure both points.

Defensively The Magpies were superb, though United were well organised enough and never looked likely to be breached - as a result a stalemate was always on the cards.

MANCHESTER UNITED 5 LEICESTER CITY 2
DIVISION ONE 18 MARCH 1967

UNITED SOUGHT TO extract revenge on Leicester for the defeat that had marked the end of last season's title dreams. Best was happy to contort defenders, then seek out a teammate and assist the push for others to score rather than himself. David Herd grabbed one after 90 seconds but if The Reds were to claim the title it was to be without him. The thirty-two year old broke his leg in the act of scoring to effectively finish his season and, eventually, his United career.

Denis Law, Bobby Charlton, John Aston and David Sadler added to the afternoon's tally and boosted United's goal average. Something that might prove useful in the final shake up.

LIVERPOOL 0 MANCHESTER UNITED 0
DIVISION ONE 25 MARCH 1967

WITH LIVERPOOL LOSING at Burnley the previous week it was all to play for when the top two met at Anfield. There was usually some significance to any clash of the two Reds but a result either way would more than likely decide the title.

With the exception of David Herd, United were at full strength. Liverpool made changes; Roger Hunt returned for Manchester born Alf Arrowsmith. Emlyn Hughes, making his third outing for the home side, switched from central defence replacing Gerry Byrne at left back where he would be pitched against George Best with Willie Stevenson coming in to add some guile in midfield.

Little quarter was given by either side and with each wary of commiting men forward, chances were at a premium. So much so that the game, somewhat predictably given the prize on offer, finished goalless. Both defences and midfields cancelled each other out. For United a fifth successive away draw allowed the gap to remain at a couple of points and certainly favoured them in terms of the title.

FULHAM 2 MANCHESTER UNITED 2
DIVISION ONE 27 MARCH 1967

LIVERPOOL BLEW THEIR title ambitions by recording successive home draws this time with Arsenal giving United a chance to all but wrap up the championship yet Fulham earned a hard fought 2-2 draw at Craven Cottage meaning United could not extend their advantage at the top.

Allan Clarke, an England under-23 international and one time target for Matt Busby, opened the scoring after 18 minutes but just before the break George Best pulled United level. This was his first goal since December and came after he jinked from side to side following a pass from Denis Law. A number of Fulham defenders, already with thoughts on the refuge of their dressing room, lost their bearings and Best's run ended with a shot that squeezed between Tony Macedo and the post.

Les Barrett gave Fulham the lead once more in the final quarter but Nobby Stiles, with his first goal since the opening game of the season, grabbed a share of the points with six minutes left.

Just before the home side made it 2-1 George had had a good chance to give United an advantage. The keeper managed to save with his legs but with cover still trying to get back and Macedo committed to narrowing the angle, passing the ball to Law would undoubtedly have seen the ball hit the net, much to the Scotsman's frustration.

MANCHESTER UNITED 2 FULHAM 1
DIVISION ONE 28 MARCH 1967

A QUICK DASH from London to Manchester in order to contest the return fixture with Fulham didn't leave Paddy Crerand and Denis Law much time for running repairs on knocks suffered at Craven Cottage. Though United were finding the net, they were not as prolific as they should have been and were clearly missing David Herd. Fortunately defenders were helping out at both ends.

Twenty-four hours earlier it had been Nobby Stiles, today it was Bill Foulkes who popped up to head in just minutes from the end, adding to yet another Stiles goal. United's approach play was good but ultimately lacked end product until Bill's header. George Best was the most dangerous player on view but no one was able to capitalise on his approach work.

MANCHESTER UNITED 3 WEST HAM UNITED 0
DIVISION ONE 1 APRIL 1967

AN EARLY GOAL from Bobby Charlton finally saw at least one of the attackers repay their backline for bailing them out in recent games. Charlton's drive rounded off a superb charge down the flank by Best who picked out the England international in a great position.

United remained dangerous and the team most likely to score but couldn't add to their lead until the final minutes when Denis Law and George Best converted

opportunities. Law missed a penalty for the first time since a 5-0 win over Bolton back in February 1964, hitting a post. It would have added to the scoreline which, though deserved, on the balance of play seemed unlikely given the wastefulness shown.

West Ham had few chances but with games running out wins were vital and it seemed Best, Charlton and Law were running into form at just the right time.

SHEFFIELD WEDNESDAY 2 MANCHESTER UNITED 2
DIVISION ONE 10 APRIL 1967

WEDNESDAY'S CUP COMMITMENTS saw the game re-arranged for the following Monday evening and if The Owls were tired United seemed ready to benefit. Paddy Crerand was in the thick of the action, seeking to win every early battle in central midfield.

George was forced to limp off after harsh treatment which saw him miss out on winning an international cap the following night. However, he withstood the initial challenges and was in no mood to allow the hard work he had put in over recent weeks go to waste.

He didn't spare himself this evening, setting up Bobby Charlton with a run down the wing for his first goal before similar play from Dunne allowed him to make it 2-0. United should have held on and certainly had chances to extend the lead but were pegged back for a draw. Nevertheless they retained top spot in the league.

MANCHESTER UNITED 3 SOUTHAMPTON 0
DIVISION ONE 18 APRIL 1967

ANOTHER CLUB'S CUP exploits and the international calendar meant games had to be fitted in to a hectic April. Fortunately an extra few day's rest gave Best the chance to recover and take his place on the right hand side in an unchanged side.

Law and Charlton were the real stars of the late show which secured victory, setting each other up for the first two goals scored.

David Sadler headed in a John Aston cross to round off the night. Southampton were kept quiet by a well-organised defence. Best floated around but lacked any real sting even though his skills were easy on the eye.

MANCHESTER UNITED 3 ASTON VILLA 1
DIVISION ONE 19 APRIL 1967

UNITED FANS EAGER to see Old Trafford witness another great occasion were buoyed by George Best who seemed on a one man mission to sate their desire. He was running freely at defenders with pace and trickery. Yet their joy was thwarted by Willie Anderson who scored early for Villa. The former United winger had been sold to the Midlands side just three months earlier for £20,000 but, having made just one appearance he now re-appeared to dent his former colleague's title hopes.

United nerves were calmed when the man who had made Anderson surplus to requirements, John Aston, levelled. Law headed United in to the lead and Best's curling effort from mid-range put The Reds on the brink of a record equalling seventh championship crown.

SUNDERLAND 0 MANCHESTER UNITED 0
DIVISION ONE 22 APRIL 1967

SUNDERLAND WOULD BE key figures in the title's destination even though they lay in mid-table. With upcoming games against Nottingham Forest and Liverpool, as well as this fixture with United, their performances would provide the remaining championship challengers with a chance to catch The Red Devils.

Liverpool, following one win in seven games, trailed by six points but had a game in hand while Forest were closer but were still looking for their first championship crown. As long as United took the majority of the eight points available, the title would be theirs.

However, The Rokerites were not prepared to give anyone an easy game. United's attacks on goal were sporadic but the opportunities created were decent and they should have done better. Nevertheless the pattern since Boxing Day was maintained as United recorded their eighth away draw in a row.

WEST HAM UNITED 1 MANCHESTER UNITED 6
DIVISION ONE 6 MAY 1967

THOUGH A SINGLE point would be enough to reclaim the championship trophy, and there was another game to go after this for United as insurance, there was little chance of any of the travelling party accepting the minimum requirement. Manchester City could have handed the title to The Reds before this game by beating Forest in midweek but lost 2-0 at The City Ground.

United and Best in particular could never tolerate any player simply going through the motions and wanted to win with style courtesy of their own efforts rather than at the hands of others.

Bobby Charlton prised open a defence which had leaked its fair share of goals over 40 games within two minutes with the type of drive he had been perfecting his whole career.

Paddy Crerand scored the 29th opposition league goal at Upton Park so far that term with a firm header from John Aston's cross before ten minutes had gone and within moments Bill Foulkes had made it 3-0 converting a chance created after he had challenged rookie keeper Colin Mackleworth. It was the young stopper's second league game and he was no match for the battle-hardened centre-half.

George Best made the score sheet after a quarter of an hour. Nobby Stiles ran forward from the centre of defence and found Best who had drifted in from the wing. Controlling it on his right foot he then teed up a shot on his left. Mackleworth was grasping at thin air as the ball beat him for pace and hit the net.

John Charles, known as Charlo to distinguish him from the Welsh international forward by the same name, pulled one back soon after the break but United simply reasserted themselves regaining a four goal cushion through a Denis Law penalty and completed the scoring when Law got on the end of a perfectly weighted George Best centre.

The final strike typified so many of United's goals that term. George Best may only have scored ten league goals but he made more than treble that for others, particularly Law who hit 23 to finish top scorer. The *Sunday Express* described the win as "the finest display of football since the war." Matt Busby certainly agreed. He felt the win was his finest hour.

There could have been few better displays by English clubs and many of those which had been on a par would have been produced by other Busby sides.

MANCHESTER UNITED 0 STOKE CITY 0
DIVISION ONE 13 MAY 1967

UNITED WOUND DOWN the campaign with a goalless draw against mid-table Stoke City though the game was not without incident and United could well have earned a 25th win of the season.

Denis Law was ruled out so George Best, sporting a short haircut, filled in as an inside forward. Unlike the biblical Samson, the Irishman found that his powers had not been diminished and gave the Stoke defence a real testing.

However, despite good approach play the story of the season continued as a lack of true fire power kept the ball the wrong side of the goalline. There was of course no pressure on United and Stoke almost took advantage of the relaxed atmosphere, missing several chances during the game.

1966-67

In what would prove to be United's last championship season for 26 years, the triumvirate of Best, Law and Charlton did sufficient to ensure another shot at winning the European Cup. Liverpool had led the league until January but on gaining top spot after a 0-0 draw at Newcastle in March, United didn't relinquish pole position ending the season with 20 games without defeat from Boxing Day.

One of the key acquisitions was the arrival of Alex Stepney in September, a move that shored up a hitherto leaky defence while positional switches gave the side an added dimension. David Sadler moved to centre forward while David Herd dropped back to inside-left where he linked up with George Best who had switched flanks to accommodate John Aston whose direct running made John Connelly surplus to requirements after barely more than half a dozen appearances. The side had evolved with United going undefeated at home, winning a remarkable 17 out of 21 games and keeping 13 clean sheets in the process. Only the 2-1 FA Cup defeat by Norwich City blighted the home campaign but the manner in which United repaired themselves after that ignominious cup exit to take the title underlined the quality and spirit of the side.

Though there was still a focus on youth, substantial investment had been made to ensure United remained a force both domestically as they moved towards Busby's dream of conquering Europe. Denis Law was predictably the top scorer and brushed off a pre-season dispute with the club which had threatened to undermine his United future. George Best proved that his knee was back to full strength and completed his first ever-present season. He was the only player to appear in every fixture over the course of 45 league and cup games.

Without a European stage to showcase his talents, Best still managed some captivating performances, contributing heavily to United's league success, notably in the awe-inspiring 6-1 win at West Ham that clinched the league. Nevertheless, the season was always going to be a little prosaic without a continental adventure to thrill the fans. United's absence from foreign fields was especially hard to take as Celtic, rather than United, became the first British club to win the European Cup, beating Inter Milan 2-1 in Lisbon. Now, of course, courtesy of the title victory, the following season's aspirations hung almost entirely on becoming the first English club to lift the big trophy.

DATE	OPPONENT	VENUE	SCORE	ATT'D	1	2	3	4	5	6	7	8	9	10	11
20 August	WBA	Old Trafford	5-3	41,343	Gaskell	Brennan	Dunne(A)	Fitzpatrick	Foulkes	Stiles[1]	Best[1]	Law[2]	Charlton	Herd[1]	Connelly
23 August	Everton	Goodison Park	2-1	60,657	Gaskell	Brennan	Dunne(A)	Fitzpatrick	Foulkes	Stiles	Best	Law[2]	Charlton	Herd	Connelly
27 August	Leeds United	Elland Road	1-3	45,092	Gaskell	Brennan	Dunne(A)	Fitzpatrick	Foulkes	Stiles	Best[1]	Law	Charlton	Herd	Connelly
31 August	Everton	Old Trafford	3-0	61,114	Gaskell	Brennan	Dunne(A)	Crerand	Foulkes[1]	Stiles	Connelly[1]	Law[1]	Charlton	Herd	Best
3 September	Newcastle United	Old Trafford	3-2	44,448	Gregg	Brennan	Dunne(A)	Crerand	Foulkes	Stiles	Connelly[1]	Law[1]	Charlton	Herd[1]	Best
7 September	Stoke City	Victoria Ground	0-3	44,337	Gregg	Brennan	Dunne(A)	Crerand	Foulkes	Stiles	Connelly	Law	Charlton	Herd	Best
10 September	Tottenham Hotspur	White Hart Lane	1-2	56,295	Gaskell	Brennan	Dunne(A)	Crerand	Foulkes	Stiles	Best	Law[1]	Sadler	Herd	Charlton
17 September	Manchester City	Old Trafford	1-0	62,085	Stepney	Brennan	Dunne(A)	Crerand	Foulkes	Stiles	Best	Law[1]	Sadler	Charlton	Aston
24 September	Burnley	Old Trafford	4-1	52,697	Stepney	Brennan	Dunne(A)	Crerand[1]	Foulkes	Stiles	Herd[1]	Law[1]	Sadler[1]	Charlton	Best
1 October	Nottingham Forest	City Ground	1-4	41,854	Stepney	Brennan	Dunne(A)	Crerand	Foulkes	Stiles	Best	Charlton[1]	Sadler	Herd	Aston
8 October	Blackpool	Bloomfield Road	2-1	33,555	Stepney	Dunne(A)	Noble	Crerand	Cantwell	Stiles	Herd	Law[2]	Sadler	Charlton	Best
15 October	Chelsea	Old Trafford	1-1	56,789	Stepney	Dunne(A)	Noble	Crerand	Cantwell	Stiles	Herd	Law[1]	Sadler	Charlton	Best
29 October	Arsenal	Old Trafford	1-0	45,387	Stepney	Dunne(A)	Noble	Crerand	Cantwell	Stiles	Herd	Law	Sadler[1]	Charlton	Best
5 November	Chelsea	Stamford Bridge	3-1	55,958	Stepney	Brennan	Noble	Crerand	Foulkes	Stiles	Herd[1]	Aston[2]	Sadler	Charlton	Best[1]
12 November	Sheffield Wednesday	Old Trafford	2-0	46,942	Stepney	Dunne(A)	Noble	Crerand	Foulkes	Stiles	Herd[1]	Law	Sadler	Charlton[1]	Best
19 November	Southampton	The Dell	2-1	29,458	Stepney	Dunne(A)	Noble	Crerand	Cantwell	Stiles	Herd	Law	Sadler	Charlton[2]	Best
26 November	Sunderland	Old Trafford	5-0	44,687	Stepney	Dunne(A)	Noble	Crerand	Sadler	Stiles	Best	Law[1]	Charlton	Herd[4]	Aston
30 November	Leicester City	Filbert Street	2-1	39,014	Stepney	Dunne(A)	Noble	Crerand	Sadler	Stiles	Best[1]	Law[1]	Charlton	Herd[1]	Aston
3 December	Aston Villa	Villa Park	1-2	39,937	Stepney	Dunne(A)	Noble	Crerand	Sadler	Stiles	Best	Law	Charlton	Herd[1]	Aston
10 December	Liverpool	Old Trafford	2-2	61,768	Stepney	Brennan	Noble	Crerand	Sadler	Dunne(A)	Best[2]	Ryan	Charlton	Herd	Aston
17 December	WBA	The Hawthorns	4-3	32,080	Stepney	Brennan	Noble	Crerand	Sadler	Stiles	Best	Law[1]	Charlton	Herd[3]	Aston
26 December	Sheffield United	Bramall Lane	1-2	42,752	Stepney	Dunne(A)	Noble	Crerand	Foulkes	Sadler	Best	Law	Charlton	Herd[1]	Aston
27 December	Sheffield United	Old Trafford	2-0	59,392	Stepney	Dunne(A)	Noble	Crerand[1]	Foulkes	Sadler	Best	Law	Charlton	Herd[1]	Aston
31 December	Leeds United	Old Trafford	0-0	53,486	Stepney	Dunne(A)	Noble	Crerand	Foulkes	Sadler	Best	Law	Charlton	Herd	Aston
14 January	Tottenham Hotspur	Old Trafford	1-0	57,366	Stepney	Dunne(A)	Noble	Crerand	Foulkes	Sadler	Best	Ryan	Charlton	Herd[1]	Aston
		Maine Road	1-1		Stepney	Dunne(A)	Noble	Crerand	Foulkes[1]	Stiles	Ryan	Charlton	Sadler	Herd	Best

Date	Opponent	Venue	Score	Att.											
25 February	Blackpool	Old Trafford	4-0	47,158	Stepney	Dunne(A)	Noble	Crerand	Foulkes	Stiles	Best	Law¹	Sadler	Charlton²	Aston
3 March	Arsenal	Highbury	1-1	63,363	Stepney	Dunne(A)	Noble	Crerand	Foulkes	Stiles	Best	Law	Sadler	Charlton	Aston¹
11 March	Newcastle United	St James' Park	0-0	37,430	Stepney	Dunne(A)	Noble	Crerand	Foulkes	Stiles	Best	Law	Sadler	Charlton	Aston
18 March	Leicester City	Old Trafford	5-2	50,281	Stepney	Dunne(A)	Noble	Crerand	Foulkes	Stiles	Best	Law¹	Charlton¹	Herd¹	Aston¹
25 March	Liverpool	Anfield	0-0	53,813	Stepney	Dunne(A)	Noble	Crerand	Foulkes	Stiles	Best	Law	Sadler	Charlton	Aston
27 March	Fulham	Craven Cottage	2-2	47,290	Stepney	Dunne(A)	Noble	Crerand	Foulkes	Stiles¹	Best¹	Law	Sadler	Charlton	Aston
28 March	Fulham	Old Trafford	2-1	51,673	Stepney	Dunne(A)	Noble	Crerand	Foulkes¹	Stiles¹	Best¹	Law	Sadler	Charlton	Aston
1 April	West Ham United	Old Trafford	3-0	61,308	Stepney	Dunne(A)	Noble	Crerand	Foulkes	Stiles	Best¹	Law¹	Sadler	Charlton¹	Aston
10 April	Sheffield Wednesday	Hillsborough	2-2	51,101	Stepney	Dunne(A)	Noble	Crerand	Foulkes	Stiles	Best	Law	Sadler	Charlton²	Aston
18 April	Southampton	Old Trafford	3-0	54,291	Stepney	Dunne(A)	Noble	Crerand	Foulkes	Stiles	Best	Law¹	Sadler¹	Charlton¹	Aston
22 April	Sunderland	Roker Park	0-0	43,570	Stepney	Dunne(A)	Noble	Crerand	Foulkes	Stiles	Best	Law	Sadler	Charlton	Aston
29 April	Aston Villa	Old Trafford	3-1	55,782	Stepney	Brennan	Dunne(A)	Crerand	Foulkes	Stiles	Best¹	Law¹	Sadler	Charlton	Aston¹
6 May	West Ham United	Upton Park	6-1	38,424	Stepney	Brennan	Dunne(A)	Crerand¹	Foulkes¹	Stiles	Best¹	Law²	Sadler	Charlton¹	Aston
13 May	Stoke City	Old Trafford	0-0	61,071	Stepney	Brennan	Dunne(A)	Crerand	Foulkes	Stiles	Best	Ryan	Sadler	Charlton	Aston

FA Cup

Date	Opponent	Venue	Score	Att.											
28 January	Stoke City	Old Trafford	2-0	63,500	Stepney	Dunne(A)	Noble	Crerand	Foulkes	Stiles	Best	Law¹	Sadler	Herd¹	Charlton
18 February	Norwich City	Old Trafford	1-2	63,409	Stepney	Dunne(A)	Noble	Crerand	Sadler	Stiles	Ryan	Law¹	Charlton	Herd	Best

League Cup

Date	Opponent	Venue	Score	Att.											
14 September	Blackpool	Bloomfield Road	1-5	15,570	Dunne(P)	Brennan	Dunne(A)	Crerand	Foulkes	Stiles	Connelly	Best	Sadler	Herd¹	Aston

1967-68
THE PINNACLE

A worldwide tour followed the title win. Friendlies took place in Los Angeles, then New Zealand and Australia effectively extending the season to late June. Many young stars were amongst the travelling party and even though George deserved a rest, his profile meant he had to attend.

The summer sport continued when City and United swapped goalposts for willow to play a cricket 'derby' at the other Old Trafford. George displayed an aptitude for keeping wicket. So much so that Matt Busby may even have wondered whether he should take the gloves on the football field in an emergency. However, when his old drinking partner Mike Summerbee stepped up to the crease he couldn't resist having a bowl.

Some felt this extensive travelling would end up hurting United later in the campaign as the players had been afforded little more than six weeks full rest before beginning their defence of the championship and assault on the European Cup which for various reasons had continued to elude Matt Busby.

MANCHESTER UNITED 3 TOTTENHAM HOTSPUR 3
CHARITY SHIELD 12 AUGUST 1967

OLD TRAFFORD WITNESSED one of Bobby Charlton's most spectacular efforts from distance after he was set up by Denis Law and Brian Kidd. It was a beautifully crafted goal set up initially by Law who took the ball in his own half then beat three players before passing to Kidd on the left wing. Law bustled through taking a return ball before playing it into space just yards ahead of Charlton. The England man struck the ball over Pat Jennings and into the net at The Stretford End.

This was the first glimpse the majority of United fans had had of Kidd who starred during the American tour and United's spell in The Antipodes. A down to earth, dyed-in-the-wool red, Kidd's father drove the 112 and 113 buses that transported many of the spectators inside Old Trafford. He played at inside-left with Bobby Charlton as a central forward. David Sadler was the unlucky man left on the bench.

However, by the time Charlton's strike had stretched the net Spurs were already 2-0 up. Jimmy Robertson scored in the second minute, then Jimmy Greaves got the ball midway inside the United half and burst towards the area beating Stiles before squaring for Robertson who had the relatively simple task of rolling in after all the hard work had been put in by Greaves.

Spurs goalkeeper Pat Jennings stretched the lead in the seventh minute. Breezy conditions affected the Ulsterman's downfield punt and as Alex Stepney advanced too far, he was embarrassed by a particularly high bounce.

United finally asserted themselves on the game following Charlton's equaliser. Frank Saul pulled the Londoners clear once more but Denis Law netted after a

Bobby Charlton shot was half saved and allowing him to pick up the scraps.

The 3-3 draw was a tantalising foretaste of what was to come over the next nine months.

EVERTON 3 MANCHESTER UNITED 1
DIVISION ONE 19 AUGUST 1967

A HIGHLY ANTICIPATED league campaign started with a couple of Merseyside v Manchester clashes. City hosted Liverpool with United travelling to Everton. The Goodison side were well fancied to mount a stiff challenge for the title and set about demonstrating their credentials against the champions by taking the lead through Alan Ball on 13 minutes.

The Reds saw more of the ball immediately after the goal but were

disappointing in and around the area gifting possession very cheaply. Everton had no such problems and when they had chances more often than not either took them or tested Alex Stepney.

Ball excelled and ran midfield scoring another before Alex Young made it 3-0. Bobby Charlton hit a consolation late on as United made a disappointing start to the defence of their league crown. Incidentally, City and Liverpool drew 0-0.

MANCHESTER UNITED 1 LEICESTER CITY 1
DIVISION ONE 26 AUGUST 1967

A KNEE INJURY made Best one of many doubts for Leeds United's visit during the week, though he did manage a return against Leicester, taking his place on the right. Paddy Crerand on the other hand finally succumbed to an injury suffered in the opening league game allowing David Sadler his first start of the season.

Leicester came into the game on the back of two defeats and put centre half John Sjoberg into attack hoping to mix things up a bit but the tall Scot was well patrolled by Bill Foulkes. Brian Kidd's introduction had caught the imagination but seemed to disrupt the partnership

of Best, Law and Charlton who, despite looking good at various points were failing to gel as a unit. John Aston was going through a tough spell which didn't help but he was not solely to blame.

The problems were evident once more as most of the strikers and midfielders remained on different wavelengths. Crerand's absence was also felt. When chances were crafted The Reds found Peter Shilton as safe as his growing reputation suggested he would be. Despite an ankle injury the young keeper was outstanding though he was beaten by Bill Foulkes.

WEST HAM UNITED 1 MANCHESTER UNITED 3
DIVISION ONE 2 SEPTEMBER 1967

TEENAGER Francis Burns made his debut at left back with Shay Brennan out, Tony Dunne covered on the right. Law and Aston were also ruled out meaning George switched flanks to partner Burns. David Sadler came in at inside right.

There was some crowd trouble before the match began. Unfortunately United fans made up the majority of the half dozen or so ejected from Upton Park.

The Hammers, seeking to avenge the 6-1 defeat which earned United the title last season, attacked from their first touch. United's threat was only sporadic. Best put one of the clearest chances just wide after linking with Jim Ryan while Bill Foulkes made two superb goalline clearances and the game stayed goalless until the break.

A solid defence enabled the forwards and midfield more licence to attack in the second period. Sadler was pivotal in a reprise of the role he played so effectively at the end of last term, assisting in Kidd's opener and then hitting a rasping drive to make it 2-0. West Ham reduced the arrears but saw the two goal deficit restored when Paddy Crerand set up Jim Ryan.

SUNDERLAND 1 MANCHESTER UNITED 1
DIVISION ONE 6 SEPTEMBER 1967

SUNDERLAND HAD MADE one of their finest ever opening sequences to a season. Though missing Denis Law, United still fancied a good result at Roker Park and this performance certainly suggested as much and was worth more than the 1-1 draw earned.

When Kidd nodded home a Crerand cross, United seemed to be on course for a routine victory and with Charlton exceptional United appeared to have rediscovered the forward link play so obviously missing thus far.

That was until Colin Suggett's equaliser. Still the visitors would have taken both points had it not been for Jim Montgomery who made extraordinary saves from Best, Burns and Sadler in the opening period.

United were still solid in defence and thwarted a more dangerous looking Sunderland in the second half.

MANCHESTER UNITED 2 BURNLEY 2
DIVISION ONE 9 SEPTEMBER 1967

DENIS LAW REMAINED sidelined and was joined by Nobby Stiles who was substituted at Sunderland. These were the only setbacks for Matt Busby who was pleased with most of his side's showings in all areas even if he would have preferred to see his charges make games safe rather than rely on resilience at the back.

Burnley took the game to United and

were the more likely to score all afternoon. They certainly enjoyed better chances than The Reds. However two clear opportunities still fell to Best who skied the first then sent another across the face of goal. It seemed the home side would rue those misses misses when Burnley went ahead through an Andy Lochhead header. The same player grabbed another not long after.

Yet United managed to salvage a point. Francis Burns scored four minutes from the end to provide some hope and a Paddy Crerand equaliser two minutes into injury time completed an undeserved comeback.

Best had a quiet game by his own standards and was certainly disappointing in front of goal but finally clicked towards the close.

SHEFFIELD WEDNESDAY 1 MANCHESTER UNITED 1
DIVISION ONE 16 SEPTEMBER 1967

UNITED CONTINUED TO find themselves pitched against the early pacesetters with a visit to Hillsborough - a ground with few happy memories over recent times, they had failed to register a win there in ten visits.

Wednesday had only dropped four points thus far and ran strongly at United who were grateful for some timely interceptions including one or two which could only be considered last ditch.

Best was fairly unadventurous early on and rarely an attacking force except in glimpses but made one run from the full-back position after lending a hand in

defence. He weaved past a host of players on a mazy, 90 yard run. The dribbling was only punctuated by a quick 1-2 with Bobby Charlton but Ron Springett advanced and smothered the ball at George's feet.

Stepney had had little to do before Wednesday took the lead with a goal most thought to be offside. Best got himself on the end of a Burns' free-kick to equalise. David Sadler was withdrawn into defence and that restricted United's attacking options but Busby felt his presence was required more in the backline during the second period.

MANCHESTER UNITED 4 HIBERNIANS 0
EUROPEAN CUP 1ST RD 1ST LEG 20 SEPTEMBER 1967

MINNOWS HIBERNIANS, WHO had denied Sliema Wanderers a fourth successive Maltese title by a single point, were not expected to cause many problems and were soundly beaten with United barely forced to raise a canter for 90 minutes. Only half a dozen teams contested the Maltese title, so the Mediterraneans had little chance to play teams of United's

calibre outside UEFA competition.

Though coached by Father Tagliaferro, Hibernians quickly found themselves without a prayer courtesy of two well taken goals by Denis Law including the second of the night which was as good as anything Old Trafford had seen that term. The ball was lashed in from distance. David Sadler hit the other two.

MANCHESTER UNITED 3 TOTTENHAM HOTSPUR 1
Division One 23 September 1967

United had drawn four of their last five games but fell behind early when Frank Saul put Alan Gilzean through on four minutes. The scorer outwitted the attending defenders before firing past Stepney. Rather than let their heads drop, United responded in kind with Best equalising two minutes later.

After the goal The Reds remained the better side occupying very capable central defenders in Mike England and Alan Mullery through Bobby Charlton's visionary passing.

Frustratingly it actually seemed like all the hard work would not pay off when Denis Law had an excellent goal disallowed for offside and missed a penalty. That was until Best hit another and Law rounded matters off late on.

HIBERNIANS 0 MANCHESTER UNITED 0 (AGG 0-4)
European Cup 1st Rd 2nd leg 27 September 1967

Amongst the 25,000 present at The Empire Stadium in Gzira was a huge contingent of Maltese based United supporters enjoying the rare chance to see their favourites play in their home country.

Names such as Nobby Stiles, Bobby Charlton, Denis Law and George Best were revered in Malta. Most would have been disappointed had George not made the game as Hibernians were only participating in the European Cup for the second time. George's non-appearance seemed a distinct possibility when he had three teeth out soon after the Spurs game.

Remarkably it was the fans supporting the home side who left happiest. United were always in control of the tie but a goalless draw was a relatively poor showing although the surface didn't help.

Best, always keen to please a crowd, tried some flicks and tricks which lesser skilled players such as the Maltese side couldn't live with. As a consequence a rather pallid atmosphere was lifted.

However, the strange hard baked and sandy surface was the real winner as it thwarted both Best and United. Keeper Freddie Mizzi had a tough work out but United's shot shy strikers gave him the chance to claim a famous clean sheet.

MANCHESTER CITY 1 MANCHESTER UNITED 2
DIVISION ONE 30 SEPTEMBER 1967

CITY FIELDED NEW keeper Ken Mulhearn after Harry Dowd broke a finger in training and The Blues enjoyed a good opening, going ahead on five minutes through Colin Bell who looked dangerous throughout. City were in such control that Alex Stepney was required to pull off two superb saves to deny the midfielder a hat-trick. But as quickly as City established their dominance they found it snatched away by Bobby Charlton who scored two smart, quick-fire goals to turn the tide.

The home side had to work hard to keep it at 2-1 during the second half.

MANCHESTER UNITED 1 ARSENAL 0
DIVISION ONE 7 OCTOBER 1967

THOUGH JUST 21 years of age, George had already penned an autobiography - The Best of Both Worlds - with the help of journalist James Mossop. He did of course have plenty to write about in his football career but huge swathes of the text were censored by United. Matt Busby instructed the publishers that chapters dealing with girls and other players who Best termed 'nasties' were pulled a few days before United entertained Arsenal in order to ensure neither club nor player were hauled over the coals for bringing the game into disrepute. It wasn't the most extreme example of hedonism a professional footballer had ever indulged in but maybe with hindsight an indication of where future controversies would lie.

David Sadler was taken out of the attack once again to play at centre half with Foulkes out. Aston came in on the left with George back on the right. Arsenal, a robust and defence-orientated outfit similar to the blueprint established by Don Revie's Leeds, looked to exploit their many physical advantages. As a result the game found itself stopped for freekicks.

Inevitably Ian Ure mixed it with Denis Law and both were sent off for constant foul play and retaliation. At the same time The Gunners possessed a credible goal threat and Alex Stepney had to pull off a run of fine saves. John Aston's winner took United up to a season's high of third place.

SHEFFIELD UNITED 0 MANCHESTER UNITED 3
DIVISION ONE 14 OCTOBER 1967

JOHN ASTON'S RETURN to the type of indifferent form which saw his performances maligned on the terraces after a great showing against Arsenal was a disappointment but the Blades, joint bottom of Division One, were still easily dispatched. United's most dangerous approaches came from Best on the right who looked potent alongside Kidd at inside-forward.

A greasy surface resulting from heavy rain gave nimble players increased speed over the ground. A cross was converted by Aston was one of the winger's few solid contributions but Sheffield could so easily have levelled with a glorious chance soon after. As so often that season the home side were found wanting in attack.

Blades keeper Alan Hodgkinson, who often produced his best form against the big clubs, made a number of good saves but had no answer to Brian Kidd before Denis Law rounded matters off from the spot. United remained third, a point behind leaders Liverpool and Sheffield Wednesday in second.

NORTHERN IRELAND 1 SCOTLAND 0
EUROPEAN CHAMPIONSHIP QUALIFIER 21 OCTOBER 1967

GEORGE BELIEVED THAT this match was one of his best ever and certainly the best for his country. Scotland, missing Billy Bremner, Jim Baxter, Jimmy Johnstone and Bobby Lennox through suspension, may still have struggled with these first choices present as, summing up his mood prior to the game, George felt a sensation that this would be his day - a feeling any player, even Best, only got on rare occasions.

It was the day George Best played Scotland on his own and led many illustrious defenders a merry dance. The more fancied Scottish XI contained four members of Celtic's European Cup winning side. It is also worth considering the absence of Newcastle's David Craig for the Irish who were forced to plunder their own league for a replacement rather than draw extensively from the English club scene.

The home side were unlucky not to win by more than a single goal in this European Nations Cup qualifier. The group pitted the home nations against one another as the British Championship series doubled up as qualifiers for the tournament finals in Italy.

On a perfect autumn night in Belfast

George was nothing short of astounding and took on players for fun. One of his mazy dribbles set up the winner for Coventry City's Dave Clements who had the simple task of converting past the prone Scottish keeper.

There had been a suggestion that Best was a little less committed to international than club matters and perhaps this was the reason George turned it on. The truth of the matter was that Northern Ireland had three or four good players other than George with the balance of squads drawn from Second and Third Division sides or even part-timers from the Irish League.

Northern Ireland struggled without him as proved by the 0-0 draw achieved with Wales in the last international game played and Best was only at his best when surrounding by players of equal talent. Consequently it often looked like he was performing well within himself. On most days playing eleven players on your own was a huge task but not today.

In goal Ronnie Simpson, who had kept Inter Milan at bay in that European Cup final, was as severely tested by Best within the opening exchanges as he had been by the Italian giants throughout the entire 90 minutes in Lisbon. The Glaswegian, winning just his third cap, fielded a shot from all of 30 yards out and looked fairly assured getting at least a fingertip to everything hit at him from Best who seemed to decide that he couldn't trust many others to complete his handiwork.

Derek Dougan almost got his head on to a cross after Best tore down the left wing and beat Tommy Gemmell at will. Indeed such was Gemmell's roasting on the night that he asked whether Eddie McCreadie on the left fancied a change of scene. Remembering a number of hidings he had been given by George at club level with Chelsea he less than

politely declined. Centre back Arthur Stewart who, like Best, had turned in a sterling performance against Benfica in the European Cup during his time with Glentoran was outstanding at the back helping break up a number of Scottish attacks.

Best later described this performance as his 'game for Belfast'. Within a few years the Troubles in Northern Ireland precluded international football from the province - so this game has attained legendary status among the country's football supporters.

MANCHESTER UNITED 4 COVENTRY CITY 0
DIVISION ONE 25 OCTOBER 1967

FORMER UNITED FULL-BACK Noel Cantwell, now manager of Coventry City, made a quick return to Old Trafford with his charges. He would have been hopeful that his extensive inside knowledge would assist in causing an upset but few sides could have responded to United and Best in this mood.

Continuing his form from Belfast,

Best found the net with a long range shot through a forest of legs which gave the keeper no chance.

Bobby Charlton showed that anything George could do he could do at least as well lashing home a shot after a run from half way. Two Aston goals completed the scoring and gave the left sided wingman his fourth goal in three games.

NOTTINGHAM FOREST 3 MANCHESTER UNITED 1
DIVISION ONE 28 OCTOBER 1967

DENIS LAW BEGAN a six week suspension 48 hours after this game leading to speculation that United wanted to sign Bobby Tambling. He was one of a group of players Matt Busby had enquired about but permission to discuss terms had been refused by Chelsea. Youngster Frank Kopel, who had been introduced from the bench against Burnley six weeks earlier, made a full debut at Nottingham

Forest covering for Tony Dunne.

Forest had been runners-up to United in the league last season and in Joe Baker and Frank Wignall had two strikers determined to underline their reputations by excelling against The Reds. Baker had hit the net twice by half time as United's new look defence took time to settle.

The champions came back as a force in the second half prompted by Best who scored another superb goal and hit a post with an equally well struck shot. He was an obvious figurehead of revival but the spiritual leader was Paddy Crerand who took charge of midfield and linked defence to attack.

Law had a quiet time - maybe understandably with his lengthy suspension looming larger as every minute passed.

MANCHESTER UNITED 1 STOKE CITY 0
DIVISION ONE 4 NOVEMBER 1967

GEORGE BEST WAS drafted in as Law's immediate successor at inside left with Jim Ryan taking over on the right wing. Potentially nine games were coming up without the Scottish international but a good performance by a youthful side gave confidence that the wait would not be as arduous as it may have seemed. George took well to his new responsibilities attempting to ensure his usual style didn't interfere with the inside forward's need for directness not just in shooting but finding a better placed colleague when necessary.

Great anticipation and a real striker's instinct saw him latch on to Calvin Palmer's back pass and fire a snap shot at Gordon Banks who saved but was helpless as Charlton knocked home the loose ball.

LEEDS UNITED 1 MANCHESTER UNITED 0
DIVISION ONE 8 NOVEMBER 1967

ALREADY MISSING DENIS Law, United had another important man ruled out when Nobby Stiles was struck down with cartilage trouble. This was the fourth game he had missed and the prognosis was that he would not return until Christmas at the earliest but most probably even later.

A 24th minute goal from Jimmy Greenhoff only emphasised his continued absence. The shot appeared too weak to beat a keeper like Alex Stepney until it became clear that in attempting to clear Paddy Crerand had actually diverted the ball in. United were for the most part disappointing, although they did force Gary Sprake to make a number of fine saves throughout the course of the game including a sensational last gasp effort from a George Best volley close in which Sprake somehow managed to palm to safety.

United attempted to attack but were caught high upfield for the goal and once behind had little option but to persist with the game plan. The only problem was that the attack lacked a figurehead further emphasising The Lawman's absence.

LIVERPOOL 1 MANCHESTER UNITED 2
DIVISION ONE 11 NOVEMBER 1967

ONCE AGAIN WHEN United and Liverpool met it was as the league's top two clubs and the home side delivered notice that their aspirations to retain the crown were still very much alive. The match was tight as both teams attempted to put markers down but with Liverpool at home the crowd's hopes and expectations were on them.

United seemed to forget the chinks shown in their defensive armour at Elland Road and in fact were nothing short of outstanding despite their host's territorial advantage. What made their victory even more remarkable was that the Merseysiders had a 100% record at Anfield with 18 goals scored having chalked up a number of notable victories over many other high flying clubs. However, once United got in front they

stayed there. Liverpool were helpless to stop the flow from George Best who opened the scoring from a Bobby Charlton set up.

A lesson had been learned from the Leeds game and when attacks were broken down the ball was quickly moved through midfield with Bobby Charlton setting up play. Until that point United had seen very little of the ball at the business end of the field.

Liverpool continued with their strategy roared on by The Kop but fell into the same trap with Best supplying the sucker punch again. He could have bagged a hat-trick, a first at this level, near the end had his shot not flown narrowly wide. Roger Hunt halved the deficit with seven minutes to go but United closed out the game with few alarms.

FK SARAJEVO 0 MANCHESTER UNITED 0
EUROPEAN CUP 2ND RD 1ST LEG 15 NOVEMBER 1967

MATCHES BEHIND THE Iron Curtain were typically tough and uncompromising affairs. The closed nature of their football meant few western teams knew what to expect and even those who did often struggled to come to terms with sometimes primitive conditions. Any kind of positive result was to be celebrated and even a small deficit suited most.

Without Denis Law or Nobby Stiles United overcame the hostility on and off the pitch taking a very creditable goalless draw back to Old Trafford. Sarajevo were struggling domestically and floundering

near the bottom of the Yugoslav league with any chance of retaining their title long since gone. It also meant their only hope of a European Cup return was to win it outright. United on the other hand had just gone top of the league after beating Liverpool. The contrast couldn't have been starker and nor could the obvious gulf in class between the two sides.

The Yugoslavs decided their only chance to progress was to reduce the game into a bad-tempered affair. And, although they often seemed likely to be reduced to ten men, in the end it was through injury to

Bosko Proanovic rather than disciplinary reasons. As may be expected, George Best was singled out for treatment so too was Brian Kidd but both managed to keep their heads. Only John Fitzpatrick showed any signs of allowing things to get to him and a snap reaction to an incident led to a booking.

MANCHESTER UNITED 3 SOUTHAMPTON 2
DIVISION ONE 18 NOVEMBER 1967

MATT BUSBY'S 4-3-3 formation was obtaining results both at home and abroad. It suited United in any case but never more so than in the absence of Denis Law as it bolstered the forward line and provided extra bodies in midfield at vital times.

Aston scored the first and Brian Kidd, playing as a winger, cut in to snatch a second. But The Saints could never be written off with a strike partnership of the quality of Ron Davies and Martin Chivers. Both made life difficult by switching positions and the tactic paid off when Davies reduced the arrears.

However, a howitzer by Charlton after a surge down the centre made the game safe.

CHELSEA 1 MANCHESTER UNITED 1
DIVISION ONE 25 NOVEMBER 1967

BEST WAS STRUGGLING with injury prior to this game. Tony Dunne was also a doubt although both made it. George, along with John Aston who he partnered down the left flank, provided most threat to The Pensioners. Aston was skipping into some form after another lean spell and was grateful to link up with Best who understood the wingman's game well. Both made good runs but built little of any note in the penalty area.

Chelsea came back in to it and Peter Osgood in particular made better use of the ball than any United player, forcing Stepney into a host of excellent saves. Ron Harris was given the task of keeping The Reds' number 10 shackled and did so in uncompromising fashion. A late Brian Kidd header ensured a share of the points.

MANCHESTER UNITED 2 FK SARAJEVO 1 (AGG 2-1)
EUROPEAN CUP 2ND RD 1ST LEG 29 NOVEMBER 1967

UNITED TOOK AN early lead through John Aston who lashed in after 11 minutes but had to contend with the same aggressive tactics faced in Yugoslavia a fortnight earlier. Nobody suffered more than George Best who was scythed down at almost every opportunity the Sarajevo players had. He still managed to slip free more than once and made it 2-0 in the final quarter heading in Brian Kidd's centre from the right which Refick Muftic could only touch in.

However, a price was almost paid. The keeper had tried to plunge the United man into trouble a few minutes earlier after George took a swing at him. The hand missed but that didn't stop Muftic acting as if he had been laid out by Henry Cooper. Clasping over his jaw he staggered around his area as if ready to take a standing count, if not keel over.

The referee had not been fooled but the Sarajevo players took their revenge out on Best, hacking him down. Fahrudin

Prljaca saw red for one over enthusiastic challenge too many and though Delalic scored with three minutes to go United went through to the quarter-finals.

After the game had ended Muftic punched Matt Busby but, content with seeing the back of Sarajevo and knowing they were unlikely to clash again for some years, the United boss refused to report the incident.

MANCHESTER UNITED 2 WEST BROMWICH ALBION 1
DIVISION ONE 2 DECEMBER 1967

PRIME-MINISTER HAROLD Wilson was just one of many spectators in attendance for the visit of West Bromwich Albion who witnessed a devastating show by George Best at his most imperious for the league leaders. Remarkably West Brom, who had recently beaten Spurs amongst others, had started off well with Dick Krzywicki and Jeff Astle just two of the dangers of which Alex Stepney and his backline had to be wary.

However, if the visitors felt they could

catch United following a tough European tie, they were mistaken. The Reds came back into the game strongly. George's willingness to run and take the ball prompted a positive response from his teammates.

The Irishman created and finished two goals to open up a deserved lead. The Baggies rallied and scored through John Kaye and though they remained a threat there were no serious concerns for United who finished strongly.

NEWCASTLE UNITED 2 MANCHESTER UNITED 2
DIVISION ONE 9 DECEMBER 1967

ICY CONDITIONS REQUIRED caution as one slip could prove costly on this surface. Newcastle settled quickest, forcing a fine save from Alex Stepney. George Best made light of the thin sheet of crumbly ice between his studs and the soft turf. With all the poise of an Olympic skater he glided upfield before drawing a fine save from Jack Marshall.

It wasn't until the second half that things started to happen when The Magpies went 2-0 up through Tommy Robson and

Jim Iley. United barely deserved to trail, let alone by a couple of goals. Chasing the game The Reds poured forward in huge numbers.

Brian Kidd headed in with six minutes remaining but a share of the points looked remote until Tony Dunne struck in the dying seconds with a cross shot which fooled the keeper. The equaliser may have involved a slice of fortune but the point it secured was well deserved.

MANCHESTER UNITED 3 EVERTON 1
DIVISION ONE 16 DECEMBER 1967

EVERTON ALWAYS TENDED to draw a decent crowd on their visits to Old Trafford and 63,000 turned out to beat the season's previous highest attendance set in October against Arsenal. It was little wonder as the game marked the return of The King - Denis Law, from suspension. Shay Brennan missed out in the reshuffle as Denis re-took his inside-left spot allowing Best to move back to the right wing.

It was almost as if the Scot had never been away as Law got straight into the thick of the action in a very open beginning to the game which allowed him plenty of space and the chance to assist David Sadler who headed powerfully past Gordon West.

Later Law grabbed a goal as did John Aston. Alex Young pulling one back for Everton before the close in a reversal of the scoreline in the season's opener. Bobby Charlton and George Best were equally impressive and it had to be noted that although United played well enough without their star striker, The Holy Trinity's reunification really sparked The Reds.

LEICESTER CITY 2 MANCHESTER UNITED 2
DIVISION ONE 23 DECEMBER 1967

WITH NOBBY STILES almost ready for a return and named in the reserve side to face Leeds, the first team travelled to Leicester. United looked set for a return to full strength at just the right time. David Herd was also called into the second string nine months after breaking his leg.

Law continued his high octane return to the scene, testing The Foxes who had to be vigilant throughout the initial exchanges before the Scot scored. Bobby Charlton also notched but Leicester re-established their hold on this fixture after two seasons, managing to square matters before the end.

MANCHESTER UNITED 4 WOLVES 0
DIVISION ONE 26 DECEMBER 1967

AN INSPIRATIONAL DISPLAY by George Best saw Wolves totally outclassed and dominated. It was a nightmare for the Black Country outfit and their support but a Christmas treat for the United fans.

George just couldn't be tamed. He was full of skills few players could emulate but underneath all that glitz was a huge work ethic built on determined running and a desire to do his utmost for the team. As usual that didn't always include parting with the ball at the right time. He couldn't be shaken off by the Wolves defenders nor persuaded to pass for colleagues starved of possession. However, no one could argue with the situation when two superb goals were cracked in.

In the end the score flattered Wolves as, had Best lifted his head from time-to-time, he might have made more of the freedom he created. Brian Kidd and Bobby Charlton made it 4-0 before an hour had been played and at that stage United eased up mindful of the busy programme to come.

Psychologically this was a huge boost for The Reds and a mightily impressive way for the leaders to throw down the gauntlet to title rivals.

WOLVES 2 MANCHESTER UNITED 3
DIVISION ONE 30 DECEMBER 1967

DEREK DOUGAN WAS a dangerous forward whose presence had been missed at Old Trafford and his return looked set to bolster Wolves. Unfortunately he was forced out with less than an hour before kick-off with a recurrence of his injury.

Best, eager to reassert his form of 96 hours earlier, was champing at the bit for the ball but was thwarted by defenders who had learned their lesson from Old Trafford.

Understandably Wolves had more confidence at Molineux particularly in attack. United were stretched far too often resulting in Dougan's deputy Pat Buckley heading in. The same player doubled the lead with United taking 15 minutes to respond. Goals from Brian Kidd, Bobby Charlton and John Aston saw United through, though narrowly.

MANCHESTER UNITED 3 WEST HAM UNITED 1
DIVISION ONE 6 JANUARY 1968

AN EARLY GOAL for Bobby Charlton gave The Reds an edge in a game that marked a departure for the United strike force as Denis Law sat deeper than usual.

It allowed the wingers to support attacks and Busby's tactics paid off handsomely as both Best and Aston netted.

MANCHESTER UNITED 4 SHEFFIELD WEDNESDAY 2
DIVISION ONE 20 JANUARY 1968

ALEX STEPNEY WAS declared fit despite bruised fingers but, with an FA Cup clash against Spurs only a week away, United were praying for no further set backs, especially as Bill Foulkes and Nobby Stiles were likely to be out for some time.

David Sadler had done so well as a central defender that he had been capped

twice by England in the same position alongside Bobby Moore. Today he partnered John Fitzpatrick as he had a fortnight earlier and both were called into action to deal with an Owls side keen to make their mark.

A couple of goals were conceded to Jack Whitham. However, by this stage United were well ahead and coasting courtesy of two fantastic goals from George who was now the club's leading marksman

for the season. Brian Kidd also scored. Fortunately so as Whitham came within a whisker of scoring a hat-trick.

MANCHESTER UNITED 2 TOTTENHAM HOTSPUR 2
FA Cup 3ᴿᴰ Rᴅ 27 Jᴀɴᴜᴀʀʏ 1968

Jɪᴍᴍʏ Gʀᴇᴀᴠᴇs ᴡᴀs unexpectedly dropped for the cup holders after a poor showing in recent weeks. He had been tried in various positions across the front line as well as outside left but a change of scene didn't seem to lift him. It was the first time he had been left out of the side for any reason other than injury since joining Spurs in 1961.

It was a huge lift for United as, despite his form, everyone realised the drought couldn't last forever but when Chivers netted after four minutes it seemed any delight at seeing Greaves in the stands was misplaced. George Best equalised

minutes later. Both were splendidly taken strikes with the Irishman's coming after a lengthy dribble which saw him ghost past the cover.

Bobby Charlton's first cup goal in four years put United ahead but was only good enough for a draw as Chivers hit another minutes from the end. The home side were grateful for three world class Alex Stepney saves. John Fitzpatrick had been detailed to take care of Chivers and did well but was powerless to halt him due to the striker's excellent movement.

TOTTENHAM HOTSPUR 1 MANCHESTER UNITED 0 (AET)
FA Cup 3ᴿᴰ Rᴅ Rᴇᴘʟᴀʏ 31 Jᴀɴᴜᴀʀʏ 1968

Dᴀᴠɪᴅ Hᴇʀᴅ ᴇᴀʀɴᴇᴅ a recall but, keen to limit Spurs, Matt Busby took a squad with plenty of defensive options to White Hart Lane. A predictably tight game ensued which was only settled in the 14th minute of extra-time. However, there was more than a touch of controversy about the winner. Alex Stepney protested that Mike England had fouled him and before the keeper's manhandling Tony Dunne felt he had been shoved in the back by Alan Gilzean.

Referee Jack Taylor waved the complaints away but it should be noted that the official made an error by allowing United to start both periods of extra-

time. John Fitzpatrick swapped targets marking Gilzean while David Sadler shackled Martin Chivers. With Denis Law's knee injury rumoured to have all but ended his season Best floated across the line and proved a problem for the Spurs defence including his marker Cyril Knowles a former Manchester United trialist who had a reputation for being not just a competent mover with the ball but a tough tackling full back.

That standing was almost ruined by the wingman and it took a Pat Jennings save at his feet to snuff out George and United's clearest chance.

TOTTENHAM HOTSPUR 1 MANCHESTER UNITED 2
DIVISION ONE 3 FEBRUARY 1968

OFFICIAL STATEMENTS ABOUT Law's injury remained vague as Matt Busby maintained the Scottish international was in contention for the following weekend's derby after it became clear he would not make the side for another shot at Spurs. Foulkes and Stiles were said to be close to full fitness and in with a chance but both found themselves out for at least another match.

United's hopes of revenge waned as early as the second minute when Chivers netted after a precise pass from Alan Mullery which gave the United rearguard little chance to close the striker down.

Yet Paddy Crerand stepped up his game, providing the type of showing he should have put in earlier that week to establish a stronghold in midfield which others could exploit. George Best

equalised when he smashed the ball through a crowded area. Quite how he managed to net cleanly and without a deflection was a mystery. Tireless running won a penalty but when Bobby Charlton hit it straight at Pat Jennings it seemed United would have to settle for a draw. However, determined to make up for his poor effort, Charlton took it upon himself to find a way through and two minutes from time his determination paid off.

The England international seized the ball near his own area. Surged through defence and then midfield in a dribble which took him across the width as well as length of the field before demonstrating how lucky the keeper had been from the spot kick with an unstoppable drive.

BURNLEY 2 MANCHESTER UNITED 1
DIVISION ONE 17 FEBRUARY 1968

NOBBY STILES MADE a welcome return to the fold although John Fitzpatrick was unlucky to see his three game run in the first team end as a result. Denis Law made another comeback with David Herd missing out and asked to continue his quest for match fitness in the reserves. The reinforcements were pleasing as Burnley had yet to be beaten at home.

Best was given a taste of the type of afternoon which lay ahead when he was knocked to the ground by Andy Lochhead before a minute had passed. He didn't even have the ball at the time

having sensed the danger and offloaded. The next time the Burnley man got a touch George threw himself into a tackle which grounded Lochhead and earned censure from referee Hindley.

It was worth a dressing down for Best who ensured everyone with a mind to launch into him would at least think twice and with justice dispensed he could concentrate on his game. A charge down the right brought a perfect cross for Law who saw his effort hit keeper Harry Thomson. United and Clarets players scrambled to poke the ball over the line or knock it to safety with the latter winning out. However, there wasn't long to wait before the visitors took the lead. Best had the simple task of rolling the ball into an empty net but had done all the hard work after a run then check inside to beat Colin Waldron with an impudent dribble and Thomson who had to charge out rather than allow himself to be made a fool of.

In this form George was a problem for any backline but United's failure to capitalise on the panic he created was a huge disappointment and ultimately proved to be costly as two goals in five minutes won the game for Burnley.

At stages the Clarets were down to ten men with Lochhead unable to continue for a spell and then permanently weakened by Frank Caspar's dismissal. Somehow Burnley managed to hold on despite United battering their goal and creating decent chances. Law could have grabbed a hat-trick had he been a little sharper following his injury lay-off.

ARSENAL 0 MANCHESTER UNITED 2
DIVISION ONE 24 FEBRUARY 1968

BOBBY CHARLTON MISSED out through injury and was replaced by John Fitzpatrick who, though he wore the number nine shirt, sat deep in midfield alongside Paddy Crerand. It was a more defensive set up than United were used to but one that Matt Busby seemed keen to try out with one eye on Europe. Brian Kidd should have scored after a defence splitting pass put him through but he checked back to get himself in a better position to shoot then slipped.

Denis Law celebrated his birthday with a new task - playing as a scheming forward just behind Kidd linking the central striker with the engine room. It created additional space on the flanks and it was a situation tailor made for George who jigged impishly through Arsenal's cover and had the home side on the back foot throughout.

Peter Storey, a player Best had a particularly low opinion of, was so worried by one run that after poaching the ball he feared he could be caught in possession so looked for the outlet of his keeper. He only succeeded in putting through his own goal. The scoring was completed by an excellent shot which again saw George beat a host of defenders in a crowded penalty area with a shot which found the net through a forest of legs.

MANCHESTER UNITED 2 GORNIK ZABRZE 0
EUROPEAN CUP QF 1ST LEG 28 FEBRUARY 1968

THOUGH LITTLE KNOWN, Polish side Gornik Zabrze barred the way to a place in the last four and could not be taken lightly. European Cup holders Celtic had been knocked out in the opening round by Dynamo Kiev who in turn had perished by a slender margin to Zabrze.

Key amongst the Pole's armoury was inside-forward Włódzimierz Lubanski who had scored most of the goals on the way to the last eight and was in devastating form in domestic football. Understandably he operated as a lone striker only supported in real numbers during a counter-attack was mounted or when holding up the ball - a real asset of his game. Otherwise Zabrze came to defend and in centre-back and captain Oslizlo had no better man to organise the troops.

United, missing Law, retained their now customary 4-3-3 formation but poured forward when allowed, hitting the visitors with all but the kitchen sink for the entire 90 minutes but even when Oslizlo and his colleagues were beaten keeper Kostka was nothing short of magnificent. However

the Polish keeper didn't expect the main threat to come from a colleague so he was taken unawares when Florenski put through his own goal on the hour. The defender was attempting to divert George Best's low angled cross delivered after a dance along the goal line provided a yard of space to exploit.

A one goal deficit would have been a good score to take back to Poland but the lead was doubled in the final minute when Brian Kidd back-heeled a Jimmy Ryan shot which travelled through a crowd of bodies. Kostka saw nothing until the ball was beyond him and Kidd was left with the easiest of tap-ins.

MANCHESTER UNITED 1 CHELSEA 3
Division One 2 March 1968

WITH GEORGE BEST in super form and in the greatest goalscoring run of his career, the Old Trafford crowd arrived expecting to witness his 50th league goal for United. His effort at Arsenal had left him one short of the milestone.

Perhaps the expecatation weighed more heavily on the Irishman than expected as Best attempted to score with virtually every touch. He almost scored in the opening minutes following a David Sadler clearance. He beat Ron Harris and David Webb to go one-on-one with Peter Bonetti but couldn't get a shot away before the keeper pounced on the ball.

Otherwise United were very lethargic and lacked the spirit which had served the club so well over recent months. Apart from the early chance, Harris kept Best extremely quiet and the only other

opening he had came from a penalty kick which he blasted over the bar. A real shock given the accuracy of Best's shooting.

Chelsea were making great progress under Dave Sexton and inflicted United's first home defeat in 47 months and 38 games. Brian Kidd equalised a Bobby Tambling goal after being played in by Jimmy Ryan but there was no way back once Chelsea grabbed the lead again. The visitors were well on top and with Alex Stepney visibly injured it was only a matter of time before the game was made safe with a third.

GORNIK ZABRZE 1 MANCHESTER UNITED 0 (AGG 1-2)
EUROPEAN CUP QF 2ND LEG 13 MARCH 1968

THE LACK OF A weekend game meant more time to prepare for the clash with the Polish champions but freezing temperatures, blizzards and a bone hard pitch caused concern for Matt Busby who felt that the match should be postponed until the temperatures were more clement. His appeals fell on death ears with the game kicking-off on schedule.

Forward play was the last thing on United minds and this time even Best conceded that discretion was the better part of valour although in the dressing room he had been the only player willing to go out when the matter was put to a vote of the squad. He probably viewed the conditions as another challenge to

master.

United defended well, David Sadler acted as a sweeper and John Fitzpatrick in particular put in some sterling work helping to keep things tight. Only one goal was scored and that came through the predatory instinct of Lubanski who picked up a loose ball after a free-kick had bounced off the wall and fell kindly. Alex Stepney stood little chance.

As a test of United's European aspirations passage through to the semi-finals was well deserved and United's obdurate performance in such testing conditions was testimony to their determination to win the cup.

COVENTRY CITY 2 MANCHESTER UNITED 0
DIVISION ONE 16 MARCH 1968

A PRESENCE AT the penultimate stage of the European Cup may have been safely negotiated but there was no escaping the probability that this had come at the expense of successfully defending the title. United held a useful lead over Liverpool at one stage but the gap had narrowed while Manchester City and Leeds had joined the fray.

Defeat to struggling Coventry, who had been hammered with ease at Old Trafford, gave neighbours City an advantage they ultimately would not relinquish despite a few set backs. Relegation battlers Coventry had spent a significant sum of money on transfer deadline day buying forward Ernie Hunt of Everton and Huddersfield

Town's full back Chris Cattlin. United were rumoured to have placed bids for as many as half a dozen players, with some approaching the £150,000 domestic record fee. However, each club refused permission to speak to the targets.

Yet somehow the Sky Blue strugglers, under former United stalwart Noel Cantwell, managed to win with goals from Ernie Machin and another former Red Maurice Setters.

MANCHESTER UNITED 3 NOTTINGHAM FOREST 0
Division One 23 March 1968

Alongside the Manchester clubs and Liverpool only Leeds United had genuine title pretensions. The lead virtually switched between the four week by week. Leeds beating City gave United a chance to reclaim top spot which they duly did courtesy of a professional performance and goals from Shay Brennan who netted for the first time in six years, Francis Burns and David Herd.

Forest keeper Peter Grummitt, a man who had often saved his finest for United, was out with Brian Williamson deputising. David Herd made his first home appearance since breaking a leg the previous year with Brian Kidd, subbed against Coventry, dropped before his suspension was due to start the following Monday.

John Fitzpatrick earned his first chance to play at Old Trafford for the senior side.

He had normally been utilised on the road as Matt Busby sought to keep things tight. The threat of Forest picking up an away win was cited as the reason for such caution.

The lack of another match in Europe until late April gave The Reds time to concentrate on the league. The entire team looked slick with Best hugging the touchline but he failed to get a telling ball past the defence or keeper until Herd scored a quarter of an hour in. Alex Stepney made a great save from Joe Baker early on but the backline ensured there were few chances after that.

A swift break out of defence was often the most telling mode of attack for United and the lack of pressure allowed each of the full backs to venture forward often and the fact that both found the net was no coincidence.

MANCHESTER UNITED 1 MANCHESTER CITY 3
Division One 27 March 1968

Denis Law was unexpectedly named in the squad and given until the last minute to prove his fitness. Law's inclusion highlighted the importance of the match - this was possibly the most important Manchester derby game ever and would in effect decide the destination of the title as just two points separated City and United at the start of play.

George Best suggested United would comfortably establish supremacy within 38 seconds. With almost his first touch he beat Tony Book and the City captain

could only look on as George advanced towards goal, drew keeper Ken Mulhearn, sold him a dummy and then stroked the ball into the empty net.

Colin Bell showed that George was not the only skilful player on duty that evening by rounding off a flowing move he had begun deep inside his own half to draw City level.

The visitors were in a real purple patch at the time and went ahead when George Heslop, a centre back who had never scored in over 100 appearances prior to this game, headed in Tony Coleman's free-kick. United had chances to level but a Francis Lee penalty, conceded after Francis Burns made a clumsy challenge on Colin Bell, finally saw City through.

George was one of, if not the, most consistent United player on duty and created chances. It was just a shame that no one managed to convert them. One cross rolled inviting across the six yard line and just needed a touch to force it in. Unfortunately Law failed to connect and City's win took them top of the table on goal average.

STOKE CITY 2 MANCHESTER UNITED 4
DIVISION ONE 30 MARCH 1968

UNDERGRADUATE ALAN GOWLING, studying for a degree in economics as well as playing in the Central League, looked a very good prospect and had hit 23 goals for the stiffs.

His graduation to the top flight was well deserved on that basis. George Best opened the scoring on two minutes then Gowling netted but goals from George Eastham and Peter Dobing made it 2-2 at the break. John Aston and Jim Ryan rounded off a deserved win.

MANCHESTER UNITED 1 LIVERPOOL 2
DIVISION ONE 6 APRIL 1968

DENIS LAW, NOBBY STILES, David Herd and Tony Dunne all faced late fitness tests for this crunch home match with Liverpool with only the latter pair making the cut. Dunne replaced Shay Brennan. Alan Gowling was retained after being excused from the England amateur team training camp preparing for the summer Olympics in Mexico. The visitors had Tony Hateley back to full fitness but Tommy Smith was ruled out so the less ferocious Ian Ross came in at right half.

For the third successive game George opened the scoring early. However, Ron Yeats equalised before Roger Hunt put Liverpool ahead. Recent defeats had seen United lose a decent margin at the top and they now shared top spot. Going behind put United in a tricky position as the defence that had served so well was left unguarded with midfield pushing on to support the attack.

Liverpool's Tommy Lawrence made some good saves but the Anfield side dominated possession and defended their lead well to close the game out.

FULHAM 0 MANCHESTER UNITED 4
DIVISION ONE 12 APRIL 1968

A BUSY 72 hours, which would see United travel to the south coast then back to Manchester, saw Brian Kidd make a successful return from suspension, finding the net along with Denis Law and Best who hit a couple to round off a more than competent performance.

SOUTHAMPTON 2 MANCHESTER UNITED 2
Division One 13 April 1968

A visit to The Dell completed away games with two relegation candidates in the space of 24 hours. Bill Foulkes made a welcome comeback as United finally started to see those stars who had missed a number of games over recent weeks return.

Somehow United managed to go behind and stay there until Bobby Charlton and Best, with his sixth goal in five games, found the net. Extending the run had proved difficult for George who was well patrolled by Saints 'star man' left back Denis Hollywood.

MANCHESTER UNITED 3 FULHAM 0
Division One 15 April 1968

United made a fast start to this match with Brian Kidd putting a good chance wide within 30 seconds after a skilful run down the right from Best. Bobby Charlton hit the first goal of the game after 13 minutes with a superb shot following a burst through the middle.

The lead was extended just past the half hour after a lively dart by Best down the wing which ended in a shot from an almost impossible angle: George cut along the byline surrounded by defenders. Most players would have looked for a corner but not Best who took aim. It was an audacious effort but hit so well that it squeezed past the keeper clipping the angle of post and crossbar. No other player in the world could have hoped to pull it off, no other player in the world would have attempted it.

The strike surpassed Denis Law's overall total in the league the previous season. With four games remaining it seemed he may push the tally on towards 30. This particular shot encapsulated the type of game the winger was having. Fred Callaghan, who was marking Best, was replaced by Brian Nichols but the substitute full back was just as helpless as his colleague. It was only a string of good saves, crosses plucked out of the air or chances being denied through blocks plus wayward finishing which kept the score down until Best beat two defenders then crossed for Aston in the 85th minute.

Having looked back amongst the pack a couple of weeks ago United had managed to build a three point gap with a string of back to back wins while other contenders dropped points. City had three games in hand so were a livelier threat than Liverpool whose chances looked slim to none,

MANCHESTER UNITED 1 SHEFFIELD UNITED 0
DIVISION ONE 20 APRIL 1968

AFTER MISSING THE previous game Alex Stepney and Nobby Stiles, who had sat out a few more games, returned. If there was a temptation to rest the big guns Matt Busby resisted it with United's two main objectives for the season still very much up for grabs. Even Best, who strained a leg muscle in training, was not stood down as a precaution.

Denis Law scored the only goal of the game after five minutes and though United may have been expected to hammer home that early advantage the remainder of the game was sterile. Indeed United were at sixes and sevens defensively. Stepney made some good saves and other timely blocks kept The Blades at bay.

MANCHESTER UNITED 1 REAL MADRID 0
EUROPEAN CUP SF 1ST LEG 24 APRIL 1968

REAL MADRID, THE champions of two seasons ago, would have to be conquered if United were to become the first English team to reach a European Cup final. The Spaniards had dominated the competition over its opening years winning the first five finals and usually reaching the latter stages every year in which they qualified. United's record was nearly as impressive - they hadn't failed to make a semi-final in their three previous campaigns, yet the final had always eluded them.

Needless to say, this was an eagerly anticipated clash with Old Trafford a 63,500 sell out and a world-wide television audience estimated at 200 million taking in the action.

The stakes were high and despite their more recent success Madrid realised that United were a huge danger and possessed some of the greatest players of their era.

Spanish skipper Francisco Gento was the sole survivor of the Real team that had faced the Busby Babes in 1957. His organisation was key in Madrid's bid to keep things tight. United, invited on to the front foot by the wily visitors, were happy to make the running although they were frequently thwarted by a tight backline.

Paddy Crerand hit a post following a corner but the rearguard was beaten only once, just before half-time, when Brian Kidd found John Aston on the wing. The ball was played inside for Best who had found space 15 yards out. His turn and shot lashed just under the bar gave United a slim advantage.

Brian Kidd should have doubled the lead late in the game but blazed over and the narrow win gave United a psychological edge. A number of weaknesses had been identified in an ageing Real team.

The only disappointment was The Reds inability to truly exploit their superiority. It was something to defend but in the white heat of the Stadio Santiago Bernabeu many experts thought it would not be enough.

WEST BROMWICH ALBION 6 MANCHESTER UNITED 3
DIVISION ONE 27 APRIL 1968

A TEAM THAT George routinely scared the life out of finally gained revenge just three days after United's exhausting win over Real.

This shock result all but guaranteed that the league championship would make the short journey to Maine Road.

The Throstles were comfortable in mid-table but the result and particularly

the severity of the defeat was a shock. Though Denis Law found the net he had struggled since picking up a knee injury and a short lay off had seemingly done him few favours. He had looked off the pace for weeks and struggled to cope with this match. Few players excelled as United suffered their biggest defeat of the season.

MANCHESTER UNITED 6 NEWCASTLE UNITED 0
DIVISION ONE 4 MAY 1968

NEWCASTLE WOULD FACE Manchester City in the final round of league games held in seven days time. United were looking to relegate them this week and then rally sufficiently to deny their neighbour's points.

The prospect remained a likely one as, although City claimed a very impressive 3-1 win at White Hart Lane, United and George Best in particular (who had been named European Footballer of the Year

that very day) hammered The Magpies without remorse.

Even George had mauled few teams to quite this extent since his days as a junior and a first professional hat-trick was just reward for his contribution, even if it did include a couple of penalties. One of the spot kicks was awarded for a foul on Best himself when he looked certain to score and the other for a foul on two-goal Brian Kidd. David Herd also found the net.

MANCHESTER UNITED 1 SUNDERLAND 2
DIVISION ONE 11 MAY 1968

WITH CITY AND United tied on 56 points going into the final game of the season the Blues held a significant advantage, leading on goal average. That meant United had to beat Sunderland to claim the title and hope that City failed to win. However, The Rokerites were deserved victors here, denying United the championship with a doughty performance. Meanwhile City enjoyed a 4-2 win at Newcastle to claim the title. Mike Summerbee provided an

early lead and despite being pulled back twice City held on for a 4-3 win.

United had undergone an atrocious start and Sunderland led 2-0 after the first five minutes as Colin Suggett and George Mulhall found the net with ease. Though Best was as irresistible as he had been the previous week and scored shortly before half-time the team as a whole lacked any real drive with only Brian Kidd impressing alongside the Irishman. Thoughts of the job to be completed in Madrid were no doubt a distraction. Consequently the game was a scrappy affair during which United pressed for an equaliser but there was to be no grandstand finish.

Conspiracy theorists of a blue persuasion had a field day when the League Championship trophy, which had been left in United's boardroom in anticipation of a red victory, went missing during the game making a mysterious re-appearance at Maine Road the next day.

REAL MADRID 3 MANCHESTER UNITED 3 (AGG 3-4)
EUROPEAN CUP SEMI-FINAL 2ND LEG 15 MAY 1968

NEEDING TO DEFEND the lead Best had provided from the first leg, United found themselves 3-1 down by the break. 120,000 Spaniards had roared Real into the lead and most believed that by half-time the tie was over.

The absence of Denis Law, now not due to return until the following season, was a huge blow as it robbed the side of a source of goals. Best had moved infield to partner Brian Kidd while Paddy Crerand switched to the right with Nobby Stiles coming into centre midfield alongside Bobby Charlton to look after Amancio who returned to the Real side.

Yet Real played like champions and took the lead when Pirri headed in from a free-kick delivered from Amancio after half an hour. Gento made it 2-0 ten minutes later but a vital own goal from Zoco, who deflected Kidd's lob into the net, gave United some hope after a torrid opening. Nevertheless Amancio restored Real's advantage just before the half concluded with a well taken effort on the turn which fizzed past Alex Stepney.

In the time afforded to him Matt Busby galvanised his troops like never before. Reminding them that United were only 2-3 down on aggregate and another goal would see them into a play-off in Lisbon

he pushed David Sadler from centre-back to centre-forward and the formation shifted from 4-4-2 to 4-3-3. It was all out attack and as he had two years earlier against Benfica, George Best took hold of the game.

United's resurgence was undoubtedly helped by the attitude of their opponents who emerged from their dressing room in over-confident mood. The Spaniard's party pieces and fancy tricks early in the second half gave United a toe-hold in the game. On 70 minutes Pat Crerand's free-kick was flicked on by Best for his roommate Sadler to tap home.

Now United held the psychological advantage and continued to attack, lest Madrid re-discover their first half form. Within five minutes United went ahead 4-3 on aggregate.

Best may have been tempted to crown a mazy run, during which he had brushed off the attentions of several challengers, with a shot but having seen a red shirt in the middle he delivered to the striker's feet only to discover - first to his horror, then to his relief - that the recipient was none other than Bill Foulkes, who cooly slotted home.

Foulkes, a survivor of the Munich Air Disaster, was a man unaccustomed to life in the opposition penalty area - as 9 goals over 19 seasons suggests. Yet his calm side-foot seemed heaven sent...

At the final whistle Matt and most of the team were in tears. After 12 years of struggle his dream of beating Real Madrid had been realised.

The final was regarded as a formality - United seemed destined to become champions of Europe.

MANCHESTER UNITED 4 BENFICA 1
EUROPEAN CUP FINAL - WEMBLEY - 29 MAY 1968

UNITED TOOK ON Benfica for the first time since that infamous Lisbon night two years ago, in the final of the 1968 European Cup final. The Portuguese side's progress had been shuddering rather than steady but as four-time finalists they certainly had the edge in terms of experience, even if their triumphs had been during the early part of the decade.

Benfica had looked anything but potential finalists early on. Northern Ireland champions Glentoran were only beaten on away goals with The Glens claiming a creditable 0-0 draw in Lisbon. The margin of victory over St Etienne had also been narrow but comfortable wins over Vasa Budapest and Juventus suggested that Benfica had come into decent form at just the right time.

Still smarting from the hat-trick Best had scored in the European Cup tie two years earlier, Benfica needed little reminder of the danger he posed and decided to focus many of their efforts on thwarting him. That particular part of the job went well for a long while but it did leave gaps in other areas. Most notably for Bobby Charlton who grabbed the lead early in the second half, heading in from David Sadler's cross. Minutes later Eusebio hit the bar with a shot from 20 yards.

United dominated for most of the time that remained but seemed to tire towards the end and, with 10 minutes to go, Benfica levelled, Jaime Graca netting from close range. Eusebio almost won it during injury time when one-on-one with Alex Stepney but a superb save by the keeper, who refused to commit himself, took the game into extra-time.

Benfica were enjoying the better of the opening exchanges in extra time and were on the attack when the ball was cleared upfield. Lurking in the centre circle George made ground towards its flight, took possession from a flick on and moved forward from just inside the opposition half. Best danced through the backline humiliating skipper Mario Coluna on his way into the area and bore down on keeper Enrique. A shimmy left him diving before the ball was released. From then on the task of stroking the ball into an empty net was a simple one.

Later George claimed that he wanted to run on taking the ball up to the line and then head it over the line but even he felt this would be too risky and that a defender could have got back in the time it had taken.

Soon after Brian Kidd celebrated his 19th birthday in real style by extending the lead. Benfica had finally been beaten and offered very little until the final whistle by which time Charlton had scored his second with a trademark finish from close range.

Bobby was reduced to tears once the whistle went but was one of the first players to reach his manager who was also weeping. Both survivors knew exactly what this day meant. It was without doubt the greatest night of Matt Busby's career and an event which he said eased the pain and guilt of taking his team into Europe. Still, there were mixed emotions.

Thoughts were also spared for Denis Law who had done as much as anyone else to get United to the pinnacle of the game but was forced to watch from afar as TV pictures were beamed to his hospital bed as he recovered from an operation on his damaged cartilage. Francis Burns had also lost his place in the team just before the final despite making the starting XI for the first seven European games and then some weeks in April as a deputy for Shay Brennan.

Having finished as United's top scorer in the league with 28 and having assisted in many of the other 61 goals United scored that term George was a shoo-in for the English player of the Year Awards. He was predictably named Northern Ireland's top footballer but his exploits in Europe ensured he was acclaimed as the continent's player of the year too. Bobby Charlton and Denis Law had won the same accolade within the past four years but neither were as young as George Best at that time and had served several seasons as professionals. At just 22 the unassuming young man who had come to Manchester from Belfast had won two English titles and now the European Cup.

Finally, winning the European Cup was the only thing that could have eclipsed winning the title but with the championship crown passing to City it was hard for anyone to dispute that Manchester was the capital of British football. Not only that but it seemed that United could dominate for years to come.

Old hands like Bobby Charlton were still capable of classy displays and, alongside Denis Law and local discoveries such as Brian Kidd (who had bagged 15 goals in his debut season) United still appeared to have a squad capable of challenging for honours.

BY GEORGE, HE'S DONE IT!
George Best wheels away in celebration after beating Benfica keeper Enrique to give United a lead they would not relinquish in the 1968 European Cup Final.

1967-68

George later admitted that he remembered little about the ensuing celebrations after the European Cup Final - either leaving the stadium, at the after-match party or the triumphant return to Manchester. After such an exhausting game and the euphoria of the win any player could be forgiven for taking a drink but George later admitted that his taste for alcohol was devoloping by this stage.

Nevertheless the public cared little idea about Best's nocturnal activities as he was regularly producing moments of genius on the pitch. Best had emerged as the finest player at the club, certainly the most talented in the English game and, some argued, the pre-eminent player in the world.

George was United's leading scorer with 28 and was the league's joint top scorer, sharing the accolade with Southampton's Ron Davies. The absence of Denis Law for the latter part of the campaign was a factor in Best's ouput as he played in a more central position but his strike rate only underlined his ability in all forward positions.

From the opening day of the season United suffered just two defeats in 25 games but despite holding a five-point lead at the top of the table with the home straight in sight, the quest for European glory plus the loss of Denis Law knocked United out of their stride allowing City to overhaul the deficit and win the title by two points. The 3-1 reverse at Old Trafford in March's derby game ultimately proving the decisive factor.

City's victory in the title race was somewhat overshadowed by United's emotional triumph at Wembley later that month. Yet the success of both Manchester teams established the city as the capital of football. Manchester was certainly buzzing and, if Liverpool could claim The Beatles and London the title of fashion capital of the world, Mancunians of all perusasions were more than satisfied with the exploits of their footballers and the magnetism of one in particular.

And in George Best their city witnessed perhaps the greatest sight of the sixties, the bewildering, bewitching and, sometimes, baffling play of the greatest footballer in the world vanquishing the best the game could throw at him. Even City fans found themselves lost in admiration for the Ulsterman and you can't get higher praise than that.

By 1968 each football match involving George Best seemed to be an event, 'A Happening' in sixties parlance, with the main man performing to his own unscripted staccato rhythm. Not that there was much peace and love knocking about in the English First Division - professional footballers loved nothing more than nullifying the threat of the Ulsterman. That, of course, was all part of the appeal, with the opposition playing the role of unwitting accomplices in George's latest attempts to defeat the forces of negativism. Or at least that might have been how one critic may have seen it...

To Old Trafford regulars he was merely the Best Player in the World, how he performed in the seasons to come would determine the club's future progress.

DATE	OPPONENT	VENUE	SCORE	ATTD	1	2	3	4	5	6	7	8	9	10	11
19 August	Everton	Goodison Park	1-3	61,452	Stepney	Brennan	Dunne(A)	Crerand	Foulkes	Stiles	Best	Law	Charlton¹	Kidd	Aston
26 August	Leicester City	Old Trafford	1-1	51,256	Stepney	Brennan	Dunne(A)	Sadler	Foulkes¹	Stiles	Best	Law	Charlton	Kidd	Aston
2 September	West Ham United	Upton Park	3-1	36,562	Stepney	Dunne(A)	Burns	Crerand	Foulkes	Stiles	Ryan¹	Sadler¹	Charlton	Kidd¹	Best
6 September	Sunderland	Roker Park	1-1	51,527	Stepney	Dunne(A)	Burns	Crerand	Foulkes	Stiles	Ryan	Sadler	Charlton	Kidd¹	Best
9 September	Burnley	Old Trafford	2-2	55,809	Stepney	Dunne(A)	Burns¹	Crerand¹	Foulkes	Fitzpatrick	Ryan	Sadler	Charlton	Kidd	Best
16 September	Sheffield Wednesday	Hillsborough	1-1	47,274	Stepney	Dunne(A)	Burns	Crerand	Foulkes	Stiles	Best¹	Sadler	Charlton	Law	Kidd
23 September	Tottenham Hotspur	Old Trafford	3-1	58,779	Stepney	Dunne(A)	Burns	Crerand	Foulkes	Stiles	Best²	Sadler	Charlton	Law¹	Kidd
30 September	Manchester City	Maine Road	2-1	62,942	Stepney	Dunne(A)	Burns	Crerand	Foulkes	Stiles	Best	Sadler	Charlton²	Law	Kidd
7 October	Arsenal	Old Trafford	1-0	60,197	Stepney	Dunne(A)	Burns	Crerand	Sadler	Stiles	Best	Kidd	Charlton	Law	Aston¹
14 October	Sheffield United	Bramall Lane	3-0	29,170	Stepney	Dunne(A)	Burns	Crerand	Sadler	Stiles	Best	Kidd¹	Charlton	Law¹	Aston¹
25 October	Coventry City	Old Trafford	4-0	54,253	Stepney	Dunne(A)	Burns	Crerand	Sadler	Fitzpatrick	Best¹	Kidd¹	Charlton¹	Law	Aston²
28 October	Nottingham Forest	City Ground	1-3	49,946	Stepney	Kopel	Burns	Crerand	Sadler	Fitzpatrick	Best¹	Kidd¹	Charlton	Law	Aston
4 November	Stoke City	Old Trafford	1-0	51,041	Stepney	Dunne(A)	Burns	Crerand	Foulkes	Sadler	Ryan	Kidd	Charlton¹	Best	Aston
8 November	Leeds United	Elland Road	0-1	43,999	Stepney	Dunne(A)	Burns	Crerand	Foulkes	Sadler	Ryan	Kidd	Charlton	Best	Aston
11 November	Liverpool	Anfield	2-1	54,515	Stepney	Dunne(A)	Burns	Crerand	Foulkes	Sadler	Fitzpatrick	Kidd	Charlton	Best²	Aston
18 November	Southampton	Old Trafford	3-2	48,732	Stepney	Dunne(A)	Burns	Crerand	Foulkes	Sadler	Fitzpatrick	Kidd¹	Charlton¹	Best	Aston¹
25 November	Chelsea	Stamford Bridge	1-1	54,712	Stepney	Brennan	Dunne(A)	Crerand	Foulkes	Sadler	Burns	Kidd¹	Charlton	Best	Aston
2 December	WBA	Old Trafford	2-1	52,568	Stepney	Brennan	Dunne(A)	Crerand	Foulkes	Sadler	Burns	Kidd	Charlton	Best²	Aston
9 December	Newcastle United	St James' Park	2-2	48,639	Stepney	Brennan	Dunne(A)¹	Crerand	Foulkes	Sadler	Burns	Kidd¹	Charlton	Best	Aston
16 December	Everton	Old Trafford	3-1	60,736	Stepney	Dunne(A)	Burns	Crerand	Foulkes	Sadler¹	Best	Kidd¹	Charlton¹	Law¹	Aston
23 December	Leicester City	Filbert Street	2-2	40,104	Stepney	Dunne(A)	Burns	Crerand	Foulkes	Sadler	Best	Kidd	Charlton¹	Law¹	Aston
26 December	Wolves	Old Trafford	4-0	63,450	Stepney	Dunne(A)	Burns	Crerand	Foulkes	Sadler	Best²	Kidd¹	Charlton¹	Law	Aston¹
30 December	Wolves	Molineux	3-2	53,940	Stepney	Dunne(A)	Burns	Crerand	Foulkes	Sadler	Best¹	Kidd¹	Charlton¹	Law	Aston¹
6 January	West Ham United	Old Trafford	3-1	54,498	Stepney	Dunne(A)	Burns	Crerand	Sadler	Fitzpatrick	Best¹	Kidd¹	Charlton¹	Best	Aston¹
20 January	Sheffield Wednesday	Old Trafford	4-2	55,254	Stepney	Dunne(A)	Burns	Crerand	Sadler	Fitzpatrick	Best²	Kidd¹	Charlton¹	Law¹	Aston¹
3 February	Tottenham Hotspur	White Hart Lane	2-1	57,790	Stepney	Dunne(A)	Burns	Crerand	Sadler	Fitzpatrick	Best¹	Kidd¹	Charlton¹	Law¹	Aston
17 February	Burnley	Turf Moor	1-2	31,965	Stepney	Dunne(A)	Burns	Crerand	Sadler	Stiles	Best¹	Kidd	Charlton	Herd	Aston
24 February	Arsenal	Highbury	2-0	46,417	Stepney	Dunne(A)	Burns	Crerand	Sadler	Stiles	Best¹	Kidd	Fitzpatrick	Law	Aston
2 March	Chelsea	Old Trafford	1-3	62,978	Stepney	Dunne(A)	Burns	Crerand	Sadler	Stiles	Best	Kidd¹	Charlton	Ryan	Aston
16 March	Coventry City	Highfield Road	0-2	47,110	Stepney	Brennan	Burns	Crerand	Sadler	Stiles	Best	Kidd	Charlton	Fitzpatrick	Herd
23 March	Nottingham Forest	Old Trafford	3-0	61,978	Stepney	Brennan¹	Burns¹	Crerand	Sadler	Stiles	Fitzpatrick	Herd¹	Charlton	Best	Aston

Date	Opponent	Venue	Score	Att.											
27 March	Manchester City	Old Trafford	1-3	63,004	Stepney	Brennan	Burns	Crerand	Sadler	Stiles	Fitzpatrick	Law	Charlton	Best¹	Herd
30 March	Stoke City	Victoria Ground	4-2	30,141	Stepney	Brennan	Burns	Crerand	Sadler	Fitzpatrick	Best	Gowling¹	Charlton	Herd	Aston¹
6 April	Liverpool	Old Trafford	1-2	63,059	Stepney	Dunne(A)	Burns	Crerand	Sadler	Fitzpatrick	Best¹	Gowling	Charlton	Herd	Aston
12 April	Fulham	Craven Cottage	4-0	40,152	Stepney	Dunne(A)	Burns	Crerand	Sadler	Stiles	Best²	Kidd¹	Charlton¹	Law¹	Aston
13 April	Southampton	The Dell	2-2	30,079	Stepney	Dunne(A)	Burns	Crerand	Foulkes	Sadler	Best¹	Kidd¹	Charlton¹	Gowling	Aston
15 April	Fulham	Old Trafford	3-0	60,465	Rimmer	Dunne(A)	Burns	Crerand	Foulkes	Sadler	Best¹	Kidd	Charlton	Law	Aston¹
20 April	Sheffield United	Old Trafford	1-0	55,033	Stepney	Brennan	Dunne(A)	Crerand	Sadler	Stiles	Best	Kidd	Charlton	Law¹	Aston
29 April	WBA	The Hawthorns	3-6	43,412	Stepney	Dunne(A)	Burns	Crerand	Sadler	Stiles	Best	Kidd²	Charlton	Law¹	Aston
4 May	Newcastle United	Old Trafford	6-0	59,976	Stepney	Brennan	Dunne(A)	Crerand	Foulkes	Sadler¹	Best³	Kidd²	Charlton	Gowling	Aston
11 May	Sunderland	Old Trafford	1-2	62,963	Stepney	Brennan	Dunne(A)	Crerand	Foulkes	Stiles	Best¹	Kidd	Charlton	Sadler	Aston
Charity Shield															
12 August	Tottenham Hotspur	Old Trafford	3-3	54,106	Stepney	Brennan	Dunne(A)	Crerand	Foulkes	Stiles	Best	Law¹	Charlton²	Kidd	Aston
FA Cup															
27 January	Tottenham Hotspur	Old Trafford	2-2	63,500	Stepney	Dunne(A)	Burns	Crerand	Sadler	Fitzpatrick	Best¹	Kidd	Charlton¹	Law	Aston
31 January	Tottenham Hotspur	White Hart Lane	0-1	57,200	Stepney	Dunne(A)	Burns	Crerand	Sadler	Fitzpatrick	Best	Kidd	Charlton	Herd	Aston
European Cup															
20 September	Hibernians	Old Trafford	4-0	43,912	Stepney	Dunne(A)	Burns	Crerand	Foulkes	Stiles	Best	Sadler²	Charlton	Law²	Kidd
27 September	Hibernians	Empire Stadium	0-0	25,000	Stepney	Dunne(A)	Burns	Crerand	Foulkes	Stiles	Best	Sadler	Charlton	Law	Kidd
15 November	Sarajevo	Stadion Kosevo	0-0	45,000	Stepney	Dunne(A)	Burns	Crerand	Foulkes	Sadler	Fitzpatrick	Kidd	Charlton	Best	Aston
29 November	Sarajevo	Old Trafford	2-1	62,801	Stepney	Brennan	Dunne(A)	Crerand	Foulkes	Sadler	Burns	Kidd	Charlton	Best¹	Aston¹
28 February	Gornik Zabrze	Old Trafford	2-0	63,456	Stepney	Dunne(A)	Burns	Crerand	Sadler	Stiles	Best	Kidd¹	Charlton	Ryan	Aston
13 March	Gornik Zabrze	Stadion Slaski	0-1	105,000	Stepney	Dunne(A)	Burns	Crerand	Sadler	Stiles	Fitzpatrick	Charlton	Herd	Kidd	Best
24 April	Real Madrid	Old Trafford	1-0	63,500	Stepney	Dunne(A)	Burns	Crerand	Sadler	Stiles	Best¹	Kidd	Charlton	Law	Aston
15 May	Real Madrid	Bernabeu	3-3 +	125,000	Stepney	Brennan	Dunne(A)	Crerand	Foulkes¹	Stiles	Best¹	Kidd	Charlton	Sadler¹	Aston
29 May	Benfica	Wembley	4-1	100,000	Stepney	Brennan	Dunne(A)	Crerand	Foulkes	Stiles	Best¹	Kidd¹	Charlton²	Sadler	Aston

1968-69
THE END OF AN ERA

Football had seen very few of its number knighted. In fact, prior to Matt Busby receiving the honour from The Queen in the summer which followed his European triumph, only Walter Winterbottom, Alf Ramsey and Stanley Matthews had received knighthoods. Busby's triumphant night at Wembley Stadium ensured he was given a similar status at the earliest opportunity to add to his CBE from a decade earlier.

Many felt that he would call it a day prior to the 1968-69 campaign opening but Matt felt he still had a job to do. One of his first tasks was to deny George captaincy of the side. Best had sought a meeting with his manager to discuss his future and that of the team. He cut to the chase suggesting that Bobby Charlton, Paddy Crerand and Denis Law should be allowed to leave and the side built around him.

As the focal point of the side Best also felt he should be the designated leader on the pitch. Matt rejected any such notions and told George that he felt him too immature.

MANCHESTER UNITED 2 EVERTON 1
DIVISION ONE 10 AUGUST 1968

UNITED KICKED OFF the season as European Champions with a clean bill of health and a full strength squad to pick from. Denis Law was back to fitness after his cartilage operation and a good pre-season cleared any doubts about his long term future.

Everton were superb from until midway through the first half when United scored against the run of play. Alex Stepney excelled and his display proved just as vital as the two finest outfield players, and

scorers, that afternoon Bobby Charlton and George Best.

George hit United's first after a pass from Charlton and returned the compliment as a twisting run ended with the England man's emphatic finish at least equal to his colleague's earlier effort.

It was unfortunate that only a few players could take their lead from Best who often found himself isolated while in possession, with few willing targets to aim at.

WEST BROMWICH ALBION 3 MANCHESTER UNITED 1
DIVISION ONE 14 AUGUST 1968

UNITED WERE CAUGHT cold for the second game in a row by a busy side determined to prove their worth against Europe's premier club. Jeff Astle nodded in on four minutes as United's backline was exposed. Alex Stepney was not as

confident as he had been four days earlier and it showed in the eventual scoreline.

Bobby Charlton hit one back before the interval but Albion deserved their victory.

MANCHESTER CITY 0 MANCHESTER UNITED 0
DIVISION ONE 17 AUGUST 1968

THIS WAS PERHAPS the highest profile Manchester derby ever between the champions of England and Europe. Yet though Manchester, the capital of British and European football, was bracing itself for a goal-fest, that is not how the match turned out. Paddy Crerand and Shay Brennan were left out while Denis Law, who hoped his old problem had not flared up again, and Bill Foulkes were missing through injury.

George Best, serving a re-jigged front line in which Brian Kidd acted as an out and out striker, missed an early chance from close range. This was remarkable given Best's level of consistency and ability in that department. However, he refused to let the incident play on his mind and worked tirelessly down the flank creating good quality chances throughout.

Neither side wanted to yield much given their respective status in the game and the result was a continental style stand-off in which both sides failed to take by the scruff of the neck.

It would prove a learning curve for City as they prepared to make their debut in the European Cup against across teams happy to do this over two legs and see what they could grab. The Blues subsequent failure in their only outing in the European Cup against Fenerbahce summed up their tactical naivety.

United made more and better chances but were rocked by a broken leg for Wembley hero John Aston which looked to have ended his season at such an early stage.

MANCHESTER UNITED 1 COVENTRY CITY 0
DIVISION ONE 21 AUGUST 1968

FRANCIS BURNS MUST have impressed during training as the specialist left back was asked to partner Brian Kidd. With Aston injured, Best was asked to turn out on the left with Jim Ryan taking the right side of midfield. George had to pass a fitness test before he could be named on the teamsheet and despite initial doubts over his participation, he proved to be the star player of the evening, shining as other's contributions fell below the standard expected by United players.

The Irishman hammered Bill Glazier in goal with shots or created chances which others spurned.

Jimmy Ryan hit the winner, chipping in after a pass from Bobby Charlton who could at least lift his performance in phases but would not have been happy with his overall contribution. It was enough but United required more if remaining Kings of Europe or topping the First Division was to be a realistic aim.

MANCHESTER UNITED 0 CHELSEA 4
DIVISION ONE 24 AUGUST 1968

SO MUCH FOR Matt Busby having a large squad to choose from: John Fitzpatrick succumbed to ankle and shin injuries giving Paddy Crerand a route back into the side. Yet there was no time for United to settle before Tommy Baldwin netted. The right winger hit a shot Stepney had no chance of saving. The sheer pace meant he barely got into the air as the ball whizzed past him. Bobby Tambling doubled the lead and by half time United were 3-0 down.

A relentless display by Ron Harris kept George Best in check and as a team Chelsea kept United quiet allowing only pot-shots. George managed to get one away but was too far from goal.

MANCHESTER UNITED 3 TOTTENHAM HOTSPUR 1
DIVISION ONE 28 AUGUST 1968

WILLIE MORGAN, MAKING his debut, had been the subject of a lengthy transfer saga before United paid £117,000 for the Scottish international winger. His looks and the position he played led many (not least Willie himself) to believe he was the equal of Best. In reality Morgan was a good international winger in his own right as his record for United shows, though someway short of the genius he believed himself to be.

Denis Law returned and finally seemed to scotch rumours about his United career being at an end. John Fitzpatrick came back at the first opportunity and scored twice. Francis Burns was omitted from the team ending the striking experiment as there were no opportunities at the back where Shay Brennan replaced Frank Kopel. Paddy Crerand was a further casualty.

Morgan's contribution was distinct and complimentary not only with his international teammate Law but George Best and Bobby Charlton who was allowed to slip in to central midfield - an area which suited his game. David Sadler kept Martin Chivers out of harms way for the second successive clash with Spurs.

SHEFFIELD WEDNESDAY 5 MANCHESTER UNITED 4
DIVISION ONE 31 AUGUST 1968

DENIS LAW'S 200TH league game was one to remember but not for all the right reasons. United led 4-2 at the break yet somehow allowed The Owls to come back and edge it by the odd goal in nine.

Many in the pressbox needed calculators to keep up with the scoring as Jack Whitham gave Wednesday a lead which George Best equalised. Wednesday went ahead once more before Law levelled. Law hit another with Bobby Charlton seeming to have provided breathing space. and Wednesday looked all but out it though, for some reason, United conspired to shoot themselves in the foot.

Basic errors gifted the position away. A Nobby Stiles own goal and Whitham's hat-trick included one goal which followed Alex Stepney dropping the ball.

MANCHESTER UNITED 1 WEST HAM UNITED 1
DIVISION ONE 7 SEPTEMBER 1968

UNITED LAY IN mid-table with seven points from as many games before kick-off. Having conceded four to Chelsea and five to Wednesday, Bill Foulkes and Francis Burns were rushed back with Brennan and Kidd omitted.

The alternations had the desired effect as deep-lying players anchored the midfield. Unfortunately United's attack suffered as safety-first football dominated the game.

West Ham were rarely a threat yet emerged with a point despite Denis Law nodding in a George Best centre from a yard out. Best had been one of the few players to shine at the start of the season and, confident that all was well behind him, he ran hard at the opposition.

Geoff Hurst managed to equalise following a burst from defence by Harry Redknapp which caught The Reds half asleep. United's frustration at allowing West Ham to nick a point had to be tempered with the realisation that they had at least stemmed the flow of goals conceded.

BURNLEY 1 MANCHESTER UNITED 0
DIVISION ONE 14 SEPTEMBER 1968

WILLIE MORGAN LINED up against the side he had joined as a 15 year-old trainee for the first time. His career had moved on and the money offered was too good for The Clarets to turn down but the Lancashire club had the last laugh when Brian O'Neill hit a screamer from 30 yards to earn both points.

George was well contained by Les Latcham and, with the Ulsterman quiet, the rest of the team had more work to do. Denis Law was also well marked meaning The Reds were effectively two key men down. Morgan, who Burnley manager

Harry Potts knew only too well, was guarded by Dave Merrington. As a result

very few chances were created though one shot from Best flew narrowly wide.

WATERFORD 1 MANCHESTER UNITED 3
European Cup 1st Rd 1st leg 18 September 1968

IRISH CHAMPIONS WATERFORD were not the sternest test but there again United didn't need to meet another of the bigger clubs at this stage and, as holders, had every right to get a chance of settling into the role against a team of minnows.

Law and Best, at their awe inspiring peak, linked well. George set up two goals and Brian Kidd the other as Denis

notched a hat-trick. Lots of players visibly gained confidence from the performance.

Despite being from Northern Ireland, George was acclaimed in Dublin and had his clothes torn off by fans of both sexes. One of his jumpers was shredded as hands grasped at the chance of an unusual souvenir.

MANCHESTER UNITED 3 NEWCASTLE UNITED 1
Division One 21 September 1968

UNITED WOULD LEAVE for Argentina and a clash with Estudiantes in the World Club Championship directly after the final whistle. Nonetheless Newcastle were soundly beaten at Old Trafford as Willie Morgan, who was ineligible for Europe, returned.

Tricky forward Wyn Davies was missing after a midweek injury in the Fairs Cup which was a relief to the United backline but there was no respite for the Newcastle defence who found that Law and Best continued where they left off in Ireland.

This time it was George hitting the net

first with a clinical but remarkable strike from 10 yards. He was no more than a yard or so away from the touchline but rather than cross George bent his shot past Coleraine born Iam McFaul.

Law smashed one from long distance which crashed into the roof of the net before George grabbed the third to make the game safe by the half hour. Minds then seemed to focus on Buenos Aires as Tommy Gibb got a late consolation but there was little chance of a Magpie recovery.

ESTUDIANTES DE LA PLATA 1 MANCHESTER UNITED 0
Intercontinental Cup 1st leg 25 September 1968

As EUROPEAN CHAMPIONS United met their South American equivalents, Copa Libertadores winners Estudiantes de la Plata of Argentina, to decide who would be crowned World Champions. It was estimated that the clash could earn

United a six figure fee. However, many questioned whether the profit would be worth the aggravation. A bad atmosphere had been created before a ball had been kicked. United had been treated shabbily at functions and when a bumpy pitch attracted criticism from manager Matt Busby the Argentine media made his comment out to be sour grapes.

The first leg, played in Buenos Aires, was something of a bloodbath with foul rather than fair means employed by the South American side. Best was subjected to the worst of this which included blatant hacking, hair pulling and spitting. Bobby Charlton needed two stitches in a wound suffered during a challenge which the club doctor believed could have broken his leg, though he wasn't the only United player requiring treatment. Denis Law had his hair tugged as early as the opening minute.

George had adjusted to some of the more skulduggerous means of halting him over the years and always managed to remain calm regardless of the provocation but just 15 minutes into the first leg with a referee seemingly happy to wave play on in any circumstances he simply abandoned any hopes of competing equally and gave up chasing 50-50 balls.

Celtic had faced Argentine opponents the previous year and suffered similar consequences. Keeper Ronnie Simpson

had stones thrown at him as he came out of the tunnel and was carried off. Celtic, who had won the 1st leg in Glasgow, took the lead but lost 2-1. The goals were scored after half-time when Jock Steins' side had been kept in the changing rooms for almost 30 minutes. With their air conditioning cut off the Celtic players refused to return until they had cooled down with a shower. A re-match in Montevideo, Uruguay was arranged 72 hours later.

Violence more horrific than that which had gone in the preceding games followed with Celtic reduced to seven men as a result.

A year on, Nobby Stiles was the focus of Argentinian ire as he was head butted and left with a cut over his eye. Remonstrations against an offside flag saw him sent off late on. Frustrations had simply boiled over. Nobby had suffered for being part of Sir Alf Ramsey's World Cup winning side. The England boss had described the Argentine side as "animals". Such as it mattered Marcos Conigliaro headed the winner in this game.

MANCHESTER UNITED 7 WATERFORD 1
EUROPEAN CUP 1ST RD 2ND LEG 2 OCTOBER 1968

WATERFORD GAVE ALEX Stepney plenty to do early in the second leg and gained plaudits from the Old Trafford crowd for their spirit alone. They could only be admired for failing to be daunted by the glamour of the stage or their 3-1 deficit from the opening leg.

Denis Law went one better than his

hat-trick a fortnight earlier while Francis Burns, Nobby Stiles and Bobby Charlton scored one a piece. On the same night Manchester City exited the competition to Fenerbahce of Turkey.

MANCHESTER UNITED 0 ARSENAL 0
Division One 5 October 1968

JOHN FITZPATRICK CAME in for David Sadler who injured an ankle against Waterford. He was the only change to the eleven caused by injury as a host of wounded players managed to make a sufficient recovery.

A relatively poor game was played out as United's European curse struck again in the subsequent league game. Denis Law could have bagged at least two. His closest shave was having one cleared off the line but it should also be noted that he managed to squander one or two other decent chances. Arsenal mounted a stiff defence which nullified almost every attack mounted.

TOTTENHAM HOTSPUR 2 MANCHESTER UNITED 2
Division One 9 October 1968

THE REDS FAILED to win but provided a timely boost as despite being 2-0 down within the first quarter, they came back to claim a draw. A 25-yard volley from Paddy Crerand pulled one back. Denis Law, following up quickly with a snap shot from a narrow angle, scored the equaliser while Carlo Sartori, on as a substitute for Burns, almost hit the winner.

Despite allowing a couple of early goals in, United's improved display at the back kept Spurs in check once the scores had been levelled.

MANCHESTER UNITED 1 ESTUDIANTES DE LA PLATA 1
Intercontinental Cup 2nd leg 16 October 1968

GEORGE WAS ONE of eight star names to miss out against Liverpool (United lost 2-0 at Anfield) at the weekend but was restored to the side as United set about turning the second leg of this tie around. Like every other player Best fought hard to regain parity but with Denis Law's loss early on, the task became an uphill struggle.

Six minutes in a free-kick found Estudiantes' Juan Ramon Veron (the father of future £28 million signing Juan Seba Veron) and he netted at the far post.

Like the first game, play was niggly and littered with fouls. After almost three hours of keeping an even temperament and despite extreme provocation, Best finally snapped retaliating to something which fell marginally short of an assault by Hugo Medina, which saw both players dismissed. George had been incensed by some of the treatment meted out to his colleagues especially Denis Law who had been carried off the field after a clattering by the keeper. After Medina kicked his shins with no intention of challenging for the ball and then spat at Best for good measure, the red mist descended.

He had been singled out for rough treatment before the game had started and labelled a cry baby. In this instance he proved anything but and smacked the South American in the jaw then walked towards the dressing rooms before he was formally dismissed. He had already struck Argentine skipper Oscar Malbernat.

Just minutes remained when United squared the tie on the night. Willie Morgan fired home from a Paddy Crerand set-piece and the scorer seemed to have turned provider in the final seconds when passing to Brian Kidd who hit the ball in but saw his effort cancelled out by a referee who had already blown his whistle to signal the end of the game and the beginning of Estudiantes de la Plata's reign as World Champions.

Events caused the start of a very bad tempered exchange between the Football Association and their South American equivalents. Estudiantes said they wanted to withdraw from pre-arranged friendlies with Arsenal and Birmingham City the following week despite contracts being signed and both clubs having gone to various lengths and expense to host ties.

When the Argentine players returned home Daniel Onega was jailed by his local police chief for his part in the brawl at Old Trafford. There is no record as to whether the officer was a United fan or just keen to let everyone within his jurisdiction know that such activity had its consequences. A strike was subsequently threatened by the country's professionals.

United's experience of the Intercontinental Cup was no better than Celtic's the year before in which John Hughes had been dismissed for the Hoops. This time Best saw red but few United fans thought any worse of him for that.

MANCHESTER UNITED 1 SOUTHAMPTON 2
DIVISION ONE 19 OCTOBER 1968

CARLO SARTORI CAME in for Brian Kidd as Best shook off the controversy of his early bath and looked sharp, knocking accurate passes over distances which brought ripples of applause from the Old Trafford crowd but his early efforts fizzled out.

Two errors led to Southampton's goals but poor performances across the pitch didn't help either.

Best wasted possession too often as he attempted to beat The Saints singlehandedly - nevertheless he did score an excellent goal which emphasised his bravery. His zest for the game and balletic poise came to the fore on that occasion but otherwise he was held in check.

NORTHERN IRELAND 4 TURKEY 1
WORLD CUP QUALIFIER 23 OCTOBER 1968

A COMFORTABLE AND predictable home win in qualifying group four at Windsor Park was plain sailing from the moment George Best hit the first goal of the game.

Eric McCordie netted just before the break with Ogun replying for the Turks. Dougan and Campbell rounded matters off on the resumption.

George was talked to for seeming to not give his all during the last few minutes. He had been swamped by his home town crowd countless times and rather than find himself engulfed in admirers tugging at his hair and kit he stayed close to the area just in front of the tunnel. As expected hundreds of spectators jumped over the barriers on the final whistle while George sprinted down the tunnel to the sanctuary of the home changing room.

QUEENS PARK RANGERS 2 MANCHESTER UNITED 3
DIVISION ONE 26 OCTOBER 1968

THE DESIRE AND tenacity lacking against Southampton returned in abundance for the trip to Loftus Road but United were still wasteful with countless opportunities wasted. Willie Morgan, without doubt the player of the moment, continued to shine but George Best wasn't far behind and scored the first goal. The effort deflected off centre half Ron Hunt but there was no mistake about the absolute quality of his second - a chip that beat the keeper for pace as well as direction. Law hit a third from close range to make the final score 3-2.

Overall the performance was shaky but two points at this stage of the campaign were all important.

MANCHESTER UNITED 0 LEEDS UNITED 0
DIVISION ONE 2 NOVEMBER 1968

DENIS LAW AND Shay Brennan were doubts before the game but returned to face title favourites Leeds. Don Revie's change in ethos plus a little more money allowed him to make The Tykes a more attacking side who attracted better players rather than the dour outfit of previous years. They certainly got into their stride quicker than The Reds and would have gone ahead had Mick Bates not proved so wasteful when unmarked in the area.

Johnny Giles had a huge effect on the Yorkshire club's approach. The former United man guided his present side well and used his experience to dictate the play from the hub of midfield.

For United it was the final ball which proved the biggest problem. This only increased a sense of annoyance on and off the pitch. That said, Gary Sprake made two exceptional saves from Law when United finally did bed in but this was a game decided in the white heat of midfield by a handful of players, each good enough to nullify the other. A goalless draw was the only logical conclusion and both sides deserved at least a point.

SUNDERLAND 1 MANCHESTER UNITED 1
DIVISION ONE 9 NOVEMBER 1968

BEST WAS A lingering doubt for the journey to Roker Park with a groin strain though Denis Law, who was a regular fixture at late fitness tests, failed to make the cut this weekend. Carlo Sartori stepped in to the attack partnering George on the left.

Heavy mud was a problem for defenders and forwards alike. Well most forwards. Best seemed happy enough and at times displayed astounding skills which many would have struggled to match on a perfectly manicured surface. George drove United forward with his imminent European suspension (as a result of his dismissal in the World Club match) uppermost in his mind. However, for all this good work, United couldn't find the net.

Gordon Harris struck against the run of play in the opening period during Sunderland's only real sustained attack of the first half. Matters were not squared until the final couple of minutes when a Nobby Stiles shot, which was nothing more than a speculative punt at goal, hit Jim Hurley and deflected past Jim Montgomery.

MANCHESTER UNITED 0 IPSWICH TOWN 0
DIVISION ONE 16 NOVEMBER 1968

IN THE ABSENCE of Best, United built a handy 3-0 lead in the opening leg of their second round European Cup tie against Anderlecht. It was certainly a huge mountain for the Belgian champions to climb.

Back in the league, centre-half Steve James was withdrawn from the reserve game with Derby County to deputise for the 'flu ridden David Sadler for his second first team appearance. United had been linked with Ian Ure of Arsenal but 18 year-old James refused to be affected and settled well into United's makeshift backline.

Later, Brian Kidd was forced off and Shay Brennan continued although clearly injured. Ipswich also lost key men but with an extra defender on the bench mounted a stubborn resistance.

Unfortunately nobody, Best included, could string something together and The Reds tamely surrendered to a third successive league draw.

STOKE CITY 0 MANCHESTER UNITED 0
DIVISION ONE 23 NOVEMBER 1968

AS THE INJURY jinx continued United lost the services of Denis Law, Shay Brennan, Brian Kidd and David Sadler who were all ruled out days prior to the game. George Best was suspended for the second leg of the European Cup tie in Belgium and an arguably weaker side than would be needed for that match took to the field at the Victoria Ground. It could only be hoped that those on display would raise their game in the hope of gaining selection.

That was certainly the case defensively but the strikers toiled. As ever Best was outstanding and ran Stoke ragged but no one could capitalise on his work.

When confronted with a chance everyone, including the man himself, seemed to shrink. Far too many efforts flew wide when the target should have been hit and when the accuracy was there Gordon Banks proved himself the equal of all efforts, flinging himself to all corners of his net with Bobby Charlton the most profligate in front of goal.

MANCHESTER UNITED 2 WOLVES 0
DIVISION ONE 30 NOVEMBER 1968

ANDERLECHT HAD PROVIDED A real fright in midweek, almost overturning the lead built at Old Trafford and, had it not been for Carlo Sartori's away goal, they would have forced extra-time. The scorer kept his place while George Best, his ban now served, was keen to make further amends for the indiscipline he believed had let his colleagues down and put hopes of retaining the European Cup in jeopardy.

Consequently Best took to this game with real vigour. From the off he was looking to get involved in almost every area of the pitch.

Forwards inevitably benefited from such industry and Sartori hit a post after good work from the winger. But the first hour was frustrating, punctuated by surges from Best who opened the scoring after taking a pass from Paddy Crerand, then running the ball inside his full back before hitting a superb low shot.

Law netted from a Willie Morgan cross with a header. The pace of the move was stunning and gave Wolves no chance to react.

LEICESTER CITY 2 MANCHESTER UNITED 1
DIVISION ONE 7 DECEMBER 1968

LEICESTER HAD SACKED their long serving manager Matt Gillies after a disappointing start to the season capped by a 7-1 defeat to lowly Torquay. Future United boss Frank O'Farrell was tipped to take over. George Best looked to compound their misery and picked up the ball 30 yards out within the opening minutes. His mazy run was only halted by a sturdy challenge from Peter Rodrigues.

However, Leicester didn't allow United to dominate and even after going behind to a Denis Law penalty on 13 minutes looked to gain parity, which they did when David Nish converted a spot kick. The Foxes were prepared to work hard to keep The Reds out and could rely on Peter Shilton who had a great game. Rodney Fern hit what proved to be the winner just after half time though there was a fair slice of luck involved. The ball struck Nobby Stiles and bounced kindly for the forward who gave Alex Stepney no chance.

MANCHESTER UNITED 1 LIVERPOOL 0
DIVISION ONE 14 DECEMBER 1968

DESPITE FAILING TO score for the past three games, Roger Hunt came to Old Trafford chasing Liverpool's goalscoring record. With United's recent form at the back he seemed a decent bet to break Gordon Hodgson's mark set 32 years earlier. The Merseyrider's led the table by four points and though Matt Busby was keen to ensure George Best was fit after damaging his instep he sensationally dropped Willie Morgan in favour of shoring up the back four.

The foot injury had forced the winger to miss his country's World Cup qualifier with Turkey during the week. Steve James, who had made his debut in the match at Anfield, came in at centre half as Sadler went to inside right to play alongside Best.

A greasy surface caused more than one player to slip but both sides managed to cope well in key areas of the field. Tommy Lawrence thwarted a busy United side when called upon but United grew in confidence as the game wore on.

Typically George coped best with the conditions which should really have had slowed the speedy player down but he seemed to glide over the muddy surface, receiving a pass from Bobby Charlton to set up the only goal of the game. His graceful run down the wing setting up a chance for Law who made no mistake.

SOUTHAMPTON 2 MANCHESTER UNITED 0
DIVISION ONE 21 DECEMBER 1968

UNITED WERE BACK to their lackadaisical ways and had a disastrous start as Ron Davies and Mike Channon put Southampton 2-0 up in the opening minutes. The Reds had no cutting edge and despite some excellent approach play by Best, the winger and his colleagues finished poorly. Consequently George began to take more and more things upon himself. It proved an impossible job, even for someone of his ability.

Denis Law hit a post and Sartori went close while Nobby Stiles got the ball over the line but did so with his fist.

ARSENAL 3 MANCHESTER UNITED 0
DIVISION ONE 26 DECEMBER 1968

A VOTE AMONGST Europe's sports press had ended with George Best being named European Player of the Year. He edged out Bobby Charlton, who had won the accolade two years earlier, by 61 votes to 53. Most other contenders polled a good deal less than the United stars.

As if to celebrate the award Best ripped

at Arsenal throughout the first half but gained no reward for either himself or any of his colleagues. He set up Denis Law who hit an air shot with the goal at his mercy two minutes in. In the next attack George beat five defenders but put in a weak effort on goal.

Events during the last half hour of the game more or less cost United any hope slim hopes of winning the title. Paddy Crerand was lost to injury and after that United fizzled out.

The Gunners took full advantage with headed goals from George Armstrong, David Court and John Radford.

EXETER CITY 1 MANCHESTER UNITED 3
FA Cup 3rd Rd 4 January 1969

EXETER SAT 91ST of the 92 Football League clubs on the morning they welcomed Manchester United to their homely St James Park ground but, as Sir Matt's side knew only too well, no team could be taken lightly in this competition. John Mitten, son of former Reds winger Charlie, played at inside-forward for The Grecians. He had had a trial at Old Trafford seven years previously after brief stints with Mansfield Town, Newcastle United and Leicester City but failed to make the grade.

Alan Banks, who had plundered six goals in eight league games for Liverpool, scored for Exeter on 15 minutes though United could already have been a goal down at that point as Alan Pinkney

rattled a volley directly at Alex Stepney after a free-kick had been cleared. Such was the ferocity of the shot that had the shot been a foot or so either side of the keeper, it would have gone in.

The home side managed to contain the superstars who enjoyed plenty of possession even if they could do very little of consequence with it. Only when John Fitzpatrick scored from close range just before the break did United finally assert themselves. A John Newman own goal in a melee caused by United's pressure and Brian Kidd's late effort settled it. George Best, like many of his colleagues, had plenty of pretty play but no end product until he was withdrawn 20 minutes from time with an ankle injury.

LEEDS UNITED 2 MANCHESTER UNITED 1
Division One 11 January 1969

SOMEWHAT SURPRISINGLY BRIAN Kidd was given the afternoon off but the decision worked to the benefit of John Fitzpatrick who deserved his chance. Best made a complete recovery from his ankle injury after a few days light training.

Leeds had a cup replay in midweek but showed no signs of tiredness as

they set about grabbing an early goal. United did well to hold out before Alex Stepney misjudged a Peter Lorimer cross to give Mick Jones the simple task of heading into an unguarded net. United had a goal disallowed when referee John Gow signalled for a direct free-kick but controversially ruled out the resulting effort.

Once again George was kept quiet by Paul Reaney and with Denis Law not a force in the game either, The Reds were well shackled. Only goalscorer Bobby Charlton could claim to have had a decent game. Leeds kept the initiative grasped in the opening minutes until the end.

MANCHESTER UNITED 4 SUNDERLAND 1
DIVISION ONE 18 JANUARY 1969

HAVING WON EVERY honour in the game and been in charge of United since the end of World War Two, Sir Matt Busby finally bowed to the inevitable and announced his retirement on 14th January 1969. With his 60th birthday fast approaching and having done all in his power to return United to the pre-eminence they had enjoyed in Edwardian times, nobody could deny him the chance to part on his own terms. He would remain involved as a General Manager to assist the new man but day-to-day control of the team would be relinquished.

A club statement broke the news. Many candidates were linked within the first few days but the United players didn't let off field matters prove a distraction. Sixth from bottom of the league before the game against Sunderland commenced, neither they nor their boss could allow it.

Alex Stepney was dropped after a poor showing at Elland Road while Paddy Crerand was back on the sick list giving Willie Morgan a chance to re-stake his claim to a regular place in the side. His cause was done the power of good with a clever flick on for Best who in turn found Denis Law. An overhead kick from the striker hit a defender and although the ball stuck in the mud it was eventually cleared.

A foul on Best gave Bobby Charlton a chance to send in a free-kick which the winger stretched to head but he couldn't quite get enough elevation in his leap. The ball carried through to Law who netted. The goal was ruled out but no one seemed quite sure whether it was for offside or handball against Best. However, there was no denying the Scot soon after.

The midfield finally gelled with the attack - Morgan and Best were outstanding in creating chances for Law who scored his second hat-trick of the season. The middle goal was an aerial volley at waist height but it wasn't just the goals but his sharpness which was so impressive. Jimmy Rimmer had little to do but pick the ball out of the net for the Sunderland goal.

MANCHESTER UNITED 1 WATFORD 1
FA CUP 4TH RD 25 JANUARY 1969

JUST HOURS BEFORE the game George Best was bed ridden with a heavy cold and seemed destined to miss the tie but he reported for duty declaring himself fit to play. Francis Burns was out after his third cartilage operation in recent years. Tony Dunne switched to the left with Frank Kopel introduced on the right.

A robust approach from the Third Division leaders paid handsome dividends. Best, amongst others, was buffeted to the ground on countless occasions. Outside right Stewart Scullion stunned Old Trafford as early as the third minute by not only comprehensively beating Bobby Charlton but hitting a rising 20 yard drive just after he had done so. The ball flew past Jimmy Rimmer and into the top corner.

United's equaliser was fortunate. A panicked defender headed the ball out of his own keeper's hands when Mike Walker seemed the favourite to take Dunne's cross. Law scrambled it in. Best struggled against his cold which seemed to hinder his performance more and more as play wore on. Charlton and Law were also disappointing though had less excuse.

IPSWICH TOWN 1 MANCHESTER UNITED 0
DIVISION ONE 1 FEBRUARY 1969

JOHN FITZPATRICK EMPHASISED his value to the side by slotting in at right back and had plenty to do as Ipswich failed to bow to reputations and barely allowed United a chance to settle while remaining resolute at the back.

The Reds enjoyed a better second half but misses proved costly, in particular two from Bobby Charlton which should have been converted.

An own goal from Tony Dunne decided the game. He attempted to stop Chris Barnard reaching a through ball but only succeeded in lifting it over his keeper's head, as United failed to find a way to goal yet again.

WATFORD 0 MANCHESTER UNITED 2
FA CUP 4TH RD REPLAY 3 FEBRUARY 1969

A BRACE FOR Denis Law earned United a tie with Birmingham in the next round. The first was a header after a spellbinding run and cross from George Best with the second a predatory finish from inside the area. However, other than those two moments, United rarely threatened despite some very silky approach play.

Watford represented little threat in attack and when they did reach danger areas, they were dealt with easily.

BIRMINGHAM CITY 2 MANCHESTER UNITED 2
FA Cup 5th Rd 8 February 1969

DENIS LAW had been injured during his match winning performance at Vicarage Road but, along with Steve James, made the starting line-up. Birmingham had one or two doubts but declared a fairly clean bill of health. A penalty during the last ten minutes earned Birmingham another chance at Old Trafford but United should have been in command by this time having led twice and looking comfortable until conceding disappointing goals.

Malcolm Beard scored the first equaliser with a free-kick replying to Denis Law's effort just before the hour. Law had been denied a couple of times by sensational saves from Jim Herriot but the keeper could only watch as Willie Morgan sent an effort on to the bar. He was then beaten by George Best but within two minutes central defender Dave Robinson had converted a spot kick to earn the Blues an Old Trafford replay.

WOLVES 2 MANCHESTER UNITED 2
Division One 15 February 1969

A BIG FREEZE gripped the country but the Molineux groundsman's sterling efforts were rewarded with kick-off as scheduled and Wolves led 2-0 by the break. Nobby Stiles and Denis Law were missing with David Sadler and Carlo Sartori coming in. The Reds looked uncomfortable upfront dithering over chances throughout the first half. However, the resumption saw things click with Bobby Charlton and George Best pegging the home side back. Skipper Charlton offered a clarion call and led by example.

His volley from a Morgan cross on 47 minutes brought belief and with enough time to complete the recovery United's confidence grew and continued to do so before Brian Kidd set up a header for Best to level.

Wolves were exposed whenever United attacked as Willie Morgan and Best created space. Only the troublesome surface, which seemed to ice over during the game, caused trouble underfoot stopped either winger creating a possible winner.

MANCHESTER UNITED 6 BIRMINGHAM CITY 2
FA Cup 5th Rd Replay 24 February 1969

LEICESTER CITY WERE due at Old Trafford the weekend preceding this cup replay but the weather's intervention meant there would be an extra 48 hours rest for both teams. Stiles returned with Sadler relegated to the bench. Morgan

and Best started where they left off against Wolves and inspired the team, especially Law, who could only benefit from their work. By the end of the game he had netted a highly impressive 34 goals from 33 FA matches.

Jimmy Greenhoff had actually given Birmingham a fourth minute lead after some poor defending but a trip on John Fitzgerald, who made a rare foray into the opposition penalty area, provided a chance to level. Paddy Crerand's chip seized the lead and from that point on

United were the dominant force. Two further goals for Law plus one each for Kidd and Morgan gave United six. Phil Summerill scored for the Midland side near the end but the result was still a massive boost for the return of European competition two days later.

MANCHESTER UNITED 3 RAPID VIENNA 0
European Cup QF 1st leg 26 February 1969

THE QUEST TO retain the European Cup had become all important with the league now beyond United. The victory against Birmingham City had only been completed 48 hours before United hosted the Austrians and many thought The Reds vulnerable going into the quarter-final. Rapid coach Rudolf Vytlacil had watched the FA Cup tie and felt the rigorous nature of the game would take its toll. He would ensure his side refused to give United as much room as Birmingham had afforded.

The Austrian champions had beaten Rosenberg and then shocked Real Madrid on away goals after a 2-1 defeat at The Bernabeu to reach the last eight and fancied their chances of taking another huge scalp. But he reckoned without George Best.

Much to United's relief John Fitzgerald

was declared fit and the backline was outstanding despite the tender years of certain members. Best ran and ran at Rapid and scored his first of the evening just before the break, hitting in a rebound following a Denis Law shot after Willie Morgan's cross had created the initial chance. It was Morgan's European bow as he had been ineligible for the first half of the competition. Good work from Charlton and Brian Kidd set up a chance for the debutant.

Nobby Stiles' wife had given birth earlier in the day and he celebrated further when his chipped pass to Best created a third. In addition to the three chances taken, United had many other efforts on goal plus two good penalty shouts for fouls on Charlton and Best during a spell when Vienna found themselves turned inside out. In the end the 3-0 scoreline

MANCHESTER UNITED 0 EVERTON 1
FA Cup 6th Rd 1 March 1969

In keeping with most clashes between United and Everton, this match lived up to its billing as a heavyweight encounter. Both sides sought to land early blows and by the end a knock-out victory with passage to the last four as a reward.

Each had chances to go ahead although Everton really should have grasped one of theirs but Jimmy Husband headed wide of an open goal. Joe Royle eventually netted but try as they might United found no way through a well-drilled defence.

Gordon West was excellent when called upon and withstood everything thrown at him. It was a shame that United exited at this stage as the deeds of Best, Morgan and Kidd deserved far more.

George's sense of injustice became clear when he got involved in a scuffle with Everton winger Johnny Morrissey towards the end.

RAPID VIENNA 0 MANCHESTER UNITED 0
European Cup QF 2nd leg 5 March 1969

Though he seemed to have recovered from a knee strain, Denis Law was ruled out of the second leg of the European Cup quarter-final. It was a set back but not one likely to threaten The Reds survival in the competition. At any rate the emphasis would not be on all-out attack. United had earned that luxury after such a good performance at Old Trafford.

This was a different type of display but one that was technically very sound. As a visiting side United sat fairly deep trying not to offer chances though when the opportunity to attack arose the midfield was able to press with real purpose. The ball found itself upfield pretty often where Brian Kidd could be relied upon to retain it and await reinforcements. George Best was a vital link between the midfield and lone striker.

Vienna threw what they could at United but didn't have enough quality to push themselves through a very solid wall.

MANCHESTER UNITED 0 MANCHESTER CITY 1
Division One 8 March 1969

An arduous midweek game expanded United's already lengthy injury list. In addition to Law, Steve James and Tony Dunne were now doubts for the 80th Manchester Derby though on a positive note Bill Foulkes returned and John Aston had recovered from the broken leg he sustained in the first derby of the season by taking his place on the bench. By contrast City were able to pick from a full strength squad which showed early on as the Blues enjoyed a terrific start.

United's front line, as excellent as it had been in Austria, wasn't short of ammunition courtesy of Morgan and Best patrolling the flanks. It was unfortunate that for all their neat play Brian Kidd and others could not seize their chances. At the back only Mike Summerbee's goal before half time was a let down. It proved to be the winner.

Although United threw more and more into attack as the minutes ticked by it became clear City were leading a charmed life. Late on Kidd hit the bar and Bobby Charlton saw an effort cleared off the line.

EVERTON 0 MANCHESTER UNITED 0
DIVISION ONE 10 MARCH 1969

JUST NINE DAYS previously Everton had exposed United's backline a number of times and progressed to the semi-finals of the FA Cup as a result. The Reds managed to plug the same holes and withstand a barrage of attacks thereby gaining some measure of credibility.

The second half was United's time to push forward after soaking up the pressure. Many players went close. So many infact that no one could quite understand how the deadlock remained unbroken.

George was frustrated at seeing his colleagues efforts saved or put wide. His irritation boiled over and for the second time in just over a week against Everton his temper got the better of him. This was not surprising given the charged nature of the occasion but constantly disputing decisions saw him talked to sternly by the referee.

CHELSEA 3 MANCHESTER UNITED 2
DIVISION ONE 15 MARCH 1969

THE DRAW AT Goodison Park was a hard fought result which should have yielded more. It left United fifth from bottom of the table, just six points ahead of the drop zone. However, a watching brief still had to be maintained. Later in the week former youth team captain Bobby Noble was forced to retire. The 23 year-old, once widely tipped as a future England star, had failed to recover from a car accident in April 1967. Though the physical injuries had mended his vision and co-ordination remained a problem.

It was a stark demonstration of the fickle nature of a footballer's career. Players such as George Best, who came through the system alongside Noble, couldn't help but think they were lucky it wasn't them. Then again George always played with such abandon demonstrating a sound philosophy; each match could be your last, so savour them all.

Bobby Charlton became the latest name to miss out through injury. United may have wanted to keep things tight for a while but were robbed of the opportunity when David Webb netted from a corner with seconds played. The Reds were forced to attack but went 2-0 down on 27 minutes. Steve James pulled one back from a David Sadler free-kick to register his first goal as a senior player. United had a good shout for a penalty turned down after a challenge on Willie Morgan but earned a spot-kick when Brian Kidd went down under a challenge. Denis Law dispatched his shot with great accuracy.

Ron Harris, usually so effective when deployed against George Best, for once failed to tame the winger who looked a goal threat every time he took the ball. However, his chances were reduced as, in and around the danger zone, he was well marshalled as Chelsea got numbers back. Especially once they grabbed what proved to be a late winner.

MANCHESTER UNITED 8 QUEENS PARK RANGERS 1
DIVISION ONE 19 MARCH 1969

JOHN ASTON MADE his first start since breaking a leg back in August, as a make-shift centre forward. Bobby Charlton remained out but the reshuffle in attacking perssonel failed to see United score as freely as their work deserved until Willie Morgan netted before the interval.

Two excellent goals by Best after teasing runs and an excellent overall contribution earned him the plaudits and the man of the match award.

Rodney Marsh, one of the few players who could be compared to George Best, pulled one back for QPR but Rangers had no answer to United who hit five more very quickly through Nobby Stiles, Brian Kidd, John Aston and Willie Morgan who completed a hat-trick - his first and as it turned out only treble for United.

MANCHESTER UNITED 1 SHEFFIELD WEDNESDAY 0
DIVISION ONE 22 MARCH 1969

AN UNDERSTANDABLY CONFIDENT side welcomed Sheffield Wednesday to Old Trafford. Willie Morgan was passed fit and hoped to add to his treble of midweek. However, he and every other United player had to be patient as The Owls proved very impressive during the opening phases.

Best was given a roaming brief and proved to be the man of the match yet again as he gradually helped The Reds find a way back into the game by prompting attacks. Some decent chances were wasted but George managed to find the net. Denis Law had a poor penalty saved by Peter Springett.

MANCHESTER UNITED 1 STOKE CITY 1
DIVISION ONE 24 MARCH 1969

HAD A LESSER keeper than Gordon Banks been on duty for Stoke, United would have won this game with ease. However, the stopper regarded as one of the greatest in the world underlined his credentials thwarting George Best amongst others on a number of occasions.

He was only beaten when completely helpless to prevent Aston's tap-in during a scramble for possession yards out. Willie Stevenson deservedly equalised, as Banks, for one, didn't merit being on the losing side.

WEST HAM UNITED 0 MANCHESTER UNITED 0
DIVISION ONE 29 MARCH 1969

MORE WAS EXPECTED of George Best when other stars were missing and, with Willie Morgan now added to the injury list, the burden of his workload got even heavier.

At the end of a long, demanding month George found the going tough. He was still threatening going forward but seemed to have less fuel in his tank than usual. When that little extra was needed the thrusters seemed to misfire.

Both sides appeared lethargic and with The Hammers out of the running for a spot in the Fairs Cup (due to the performance of other London clubs) they were more than happy to contain The Reds.

NOTTINGHAM FOREST 0 MANCHESTER UNITED 1
DIVISION ONE 31 MARCH 1969

WITH PLENTY OF fitness worries for established first teamers, as well as fringe players, Matt Busby's resources were strecthed ever further. As a result many players were asked to fill in in areas they were not always accustomed to. For instance, Nobby Stiles covered at left back. Another player given a new responsibility was George Best who was nominated as skipper and penalty taker after Denis Law's patchy record from the spot. Law had missed three out of the six penalties taken that term and, without a goal in five games, was less than confident about the task.

When United were awarded a 68th minute spot kick after Terry Hennessy had held Brian Kidd, Best coolly dispatched the kick, sending Alan Hill the wrong way.

A couple of penalties could have been awarded up to that point for what could most politely be termed the over-enthusiastic checking of George Best by Hennessy, but on both occasions the Forest defender escaped sanction. One of them came in the first five minutes and left Best with a sore ankle which kept nagging him throughout the game.

Rain lashed down throughout and the sodden turf was not handled well by most players. Of course George Best excelled regardless of the surface. Another sparkling display had the Forest defence running around in circles.

MANCHESTER UNITED 2 WEST BROMWICH ALBION 1
DIVISION ONE 2 APRIL 1969

FOR THE SECOND time in three days George Best secured the points as United's other forwards were miserable in front of goal.

Like the majority of United games this term, excellent build-up play was regularly let down by woeful finishing. The effect was that few players wanted to take responsibility. Best's confidence was rarely low, though he had to get over his own jitters to finally provide some direct threat on The Baggies goal.

When Albion took the lead it only underlined the profligacy of United's shooting. Then, in the dying minutes, George got first an equaliser and then, with seconds remaining, an unstoppable winner that gave the keeper no chance.

MANCHESTER UNITED 3 NOTTINGHAM FOREST 1
DIVISION ONE 5 APRIL 1969

DENIS LAW RETURNED after missing the game with West Bromwich Albion and replaced Jim Ryan who had pulled a thigh muscle. Bobby Charlton, though close to a return and considered a possible starter right up to the last hour, was forced to sit out a ninth successive game - his longest lay off by some distance. Forest made two changes from the side which faced United at the beginning of the week omitting Ronnie Rees and Colin Hall.

Within two minutes Alex Stepney was forced to face a penalty from Joe Baker whose low, hard shot was well saved. Willie Morgan scored on 11 minutes to edge United ahead. A good midfield display built the foundations for the shift. Denis Law often dropped back rather than looking to go forward which helped as did Kidd who had been running tirelessly for a number of games. He was appreciated by his colleagues but superb lay-offs for Best and then Morgan to fire home two more made sure his contribution was more widely recognised.

Ten points from a possible twelve, over half of which could be attributed to the exploits of George Best, had put United into real contention for a spot in next season's Fairs Cup but their real aim remained retaining the European Cup.

COVENTRY CITY 2 MANCHESTER UNITED 1
DIVISION ONE 8 APRIL 1969

HITTING THREE GOALS a few days before travelling to Coventry City should have provided a renewed confidence in attack but the past months had been strewn with high scoring encounters followed by games in which United struggled. Yet again The Reds were toothless and against a team hard pressed to avoid the drop - this spelled trouble.

Bad errors from Alex Stepney allowed the Sky Blues to score both their goals. Bobby Charlton was back and looked solid but too many players lacked the same drive. John Fitzpatrick pulled one back from a Brian Kidd centre but it was too little too late. Any team under the charge of Noel Cantwell was unlikely to be caught out twice.

Despite defeat at Highfield Road, results elsewhere meant United were all but safe and Matt Busby finally felt that the decision to make Wilf McGuiness his chief coach could be released. The decision had been taken three months earlier when it was discovered that others on the short list were unwilling to fill the big man's shoes. Dave Sexton had been one of the main contenders for the post but stated he wished to remain at Chelsea.

A statement was issued on 9th April 1969 and even McGuiness himself only found out hours after the Coventry game when he was asked to wear a tie on reporting for work at Old Trafford the following day.

At 31 years of age Wilf was charged with stepping up from the reserves to the first team with total responsibility for all matters on match day. He was an experienced coach who had proved himself beyond club level as part of the England set up during the 1966 World Cup. He had also managed the national side's youth team.

NEWCASTLE UNITED 2 MANCHESTER UNITED 0
DIVISION ONE 12 APRIL 1969

OUT OF PATIENCE with an error prone Alex Stepney, Matt Busby gave Jimmy Rimmer a chance to stake his claim after some quality performances in the reserves. He had been told that as long as he performed well he would remain in the side regardless of the magnitude of the game. Giving youngsters their chance was of course nothing new for the United manager, though he would have been relieved to see the inexperienced keeper show his mettle as, apart from a run by Best which dragged Newcastle defenders across the pitch and earned a corner, it was all Newcastle. Unfortunately he was powerless to save Bryan Robson's penalty on eight minutes awarded for a Steve James trip on Tommy Gibb.

Best had a good shot well saved but otherwise United were poor and merited little. Alan Foggon wrapped things up six minutes from the close. It could have been a far heavier defeat but for the bravery of Rimmer which saw him treated for injuries five times.

MANCHESTER UNITED 2 BURNLEY 0
DIVISION ONE 19 APRIL 1969

BILL FOULKES RETURNED to defence as Matt Busby looked to stiffen up United's resistance at the back and test his fitness for the European Cup semi-final clashes with AC Milan. Steve James was the casualty. John Aston and Shay Brennan were also back in place of Bobby Charlton and David Sadler who both suffered injuries at Newcastle.

Burnley had a poor record away from Turf Moor and had suffered some heavy defeats. Prior to the game George Best was presented with his European Player of the Year trophy from Max Urbini editor of *France Football*. He was all smiles but this masked a desire to obtain two points and with the trophy in his possession there was no better time to turn on the style. Brian Kidd also impressed as The Reds maintained a very high standard of forward play.

The visitors proved themselves to be dangerous on the break although they were undone by a clinical finish from Best who guided a majestic Paddy Crerand centre into the net. Denis Law should have scored with his head although Harry Thomson got a hand on John Aston's cross which seemed to put the Scot off.

Balls from wide areas caused The Clarets real problems so much so that an under pressure Colin Waldron put the ball through his own goal after another superb cross. However, the match ended on a bad tempered note with Law and Stiles involved in clashes.

AC MILAN 2 MANCHESTER UNITED 0
European Cup SF 1st leg 23 April 1969

QUITE WHAT AC Milan's scouts made of United's Jekyll and Hyde performances is a mystery. Various agents had been dispatched from Italy since the draw was made but they would have been hard pressed to settle on a uniform opinion. With the exception of a handful of players The Reds often performed so poorly that most would have fancied their chances but occasionally, when everything clicked, they had the capacity to look like European Champions.

Then again the Milanese may have suspected that United's powder was being kept dry for the European Cup and knew what the side were more than capable given their status as holders. Yet the Red's defence of the European Cup floundered early on at the San Siro.

Angelo Sormani found the net on 33 minutes though there were a number of close shaves before this which required Jimmy Rimmer's attentions. He was United's star performer on the night which highlighted not only Milan's dominance but the extent of his contribution. United trailed 2-0 just after half-time when John Fitzpatrick was dismissed for aiming a kick at Swedish winger Kurt Hamrin. The defender had been elbowed and received numerous shirt pulls before this but the referee could only make his decision on what he saw which was the aftermath of the altercation.

Despite a numerical disadvantage United were strong enough to limit the damage and give themselves half a chance at Old Trafford. For Milan, Angelo Anquilletti gave George Best no chance. His colleagues at the back were equally tight and only beaten the odd time which didn't breed confidence. Milan were not the easiest team to peg back in any circumstance, especially as United now entered the home leg with a two goal deficit to overturn.

NORTHERN IRELAND 1 ENGLAND 3
Home International 3 May 1969

ENGLAND WERE EXPECTED to get their bid for the British Championship off to a comfortable start despite journeying to Windsor Park for the opening tie of the series. However, the game started slowly and it wasn't until the 40th minute that an attack of any real merit was mounted by the visitors. Francis Lee of Manchester

City lobbed the ball over a defensive wall from a free-kick into the path of Martin Peters who headed into the ground and in. The West Ham forward had been left unmarked despite having a reputation for ghosting into the box at set pieces.

Northern Ireland came into the game in fits and starts with Best at the centre of the most constructive moves and hugely threatening while in possession. Unfortunately his colleagues failed to supply him with the ball regularly enough and the man-to-man marking job effected by Keith Newton of Blackburn Rovers kept him at bay. The end result was that George dropped back into deeper positions attracting even more attention. He often broke through the ranks but Derek Dougan wasted the best chances created.

Eric McMordie, who had accompanied Best on his original voyage across the Irish Sea to Manchester back in 1961, was less profligate grabbing an equaliser when George's overhead scissor-kick rebounded back off a defender and fell nicely for him to head home.

However, England regained the advantage with a goal from Lee which George himself would have been proud of. A devastating solo dribble brought the City striker a clear shot on goal - his smooth left foot finish nestling in the corner of the net.

Lee was also on hand to notch the final goal of the match from the spot after Geoff Hurst was bundled over in the area. Pat Jennings got his hands on the ball but could only deflect it high into the net.

SCOTLAND 1 NORTHERN IRELAND 1
HOME INTERNATIONAL 6 MAY 1969

THE LOWEST EVER crowd for an international at Hampden Park - 7,843 - witnessed a drab affair to match the Glasgow weather. Rain fell heavily all day but increased rapidly in the build up to kick-off.

Scotland had beaten Wales 5-2 a few days earlier in a game riddled with defensive errors on both sides and they clearly hadn't resolved any issues in training. The Irish attack had the better of most exchanges, including another goal created by Best and scored by McMordie. Once again the set-up was unintentional when a floated cross dropped invitingly off the bar for the Middlesbrough striker to head in once more.

The pre-match favourites drew level soon after half-time through Colin Stein who nodded in following a clever move which drew Northern Ireland's backline out of position.

With a little more luck Best would have earned both points as he dominated and tormented Scotland until the last kick of the game - a shot from wide in the area which whizzed across goal but just the wrong side of the post. Earlier he had had a goal chalked off for a handball in the build up.

NORTHERN IRELAND 0 WALES 0
HOME INTERNATIONAL 10 MAY 1969

DESPITE THE APPROACH of summer, rain continued to plague the UK and Ireland for most of the Home International week turning the Windsor Park pitch into a quagmire. This made life difficult for even the most skilled ball player. As a result neither team carved out any gilt-edged chances and the match finished goalless. However, the point did at least ensure Northern Ireland avoided the wooden spoon. Having been beaten by Scotland and England before this game that dubious honour belonged to Wales.

MANCHESTER UNITED 1 AC MILAN 0
EUROPEAN CUP SF 2ND LEG 15 MAY 1969

OLD TRAFFORD HAD accommodated 22,500 fans to watch the first leg on closed circuit television and just over 63,000 came through the turnstiles to see if United could turn the tide and reach the final in Madrid.

Tony Dunne was due to make a welcome return after recovering from his broken jaw but was laid low by a back injury. It was a huge disappointment as he was slated to mark the dangerous Pierino Prati. Francis Burns filled in with Denis Law passed fit.

Milan were content to see the game out and only committed themselves upfield when the chance to counter-attack allowed. United continually banged on the door but with Milan masters of the defensive arts so well practised in Italy, The Reds found it difficult to break through.

Their defence was finally breached in the 70th minute when Best helped set up Bobby Charlton. It was one of the few times George had beaten Anquilletti and he made sure it counted.

United continued to batter at AC, leaving them exposed at the back but Milan failed to take their few opportunities and almost paid a high price with just under a quarter of an hour to go when Paddy Crerand's lob seemed to have crossed the line before it was cleared. The referee felt it had been intercepted before the line but TV replays demonstrated the opposite. It was also obvious to the Stretford End who pelted the goalmouth and officials with a range of missiles causing a delay which in effect killed off any momentum the home side had built up. Keeper Fabio Cudicini was knocked unconscious by one of the objects.

United played with a verve which had been missing in recent weeks and well enough to win by a comfortable margin which only heightened the disappointment as their defence of the European Cup ended. Amazingly this was to be the last European club match of George's career.

MANCHESTER UNITED 3 LEICESTER CITY 2
DIVISION ONE 17 MAY 1969

THOUGH THE DOMESTIC season had finished just under a month earlier United had to extend the campaign due to international commitments and the European Cup semi-finals. The same side which almost upset the odds against Milan was given the chance to sign off the season and both sides treated the crowd to a fantastic opening. Three goals were scored in the first four minutes.

David Nish put Leicester ahead and there were many times throughout the game when they caused United real concern. George Best equalised and six minutes later Brian Kidd edged United into the lead. Willie Morgan had also found the net by the end and the 3-2 defeat sent The Foxes down. It may have been considered some form of retribution for all the defeats suffered at the hands of the same team. The fact that it saved Coventry managed by former United legend Noel Cantwell was another bonus for those of a red persuasion.

WALES 0 REST OF THE UNITED KINGDOM 1
INTERNATIONAL FRIENDLY 28 JULY 1969

A MATCH HELD to celebrate the investiture of Prince Charles pitted the Welsh national side, missing only Wyn Davies and David Powell from their usual full XI, against the remainder of the UK football federations at Cardiff City's Ninian Park.

A rare link up between Best and Francis Lee of Manchester City was little short of breathtaking considering they had never played on the same side before and the man from Maine Road hit the only goal of the game on 33 minutes, converting from a few yards out after Derek Dougan's shot came back off the defender's legs.

The full Rest of the United Kingdom starting line up saw Best, Pat Jennings and Derek Dougan represent Northern Ireland alongside Scotland represented by Archie Gemmell, Billy Bremner and John Hughes while England contributed Terry Cooper, Alan Mullery and Francis Lee plus the Charlton brothers Jackie and Bobby.

1968-69

Matt Busby's retirement overshadowed a season that failed to live-up to expectations. By finishing eleventh in the First Division and reaching the last four in defence of the European Cup, Busby's side fell some way short of the form that had seen them dominate English football in the sixties. A lower than expected league position might have been blamed on the need to properly defend the European Cup. Yet, as the previous season had shown, a United team at their best were more than capable of competing in the league and in Europe - especially as they only played eight matches in losing at the semi-final stage, a far cry from today's bloated tournament.

A real lack of fire power was an obvious problem as taking George Best and Denis Law out of the equation just 23 goals were shared amongst the other players. Not only that but the tally had dropped from 89 to a comparatively low 57 - a mark many other clubs were able to surpass with some ease. It was clear that United were badly missing the likes of David Herd, a regular contributor of 20 goals a season while his replacement, Brian Kidd, managed a solitary league goal and Bobby Charlton a mere six from midfield.

A failure to qualify for any of the European competitions was also a huge blow for a club recognised as pioneers in this field. Indeed, United's decline was so terminal that George had already played his last game in Europe - a tragedy for both Best and lovers of his all-action style of football on the continent.

Since his European debut against Sporting Lisbon in the Cup Winners' Cup in 1964, George had scored 11 goals in 34 games. Yet the mere statistics of his European career fail to do justice to the impact he had on the continental game. He made his debut at a time when the defensive philosophies of Hellenio Herrera's Inter Milan held sway - yet Best, through his performances against the likes of Benfica and Real Madrid, showed that old-fashioned virtues of skill, daring and speed combined with his own particular brand of balletic fearlessness could expose the most committed of defences.

Even in his last European game, against a team as defensively gifted as AC Milan, the trio of George, Denis and Bobby had the Italians hanging on for dear life in the last 20 minutes and grateful to a dubious goal-line decision to reach the final. AC went on to defeat Ajax 4-1 in Madrid - the last Italian winners of the tournament until 1985.

Best himself had suffered from some problems in front of goal and after a very steady opening saw his success tail away. It seemed that some defenders had worked out a way to play him which not only limited his effectiveness in front of goal but his ability to create chances for others. Once the crosses and passes started to dry up others began to question their ability to put away the few opportunities which did come their way. That led the player to take more and more upon himself which proved to the detriment of the team.

Busby's emotional farewell marked the end of an era at Old Trafford, certainly the most pivotal in the club's history. George Best had arrived at the tail end of a managerial reign that produced three great teams, five league titles, two FA Cups and, of course the European Cup that he, more than any other British figure, helped to popularise. Having inherited a bombed out stadium, a Nissan hut for a changing room and a car park for playing practise matches, Manchester United had been transformed into a sporting behemoth that left all other English clubs in its shadow.

Moreover Busby's achievements as a manager paved the way for the likes of Shankly, Clough, Revie and the other immortals to create teams in their own image. The total control over football matters Matt demanded from the United board in 1946 still resonates today and the cult of the manager would never have existed without the great man.

Finally Manchester United, from being the second club in the city when Matt took charge, were now synonymous with fast, free-flowing football, larger than life characters and a reliance on young talent. When people talk about playing football 'the Manchester United way' it is as obvious as mentioning that the game should played in a Brazilian or Italian way. This was Busby's ultimate legacy, as much as the the trophies and titles that came the club's way.

Yet while Busby's retirement came as little surprise - for George Best, European Footballer of the Year, the departure of a father figure and his replacement by Wilf McGuinness would eventually lead to the Irishman's frustration with the game. The search for a successor to the Godfather of Manchester United had been undertaken in the greatest secrecy yet it seemed that no manager was man enough to take on Busby's legacy.

Hence the appointment from within of McGuinness. Collyhurst born Wilf was named as Chief Coach rather than manager and was responsible for tactics, training and selection. Yet the total control Busby had demanded was missing. It was clear that McGuinness would have to succeed under Busby's auspices before he could branch out on his own.

DATE	OPPONENT	VENUE	SCORE	ATT'D	1	2	3	4	5	6	7	8	9	10	11
10 August	Everton	Old Trafford	2-1	61,311	Stepney	Brennan	Dunne	Crerand	Foulkes	Stiles	Best¹	Kidd	Charlton¹	Law	Aston
14 August	WBA	The Hawthorns	1-3	38,299	Stepney	Brennan	Dunne	Crerand	Foulkes	Stiles	Best	Kidd	Charlton¹	Law	Aston
17 August	Manchester City	Maine Road	0-0	63,052	Stepney	Kopel	Dunne	Fitzpatrick	Sadler	Stiles	Best	Gowling	Charlton	Kidd	Aston
21 August	Coventry City	Old Trafford	1-0	51,201	Stepney	Kopel	Dunne	Fitzpatrick	Sadler	Stiles	Ryan¹	Kidd	Charlton	Burns	Best
24 August	Chelsea	Old Trafford	0-4	55,114	Stepney	Kopel	Dunne	Crerand	Sadler	Stiles	Ryan	Kidd	Charlton	Burns	Best
28 August	Tottenham Hotspur	Old Trafford	3-1	62,649	Stepney	Brennan	Dunne	Fitzpatrick²	Sadler	Stiles	Morgan	Kidd	Charlton	Law	Best
31 August	Sheffield Wednesday	Hillsborough	4-5	50,490	Stepney	Brennan	Dunne	Fitzpatrick	Sadler	Stiles	Morgan	Kidd	Charlton¹	Law²	Best¹
7 September	West Ham United	Old Trafford	1-1	63,274	Stepney	Dunne	Burns	Fitzpatrick	Foulkes	Stiles	Morgan	Sadler	Charlton	Law¹	Best
14 September	Burnley	Turf Moor	0-1	32,935	Stepney	Dunne	Burns	Fitzpatrick	Foulkes	Stiles	Morgan	Sadler	Charlton	Law	Best
21 September	Newcastle United	Old Trafford	3-1	47,262	Stepney	Dunne	Burns	Crerand	Sadler	Stiles	Morgan	Fitzpatrick	Charlton	Law¹	Best²
5 October	Arsenal	Old Trafford	0-0	61,843	Stepney	Dunne	Burns	Crerand	Foulkes	Stiles	Morgan	Fitzpatrick	Charlton	Law	Best
9 October	Tottenham Hotspur	White Hart Lane	2-2	56,205	Stepney	Dunne	Burns	Crerand¹	Foulkes	Stiles	Morgan	Fitzpatrick	Charlton	Law¹	Best¹
19 October	Southampton	Old Trafford	1-2	46,526	Stepney	Kopel	Dunne	Crerand	Foulkes	Stiles	Morgan	Sadler	Charlton	Sartori	Best¹
26 October	QPR	Loftus Road	3-2	31,138	Stepney	Brennan	Dunne	Crerand	Sadler	Stiles	Morgan	Kidd	Charlton	Law	Best²
2 November	Leeds United	Old Trafford	0-0	53,839	Stepney	Brennan	Dunne	Crerand	Sadler	Stiles	Morgan	Kidd	Charlton	Law	Best
9 November	Sunderland	Roker Park	1-1+	33,151	Stepney	Brennan	Dunne	Crerand	Sadler	Stiles	Morgan	Kidd	Charlton	Sartori	Best
16 November	Ipswich Town	Old Trafford	0-0	45,796	Stepney	Brennan	Dunne	Crerand	James	Stiles	Morgan	Kidd	Charlton	Law	Best
23 November	Stoke City	Victoria Ground	0-0	30,562	Stepney	Kopel	Dunne	Crerand	James	Stiles	Morgan	Best	Charlton	Fitzpatrick	Sartori
30 November	Wolves	Old Trafford	2-0	50,165	Stepney	Kopel	Dunne	Crerand	Sadler	Stiles	Morgan	Sartori	Charlton	Law¹	Best¹
7 December	Leicester City	Filbert Street	1-2	36,303	Stepney	Dunne	Burns	Crerand	Sadler	Stiles	Morgan	Sartori	Charlton	Law¹	Best
14 December	Liverpool	Old Trafford	1-0	55,354	Stepney	Dunne	Burns	Crerand	James	Stiles	Best	Sadler	Charlton	Law	Sartori
21 December	Southampton	The Dell	0-2	26,194	Stepney	Dunne	Burns	Crerand	James	Stiles	Best	Sadler	Charlton	Law	Sartori
26 December	Arsenal	Highbury	0-3	62,300	Stepney	Dunne	Burns	Crerand	James	Stiles	Best	Sadler	Charlton¹	Law	Kidd
11 January	Leeds United	Old Trafford	1-2	48,145	Stepney	Dunne	Burns	Crerand	James	Stiles	Best	Fitzpatrick	Charlton¹	Law	Sartori
18 January	Sunderland	Old Trafford	4-1	45,670	Rimmer	Dunne	Burns	Fitzpatrick	James	Stiles	Morgan	Sartori	Charlton	Law	Best¹
1 February	Ipswich Town	Portman Road	0-1	30,837	Stepney	Fitzpatrick	Dunne	Crerand	James	Sadler	Morgan	Kidd	Charlton¹	Law³	Best
15 February	Wolves	Molineux	2-2	44,023	Stepney	Fitzpatrick	Dunne	Crerand	James	Stiles	Morgan	Kidd	Charlton¹	Law	Best¹
8 March	Manchester City	Old Trafford	0-1	63,264	Stepney	Brennan	Fitzpatrick	Crerand	Foulkes	Stiles	Morgan	Kidd	Charlton	Law	Best
10 March	Everton	Goodison Park	0-0	57,514	Stepney	Brennan	Dunne	Crerand	James	Stiles	Best	Kidd	Fitzpatrick	Sadler	Aston
15 March	Chelsea	Stamford Bridge	2-3	60,436	Stepney	Fitzpatrick	Dunne	Crerand	James¹	Stiles	Morgan	Kidd	Sadler	Law¹	Best

Date	Opponent	Venue	Result	Att.											
19 March	QPR	Old Trafford	8-1	36,638	Stepney	Fitzpatrick	Dunne	Crerand	James	Stiles[1]	Morgan[3]	Kidd[1]	Aston[1]	Law	Best[2]
22 March	Sheffield Wednesday	Old Trafford	1-0	45,527	Stepney	Fitzpatrick	Dunne	Crerand	James	Stiles	Morgan	Kidd	Best[1]	Law	Aston
24 March	Stoke City	Old Trafford	1-1	39,931	Stepney	Fitzpatrick	Dunne	Crerand	James	Stiles	Morgan	Kidd	Aston[1]	Law	Best
29 March	West Ham United	Upton Park	0-0	41,546	Stepney	Fitzpatrick	Dunne	Crerand	James	Stiles	Ryan	Kidd	Aston	Law	Best
31 March	Nottingham Forest	City Ground	1-0	41,892	Stepney	Fitzpatrick	Stiles	Crerand	James	Sadler	Ryan	Kidd	Aston	Law	Best[1]
2 April	WBA	Old Trafford	2-1	38,846	Stepney	Fitzpatrick	Stiles	Crerand	James	Sadler	Morgan	Ryan	Aston	Kidd	Best[2]
5 April	Nottingham Forest	Old Trafford	3-1	51,952	Stepney	Fitzpatrick[1]	Stiles	Crerand	James	Sadler	Morgan[2]	Kidd	Aston	Law	Best[1]
8 April	Coventry City	Highfield Road	1-2	45,402	Stepney	Fitzpatrick	Stiles	Crerand	James	Sadler	Morgan	Kidd	Aston	Charlton	Best
12 April	Newcastle United	St James' Park	0-2	46,379	Rimmer	Fitzpatrick	Stiles	Crerand	James	Sadler	Morgan	Kidd	Charlton	Law	Best
19 April	Burnley	Old Trafford	2-0 +	52,626	Rimmer	Brennan	Fitzpatrick	Crerand	Foulkes	Stiles	Morgan	Kidd	Aston	Law	Best[1]
17 May	Leicester City	Old Trafford	3-2	45,860	Rimmer	Brennan	Burns	Crerand	Foulkes	Stiles	Morgan[1]	Kidd	Charlton	Law[1]	Best[1]

FA Cup

Date	Opponent	Venue	Result	Att.											
4 January	Exeter City	St James' Park	3-1	18,500	Stepney	Dunne(A)	Burns	Fitzpatrick[1]	James	Stiles	Best	Kidd[1]	Charlton	Law	Sartori
25 January	Watford	Old Trafford	1-1	63,498	Rimmer	Kopel	Dunne(A)	Fitzpatrick	James	Stiles	Morgan	Best	Charlton	Law[1]	Sartori
3 February	Watford	Vicarage Road	2-0	34,000	Stepney	Fitzpatrick	Dunne(A)	Crerand	James	Stiles	Morgan	Kidd	Charlton	Law[2]	Best
8 February	Birmingham City	St Andrews	2-2	52,500	Stepney	Fitzpatrick	Dunne(A)	Crerand	James	Stiles	Morgan	Kidd	Charlton	Law[1]	Best[1]
24 February	Birmingham City	Old Trafford	6-2	61,932	Stepney	Fitzpatrick	Dunne(A)	Crerand[1]	James	Stiles	Morgan[1]	Kidd[1]	Charlton	Law[3]	Best[1]
1 March	Everton	Goodison Park	0-1	63,464	Stepney	Fitzpatrick	Dunne(A)	Crerand	James	Stiles	Morgan	Kidd	Charlton	Law	Best

European Cup

Date	Opponent	Venue	Result	Att.											
18 September	Waterford	Lansdowne Rd	3-1	48,000	Stepney	Dunne(A)	Burns	Crerand	Foulkes	Stiles	Best	Law[3]	Charlton	Law	Sadler
2 October	Waterford	Old Trafford	7-1	41,750	Stepney	Dunne(A)	Burns[1]	Crerand	Foulkes	Stiles[1]	Best	Law[4]	Charlton[1]	Sadler	Kidd
26 February	Rapid Vienna	Old Trafford	3-0	61,932	Stepney	Fitzpatrick	Dunne(A)	Crerand	James	Stiles	Morgan[1]	Kidd	Charlton	Law	Best[2]
5 March	Rapid Vienna	Wiener Stadion	0-0	52,000	Stepney	Fitzpatrick	Dunne(A)	Crerand	James	Stiles	Morgan	Kidd	Charlton	Sadler	Best
23 April	AC Milan	Stadio San Siro	0-2	80,000	Rimmer	Brennan	Fitzpatrick	Crerand	Foulkes	Stiles	Morgan	Kidd	Charlton	Law	Best
15 May	AC Milan	Old Trafford	1-0	63,103	Rimmer	Brennan	Burns	Crerand	Foulkes	Stiles	Morgan	Kidd	Charlton[1]	Law	Best

Inter-Continental Cup

Date	Opponent	Venue	Result	Att.											
25 September	Estudiantes	Boca Juniors	0-1	55000	Stepney	Dunne(A)	Burns	Crerand	Foulkes	Stiles	Morgan	Sadler	Charlton	Law	Best
16 October	Estudiantes	Old Trafford	1-1	63,500	Stepney	Brennan	Dunne(A)	Crerand	Foulkes	Sadler	Morgan[1]	Kidd	Charlton	Law	Best

1969-70
BLOW-OUT

INEVITABY THERE WERE question marks over how Wilf McGuinness would approach managing Manchester United. Busby had not only been a visionary leader who brought success to the club but did so with a footballing philosophy and style unequalled in the English game. Now McGuinness had to not only maintain that style but add the substance required to succeed in a much more professional environment.

During this period in English football managers had altered training techniques and tactics and that had contributed to closer competition and more professionalism. McGuinness needed to add the steel United blatantly lacked during Busby's last campaign.

According to many, only an experienced man with plenty of time served at the top would be able to take on Busby's mantel. They believed McGuinness had not been the first choice and that a host of names had been linked with the post at various stages since it became known Busby would be standing down. However, it was also acknowledged that Wilf had been part of the structure for almost a decade. Few were better steeped in the ways and methods Sir Matt had employed to such effect and there was reason for optimism.

CRYSTAL PALACE 2 MANCHESTER UNITED 2
DIVISION ONE 9 AUGUST 1969

THE FIRST PRE-SEASON of the post-Busby era began well as 17 goals were scored in three friendly ties and there was a note of expectancy for the new season.

Nobby Stiles was out through suspension and Bill Foulkes recalled despite retiring and taking a place on the coaching staff. At 37 years of age and with a knee kept working by running repairs after thousands of tough tackles over the seasons, he was somewhat worryingly reckoned to be the club's best option at centre half. A lack of form by Steve James the previous season was a huge factor in the return.

United looked keen to push on up front. One of the first pieces of serious action saw a flowing move up the right with the ball before the move was switched quickly to the left. George Best advanced towards the area and his shot was put out for a corner by John Jackson. An impish skip down the middle by Best gave Willie Morgan a chance to run until he was baulked by Roger Hoy. However, it was Palace who opened the scoring after Jimmy Rimmer dropped the ball over his own line when he seemed to have been shoved.

These heavy tactics had helped The Eagles get out of Division Two and served them well in their first ever top flight game. Charlton and Best certainly found it tricky to make progress but Morgan seemed a little freer and set up a header for Charlton before the Scot netted himself to equalise at 2-2 after a set up by Law.

MANCHESTER UNITED 0 EVERTON 2
DIVISION ONE 13 AUGUST 1969

UNITED HAD FOUR defenders out with injury: John Fitzpatrick, Steve James, Nobby Stiles (who had served his ban but succumbed to an injury in training) and Tony Dunne (following an ankle knock picked-up at Selhurst Park). Somewhat predictably in those circumstances Everton totally outclassed The Reds and their 2-0 victory on the night was more

than deserved. Alan Ball got the first with an excellent drive after he found space in midfield.

The dominance of Ball centrally was crucial and meant United had limited chances. Gordon West in goal was tested by a couple of shots from Law and Best but all in all this was a disappointing opening to the home campaign.

MANCHESTER UNITED 1 SOUTHAMPTON 4
DIVISION ONE 16 AUGUST 1969

SOUTHAMPTON HAD DONE well at Old Trafford the previous term winning by the odd goal in five and were embarking on their first European campaign as a result of achieving equally impressive results elsewhere. That made them a good side to beat in terms of confidence and United's pressure turned into an advantage on eight minutes when Morgan found the net.

However, things were still not together at the back and Ron Davies scored all four

Saints goals including three from headers as the visitors raided down the flanks - usually down their left where John Sydenham gave Shay Brennan a hard time and provided telling crosses.

United were shell-shocked after such a good start and few forward players were able to react. It proved to be the 685th and last game of Bill Foulkes' distinguished career and a sad night on which to bow out of a superb United career.

EVERTON 3 MANCHESTER UNITED 0
DIVISION ONE 19 AUGUST 1969

HAVING SECURED JUST one point from the opening three games, Wilf McGuinness decided on a drastic course of action and one which would have been unthinkable just a few seasons ago. McGuinness dropped Bobby Charlton and Denis Law for the short trip down the East Lancs Road to face an Everton side which had beaten The Reds just six days earlier. Also axed were Jimmy Rimmer and Shay

Brennan following the concession of eight goals in the opening three games.

David Sadler, who had at least provided some resistance to Southampton, lined up alongside Paul Edwards. John Fitzpatrick played at right back with Don Givens and John Aston upfront.

Everton were top courtesy of a 100% record and despite those notable changes in personnel there was no transformation in United's performance. Once again the midfield was the key area and once more United had nothing to offer. Alan Ball, Johnny Morrissey and Joe Royle providing the home side with a comfortable win.

George Best had good spells and linked well with Brian Kidd at times but was still for the most part out of sorts. Whether

that would be enough for him to escape a dropping would be seen in due course. Nevertheless the McGuinness reign had begun badly with two games against that season's champions Everton, one point won out of a possible eight and 11 goals conceded.

WOLVES 0 MANCHESTER UNITED 0
DIVISION ONE 23 AUGUST 1969

LAW AND CHARLTON returned for the trip to Wolves. Jimmy Rimmer, who was deemed better at crosses than Alex Stepney, also came back. Tony Dunne looked set to return but failed to make it. Ian Ure, the first player bought by Wilf McGuinness, was introduced to arrest the defensive slide of recent weeks at a cost of £80,000. Something had to be done and on the evidence of this match

alone it seemed money well spent. There were still problems at either end but an assured performance from Ure calmed his colleagues and provided the backline with a little more belief. Most of United's attacking moves came towards the close when Best and Kidd combined well but Denis Law aggravated a groin strain he had been carrying close to the end to capping a mixed night for The Reds.

MANCHESTER UNITED 0 NEWCASTLE UNITED 0
DIVISION ONE 27 AUGUST 1969

TONY DUNNE CAME back but Law was ruled out again meaning Givens got another chance. Alex Stepney was reinstated too and although he did drop a cross he and his defence were otherwise sound.

Newcastle were just as comfortable and happy to settle for a point. The next hope was that the forwards would start to gel again. There were a couple of good chances but ultimately too little threat was posed.

MANCHESTER UNITED 3 SUNDERLAND 1
DIVISION ONE 30 AUGUST 1969

THAT DESIRE FOR more cavalier forward play came up trumps within seven minutes of the match starting as Best, who had already gone close with a header from Bobby Charlton's cross, rounded off a flowing move. Brian Kidd seemed to have been bundled over during the early stages but no penalty was awarded.

It was already looking to be a long and arduous season for Sunderland who had been thrashed 4-0 at home by Manchester City during midweek. Maybe resigned to their fate in this game The Wearsiders never looked likely to run United close. Further goals from Kidd and Don Givens, with his first for the club at senior level, made the points safe.

MANCHESTER UNITED 1 MIDDLESBROUGH 0
LEAGUE CUP 2ND RD 3 SEPTEMBER 1969

A CUP DRAW, even at the early stage of a competition, offers little more than a chance that a club can be paired with a team at the top of Division One or a team 92nd in the Football League. United did fairly well drawing Second Division Middlesbrough. However, with The Reds lowly position in the top flight there was little to choose between two sides who were only separated by a handful of league placings.

United went through courtesy of a David Sadler goal and despite some scares were relatively good value for the win.

LEEDS UNITED 2 MANCHESTER UNITED 2
DIVISION ONE 6 SEPTEMBER 1969

BEATING MIDDLESBROUGH WAS a boost but in the league United were struggling and the game at champions Leeds United would be a tough test. United's difficulties were laid bare when Wednesday's hero David Sadler managed to put through his own goal. He had jumped to challenge Mick Jones for a Johnny Giles centre but headed it over the stranded Alex Stepney. It was rough justice on the defence and particularly the keeper who had shown great anticipation and handling skills when claiming a number of high balls pumped into his area.

United had caused a few problems but George Best was kept busy by Paul Reaney. That was until after the break when the full back was caught out after the ball ran loose in the area. George gambled and was rewarded with a goal from close in. Maybe Reaney was surprised at losing a battle with the wingman. He was certainly lost for words and pace when Best got his foot to Bobby Charlton's pass then ran across the face of the area and unleashed an unstoppable effort which beat Gary Sprake all ends up with less than 10 minutes remaining. The shot was so well placed that it clipped in off the post.

The Reds looked likely to become the first side to win at Leeds in Division One for over a year. However, Billy Bremner once again showed that his game was as much about silk as steel with an elegant overhead kick to ensure a share of the spoils for Revie's men.

MANCHESTER UNITED 1 LIVERPOOL 0
DIVISION ONE 13 SEPTEMBER 1969

LIVERPOOL WERE UNBEATEN so far and their defeat to United, who held the Anfielders in attack before a Best inspired second half revival earned The Reds the points.

At times United eased the pressure on their own goal and Best cut a 'willow the wisp' figure not only high up the field but back in his own penalty area. At the business end of the pitch few Liverpool players seemed to track his runs.

He turned the tide, first beating Ron Yeats for pace before sending a cross over for Morgan to volley against the bar. Morgan's goal on 69 minutes was created when George out-jumped Yeats, nodding on for Morgan to drive low to record United's most impressive result of the season so far.

NORTHERN IRELAND 0 USSR 0
WORLD CUP QUALIFIER 10 SEPTEMBER 1969

A DOUR PERFORMANCE concluded with Northern Ireland dropping their first points of the qualification campaign. The East European side were largely responsible for such a poor game due to their over concentration on defence. Revaz Dzodzuashvili watched Best well and kept him away from creating too much danger. Without an inventive force at even half pace the home side looked stuck though still had moments.

George was patient and waited for his chances seeing more of the game later on while at the back he helped cancel out some of the few threats raised. Best went close with a header from a Jimmy Nicholson cross and McMordie set up Dougan but a good save by Evgeni Rudakov kept the scoreline blank. A scramble just yards out also failed to break the deadlock.

SHEFFIELD WEDNESDAY 1 MANCHESTER UNITED 3
DIVISION ONE 17 SEPTEMBER 1969

TWO GEORGE BEST goals within a minute changed the game and won the points for Manchester United when it seemed poor play from both sides and a host of niggly fouls would see the match amount to little more than a run of the mill draw. Brian Kidd had notched on 11 minutes, sweeping in a corner on the right Best both won and then took.

United looked untroubled at the back

until Graham Pugh equalised. Less than 10 minutes remained when Willie Morgan evaded two challenges and then found Best who hit a sweet left foot shot.

After the restart he took the ball down the left, beat a couple of men on his way to the right hand side of the area from where he unleashed yet another unstoppable shot.

ARSENAL 2 MANCHESTER UNITED 2
DIVISION ONE 20 SEPTEMBER 1969

MANY PLAYERS HAD thought as much, but Frank McClintock was possibly the first to admit it so forcibly after this latest George Best spectacular.

Despite anticipating what George would do and even when forcing him into the least threatening option, most defenders discovered there was no way of stopping Best at full tilt. The Arsenal midfielder was simply powerless to prevent himself being outstripped for both pace and skills which allowed David Sadler to net an equaliser at 2-2 and add to the goal Best himself had grabbed earlier in the game as United maintained an impressive run of results against the top teams in the country.

MANCHESTER UNITED 2 WREXHAM 0
LEAGUE CUP 3RD RD 23 SEPTEMBER 1969

UNITED HAD A very modest record in the League Cup. Reaching the fourth round was as deep as The Reds had ventured into the tournament thus far. Wrexham of Division Four rose to the occasion and nobody more than Mickey Evans who contained Best for long periods despite going down to an early goal from Brian Kidd who converted John Aston's cross and beat former Old Trafford keeper David Gaskell.

Ian Moir and Albert Kinsey, who were given little chance at United, were paired in attack and both should have scored.

Steve Ingle shot tamely at Alex Stepney when he had the goal at his mercy but it was in his strong handling of attacks as a full back that he proved his real worth to The Robins. United's progress was assured when Kidd dummied a John Fitzpatrick pass which ran to Best who hit a low shot past his former teammate.

MANCHESTER UNITED 5 WEST HAM UNITED 2
DIVISION ONE 27 SEPTEMBER 1969

THE REDS STORMED The Hammers from the start, building a 2-0 lead inside 13 minutes and although George Best was an expected star, West Ham's Clyde Best also emerged with great credit for his side despite such a wide margin of defeat. Alex Stepney had to make a number of good saves from the young Bermudan who notched his side's opener.

Bobby Charlton, who had failed to score since the opening day of the season, made it 3-1. Clyde Best sent in a cross for Geoff Hurst to head in but goals from Best and Kidd ensured United restored a comfortable lead well before the end to extend their unbeaten streak to 10 games under their new manager.

DERBY COUNTY 2 MANCHESTER UNITED 0
DIVISION ONE 4 OCTOBER 1969

UNITED'S GOOD RUN was severely tested at Derby County who had became the last Football League team to lose their unbeaten record when Sheffield Wednesday had triumphed a week previously. The Rams certainly had the better of the opening stages with two very disappointing goals from a United perspective winning the game.

Kevin Hector put the ball and Alex Stepney in the back of the net in scoring the first when he could easily have been pulled up for a foul. The same player was lucky when John Fitzpatrick got a touch on a through ball which inadvertently set him up for a second as, until that point, he had been yards offside.

It was certainly an injustice for The Reds who had two goals ruled out. Ian Ure was judged offside when Brian Kidd headed in even though the Scottish defender was yards away from the ball at the time.

Unfortunately a number of very good chances were also missed. England under-23 international Roy McFarland was detailed to mark Best but was rarely tested. George seemed out of sorts and too keen to make a mug out of the young full back rather than combine with his teammates which bought the Derby man vital time.

SOUTHAMPTON 0 MANCHESTER UNITED 3
DIVISION ONE 8 OCTOBER 1969

UNITED REVERSED THE outcome of the first clash with Southampton recording a convincing win at The Dell. Best came into the action early, testing defenders before taking the ball from Brian Kidd

and giving United the lead midway through the first half. Midfield and attack were functioning better as a unit which helped George raise his game after the disappointments at Derby.

Perhaps the pivotal moment in the match was Stepney's save from Jimmy Gabriel in the first attack The Saints mounted after going behind. Francis Burns, who looked comfortable in an unaccustomed central midfield role with Bobby Charlton, bagged the second when a John Aston cross was fumbled by Eric Martin.

A very sorry looking keeper was rounded by Kidd for the last goal of the night when one-on-one. Southampton missed Ron Davies and John Sydenham who had been so dangerous in August.

MANCHESTER UNITED 2 IPSWICH TOWN 1
Division One 11 October 1969

David Sadler reached 150 games in the league but a bruised knee kept Best's participation in doubt until the last minute. In the end he was passed fit enough to take his place in the side as was Tony Dunne. Within a minute George made it 11 goals from 11 games. sliding the ball past David Best - no relation - with great accuracy.

Ipswich struggled to cope at first, especially Mick Mills who put in a clattering challenge late on after the frustration got the better of him. The defender had a fairly decent game all things considered and even managed to equalise after 15 minutes.

An increasingly confident Brian Kidd edged United back into the lead before the break. The teenager was enjoying a leading role after a disappointing first full season.

A solid performance at the back ensured the slender lead remained safe.

BURNLEY 0 MANCHESTER UNITED 0
League Cup 4th Rd 14 October 1969

A high tempo game and one of the finest exhibitions of football the sides had put in all season, ended goalless, although it whetted appetites for the replay.

Peter Mellor saved well from Willie Morgan and Arthur Bellamy drew similar responses from Alex Stepney.

George Best had had an x-ray on his leg the previous day but was cleared to play and was quite a presence in the United side and rarely failed to be involved. He had no clear cut chances himself but fashioned opportunities for others.

MANCHESTER UNITED 1 NOTTINGHAM FOREST 1
DIVISION ONE 18 OCTOBER 1969

ANOTHER INJURY, THIS time the problem was sore shins, had to be seen off before Best could take his place. Effectively the match was decided by penalties - those both awarded and not by referee Harry New.

United were denied after a foul on George Best, which looked half a yard inside the area but was adjudged to have taken place outside. A free-kick was given on the line but wasted. David Sadler's challenge on Dave Hilley was definitely inside the area and was punished when Ian Story-Moore netted from the spot. The taker seemed to have won himself another chance as he gambled on a 50/50

challenge for the ball with Alex Stepney. The keeper arrived a second later and unceremoniously took the forward out in his attempts to stretch out a foot, however play was waved on.

With a few seconds remaining Bobby Charlton had his legs taken from underneath him. There was no penalty but this time an indirect free kick was given.

Then Charlton played Best in with a pinpoint pass after spotting a run which exposed the keeper. There was still work to do but a top drawer finish ensured a share of the spoils.

MANCHESTER UNITED 1 BURNLEY 0
LEAGUE CUP 4TH RD REPLAY 20 OCTOBER 1969

FORMER CLARET WILLIE Morgan WAS the major doubt for this League Cup replay with Burnley who decided a tight marking policy would increase their chances of keeping the increasingly dominant George Best at bay.

Les Latcham was the man charged with the responsibility and he was often joined by other defenders who put in robust efforts when they grouped around the winger.

United were weakened at the back by the absence of John Fitzpatrick during the opening period but managed to re-arrange well enough to resist, despite having to bring on forward Carlo Sartori. United were comfortable winners once a 54th minute penalty was won for Peter

Jones handling Brian Kidd's header. Burnley were under intense pressure at the time which induced Jones' moment of madness. George Best slid in the spot kick.

A knock taken in the game led to George withdrawing from the Northern Ireland squad to face the Soviet Union 48 hours after kick-off. Unfortunately, Best was the one player who could make a difference for his country in the battle to reach the World Cup finals and was forced to remain at home nursing bruised shins. As United battled on a number of fronts, six demanding games in under three weeks had taken their toll and his national team unfortunately lost out.

An unbeaten three match run had seen

Northern Ireland topped Group 4 giving them a real chance of making it to Mexico. With just two matches remaining, the prospect of a place in the finals for the first time in 12 years beckoned and with it a stage George Best would have relished.

As the Soviet Union had a game in hand, the Irish needed something from the match in Moscow - even a draw would see them through. However, defeat would all but end any hopes as a journey to Turkey, who were without a single point and had only scored one goal, was unlikely to prove a tall order for the Soviets in the final group game.

USSR recorded a 2-0 win courtesy of a goal in each half, then beat the Turks 3-1 to book their place. It should have been one of the proudest weeks of his career but this was a result which would haunt Best later on in life, as it was the closest he ever came to representing his country at an international tournament.

WEST BROMWICH ALBION 2 MANCHESTER UNITED 1
DIVISION ONE 25 OCTOBER 1969

DESPITE MISSING OUT for Northern Ireland, George was back in the United line-up for the subsequent club game at The Hawthorns but the fact he was fit just 72 hours after he should have been pulling on his county's shirt incurred the wrath of the Northern Irish FA who questioned why he had to play a club match just 48 hours before the vital international.

The fact was that George may have been rested had United had other options. Denis Law was hoping for a recall but after feeling his groin in a Lancashire Cup game earlier in the week was always battling against the odds. Willie Morgan and John Fitzpatrick were also missing. Nevertheless George still refused to wear shin-pads despite the hammerings his legs routinely took.

United were on the back foot from the start as Albion sought to earn their first home win of the season. The Reds were hampered by losing John Aston early on, although they took the lead when Brian Kidd nodded in after a corner had hit a post and bounced back into play.

However, two very deserved goals within ten minutes through the impressive Tony Brown and Bobby Hope, who lashed in after Alex Stepney could only parry a rasping shot, turned the match around.

At one stage it seemed this would be a good day for United. Brown had a penalty saved but there was no one able to capitalise on that good fortune. Best had a quiet game and as a result the United attack lacked the drive that had served them so well in recent weeks.

Away from the British club scene, some of the Estudiantes players who had behaved so poorly against United were banned after similar antics in that year's clash with AC Milan. Clash seemed to be the operative word as the match descended into something akin to hand-to-hand combat rather than football. For the record, AC won 4-2 on aggregate.

MANCHESTER UNITED 1 STOKE CITY 1
DIVISION ONE 1 NOVEMBER 1969

BEST WAS DOUBTFUL for the game with Stoke having been taken ill during training on Thursday but recovered in time. Denis Law returned, taking the number seven jersey for his first appearance in ten weeks - The Lawman looked sharp despite such a lengthy lay-off.

Harry Dowd, on loan from Manchester City, was in goal for The Potters and saw plenty of shots rain in from Best but dealt with them easily enough. Stoke's exhaustive marking forced Best to resort to chancing his arm from distance as Tony Waddington's team allowed him space on the flanks but closed him down when he got near the box.

George did have a role in United's goal, heading Tony Dunne's cross on for Bobby Charlton to net. Apart from that there wasn't much in front of him so options were limited.

Brian Kidd looked a square peg in a round hole and really struggled to partner Law effectively. A single goal lead is always precarious and Harry Burrows' shot which went in off the post gained a share of the points.

COVENTRY CITY 1 MANCHESTER UNITED 2
DIVISION ONE 8 NOVEMBER 1969

NOEL CANTWELL TOLD his troops that the key to holding United out was to stop Best at all costs, as giving him the freedom of the pitch could lead to a roasting. Their mission was to cut off his supply of the ball and his international colleague Dave Clements was the man detailed to carry out a man-to-man marking job.

The former United skipper's words were prophetic but ultimately did his side no good as George sat deeper where he had more space and still caused as much trouble as he would have done in and around the penalty area. However, Coventry were the better side going forward during the early part of the game and only failed to grab a healthy lead through poor finishing and good defending.

Three minutes before the break George Best took on three defenders in one direction then pushed the ball out for John Aston who centred for Sartori to score. Brian Kidd remained out of the side, though in fairness Sartori was doing little wrong and he saw plenty of the ball when United hauled themselves back into the match as defenders crowding Best created space.

On the other hand Denis Law for the most part couldn't apply anything like a competent finish. The adrenalin which got him through his return seemed to have deserted him although he did connect with one pass George played through the middle that left the Coventry rearguard dumfounded.

A very good finish from 20 yards gave Bill Glazier no hope and cancelled out Ernie Hunt's leveller.

DERBY COUNTY 0 MANCHESTER UNITED 0
League Cup 5th Rd 12 November 1969

DERBY WERE A side capable of challenging for honours and expertly guided by playmaker Dave Mackay, they masterminded a great attacking display and pressed hard for a goal. United defended stoically but there was no other choice. Every single player had work to do in defence but thankfully kept The Rams at bay.

United were bringing more attention to themselves away from the pitch especially with Willie Morgan and Brian Kidd being left out of various games leading to rumours of unrest.

The Reds barely threatened in the first half and although they got into the game after the resumption they were never as dangerous as their hosts. Pairings in various areas of the field were only effective on occasion.

Bobby Charlton and Francis Burns gained some control of the engine room helping Carlo Sartori and John Aston to become real dangers but more would usually have been expected from another duo - Law and Best.

Unfortunately each was kept quiet for the most part and a way through could not be fashioned with a replay at Old Trafford needed.

MANCHESTER CITY 4 MANCHESTER UNITED 0
Division One 15 November 1969

CITY WERE RELIEVED to have the two Mikes - Doyle and Summerbee - cleared of any injury doubts for this derby tussle. David Sadler was a real concern for United after having stitches in a leg wound suffered against Derby. The Reds looked to display serious intent and could have scored within seconds when Aston took a quick throw from Francis Burns then burst down the left before squaring for Law but the ball skimmed off the striker's head and out for a goal kick. Law was disappointed not to at least test Joe Corrigan and failed to get a further opportunity as that was United's sole chance of the game.

Ian Bowyer had a snap chance for the home side but couldn't adapt in time leaving Stepney with an easy save but that was the signal for one way traffic and a first City win over United at Maine Road for ten years.

Neil Young managed to squeeze one in from wide with a miscued cross. Colin Bell never stopped running in midfield and grabbed two richly deserved goals including the one which made it 4-0 a minute from the end.

From 1 to 11 City were outstanding while United looked like a team of strangers, a reflection of the shifting power in Mancunian football.

MANCHESTER UNITED 1 DERBY COUNTY 0
LEAGUE CUP 5TH RD REPLAY 19 NOVEMBER 1969

DERBY LOOKED AS impressive as they had all season in their two games with The Reds so far that term. Yet Best's genius flickered only occasionally although he essentially won the tie in the end. The ball seemed to stick between George's heels for large parts of the evening making it easy for defenders to break up United attacks. There were, of course, others capable of prising a way through defences but no one seemed able to get round the sturdy Rams defence.

Aston did score but saw his effort ruled out for foul play in the build up. Les Green made a tremendous save from Bobby Charlton and, later, a nonchalant Denis Law flick drifted just wide. However, a sublime spell where Best was untouchable sealed the win. One of his many surges during which he played a one-two with Law, showing the extent of their understanding, ended with a low shot thudding against the post and rebounding kindly for Brian Kidd. Derby had chances but nothing clear cut as United's defence watched them well although some last ditch heroics were still required.

On the same evening George Best looked so patchy, Pele claimed his 1000th goal as a professional. A 78th minute penalty for Santos against Vasco Da Gama at the Maracana Stadium saw the game stopped as players and fans hailed the Brazilian great.

MANCHESTER UNITED 3 TOTTENHAM HOTSPUR 1
DIVISION ONE 22 NOVEMBER 1969

DENIS LAW FINALLY succumbed to a long list of injuries that had plagued him over recent months. He had been replaced in the last minute of the League Cup tie and Carlo Sartori, who came on for a few seconds of the victory, partnered Brian Kidd up front. The decision to put a youngster before him gave Willie Morgan some food for thought.

Based solely upon the scoreline United seemed to win the match with ease but in reality matters were far tighter. Jimmy Greaves, possibly the greatest goalscorer of the decade, should have bagged at least a hat-trick but missed a number of chances after doing the hard work and getting in on the keeper. Alex Stepney 's anticipation had a huge effect but Greaves would have expected to finish off those types of chances.

United went ahead when Francis Burns headed in Paul Edwards' free-kick before Charlton notched after running on to a crafty headed pass from Best and claimed a brace with a thunderous effort from another free-kick before the end after Chivers had pulled one back for Spurs.

BURNLEY 1 MANCHESTER UNITED 1
DIVISION ONE 29 NOVEMBER 1969

NOBBY STILES WAS finally restored to the first team, six months after his last outing, complications following his cartilage operation having finally settled down. He had damaged the knee once again in the reserves causing further delay. Paul Edwards kept his place at the back with Stiles operating in midfield.

Snow flurries gave the surface a white tinge but failed to cause problems under foot. George Best set up Bobby Charlton in the first attack of the game but his effort was cleared. The Clarets went up the other end but were also thwarted. Bobby Charlton got through in the fifth minute after taking control of a bouncing ball, his shot seemed goal bound until Peter Mellor palmed it away, Les Latcham tried to clear but wasn't quick enough to stop George Best scoring. United continued to dominate and Best missed two very good chances but wasn't the only culprit.

A player such as Stiles coming back into the side was a real boost. It provided a passionate player who wore his heart on his sleeve and who was busy chatting away to officials, bemoaning decisions as well as engaging in terse dialogue with opponents and geeing up colleagues.

That sort of input was needed if United were to leave Turf Moor with some reward after Geoff Nulty equalised before the break. Steve Kindon was a huge threat but was contained as United registered another draw.

MANCHESTER CITY 2 MANCHESTER UNITED 1
LEAGUE CUP SF 1ST LEG 3 DECEMBER 1969

DESPITE TAKING A kick to his troublesome knee, Stiles played and Paul Edwards, who also sustained a knock at Burnley, was also cleared to play. Failing to beat City was something George always struggled to come to terms with and at the end of this game he knocked the ball out of referee Jack Taylor's hands. The official was left with no choice but to issue a further yellow card to the one brandished earlier and dismissed the Irishman. Given the serious nature of the offence - even though the incident was to all intents and purposes trivial in nature - severe sanctions were expected.

George had been incensed by a late penalty awarded when Francis Lee went over in the area under a challenge from Ian Ure. Best's complaints that Lee had dived were most vociferous. City had a very good first quarter and capitalised through a Colin Bell goal. Lee's persistence setting up the chance. United were the better team for most of the match and Best was at his most dangerous after the break. Tony Book claimed the Irishman pushed him in the build up for United's goal and that was the reason he lost possession to Charlton who shot home after setting his sights.

City caused isolated problems, primarily through the much maligned Lee who had few admirers outside Maine Road and even fewer at Old Trafford once he tempted Ure into making a tackle which led to the controversial winner. Lee, as ever, was deadly from the spot.

United were far from out of the tie with the home leg to come but the job would be tricky now City had something to defend.

MANCHESTER UNITED 0 CHELSEA 2
Division One 6 December 1969

THE TEAM WHICH broke United's long unbeaten run of 37 games at home last term were back at Old Trafford to put a spanner in the works again. Nobby Stiles, playing his first home game since returning to the side, received a rapturous reception but was made to work hard as Chelsea looked dangerous from the off.

United were grateful to Ian Ure but no one could stop danger man Ian Hutchinson after a penetrating move in the twelfth minute. The same player extended the lead soon after.

Best was well marshalled by Ron Harris, who enjoyed a measure of the winger few others could equal, but George seemed resigned to a weary afternoon and played within himself. He did better after the break but Harris had him on a tight leash which the Londoner snapped when danger appeared. The Reds only real threat came via Bobby Charlton but even the England midfielder's contribution was limited.

LIVERPOOL 1 MANCHESTER UNITED 4
Division One 13 December 1969

PADDY CRERAND was asked to cover for Nobby Stiles at inside-left for his first appearance in three months. He had spent this time in the wilderness of the reserves and while injuries to Stiles, Law, Kidd and Edwards may have been an underlying reason this was of no real concern to the Scot who looked to make all he could of the opportunity. Alex Stepney was declared fit despite experiencing pain in his shins.

Liverpool were in form and clearly up for big games like this having beaten Everton at Goodison Park the previous week. The full blooded Tommy Smith, who was often detailed to look after flair players by Bill Shankly and played on the same flank as George, was missing which must have been something of a relief to Best.

Crerand linked well with George and the pair set up the first attack of the game. However, the resulting cross was well read by Tommy Lawrence who also fielded centres from John Aston. David Sadler scored for United as a result of harrying Ron Yeats. Emlyn Hughes equalised but Ian Ure and Willie Morgan made it 3-1 as United ran away with things in the second half. A tactical switch to 4-3-3 swamped the Anfield side who could not muster an instant reply. The fourth and final goal was the finest of the day, Bobby Charlton taking a pass from Morgan after he had initially released the winger before smashing in. It was Liverpool's biggest

home defeat in five years and highlighted United's quality yet underlined their inconsistency.

MANCHESTER UNITED 2 MANCHESTER CITY 2
League Cup SF 2nd leg 17 December 1969

City held a slim lead and while United were thrashing Liverpool, the Blues had been fairly disappointing in the league game with Spurs. However, that experience could not be counted on to demoralise tonight's visitors though Denis Law and Nobby Stiles returned providing a boost while Crerand and Morgan managed to retain their places after impressive displays at Anfield.

Colin Bell was out for City, a factor which many held to be the reason behind the dreary draw with Spurs, and for a spell it seemed to continue to play on the minds of a number of players. However,

despite controlling midfield United just could not find a way through. Paul Edwards equalised an Ian Bowyer goal and Denis Law tied the aggregate scores just before the hour but only offered glimpses of his best form.

By contrast Francis Lee was a constant force and proved to be the crucial difference again. His free-kick eight minutes from the end, which was followed up by Mike Summerbee after Alex Stepney could only parry the ball, booked City's place at Wembley where they went on to beat West Bromwich Albion to lift the League Cup.

MANCHESTER UNITED 0 WOLVES 0
Division One 26 December 1969

Denis Law's recent poor form was put down to him carrying an injury and, though his absence allowed Brian Kidd a route back into the side, it only seemed likely to delay a meeting with Wilf McGuinness and Matt Busby about the Mancunian's future. Kidd had openly agitated for a return to first team action after losing his place for the previous two league games and the imminent return of Law seemed likely to bring the situation to a head.

Wolves were outplayed for the most part with keeper Phil Parkes the hero for

his bravery, safe handling and a decent run of stops including one from George Best which he managed to keep out with a leap and a strong hand. It was a save he would probably remember for the rest of his days.

Otherwise full back Derek Parkin did well against Best in a great contest which the defender shaded. However, there was one searing run George started from inside his own area that took him the full length of the pitch, leaving Wolves players in his wake only for his finishing touch to let him down.

Still with a little more bite United could and should have run out comfortable

winners. Alex Stepney was all but redundant with just one save to make.

SUNDERLAND 1 MANCHESTER UNITED 1
DIVISION ONE 27 DECEMBER 1969

IF WILF McGUINNESS sought a boost from the festive period and a couple of games against weaker opposition, he was to be disappointed as a win still eluded the new manager despite Brian Kidd establishing an early lead at Roker Park.

United sat back after registering that strike and even when Sunderland equalised through Joe Blair few could shake off the sluggishness that had crept

into their play.

Best looked dangerous in fits and starts but couldn't win the game on his own and with no one lending a hand, he struggled to create much, although he did hit the bar with a header. Willie Morgan had an effort cleared off the line as did Dennis Tueart for the Rokermen in the final seconds.

IPSWICH TOWN 0 MANCHESTER UNITED 1
FA CUP 3RD RD 3 JANUARY 1970

PRIOR TO UNITED opening their FA Cup campaign, the FA handed down a month's suspension effective from Monday 5 January and a £100 fine for Best's altercation with Jack Taylor at the end of the first leg of the League Cup semi-final with Manchester City.

Best hoped to go out with a bang but it seemed that the issue was playing on his mind, though he did force a fine save from his namesake in goal for Ipswich, Dave Best. The Ipswich stopper also did well to resist Bobby Charlton and Paul Edwards'

efforts. George played a role in United's winner, putting pressure on Mick McNeil as he tried to deal with Brian Kidd's cross. The attempted clearance was sliced and looped over the helpless keeper.

Ipswich were strongest in the opening 20 minutes but offered little other than sporadic threats after that. The fourth round draw paired United with City but George would of course miss the derby clash not to mention a chance of revenge for the League Cup exit and the incident which led to his ban.

NORTHAMPTON TOWN 2 MANCHESTER UNITED 8
FA CUP 5TH ROUND 7 FEBRUARY 1970

MUCH TO THE delight of most in a capacity 63,000 Old Trafford crowd Manchester City were vanquished 3-0 as George Best watched from the stands. During Best's absence there were also wins over Arsenal and Derby County

plus draws with West Ham and Leeds United in the league - so it appeared that United had barely missed George at all.

United came out of the hat for the fifth round against Fourth Division Northampton Town. The Cobblers had

THE COMPLETE GEORGE BEST

been languishing in mid-table for most of the campaign progressing through the competition with victories over Weymouth and Exeter City after replays. A narrow squeak with Brentwood Town followed and a win over Tranmere Rovers achieved after a replay meant they had already played eight FA Cup games.

However, there would be no question of fatigue blunting their quest for a giantkilling act. Northampton possessed a fairly experienced backline, while the youngsters in their ranks had the chance to prove their worth against some of the biggest names in the game. Town had actually played United in the league just four years previously having risen from the basement division to top flight in five seasons. Although they had held United 1-1 at The County Ground results similar to the 6-2 drubbing at Old Trafford helped them on the way to relegation and a descent which saw them fall right back to their starting place in successive seasons.

Kim Book, brother of City's Tony who had lifted the trophy as the Blues captain the previous season, was in goal for Northampton. As it turned out George could not resist putting on a show not only for those who rarely got a chance to see his skills but the United fans who had been deprived of his talent for a month and five games.

An immediate return after his suspension was not guaranteed. Together Matt Busby and Wilf McGuinness wrestled with who to drop from a winning side and the final decision to field the winger was made on the morning of the

game with John Aston making way.

Their decision was vindicated by an unbelievable 90 minute display from the Irishman that has gone down as one of the most emphatic of all time.

No one got close to Best and the Northampton crowd were treated to a host of flicks, tricks and dribbles. Best's unfortunate marker was Ray Fairfax - he later quipped that the nearest he came to Best was when the pair shook hands after the game.

Yet for 20 minutes Best and United were held at bay with The Cobblers fashioning a few half-chances. When The Reds opener came it was fairly straight-forward. A Brian Kidd cross was nodded in at the far post with George's marker unaware he had made the run until the ball hit the net.

Then David Sadler and Paddy Crerand's considered build up gained momentum in midfield before Crerand found Best in the area. With just Book to beat George feinted one way then rolled the ball in having sold the keeper a perfect dummy.

Book effected a save from another decent Best chance after Kidd and Bobby Charlton had combined little more than a minute in to the second half but as he could only parry the ball back into play George had the simple task of tapping into an empty net for his hat-trick, Best's first treble since May 1968.

Brian Kidd, who was having an excellent game, provided the assist for United and Best's fourth before finding the goal himself to make it 5-0. George had created the chance after a dazzling run which

198

took him past almost half the opposition, who had massed near the penalty area to avert complete humiliation. It didn't help as Best set-up Kidd.

Francis Burns, who had come off the bench for Bobby Charlton, was usually seen as a defender and little else but turned provider when he found Best with a ball which penetrated the Northampton backline and put the Irishman in on Book again. The finish was cool and collected.

Kidd made it seven but many wanted to see George break the competition's goalscoring record and got their wish late on: after waltzing past a handful of players and the keeper George stopped on the goal line, placed his foot on the ball, gave the United fans behind the goal a wave and tapped it over the line. If he was tempted to stoop to his knees and head the ball over as he longed to do in the European Cup final he never admitted it. In fact he seemed somewhat embarrassed by his exploits and didn't even celebrate, deciding to take a break from his exertions by leaning against the goalpost, his head bowed.

The tally set a club record as well as a mark for the most goals ever scored in one FA Cup game by a single player. Though strictly speaking another individual had scored six during a game. Denis Law, during his time with Manchester City, hit a double hat-trick against Luton Town in 1961 but the match was abandoned with twenty minutes remaining. The teams reconvened at Kenilworth Road a few days later and while Law found the net again The Hatters won through 3-1.

Dixie McNeill and Frank Large scored for the home side who also missed a penalty and the chance to halve the final deficit. Brian Kidd, who may normally have expected to gain plaudits for bagging a couple of goals and helping the club reach the quarter-finals, saw his excellent contribution virtually forgotten in all the furore after the game as record-breaker Best stole the headlines and answered the FA's ban in the only way possible.

SIX OF THE BEST
George's performance in this 1970 FA Cup-tie was memorable for several reasons, not least the fact that he hadn't played a competitive game for over a month. Here he torments another Cobblers defender on his way to his double-hattrick.

IPSWICH TOWN 0 MANCHESTER UNITED 1
DIVISION ONE 10 FEBRUARY 1970

DURING THE WEEK running up to the game sad memories were rekindled by news of a plane crash at Munich Airport in an area very close to the precise location of the disaster which claimed so many lives almost 12 years ago to the day. Fortunately most aboard the United Arab Airlines jet escaped with little more than minor injuries.

Ipswich were positive about their task but eventually found themselves worn down as David Sadler and Ian Ure exercised a vice like grip on the home side. From that point on United were in complete control.

With his tail up after that six goal haul at Northampton, Best predictably tried to get a shot off at each and every opportunity. He also attempted a range of efforts from various distances and angles. But it was Brian Kidd, who had hit the post twice, ended up as the match winner.

It seemed another goal had been scored when Dave Best attempted to clear a Willie Morgan cross but only succeeded in punching it high into the air. United got the ball in the net but the goal was disallowed after a foul committed during the melee.

MANCHESTER UNITED 1 CRYSTAL PALACE 1
DIVISION ONE 14 FEBRUARY 1970

GEORGE MADE HIS first appearance at Old Trafford in almost two months and his first of the new decade. United were title outsiders but had every chance of qualifying for Europe via the Fairs Cup should they maintain fifth place. These hopes took a knock as, despite United's dominance, Palace managed a share of the points with a penalty.

Kidd opened the scoring and that should have signalled an opening of the floodgates but the current failed to amount to much more than a trickle. Kidd could have had more and Best really should have bagged at least two but it appeared that the hype surrounding his six goals was affecting him. Other bids to score suffered as a result and made Palace's job easier than it needed to be.

Best wanted to heighten the reputation it had given him and far too often his attempts at goal were over-optimistic. Even a player of his quality could only attain that kind of performance a few times in his career.

MIDDLESBROUGH 1 MANCHESTER UNITED 1
FA Cup 6th Rd 21 February 1970

WILLIE MORGAN PLAYED despite suffering from 'flu. Boro were exceptional going forward but fortunately United's defence played well and kept The Reds in the cup. However, as United's midfielders ran to cover opposition attacks, options going forward were limited.

When they were called upon Boro's defenders were stern in their challenges. Best in particular felt many tough tackles and only caused one or two problems. Carlo Sartori notched against the run of play and had it not been for a rush of blood by Alex Stepney, who charged off his line in trying to intercept a ball he had no better than half a chance of reaching, United would have gone through. John Hickton was the comfortable winner of the race and guided the ball over the now stranded keeper and in to force a replay.

MANCHESTER UNITED 2 MIDDLESBROUGH 1
FA Cup 6th Rd Replay 25 February 1970

UNITED MAY HAVE expected to do better at Old Trafford than they had managed at Ayresome Park but were forced to admit that once again Boro were the better side even if they were helped by lapses at the back. Thankfully none of these errors were punished.

Only David Sadler and Alex Stepney, who bounced back from his latest lapse extremely well, prevented Boro from taking an early lead. In the end United went ahead following a quick break. Crerand found Best who nodded on for Bobby Charlton to finish from a yard or so out.

Boro then crowded United's area and attacked with real menace. John Hickton latched on to a mis-hit clearance to level the game but the man who was Boro's hero over the two games failed to spot Kidd lurking when attempting a back pass minutes later.

Bill Glazier felt he had no other option but to launch into a tackle conceding a penalty which Morgan steered in. Once again Best contributed little more than cameos and a short pass for the opener.

STOKE CITY 2 MANCHESTER UNITED 2
Division One 28 February 1970

LIKE UNITED, STOKE were hoping to gain entry into the Fairs Cup. Two superb goalkeepers Gordon Banks and Alex Stepney provided the benchmark many other stoppers had to measure themselves against and each proved why during this end-to-end game in which Banks was the busier. Carlo Sartori gave United the lead for a second time in three games but Stoke equalised then went ahead.

The loss of David Sadler in the second half was a blow and contributed to the home side getting their noses in front but Willie Morgan, who worked constructively all game, earned a penalty after tumbling under pressure from Banks. He picked himself up then crashed the ball home from the spot.

It was the same old story for Best who many felt was coasting and living on his recent exploits rather than looking to put in hard graft.

LEEDS UNITED 0 MANCHESTER UNITED 0
FA Cup SF 14 March 1970

THE LAST TIME United met Leeds in an FA Cup semi-final, the clash ran to a replay which the Yorkshire side won with a late Billy Bremner goal. However, those games were remembered for anything but the football played. Though Leeds had improved greatly as a team, and had been crowned as league champions the previous season, there was still an edge to their play and this match was as brutal as any other.

Brian Kidd seemed set to miss out through a bout of tonsillitis during the early part of the week but was cleared to play. Like many flair players he had little constructive use of the ball as the tie fizzled out into a scrappy, midfield bound affair.

MANCHESTER UNITED 3 BURNLEY 3
Division One 17 March 1970

BURNLEY LOOKED SET to cause an upset after taking an early lead when Jimmy Rimmer, standing in for Alex Stepney, stubbed his toe taking a goal kick. The ball went no distance as a result and Steve Kindon benefited. Pat Crerand's loose ball then allowed Dave Thomas a chance which he pushed past a now demoralised keeper. Crerand scored after a set up from the newly returned Denis Law but Thomas scored again and The Reds were 1-3 down.

David Sadler was pushed foward to beef up the forward line and one of his efforts hit a post and fell kindly for Law who netted sharply. The forward had another disallowed for offside which looked set to deprive United of reward until George Best finally made amends for some lacklustre displays in recent weeks, netting from close range as the ball bounced free, to rescue a point at the death.

CHELSEA 2 MANCHESTER UNITED 1
Division One 21 March 1970

A LENGTHY INJURY list led to a host of changes and it took some time for a re-jigged side to settle. Chelsea, on the other hand, were very smooth during the opening and stretched United. Ian Hutchinson made a habit of scoring against The Reds and further improved his record with a little less than a quarter of an hour gone. He had notched twice at Old Trafford back in October and before long had a brace at Stamford Bridge. Paul Edwards, attempting to support a move being concocted by Best and Law, was left stranded when a pass between the two left Hutchinson with a clear run.

George was full of running but little else which irritated his colleagues including Law who took up a number of good positions in vain.

In addition to the disappointment of defeat was the end of an 18-game run without defeat. Chelsea, already in the cup final after victory over Watford and third in the league, were making good on the promise shown a few seasons earlier. United would hope to be able to gain revenge in the cup final but whether The Reds would be present at Wembley remained to be seen as their replay with Leeds was only 48 hours away.

MANCHESTER UNITED 0 LEEDS UNITED 0
FA Cup SF Replay 23 March 1970

No DOUBT WARNED about their conduct by the FA, United and Leeds finally played up to the attacking abilities of both teams. United had the better of the first half and could have gone ahead many times after creating a hatful of chances. The second half saw Leeds at their strongest and, although Allan Clarke forced the ball over the line, his effort was disallowed.

Best looked somewhat off the pace and with reason. The two teams had been asked to replay at Villa Park so United left London immediately after the game with Chelsea for Birmingham. With some time to kill George, as was his wont, became very friendly with a woman who turned out to be the wife of a businessman staying at the hotel. When the coach rolled up to the entrance in order to take the players to the game just one name remained unchecked on the roll call. When Wilf McGuiness was told of George's antics he was furious and determined to send the player back to Manchester.

However, Matt Busby calmed the situation, reasoning that George Best in any condition was a player needed on the pitch. McGuinness agreed and George played in attack alongside Brian Kidd.

However, the football grapevine was red hot with the rumour which the men from Elland Road were happy to use to their advantage. None more so than former United player Johnny Giles although Jackie Charlton was given the responsibility of minding George and winding him up when Giles was otherwise engaged. The tactics worked and the winger failed to make an impact. To make matters worse he fluffed a late chance to win the game.

Rain had fallen heavily throughout the day with the pitch little more than a quagmire. The penalty areas were particularly affected. When he got the chance to go clear Best couldn't resist attempting to rub the noses of those who had teased him so mercilessly for almost an hour and a half but he struggled to exhibit his skills in these conditions. Instead of hitting the ball past Gary Sprake Best attempted one last trick. It should have given him the chance to fire into an open goal but the ball got stuck and George fell face first into the muddy turf.

Nobby Stiles, who had been at the centre of an attempted loan deal with Coventry City days prior to the transfer deadline, made his first appearance since the switch was rejected.

LEEDS UNITED 1 MANCHESTER UNITED 0
FA Cup SF 2nd Replay 26 March 1970

BEST GOT MORE change out of Reaney than he ever had in their previous meetings but lacked punch where it really mattered - in the final third of the field - at Bolton Wanderers' Burnden Park. The only exception being a deep cross which almost threatened to cross the Leeds line and should have been touched in by Willie Morgan.

The match was won by the man who scored the winner at the same stage five years earlier - Billy Bremner netting with a neat finish eight minutes in. Peter Lorimer made the most of a swirling wind, sending in a ball which Allan Clarke nodded down for Mick Jones.

The forward tried to get a shot in but it bobbled off his shins and rolled to the captain who made no mistake with his left foot.

Unusually a slow paced game followed though United tried hard to get back on terms. However, with the exception of Bobby Charlton, who gradually began to fume at his colleagues over their apparent lack of urgency, few players seemed to shine in this final episode of the cup marathon. Leeds had been hemmed in for long periods but Jones should have wrapped it up in the final minutes.

In the final, Leeds lost to Chelsea after an Old Trafford replay.

MANCHESTER UNITED 1 MANCHESTER CITY 2
Division One 28 March 1970

Both City and United had been busy over recent weeks. The Maine Road side had gone all the way in the League Cup and were still in the European Cup Winners' Cup having reached the last four. United may have won the battle in the FA Cup but otherwise The Blues had proved more than equal to The Reds and completed victories in the league and League Cup double.

As ever on these parochial occasions the midfield was the key area and again

City, despite missing important players like Colin Bell and Mike Summerbee, ruled that particular roost and were very difficult to break down at the back. That didn't stop United going ahead when a Willie Morgan shot proved too hot for Joe Corrigan to handle. Brian Kidd displayed a poacher's instinct and was on hand to net.

Neil Young robbed David Sadler close to the area but was pulled down by Alex Stepney before he had a chance to pull the trigger. Francis Lee converted the penalty. Mike Doyle hit a winner at The Stretford End after another Sadler slip to give City a double over their neighbours.

MANCHESTER UNITED 1 COVENTRY CITY 1
DIVISION ONE 30 MARCH 1970

CHANGES, BOTH IN personnel and positionally were made as United battled against fixture congestion. Understandably The Reds looked tired though, conversely, Best started sprightly and set up Kidd in the second minute after a telling run.

Coventry's rugged defence and United's struggle to break them down led to tiredness in the second half. The Sky Blues had an even easier ride when Kidd went off. Denis Law started well but was puffing hard before the end and often couldn't supplement the spirit and verve of Best who excelled until the close.

Neil Martin equalised ten minutes from the end with a well taken shot from the edge of the area which kept low.

NOTTINGHAM FOREST 1 MANCHESTER UNITED 2
DIVISION ONE 31 MARCH 1970

UNITED TOOK ON the responsibility of a second game within 24 hours, their eighth game in 17 days, in order to keep up with the league programme and journeyed to Nottingham where goals from Bobby Charlton and Alan Gowling edged a win for a much changed side.

MANCHESTER UNITED 7 WEST BROMWICH ALBION 0
DIVISION ONE 8 APRIL 1970

UNITED RECOVERED WELL from a heavy 5-1 defeat at St James Park earlier in the week to stun The Baggies by dominating the game from start to finish. George Best, back after missing the dismal showing at Newcastle, was the only scorer not to bag more than one. Bobby Charlton, John Fitzpatrick, who opened the scoring with a header, and Alan Gowling all hit a brace.

Fitzpatrick showed he had quite an aptitude in forward positions and had a hand in the five goals he didn't score. Paddy Crerand's lobbed pass for one of Charlton's goals was nothing short of sublime - great vision and weight allied with a terrific controlled finish.

George's strike sealed the margin of victory ten minutes from the end and saw him drop to his knees in thanks for hitting the net. He had seen plenty of the ball and if he had run up a few less blind alleys the final score would have been in double figures. Indifferent form and a lack of goals were clearly playing on his mind.

WATFORD 0 MANCHESTER UNITED 2
FA Cup 3rd/4th Place Play Off 10 April 1970

THE REDS WERE committed to playing a one off game at Highbury in the FA Cup against the other beaten semi-finalists Watford. It was a game nobody really wanted to contest and with the final itself being played the following day seemed nothing short of sadistic on a team that had endured so many fixtures in such a short period of time.

Within four years the tie would be phased out due to lack of fan support, the apathy of the clubs and high gate prices. As many as fifty shillings was being asked for a ticket meaning just 15,000 turned up. Most were United fans but both sides felt a need to entertain those who had parted with their cash and put on a game worthy of a semi-final.

In a very open first half the Division Two side were good value for a draw but United's experience and class won out. There were some examples of poor finishing until Kidd finished off a flowing move from Best and Morgan. The same scorer snapped up a second close to the end after Mike Walker could only paw a David Sadler free-kick to his feet.

TOTTENHAM HOTSPUR 2 MANCHESTER UNITED 1
Division One 13 April 1970

FOR A FEW MOMENTS it looked as though another lengthy ban could well be heading George's way. He was incensed by the second Spurs goal after Alan Gilzean took possession away from him then ran up the other end to score. Best felt the Spurs man had fouled him and the goal should not count. All remonstrations were waved away and he squared up to referee John Hunting but skipper Bobby Charlton stepped in when some pushing began.

Spurs had opened the scoring when Martin Chivers netted after seizing on a ball which bounced off Paul Edwards after Crerand had over-hit a pass. John Fitzpatrick pulled one back from a Charlton corner. There were other decent chances but few of enough threat to worry Spurs.

MANCHESTER UNITED 2 SHEFFIELD WEDNESDAY 2
Division One 15 April 1970

HAVING GONE INTO a 2-0 lead and seemingly condemned Sheffield Wednesday to relegation, United simply fell into submission. Best hit the opener on six minutes, slaloming his way through the defence after a Paddy Crerand pass. Bobby Charlton scored quickly after latching on to John Fitzpatrick's pass from a Willie Morgan cross.

At this point The Reds simply stopped playing. Wednesday, realising they may still be in with a shout just after the interval, reduced the deficit through former City winger Tony Coleman.

United couldn't pull themselves back together and Jack Whitham levelled after a teasing centre from Jackie Sinclair.

The Owls could still save themselves and if they beat Manchester City they would keep themselves up.

NORTHERN IRELAND 0 SCOTLAND 1
HOME INTERNATIONAL 18 APRIL 1970

THE FRUSTRATION THAT affected George at international level had started to boil over with United as he saw players of lesser ability replace the greats he had worked so harmoniously with during the early part of his career. It meant there was no escape from mediocrity on the pitch and it culminated in petulant acts such as the one which saw him dismissed while representing Northern Ireland in his home city.

Experienced English referee Eric Jennings showed Best a red card for spitting and throwing mud at him. Ireland were losing by a single John O'Hare goal at the time, though the damage could have been far worse. Best, nor any of his colleagues, could dig the side out and, feeling that decisions were going against them, players became frustrated with each other prompting the outburst.

The Irish Football Association mitigated any penalty, clearing Best to face England three days later accepting claims that he had spat at the ground and that the mud slinging was not aimed anyone in particular it was thrown in the air due to a fit of pique.

ENGLAND 3 NORTHERN IRELAND 1
HOME INTERNATIONAL 21 APRIL 1970

THERE WAS LITTLE to remember from this game, if looked at from an Irish point of view, except for an exceptional goal from George Best. England's scorers were Martin Peters, Geoff Hurst and George's United teammate Bobby Charlton who was captaining the side for the third and last time on winning his 100th cap. He was only the second England player to reach that mark following Billy Wright.

Brian Kidd was also in the starting XI along with Nobby Stiles who was marking George when he received the ball fairy central to goal. Stiles was far from the easiest defender to evade but even watching Best at close quarters every day in training couldn't assist the World Cup hero who was left flat footed by a quick turn which set up an opportunity to take on Gordon Banks. A well placed drive gave the world's best keeper no chance.

1969-70

By any standards George went through some turbulent form which coincided with the extended absences of his midfield protector Nobby Stiles who played just 13 games. Added to that was the soap opera of his personal life. The varied frustrations over United's form and his own contribution to the team had simmered for some months and finally boiled over with George sent off for tempestuous actions towards referees for both club and country.

United also suffered and though a place in the League Cup semi-finals was a positive, exiting to Manchester City was a huge blow. Perhaps of equal significance was City's double of League and European Cup Winners' Cups. The Blues were now the dominant force in the city and one win and four defeats from the five meetings with the men from Maine Road indicated that United were failing in their own backyard.

Best was still a genius when the game took his fancy but for the first time he began to show feet of clay. His consistency was lacking and, with the team now more dependent on him than ever, he could no longer expect the ageing stars Law, Charlton and Crerand to bail him out when he had an off-day.

His remarkable six-goal performance at Northampton was a case in point. In the subsequent games he tried to 'put on a show' and was found out against better defenders. When he concentrated on playing to a team pattern the results were there for all to see, it's just that George being George, he didn't always see it like that.

United's start to the season had been little short of appalling for a team of such stature. It took half a dozen games before the first league win was registered although the team's form coincided with a great run from George himself who scored nine from eight games starting with that initial win in Division One.

However, the season got harder and once again the team's fortune mirrored that of its most gifted member. Often petulant, which led to disciplinary problems, Best went through long bouts of indifferent form which may have seen a lesser player omitted from most sides. However, just one piece of magic, of which he was more than capable, could turn a game. His very presence was also an intimidation to the opposition.

In fairness many big names struggled that term: Paddy Crerand, Bobby Charlton and Denis Law all looked off their games at times. Injuries were a huge factor in the latter case. That didn't stop Matt Busby, as General Manager, transfer listing the finest goalscorer he had ever had for £60,000 almost as soon as the whistle blew on the final game of the season.

The news surrounding Law was huge but otherwise Shay Brennan was the largest name allowed to leave after a free transfer was granted. There would have to be improvements at the club. The biggest question remained who was in control - the current manager or the last one?

DATE	OPPONENT	VENUE	SCORE	ATT'D	1	2	3	4	5	6	7	8	9	10	11
9 August	C Palace	Selhurst Park	2-2	48,610	Rimmer	Dunne(A)	Burns	Crerand	Foulkes	Sadler	Morgan[1]	Kidd	Charlton[1]	Law	Best
13 August	Everton	Old Trafford	0-2	57,752	Rimmer	Brennan	Burns	Crerand	Foulkes	Sadler	Morgan	Kidd	Charlton	Law	Best
16 August	Southampton	Old Trafford	1-4	46,328	Rimmer	Brennan	Burns	Crerand	Foulkes	Sadler	Morgan[1]	Kidd	Charlton	Law	Best
19 August	Everton	Goodison Park	0-3	53,185	Stepney	Fitzpatrick	Burns	Crerand	Edwards	Sadler	Morgan	Kidd	Givens	Best	Aston
23 August	Wolves	Molineux	0-0	50,783	Stepney	Fitzpatrick	Burns	Crerand	Ure	Sadler	Morgan	Kidd	Charlton	Law	Best
27 August	Newcastle United	Old Trafford	0-0	52,774	Stepney	Fitzpatrick	Dunne(A)	Crerand	Ure	Sadler	Morgan	Kidd	Charlton	Givens	Best
30 August	Sunderland	Old Trafford	3-1	50,570	Stepney	Fitzpatrick	Dunne(A)	Crerand	Ure	Sadler	Morgan	Kidd[1]	Charlton	Givens[1]	Best[1]
6 September	Leeds United	Elland Road	2-2	44,271	Stepney	Fitzpatrick	Dunne(A)	Burns	Ure	Sadler	Morgan	Givens	Charlton	Gowling	Best[2]
13 September	Liverpool	Old Trafford	1-0	56,509	Stepney	Fitzpatrick	Dunne(A)	Burns	Ure	Sadler	Morgan[1]	Kidd	Charlton	Gowling	Best
17 September	Sheffield Wednesday	Hillsborough	3-1	39,298	Stepney	Fitzpatrick	Dunne(A)	Burns	Ure	Sadler	Morgan	Kidd[1]	Charlton	Gowling	Best[2]
20 September	Arsenal	Highbury	2-2	59,498	Stepney	Fitzpatrick	Dunne(A)	Burns	Ure	Sadler[1]	Morgan	Kidd	Charlton	Aston	Best[1]
27 September	West Ham United	Old Trafford	5-2	58,579	Stepney	Fitzpatrick	Dunne(A)	Burns[1]	Ure	Sadler	Morgan	Kidd[1]	Charlton[1]	Aston	Best[2]
04 October	Derby County	Baseball Ground	0-2	40,724	Stepney	Fitzpatrick	Dunne(A)	Burns	Ure	Sadler	Morgan	Kidd	Charlton	Aston	Best
8 October	Southampton	The Dell	3-0	31,044	Stepney	Fitzpatrick	Dunne(A)	Burns[1]	Ure	Sadler	Morgan	Kidd[1]	Charlton	Aston	Best[1]
11 October	Ipswich Town	Old Trafford	2-1	52,281	Stepney	Fitzpatrick	Dunne(A)	Burns	Ure	Sadler	Morgan	Kidd[1]	Charlton	Aston	Best[1]
18 October	Nottingham Forest	Old Trafford	1-1	53,702	Stepney	Fitzpatrick	Dunne(A)	Burns	Ure	Sadler	Morgan	Kidd	Charlton	Aston	Best[1]
25 October	WBA	Hawthorns	1-2	45,120	Stepney	Brennan	Dunne(A)	Burns	Ure	Sadler	Sartori	Kidd[1]	Charlton	Aston	Best
1 November	Stoke City	Old Trafford	1-1	53,406	Stepney	Brennan	Dunne(A)	Burns	Ure	Sadler	Law	Kidd	Charlton[1]	Aston	Best
8 November	Coventry City	Highfield Road	2-1	43,446	Stepney	Brennan	Dunne(A)	Burns	Ure	Sadler	Sartori	Best	Charlton	Law[1]	Aston[1]
15 November	Manchester City	Maine Road	0-4	63,013	Stepney	Brennan	Dunne(A)	Burns	Ure	Sadler	Sartori	Best	Charlton	Law	Aston
22 November	Tottenham Hotspur	Old Trafford	3-1	50,003	Stepney	Fitzpatrick	Dunne(A)	Burns[1]	Ure	Sadler	Sartori	Kidd	Charlton[2]	Best	Aston
29 November	Burnley	Turf Moor	1-1	23,770	Stepney	Edwards	Dunne(A)	Burns	Ure	Sadler	Best[1]	Kidd	Charlton	Stiles	Aston
6 December	Chelsea	Old Trafford	0-2	49,344	Stepney	Edwards	Dunne(A)	Burns	Ure	Sadler	Best	Kidd	Charlton	Stiles	Aston
13 December	Liverpool	Anfield	4-1+	47,682	Stepney	Brennan	Dunne(A)	Burns	Ure[1]	Sadler	Morgan[1]	Best	Charlton[1]	Law[1]	Aston[1]
26 December	Wolves	Old Trafford	0-0	50,806	Stepney	Edwards	Dunne(A)	Burns	Ure	Sadler	Morgan	Crerand	Charlton	Kidd	Best
27 December	Sunderland	Roker Park	1-1	36,504	Stepney	Edwards	Brennan	Burns	Ure	Sadler	Morgan	Crerand	Charlton	Kidd[1]	Best
10 February	Ipswich Town	Portman Rd	1-0	29,755	Stepney	Edwards	Dunne(A)	Crerand	Ure	Sadler	Morgan	Sartori	Charlton	Kidd[1]	Best
14 February	Crystal Palace	Old Trafford	1-1	54,711	Stepney	Edwards	Dunne(A)	Crerand	Ure	Sadler	Morgan	Sartori	Charlton	Kidd[1]	Best
28 February	Stoke City	Victoria Gd	2-2	38,917	Stepney	Edwards	Dunne(A)	Crerand	Ure	Sadler	Morgan[1]	Sartori[1]	Charlton	Kidd	Best

Date	Opposition	Venue	Score	Att.	1	2	3	4	5	6	7	8	9	10	11
17 March	Burnley	Old Trafford	3-3	38,377	Rimmer	Edwards	Dunne(A)	Crerand[1]	Ure	Sadler	Morgan	Sartori	Charlton	Law[1]	Best[1]
21 March	Chelsea	Stamford Bridge	1-2	61,479	Stepney	Edwards	Burns	Crerand	Ure	Stiles	Morgan[1]	Sartori	Charlton	Law	Best
28 March	Manchester City	Old Trafford	1-2	59,777	Stepney	Edwards	Dunne(A)	Crerand	Sadler	Burns	Morgan	Sartori	Charlton	Kidd[1]	Best
30 March	Coventry City	Old Trafford	1-1	38,647	Stepney	Edwards	Dunne(A)	Fitzpatrick	Ure	Sadler	Morgan	Best	Law	Kidd[1]	Aston
31 March	Nottingham Forest	City Ground	2-1	39,228	Stepney	Stiles	Dunne(A)	Crerand	James	Sadler	Morgan	Fitzpatrick	Charlton[1]	Gowling[1]	Best
8 April	West Bromwich	Old Trafford	7-0	26,582	Stepney	Stiles	Dunne(A)	Crerand	Ure	Sadler	Morgan	Fitzpatrick[2]	Charlton[2]	Gowling[2]	Best[1]
13 April	Tottenham Hotspur	White Hart Lane	1-2	41,808	Stepney	Edwards	Dunne(A)	Crerand	Ure	Stiles	Morgan	Fitzpatrick[1]	Charlton	Kidd	Best
15 April	Sheffield Wednesday	Old Trafford	2-2	36,649	Stepney	Edwards	Dunne(A)	Crerand	Sadler	Stiles	Morgan	Fitzpatrick	Charlton[1]	Kidd	Best[1]

FA Cup

Date	Opposition	Venue	Score	Att.	1	2	3	4	5	6	7	8	9	10	11
3 January	Ipswich Town +	Portman Road	1-0+	29,552	Stepney	Edwards	Brennan	Burns	Ure	Sadler	Morgan	Crerand	Charlton	Kidd	Best
7 February	Northampton Town	County Ground	8-2	21,771	Stepney	Edwards	Dunne(A)	Crerand	Ure	Sadler	Morgan	Sartori	Charlton	Kidd[2]	Best[6]
21 February	Middlesbrough	Ayresome Park	1-1	40,000	Stepney	Edwards	Dunne(A)	Crerand	Ure	Sadler	Morgan	Sartori[1]	Charlton	Kidd	Best
25 February	Middlesbrough	Old Trafford	2-1	63,418	Stepney	Dunne(A)	Burns	Crerand	Ure	Sadler	Morgan[1]	Sartori	Charlton[1]	Kidd	Best
14 March	Leeds United	Hillsborough	0-0	55,000	Stepney	Edwards	Dunne(A)	Crerand	Ure	Sadler	Morgan	Sartori	Charlton	Kidd	Best
23 March	Leeds United	Villa Park	0-0	62,500	Stepney	Edwards	Dunne(A)	Crerand	Sadler	Stiles	Morgan	Sartori	Charlton	Kidd	Best
26 March	Leeds United	Burnden Park	0-1	56,000	Stepney	Edwards	Dunne(A)	Crerand	Sadler	Stiles	Morgan	Sartori	Charlton	Kidd	Best
10 April	Watford	Highbury	2-0												

League Cup

Date	Opposition	Venue	Score	Att.	1	2	3	4	5	6	7	8	9	10	11
3 September	Middlesbrough	Old Trafford	1-0	38,939	Stepney	Fitzpatrick	Dunne(A)	Crerand	James	Sadler[1]	Morgan	Kidd	Charlton	Givens	Best
23 September	Wrexham	Old Trafford	2-0	48,347	Stepney	Fitzpatrick	Dunne(A)	Burns	Ure	Sadler	Morgan	Kidd[1]	Charlton	Aston	Best[1]
14 October	Burnley	Turf Moor	0-0	27,959	Stepney	Fitzpatrick	Dunne(A)	Burns	Ure	Sadler	Morgan	Kidd	Charlton	Aston	Best
20 October	Burnley	Old Trafford	1-0	50,275	Stepney	Fitzpatrick	Dunne(A)	Burns	Ure	Sadler	Morgan	Kidd	Charlton	Aston	Best
12 November	Derby County	Baseball Ground	0-0	38,895	Stepney	Brennan	Dunne(A)	Burns	Ure	Sadler	Sartori	Best	Charlton	Law	Aston
19 November	Derby County	Old Trafford	1-0	57,393	Stepney	Fitzpatrick	Dunne(A)	Burns	Ure	Sadler	Best	Kidd[1]	Charlton	Law	Aston
3 December	Manchester City	Maine Road	1-2	55,799	Stepney	Edwards	Dunne(A)	Burns	Ure	Sadler	Best	Kidd	Charlton[1]	Stiles	Aston
17 December	Manchester City	Old Trafford	2-2	63,418	Stepney	Edwards[1]	Dunne(A)	Stiles	Ure	Sadler	Morgan	Crerand	Charlton	Law[1]	Best

1970-71
KISSED THE GIRLS...

READING 2 MANCHESTER UNITED 3
WATNEY CUP 1ST RD 1 AUGUST 1970

THE WATNEY MANN Invitation Cup, more commonly referred to as The Watney Cup, was an invitational event specifically designed to attract a live TV audience and ensured games were settled on the night. Two teams from each of the Football League divisions entered, the teams qualifying based on high scoring the previous term. They were pitted against one another in knock-out ties.

There were no neutral venues with United travelling to Reading's Elm Park for their opening clash. On the way to the ground the team bus collided with a taxi but with nothing more than a small amount of damage the squad was soon on its way.

The Royals had scored 87 times in Division Three and though not expected to offer The Reds much of a challenge, manager Wilf McGuinness decided he should operate a little caution at first asking Bobby Charlton to sit deep. The England man, fresh from the Mexico World Cup, still scored twice in the first half adding to an early Paul Edwards goal.

Dick Habbin pulled one back but just after the break and from 3-1 down and facing elimination, Reading went at United with nothing to lose. It left space for The Reds to counterattack but Denis Law in particular could not take advantage. His pre-season touch and confidence looking anything but sure. No one had seemed overly interested in Law's availability during the summer so he returned to Old Trafford for pre-season training. In this type of form it seemed either the fee or Denis would have to be dropped if United were to move on.

Gordon Cumming reduced the arrears just before the hour. Les Chappell and Bobby Williams had proved a handful early on and remained threats. United often looked on the ropes and looked likely to suffer a knockout blow so were grateful for a host of interventions by man of the match Alex Stepney who found training through the summer as part of England's World Cup party had kept him sharp. George Best, by contrast, cut an anonymous figure.

HULL CITY 1 MANCHESTER UNITED 1
WATNEY CUP SEMI-FINAL 5 AUGUST 1970

SECOND DIVISION HULL had beaten Peterborough in their first game and proved dangerous, taking a deserved lead through Chris Chilton who volleyed in an Ian Butler cross. Alex Stepney had plenty to do before and after the goal, though at times rode his luck. There were also many

occasions for The Reds to feel grateful for David Sadler's calm under pressure. Soon after the break Butler rounded only for his shot to balloon off the crossbar. United eventually saw more of the ball but caused only isolated problems until Denis Law equalised 13 minutes from time with a deft headed finish to Willie Morgan's cross.

Along with fellow winger George Best, Morgan pressed high up the field looking to mount raids where they could. However, George still lacked pace and Hull could have had a penalty two minutes from the end of normal time which would probably have won them the game but Stepney's challenge on Ken Wagstaffe was ruled a fair, if somewhat firm one. Extra-time failed to separate the sides meaning a revolutionary means of deciding cup-ties would be tried for the first time ever. The experimental rules provided for a penalty shoot-out to decide who went through after a tied game. The same method would also be used in European competition for the first time that term.

Best became the first player to score during a penalty shoot-out in not only the UK but any UEFA sanctioned tournament after taking the initial kick and dispatching it low to the keeper's right. He was only an occasional scorer from the spot with Denis Law usually having the responsibility but The King had his penalty saved by keeper Ian McKechnie who also took his side's final effort. The Tiger's keeper hit the bar and provided United with victory. In the process of failing to score he also became the first player to save, take and miss a penalty in the same match.

The previous term McKechnie had reached the final of a specially arranged penalty shoot-out competition arranged by his club. Only Ian Butler proved himself to be of a better standard. Brian Kidd, Bobby Charlton and Willie Morgan were the other successful men from the spot. Ken Wagstaffe's miss had evened things up before McKechnie blasted over.

DERBY COUNTY 4 MANCHESTER UNITED 1
WATNEY CUP FINAL 8 AUGUST 1970

THOUGH UNITED HAD scraped through to the final, Wilf McGuinness decided against changing his side for the trip to meet Derby County who would host the game. United had already secured £4,000 plus a share of the gate receipts of the two previous games and a 40,000 plus crowd was expected at The Baseball Ground but The Reds clearly wanted to lift the trophy.

The two top division sides were probably expected to contest this match and Derby were the better side in a fairly open beginning. George Best, operating at well below full throttle, was the most potent threat at the other end. He looked to have learnt from his experience in previous games and sought to play in better placed colleagues rather than charge into the danger zone alone. He was doing as much as he could but those around him, with only a few exceptions, failed to step up their games.

John Fitzpatrick, on for the injured Willie Morgan, was one of those omitted from any blame and poked the ball out of a ruck for Best to lash home. The midfield proved a walkover for Derby who had hit four by the end with McParland, Hinton, Durban and Mackay finding the net.

MANCHESTER UNITED 0 LEEDS UNITED 1
DIVISION ONE 15 AUGUST 1970

PRIOR TO THE new season, Wilf McGuinness was officially handed the title of team manager just as had been mooted the previous year when he had been named chief coach. It was a defining moment for the club, officials and team as it marked the definitive end of Sir Matt Busby's active contribution to the first team and left players in no doubt exactly who was now in charge. Other changes to the backroom team took place, most notably the retirement of 76 year-old chief scout Joe Armstrong.

Apparent threats to kidnap Bobby Charlton's wife Norma hours prior to the new campaign commencing provided some drama. With similar threats surrounding Bobby Moore's wife Tina, the police took it seriously enough to provide the family home with a security detail, although an unconcerned Bobby, determined to concentrate on his football, sent them away.

Denis Law and Willie Morgan were ruled out after picking up hamstring and neck injuries respectively in the Watney Cup. United still made a good start without ever appearing totally comfortable but looked untidy as the match wore on. That was certainly the case in attack where good positions were often squandered as Leeds remained virtually untested.

The game was won by Mick Jones midway through the first half. His charge to meet Peter Lorimer's pinpoint centre gave Alex Stepney no chance and flew into the net. It was a simple goal in essence but one worthy of winning any game.

United's only real threat came towards the close but it proved too little too late. John Fitzpatrick and George Best had the only decent chances but even they looked ragged at stages after such a poor showing by their colleagues.

MANCHESTER UNITED 0 CHELSEA 0
DIVISION ONE 19 AUGUST 1970

BRIAN KIDD WAS added to the injury list although Willie Morgan returned in his place. Once again United only came to the fore as an attacking force in the closing stages, although they showed enough to demonstrate that Chelsea could and should have been soundly beaten.

If there was any bonus it was that woeful finishing didn't cost United. Peter Bonetti was in great form but perhaps

most importantly lucky as when he couldn't keep a ball out his defenders or good fortune did.

Once again George Best looked for colleagues throughout, only taking matters into his own hands when absolutely necessary or when a charge under his own steam was the obvious choice.

ARSENAL 4 MANCHESTER UNITED 0
DIVISION ONE 22 AUGUST 1970

HAVING NOTED THAT Best was striding back towards form, Arsenal made their thinking very clear and Peter Storey shadowed the winger. Had George looked back in the depths of the same malaise as last term The Gunners may well have given him free reign but having shown some good form and more importantly the right attitude towards building moves Bertie Mee decided to field an additional defender.

Despite sacrificing wing man Peter Marinello, who was often compared to Best for his on and off the field activities, Mee won the tactical battle. He was assisted by a wayward United defence. Ian Ure, on his return to Highbury, was little short of woeful and a pale imitation of the player who had steadied United at a vital stage the previous season. His self-induced panic spread across the backline giving Arsenal a huge advantage which John Radford seized upon scoring a hat-trick. David Sadler kept goal after Alex Stepney suffered a shoulder injury but the home side were still good value.

The largest frustration for United was that the forwards looked good when called upon but they were involved in the game less and less during the latter stages. United had chances, notably when George tried to round Bob Wilson with the game scoreless but the keeper won out after a brave challenge saw him grab the ball cleanly. Suffice it to say that United's midfield endured yet another poor game which blighted performances at both ends of the pitch.

BURNLEY 0 MANCHESTER UNITED 2
DIVISION ONE 25 AUGUST 1970

PADDY CRERAND PAID the price for a poor midfield showing, losing his place. John Fitzpatrick, who had been in a more advanced position, was asked to drop back and hold things together as the formation changed from an overtly attacking 4-2-4 to a still forward thinking but more balanced 4-3-3. Jimmy Rimmer came in for Alex Stepney. A couple of Denis Law goals won the game and provided United with a first win of the season in four attempts. The showing was more workmanlike than skilled but the points were vital as they not only got the season underway but increased confidence.

United weathered an early frenzy as Ralph Coates spearheaded various charges but rode out the storm and showed great patience. Morgan and Best look dangerous for most of the game and were set in motion by a well marshalled engine room which benefited from the changes made. Again United were poor in the latter stages but by this time had converted their dominant spells into goals. Having apparently proved not only his fitness and commitment to the cause but his return as one of the most feared forwards in the game, Law was quietly removed from the transfer list.

MANCHESTER UNITED 1 WEST HAM UNITED 1
DIVISION ONE 29 AUGUST 1970

THE REDS REVERTED to their more wayward alter egos as the win at Burnley began to look like a false dawn. Geoff Hurst scored on two minutes before United had got their minds on the game. It was a jolt which needed a swift reply which wasn't long in coming as Denis Law turned goal provider laying off the ball for John Fitzpatrick who plucked it

out of the air before ramming home.

Hurst and Jimmy Greaves were full of danger but United held out with some stout defending. At the other end Best looked a threat at various stages and after one scampering run he hit a post with an effort that deserved better.

MANCHESTER UNITED 2 EVERTON 0
DIVISION ONE 2 SEPTEMBER 1970

BRIAN KIDD RETURNED, though Willie Morgan was unfortunate to be dropped in order to allow the forward a start. Wilf McGuinness didn't want to de-stabilise a combination of Nobby Stiles, John Fitzpatrick and Bobby Charlton who had begun to inspire some confidence. Steve James made the bench for his first involvement in the senior side since a knee operation towards the end of the previous term.

Everton, last season's runway champions, hadn't won a game so far and were keen to impose their credentials. The Merseysider's were quickly into their stride and were by far the better side in a first half during which Howard Kendall had a goal disallowed and Jimmy Rimmer need to be in top form.

Rough house tactics on Best and others were repaid with the finest possible

vengeance when George turned back the clock a few seasons by taking matters into his own hands. Running at the Everton rearguard his reward came when he found the ball played to his feet and slammed the shot home crisply to register his first of the season.

It marked the beginning of a great exhibition of dribbling in the time remaining when Best took the ball from Paul Edwards in his own half then sprinted, danced and jinked for 50 yards past four players before sliding the ball out to Charlton. Bobby made the finish just as emphatic as the earlier shot which beat Gordon West. Denis Law didn't score but his all round game showed he was back to something approaching peak form.

LIVERPOOL 1 MANCHESTER UNITED 1
DIVISION ONE 5 SEPTEMBER 1970

THE CHANCE OF a win double against Merseyside opposition presented itself with a visit to Anfield. Each side dominated at various stages. Initially United had the upper hand then Liverpool responded and severely tested The Reds. Chances were carved out from all sorts of distances and angles which led to one spectacular save when Jimmy Rimmer somehow managed to divert a Bobby Graham header from five yards out.

A number of players took knocks including Denis Law who was a severe doubt until the morning of the match. George Best had dislocated a finger during the Everton game, which was a surprise considering the full-blooded nature of that clash.

Best and Law played with a verve which reminded many of their partnership from the mid-to-late 1960s. It seemed those halcyon days had passed until recent weeks.

Brian Kidd nodded in on 20 minutes from a Stiles cross but it only took moments for Liverpool to hit back through Alun Evans after Ian Ure failed to clear a Ray Clemence goalkick - the hesitancy allowed Evans space and time to shoot in.

ALDERSHOT 1 MANCHESTER UNITED 3
LEAGUE CUP 2ND ROUND 9 SEPTEMBER 1970

STOCKTON BORN ERIC Young, a 17 year-old England schools international, was called into the 13 for the visit to Aldershot joining the 11 who started against Liverpool and substitute Steve James. John Sydenham, an old foe from his days with Southampton, had dropped down the divisions to join The Shots in recent seasons but thankfully for United's defenders, he was declared unfit.

Former Liverpool forward Jimmy Melia had taken over as player/manager two years previously. He was an adept schemer at Anfield and promised his side would take United on for skills rather than attempt to out-muscle them. The Liverpudlian was as good as his word. So much so that Aldershot were by far the better side during the first half and deserved to take a lead three minutes before the break.

However, somewhat less deservedly United levelled courtesy of a flash of genius and opportunism by George Best seconds before the sides were called in. The winger controlled the ball in a tight position then lashed home after his pressure caused a moment's hesitation at the back.

Brian Kidd benefited from a little creative play on the hour. Once again some hard work chasing the ball paid off. With the ball at his feet, George headed wide and towards the byline where he found his colleague with a precise cross. All that remained was the simple task of heading in. The goal coincided with the home side losing full back Joe Jopling through concussion which effectively ended their resistance.

United were rarely required to break after taking the lead but a Denis Law goal scored after Bobby Charlton's shot was parried ensured there was no chance of Aldershot nicking a draw.

Jimmy Rimmer had to make a host of saves, many of which were of top quality, to keep things level at 0-0. The keeper must have run Best close for the accolade of match winner.

MANCHESTER UNITED 2 COVENTRY CITY 0
DIVISION ONE 12 SEPTEMBER 1970

TONY DUNNE, STRUGGLING with a thigh strain, was the player most at risk of missing out through injury and came off before the end when he started to feel twinges in his thigh. A very pedestrian first half was only lit up by George Best's improved form, though he failed to gain any reward until the hour mark when he and United burst into life. Taking an exquisite pass from Bobby Charlton, he moved through the Coventry defenders before finishing with aplomb.

Up to this point United had real problems getting the ball through to the hard working but well patrolled strikers, as the visitors rarely committed themselves in attack although when they did Jimmy Rimmer had enough about him to tidy up.

Five minutes after the opener George hit a blistering shot which was parried by Bill Glazer and fell to Charlton. Thus far the season was a mirror image of the previous campaign - a poor opening which only perked up in September as Best came into form. He had of course been tentative again during the opening phases of this term.

IPSWICH TOWN 4 MANCHESTER UNITED 0
DIVISION ONE 19 SEPTEMBER 1970

AN INJURY TO Brian Kidd allowed Alan Gowling a rare opportunity and the chance to pair up with Denis Law in attack. 17 year-old Tony Young was named as a substitute edging out fellow full back Kevin Lewis who was just a year older and travelled to Portman Road but was the unlucky 13th man.

A 4-0 defeat to Ipswich was a total shock and turned into a baptism of fire for Young who had to come on for Tony Dunne who again limped off holding his leg. With Denis Law struggling with a cold and David Sadler battling a stomach upset which left him doubled up in pain on more than one occasion, United were unable to overcome sizeable handicaps. There was little excuse however as too many fit players made life difficult for themselves. None more so than Ian Ure and Paul Edwards at centre-half.

The midfield also put in a poor showing and United's prospects looked all the worse because Best looked totally out of step and became visibly frustrated at his inability to influence events.

MANCHESTER UNITED 1 BLACKPOOL 1
DIVISION ONE 26 SEPTEMBER 1970

IAN URE AND Nobby Stiles were notable omissions, although their absence was not enforced through injury. Only Denis Law, Paul Edwards and Tony Dunne were ruled out with fitness problems. These choices provided Willie Watson with a debut at right back while Francis Burns deputised for Dunne on the left and Steve James came in at centre half. Willie Morgan made his first appearance for a month while Carlo Sartori took his place on the bench.

Blackpool, without a goal in four straight league defeats, saw the less experienced players cause them most problems while the older hands struggled. Bobby Charlton, in particular, would have cursed his limited contribution and poor shooting.

A back heel from John Fitzpatrick sent Morgan down the wing and his cross was met by Best stealing in on the other flank to score. Mick Burns equalised and after the goal Jimmy Rimmer made vital saves to keep United level. The match could have been won in the final quarter with Blackpool struggling to contain The Reds after going a man down. Best was a huge threat but couldn't quite do enough to get a goal.

WOLVES 3 MANCHESTER UNITED 2
DIVISION ONE 3 OCTOBER 1970

No CHANGES WERE made meaning the big names languished in the reserves. That included Alex Stepney now recovered but second in line as Rimmer was given an extended opportunity. What was notable was that only one player, Willie Morgan, cost a fee. The other ten plus Sartori were brought through the ranks. It was a United tradition but whether it would prove a positive remained to be seen.

A Steve James error two minutes in gifted Bobby Gould a goal and the first of what turned out to be a well merited hat-trick. United didn't deserve to lose but were caught out for the opener and well dissected by some superb forward play for the other two.

Alan Gowling, in for Law, scored when he mopped up following a Charlton shot that hit the bar. Best was a constant danger and never more so than with United chasing a game - he would have scored with a bit more luck and in the process rescued a point.

Nevertheless he still created Brian Kidd's goal which put The Reds in with a chance at 3-2 by quick thinking at a free-kick which allowed the Mancunian to twist and hit the ball in one movement. Nevertheless another away defeat left McGuinness in deep trouble.

MANCHESTER UNITED 1 PORTSMOUTH 0
LEAGUE CUP 3RD RD 7 OCTOBER 1970

DENIS LAW WAS forced to sit this League Cup tie out after narrowly failing his fitness test. Willie Watson and Steve James also missed out - a cruel twist of fate for a couple of players who had earned a chance in the first team but more so for James who had battled various injuries and then had an operation to remove his appendix midway through that recovery. Both full back berths had proved problematic over recent weeks leading to another debutant, Ian Donald, stepping in on the right.

Ure returned at centre half alongside John Aston, who had hit form and goals in the reserves, although the latter only made it as far as the substitute bench.

United, keen to go at least one better than last season in the competition, went ahead through Bobby Charlton's first goal in months. George Best had seemed destined to be the match winner as he was a constant danger to Pompey but for some reason his passing, as well as finishing, was feeble.

It meant United posed a limited threat until Charlton hit the net and they remained vulnerable to a hard working Portsmouth thereafter. David Sadler picked up an injury and with Ian Ure in poor form United struggled to progress.

MANCHESTER UNITED 0 CRYSTAL PALACE 1
DIVISION ONE 10 OCTOBER 1970

NOBBY STILES REVERTED to left half for the first time in almost 18 months after David Sadler succumbed to an ankle injury. It was the position in which he had built a formidable reputation since the early 1960s but was his fifth different role of the season after three games out. Bobby Charlton reached another milestone - his 400th league appearance. John Aston, who could have joined Birmingham but decided to stay and fight for his place, was full of running in his first opportunity in the league since April.

Palace found themselves stretched although they managed to block a goal bound lob from Best. Seeing the chance of an early breakthrough, George buzzed around the area and soon after his first effort, a testing 20 yard drive was put out for a corner by John Jackson.

However, the promising start fizzled out as United slumped. Willie Morgan's disallowed chip saw a well executed move achieve no reward and morale took a blow as good individual displays came to nothing and the team failed to gel. Palace got a chance and defeat left United fifth from the bottom. A chronic injury list was taking its toll but Wilf McGuinness couldn't rely on a dramatic improvement as some of those out had seemed way below par prior to their lay offs.

His team was also a mixture of maturity and inexperience. There were few players,

George Best excepted, at the right level of experience between youth graduates and the half dozen or so approaching their mid-30s. It seemed United's fall could be more dramatic unless action was taken.

Ian Ure's introduction a year ago had stabilised the side and a season which started badly had improved before plateauing. But for a club like United doing just enough to stay in the division was insufficient and McGuinness knew it.

LEEDS UNITED 2 MANCHESTER UNITED 2
DIVISION ONE 17 OCTOBER 1970

SOUTHAMPTON'S MICK CHANNON had been linked with United during the week since Crystal Palace had inflicted a fifth defeat of the league campaign. Though there were no direct comments made about the forward, or indeed any other player, it was clear the manager was mulling over using some of the sizeable profits Old Trafford's board had recently declared to improve his team's fortunes in front of goal.

Willie Morgan's absence increased the number of casualties though, much to the relief of United's backline Mick Jones, who boasted a good recent record against The Reds, was suffering from a stomach upset that seemed to affect his game. Leeds took the lead when Jackie Charlton smashed the ball past a static defence. A whistle had stopped the majority of players in their tracks but the noise came from the Elland Road crowd and not the referee who had waved play on. Rod Belfitt pilfered the ball from John Fitzpatrick to double the lead. United looked out of the game before it had truly started and all down to a couple of very disappointing goals.

The team effort missing against Palace somehow returned as Fitzpatrick repaid his side for a crucial lapse on the second goal before Charlton netted to level. Neither were the most clinical of strikes but were crucial to morale. There were no individual stars on the afternoon just a hard working XI which displayed great endeavour to salvage a point.

However, crucial defensive displays by Stiles and Rimmer, who got at least a fingertip to everything thrown at him, raised their contributions above everyone else's.

MANCHESTER UNITED 2 WEST BROMWICH ALBION 1
DIVISION ONE 24 OCTOBER 1970

JIMMY RIMMER'S FORM meant the manager could only consider making a change for change's sake. Alex Stepney, believing he could do no more to prove himself not only fit but in equal condition, put in a transfer request that was swiftly refused. David Sadler remained sidelined and with Nobby Stiles dropping out through an ankle problem the versatile Francis Burns switched to left-half.

A bright spot was Denis Law's long awaited return. The Scottish forward seemed to have lurched from crisis to crisis over the past few seasons but clearly hoped to pick up where he had been forced to leave off. His fire power was clearly required.

John Aston seemed to have scored but his effort was ruled out and as can often happen the team which escaped going behind scored within a minute as Tony Brown put Albion ahead. United had to summon up the same spirit as the previous week and were able to draw on their resources again.

Despite struggling in midfield Law,

who had looked uncharacteristically timid, finally emerged as a force. Bobby Hope was forced off for West Brom and that limited The Baggies' effectiveness but The Reds perseverance and fighting spirit couldn't be faulted.

Just three minutes after Law equalised he and Charlton combined for a cross which Brian Kidd nodded home. The margin of victory would have been larger had a Charlton firecracker not been ruled out for foot up.

MANCHESTER UNITED 2 CHELSEA 1
League Cup Rd 4 28 October 1970

STEVE JAMES RETURNED to fitness leading to Ian Ure's exclusion following a poor run of form. Unfortunately Law had felt his troublesome groin go again late in the match with West Bromwich Albion and with plenty of others receiving fitness tests, the fates didn't augur well.

FA Cup winners Chelsea were a good side and not the type of opposition anyone wanted to meet without key personnel. Thankfully Bobby Charlton was superb in the opening half and involved in almost every attacking move. His low shot with 30 minutes gone underlined United's dominance. The ball skidded and gained extra pace off a greasy surface giving Peter Bonetti no chance.

Chelsea equalised within five minutes following an equally unstoppable shot from John Hollins. Law was finally forced out at the break, it was a blow but United compensated and the re-jig allowed Best to shine as brightly as he had done in weeks.

Electrifying runs at defenders increased his confidence to such an extent that George decided to pick out his nemesis, Ron Harris, for ritual humiliation. For once Chopper was on the back foot and seethed with anger at failing to control his man. It only made Best determined to tease him all the more.

After six seasons of watching George Best ghost into positions when gambling on a poor back pass, one might have assumed that top flight defenders would do anything but search out their keeper when under pressure. But panic often grips players in the defensive third of the field especially with a certain Ulsterman breathing down their neck.

And so it proved as an errant backpass presented United with a goal - Bobby Charlton converting Best's pass after George had harried Chelsea's back four.

United's star man rounded off the night by hitting the second 15 minutes from time. Put through by Aston, George found the Chelsea defence had gone AWOL and although a few defenders sought to hinder his progress they were brushed aside as George approached the penalty area. With the keeper at his mercy there was still a lot to do as Ron 'Chopper' Harris sought to make up lost ground, steaming across from left half and hurling himself straight into the player with the

ball only an after thought.

With a presence of mind borne out of experience, Best altered his body position to lessen the inevitable impact. Though his knees buckled George advanced towards goal and, as if to taunt Chelsea, rounded the keeper before slotting into an empty net.

NEWCASTLE UNITED 1 MANCHESTER UNITED 0
Division One 31 October 1970

THE MIDWEEK EXPLOITS in the League Cup suggested the old George Best was back but also highlighted the fact that the campaign boasted one of the winger's poorest goals to games ratios since his debut. He had notched five all season which was a figure the Irishman was keen to boost at St James Park.

With Law out, the same 11 who finished the game against Chelsea started. Best, with his tail up after such a stunning contribution to The Reds as an attacking unit, set about ensuring The Magpies made recompense for embarrassing United 5-1 the previous term. George had missed that game through injury.

Though he built up a real head of steam

and ensured United had the better of the game, he failed to find a way through.

United paid a high price when Jimmy Rimmer failed to hold on to a wet ball as he fielded a high cross. David Sadler failed to react allowing Wyn Davies to nip in and secure Newcastle's first home win since opening day.

The result was scant reward for Best and others but particularly Bobby Charlton who was excellent in midfield but couldn't help conjure the knock-out blow. When there was a scare for Newcastle Willie McFaul was equal to it and rode his luck at times.

MANCHESTER UNITED 2 STOKE CITY 2
Division One 7 November 1970

DENIS LAW WAS back after yet another lay off and on the evidence of the previous weekend his addition was much needed. Illness saw Tony Dunne miss out and Francis Burns drop back which in turn left a midfield vacancy. Rather than be deployed as an out and out striker Wilf

McGuinness asked Denis to fill a gap between the midfield and the front two.

Along with Bobby Charlton, Best was declared fit despite picking up blisters on his feet following an indoor tournament during the week. The other members of the six-a-side competition Alex Stepney,

David Sadler, John Fitzpatrick and Carlo Sartori were all available. George's skills and close control meant he was naturally suited to that form of the game and an asset in the tight spaces most matches were played in. United had won the tournament with some ease.

Back in the traditional version of the game, further defensive frailty gifted Stoke an early lead. Just 90 seconds had elapsed when Terry Conroy stole in. United tightened up thereafter. Law proved to be a great link between midfield and attack, emphasising just how much that sort of clever and quick player was needed.

He collected a Kidd flick to equalise. Once level, The Reds dominated and looked impressive going forward. David Sadler's glanced header made it 2-1 but more flagging at the back allowed The Potters to hit back within a minute. A long ball down the centre was watched by too many players allowing John Ritchie to hold off Steve James before steering the ball past Rimmer.

It was a huge blow and while United through Best and others remained industrious, from that on the defence looked ragged under pressure and could easily have conceded another.

SPAIN 3 NORTHERN IRELAND 0
EUROPEAN NATIONS CUP QUALIFIER 11 NOVEMBER 1970

NORTHERN IRELAND LACKED real strength in depth and once one or two key men were missing looked a very ordinary side. Four players were out for the trip to Seville although Spain were still concerned by their guest's movement for the first quarter of the game. However, the loss of Derek Dougan, one of the few remaining class players, on 25 minutes led to a speedy capitulation.

Right winger Joaquín Rife and his replacement from the bench Lora kept a good tag on Best who had been working off the shoulder of the front two prior to Dougan's arm injury but was then pushed into attack.

Early in the second half George set up Terry Harkin with a free-kick. The effort was saved by José Iribar at the foot of his post. Carlos Rexach of Barcelona opened the scoring just before the break but it was the next goal from Pirri just before the hour which really broke spirits. Luis intercepted a back-pass from Tommy Jackson close to the end to wrap up the win.

NOTTINGHAM FOREST 1 MANCHESTER UNITED 2
DIVISION ONE 14 NOVEMBER 1970

WILLIE WATSON CAME back in for the dropped Paul Edwards. Francis Burns was left out to allow for Tony Dunne's return and the switch helped bolster things at the back, allowing United to record a first away win for three months.

The backline held tight in the final quarter as Forest pressed for an equaliser once they halved the deficit. Not all United's defenders were convincing but many bad habits were eradicated and Jimmy Rimmer was back in the form which had unseated Alex Stepney.

Law, playing in the hole behind the front two, was again devastating and Alan Gowling owed his twentieth minute strike to the Scot as did Carlo Sartori who made it 2-0. Bill Foulkes' midweek testimonial had clearly tired a number of players both physically and emotionally. It certainly showed in many legs in the final stages though fortunately much of the hard work had already been done.

MANCHESTER UNITED 4 CRYSTAL PALACE 2
LEAGUE CUP QF 18 NOVEMBER 1970

BRIAN KIDD AND John Aston were recalled in time for the League Cup quarter-final tie with Crystal Palace. It was tough on the previous weekend's goalscorers though Sartori was compensated by winning the battle for a place on the bench.

However, following their shock win at Old Trafford just over a month ago, no risks were about to be taken. After many seasons of taking this trophy lightly United were now keen to lift it. The small matter of a guaranteed place in Europe was a huge inducement.

Best's running bewitched The Eagles throughout but he lost the ball twice and each occasion Palace scored as a result. The visitors were handicapped by the loss of Alan Birchenall six minutes in which blunted their attack. John Fitzpatrick hit the opener from a Bobby Charlton corner just before the half-hour. On the resumption Kidd struck twice. His second whacked the crossbar and bounced over the line although Denis Law headed it into the back of the net to make sure. A deflected Bobby Charlton shot after Palace had closed the score to 3-2 via Gerry Queen and Tony Taylor rounded off the scoring.

SOUTHAMPTON 1 MANCHESTER UNITED 0
DIVISION ONE 21 NOVEMBER 1970

SOUTHAMPTON, WITHOUT RON Davies, pressed Jimmy Gabriel into service as an emergency forward. The Saints had a reputation far removed from their nickname which proved well earned on the day as Brian O'Neill forced John Fitzpatrick off. He was eventually replaced but an initial stint in which he spent five minutes getting running repairs saw United concede the only goal of the game, Gabriel popping up to head in from a lofted free-kick. Fitzpatrick was one of United's strongest players in the air which only increased the frustration.

United's defence was well worked throughout and did well to hold out especially after losing such a key figure. Through his actions O'Neill gave himself plenty of room to exploit. At the other end Denis Law was often lacklustre and Bobby Charlton could not get a grip on the game. Best tried hard but found little reward for his surges until the end of the game and even then not enough to find an equaliser. Kidd was isolated for spells and couldn't get himself into the game.

MANCHESTER UNITED 1 HUDDERSFIELD TOWN 1
DIVISION ONE 28 NOVEMBER 1970

DESPITE DEFEAT AT The Dell the same side was retained as it showed some promise. Willie Watson, who had been loaned to Huddersfield towards the end of the previous season, welcomed some familiar faces and keeper Terry Poole, a former United reserve, was making an emotional return to Old Trafford for Huddersfield's first match against United since an FA Cup tie in January 1963.

The Terriers may have been promoted the previous season but they looked assured for long periods. Frank Worthington and Brian Greenhalgh were in great form, testing United's defence and Jimmy Rimmer had to be agile. Their confidence spread to the centre of the field and inevitably they gained just reward.

Best was United's most dangerous forward and one of his runs paved the

way for United's goal with a move George completed himself. For all the finesse there was also a darker side to his game as highlighted by a punch up with winger Jimmy Lawson. Best was tugged slightly by the shirt as he began a run to support the attack and lashed out.

This marked the first time George's frustrations had shown in many months. It should have served as a warning and there would have been little complaint if he had been sent off. With an appearance before the FA pending a dismissal, Best's actions could have led to a very lengthy ban.

TOTTENHAM HOTSPUR 2 MANCHESTER UNITED 2
DIVISION ONE 5 DECEMBER 1970

UNITED NAMED AN unchanged side for the fourth successive game but could well have made a change in the number eight shirt as George missed the train to London arriving on the platform just as it pulled away. A few problems at a business appointment the club knew about was said to have been the cause and Wilf McGuinness accepted the explanation although he could have suspended the player.

George's goal the previous week was his first in over a month and generally his record had been less than prolific this campaign. Spurs were outstanding during the first half and United were lucky to survive a number of scrapes. Steve James and David Sadler were outstanding in the middle; organising and commanding their patch well. Only two Rimmer saves plus able support from Tony Dunne and Willie Watson kept it goalless.

United scored twice against the run of play but each goal was down to flashes of sheer brilliance by George Best who took an awkward cross from John Aston, controlled the ball then nonchalantly found Law who struck the first. Another tricky ball this time from John Fitzpatrick was brought down before it was crashed in to give Best his 100th league strike for the club - a mark only four other players had reached until that point.

Alan Gilzean and Martin Peters scored one a piece from Peter Knowles' crosses. A draw was the right result, even if Spurs slightly shaded events and while United would have been disappointed to lose a decent advantage, the home side's general play plus their come back from adversity, had to be admired.

MANCHESTER UNITED 1 MANCHESTER CITY 4
DIVISION ONE 12 DECEMBER 1970

DAVID SADLER FRACTURED a cheekbone during his efforts to repel Spurs which provided Nobby Stiles with a chance and, as Sadler was expected to be out for a month or so, the opportunity was due to be a prolonged one.

Glyn Pardoe, who seemed destined to miss the clash, was passed fit that morning and his appearance was a huge boost for The Blues as he always seemed to do well against Best. United capped a relatively disappointing few weeks by receiving their biggest Old Trafford Derby humiliation in 15 years. City took an early lead through Mike Doyle and only a minority of the 52,636 crowd took any pleasure in Francis Lee grabbing a hat-trick. Unusually none of his goals were from either the penalty spot or free-kicks. Jimmy Rimmer replaced Alex Stepney in goal but was blameless for any of the efforts which beat him.

Brian Kidd got a late consolation though there was a sour note to the game for City who saw Pardoe stretchered off with a broken leg. The full-back had gone into a fair challenge with George Best but fate conspired to ensure he came off worst. Though he made a comeback he rarely managed to exhibit the same form he had shown in the months leading up to this fateful day. Pardoe had been a member of the City side in that 1964 FA Youth Cup semi-final in which George had starred.

The Reds only came into the game as an attacking force in the closing stages but it was too late and even then too little was offered. Best, rocked by the injury he had inadvertently caused, was only an infrequent threat. When he mounted raids Kidd and John Aston provided little support.

Law limped off early in the second half to compound problems. City ruled the roost in midfield and United's backline was overrun as The Blues took the bragging rights for another season.

MANCHESTER UNITED 1 ASTON VILLA 1
League Cup Semi-Final 1st leg 16 December 1970

THE WINTER OF 1970 was hit by industrial action which left many homes and hospitals lit by candles. It also caused this match to be postponed from the previous week as the electricity supply for the floodlights could not be guaranteed. Both clubs and the FA had toyed with an afternoon kick off but assurances from the Electricity Board that the domestic supply would not be drained and that the pylons would remain burning throughout the game finally allowed matters to proceed.

As expected Law was missing with a bruised thigh. Carlo Sartori came in with Gowling on the bench. Villa introduced Jimmy Brown, a 17 year-old of whom much was expected. This much was clear as he had been brought in specifically to mark George Best. He had made his debut at the age of 15. Villa may have been in the Third Division but rose to the occasion and the venue. They raised their game and were not just content to defend or contain. They actively looked for goals and were rewarded by Andy Lochhead's effort on 41 minutes. The striker had a decent record with most of his teams against United.

Even before this The Reds had been tested with their defence leading a charmed life on occasions.

Brian Kidd offered little until getting in on the end of a Sartori cross just before the break to level. It was an excellent build up and finish but there was no disguising the problems.

Best was always a problem for Villa and Brown did well. There was more cutting edge in the second half although many forwards were often guilty of trying too hard against opposition which on paper should have been well beaten. The midfield was once more anonymous leading to more defensive insecurity.

MANCHESTER UNITED 1 ARSENAL 3
DIVISION ONE 19 DECEMBER 1970

WILF MCGUINNESS MADE a courageous decision to bring Willie Morgan and Paddy Crerand back with Stiles and Aston sacrificed. However, they were only two among a teamful of underperformers who could have been dropped. There were many other candidates but with Arsenal the only opposition before the vital second leg of the League Cup semi-final, surgical strikes rather than mass changes were required.

Both returnees were playing for their futures. Especially the 32 year old Crerand who had not played in the four months since The Gunners humiliated United at Highbury. Frank McClintock was back for Arsenal and ensured Crerand in particular had a lot of work to get through. A certain bite and attacking edge which had been missing for some time was evident but few others were able to take advantage of this industry. United looked especially weak in the air as McClintock, George Graham and Ray Kennedy scored with headers in the opening half. The Reds were not three goals worse but defensive lapses were costly and matters could have been graver but for John Fitzpatrick.

George Best refused to give in and took the fight to his opponents assisting Carlo Sartori to net. Best was the only real threat and although Paddy Crerand set up the forwards their finishing was once again slip-shod.

ASTON VILLA 2 MANCHESTER UNITED 1
LEAGUE CUP SF 2ND LEG 23 DECEMBER 1970

FURTHER DESPERATION AND the need to inject some adrenalin into the side saw Ian Ure recalled in place of the injured John Fitzpatrick. David Sadler returned at the first opportunity. He had made good progress during his recuperation and was declared fit ahead of schedule. Steve James missed out.

United enjoyed a good opening 20 minutes and took the lead but too many heads dropped as other efforts were missed allowing Villa, who had successfully soaked up the pressure, back into the game. Again the forwards were out of sorts as were many defenders when tested. Brian Kidd's effort on 14 minutes was equalised by Lochhead who out-muscled Ure to level.

Pat McMahon put the Villains ahead after 70 minutes with another header but the damage could have been far heavier and United would have been out of it had it not been for Jimmy Rimmer. The only other star contributor was George Best. Kidd faded after his goal with only the odd flicker of quality from others distinguishing them as top flight players.

Wilf McGuinness's gamble on experienced heads had only just failed to pay off in terms of the scoreline but was a mile off in terms of performance. Many couldn't help but wonder if he had made too many punts on personnel and systems over recent months rather than stick to a long-term plan. This defeat meant that

the knives were out for the manager in the United boardroom.

DERBY COUNTY 4 MANCHESTER UNITED 4
DIVISION ONE 26 DECEMBER 1970

THOUGH HE HAD failed to turn up for training on Christmas morning, Best did report to Old Trafford for the Boxing Day game with Derby County. Wilf McGuinness initially sent him home but after other players pleaded on his behalf, decided that the need for points (United were without a win since mid-November) was greater than the need to set an example.

The Rams were a strong side and United could not cope without Best. A £50 fine was handed down and the punishment kept quiet for some weeks until subsequent events brought it into the public arena.

The sum was of little consequence to Best who failed to let the day's events trouble him and contributed royally to a great game. United recovered from a 2-0 deficit at half time to take the lead. Snow and ice led to many errors and six goals were scored within 19 minutes highlighting the freakish nature of conditions. United's share of that tally included three during four minutes in the second-half.

A Dave Mackay free-kick provided Derby with an early lead with Frank Wignall the other scorer in the first half. On 56 minutes Denis Law began the fight back by heading in. Best hit a scorching equaliser then Law edged United ahead on the hour mark. Kevin Hector and

Archie Gemmill then sent the game see-sawing the other way but with 15 minutes remaining Brian Kidd levelled.

On the balance of play so far it could easily have ended 7-7 before the whistle but with both sides happy with a point and not wanting to risk any return for their efforts the match fizzled out.

Bobby Charlton and Paddy Crerand put in a lot of unsung work in midfield to begin the remarkable comeback.

Unfortunately, soon after the game Wilf McGuinness was relieved of his responsibilities as team manager and invited to resume his old post on the Old Trafford coaching staff. Wilf agreed and promised to keep giving his all to the club at any level. It ended a tumultuous year and a half for the man charged with succeeding Sir Matt Busby and the club. Though he had only served as team manager for 4 months and 27 days.

United had failed to achieve any success since lifting the European Cup six years earlier and had declined further under McGuinness. So much so that relegation, an unthinkable notion a few seasons ago, had become a distinct possibility. The Reds were fifth from bottom just seven points off the drop zone and 19 off the top.

The United board had little option but to end Wilf's tenure in the hotseat. He had been a popular and successful coach but failed to win many friends amongst the playing staff since taking control. There seemed every possibility of a dressing room revolt with senior players openly questioning his methods and stating that they would refuse to play under him unless something was done.

Matt Busby took over in the interim

as United sought to find a permanent replacement in the summer. Sir Matt read out a statement to the press at 11.15am on 29th December outlining the decision and the reasons for directors' actions. It made for an unhappy Christmas for the McGuinness family.

MANCHESTER UNITED 0 MIDDLESBROUGH 0
FA Cup 3rd Rd 2 January 1971

MATT BUSBY PICKED an unchanged side from the last XI Wilf McGuinness had sent out. A hard, icy pitch hindered the game's flow and many of the flair player's contributions. George Best generally struggled, though not when running with the ball, only when a Boro player attempted to win it off him. For once he had no trick to extricate himself from such situations.

Sir Matt had emphasised that play should centre around some of his most trusted attacking forces - Willie Morgan, Denis Law, Brian Kidd and George Best. Morgan had the clearest chances but failed

to make the most of them. Defensively United looked sound but Jimmy Rimmer was required to pull off some excellent saves to earn United a replay.

This goalless draw was overshadowed by a disaster in Glasgow where Rangers had been entertaining arch rivals Celtic. Home fans making their way out of Ibrox started to drift away from the stadium once Jimmy Johnstone scored for Celtic with a minute to go. Colin Stein equalised during injury time causing those who had left to turn back. Crush barriers collapsed under the renewed strain and 66 people were killed.

MIDDLESBROUGH 2 MANCHESTER UNITED 1
FA Cup 3rd Rd Replay 5 January 1971

IAN URE WAS a doubt for the replay which would see the winners face Everton in the next round. United went behind early despite a promising start. On seven minutes Hugh McIlmoyle headed in to further expose United's defensive weakness in this area. His header looped over a stranded Jimmy Rimmer who had advanced a few yards off his line. Derrick Downing made it 2-0 on 74 minutes after

John Fitzpatrick committed a foul close to the area.

George Best's header from Willie Morgan's cross seconds before the end gave United little chance of recovery.

George's selfish play was a problem. Maybe he didn't trust the ability of others or wouldn't adapt his game to his team-mates. Whatever the reason good work in midfield was wasted as he ran out of steam by the time he reached the danger area.

24 hours prior to the cup replay at Ayresome Park, Best had been in London appearing before the FA's Disciplinary Committee after receiving three bookings within a couple of months for dissent and jostling referees. A train from Piccadilly Station should have left with Best and mentor Matt Busby on board but George missed it. He arrived for the hearing three hours late. A £250 fine and a suspended six week ban were handed down. It was the heaviest punishment any player had received but given the gravity of the offences and George's history it was generally agreed that this was a fair conclusion.

Neither seemed to affect the player too much as, despite going out of the cup, Best put in a decent performance and scored United's only goal in the 2-1 defeat.

However, this game was sandwiched between two further misadventures as on the day prior to United's journey to London for a league game with Chelsea the following weekend, George missed another train already containing his teammates. Instructions that he should not travel down later were relayed. Nevertheless, George made his way to the capital in any case, for what ended up being social rather than football reasons.

He flew down on Friday evening but when he got to the team hotel in Russell Square asked his taxi driver to keep going on seeing herds of journalists and photographers at the entrance. He was thought to have returned to Manchester straight away but fancied the idea of spending the weekend away so while United battled hard to earn a 2-1 win George was in the company of Irish actress Sinead Cusack. He had arranged to meet her after the game at any rate so was able to spend more time than anticipated in her company. Photographers soon gathered outside her Islington flat waiting for the Ulsterman to leave.

Friends claimed recent defeats and his own poor form for his problem. A meeting with Matt Busby was due to take place on the Monday following the game but George failed to show. He was still in London and the posse of pressmen having found his hiding place, camped out there effectively holding him prisoner.

The United board was incensed and three hours after he was due to have attempted to make peace with the club a decision to suspend him for two weeks was announced.

Rumour had it that he was seeking a move abroad but after a meeting with Matt Busby these suggestions were scotched. George publicly apologised to his manager, club, fellow players and fans. He claimed his actions were a protest at the poor results and performances. From now on in he would be giving his all.

Headlines could concentrate on the football again - for now at least and results picked up as after the win at Chelsea, United drew at home with Burnley. The ban only covered the latter game and George would be available for United's next match at the end of the month.

HUDDERSFIELD TOWN 1 MANCHESTER UNITED 2
Division One 30 January 1971

IN TERMS OF build up, this game rekindled memories of the last time George had returned from a suspension and scored six against Northampton Town. Fans of both sides were straining at the leash to see Best's return with a bumper crowd in attendance.

During his time out George had played in a specially arranged training game and a fundraiser for the victims of the Ibrox disaster. He was asked to play at inside left here to accommodate changes required through the absence of Brian Kidd and Tony Dunne.

Former United midfielder, Belfast born Jimmy Nicholson, who missed the game at Old Trafford back in November, was keen to give a good account of himself against a manager he had last played for in the early 1960s. Nicholson put in a great performance as Huddersfield tested The Reds but for once United's defence held firm with Paul Edwards in particularly good form and Alex Stepney doing well after his return to the side under Busby.

Denis Law was eventually carried off with a gashed shin but put United ahead in a move Best initiated with a run through midfield before passing to Willie Morgan who took on a defender before crossing. Unfortunately David Sadler conceded a penalty which allowed the home side to level but a foul on Alan Gowling led to a free-kick which Morgan took. His effort found the wall but fell to John Aston who hit it sweetly on the volley.

After the game the true nature of Law's injury came to light. The cut was actually caused by Edwards. The striker had drifted back to lend a hand and after deciding to put in a ball winning tackle his challenge was followed by a lunge into the melee from his teammate.

CYPRUS 0 NORTHERN IRELAND 3
European Championship Qualifier 3 February 1971

NORTHERN IRELAND HAD gone nine internationals without a win before beating Cyprus in Nicosia. They were totally dominant but only managed to find the net after the break when Bryan Hamilton dribbled through but hit the bar, Jimmy Nicholson picked up the pieces.

Just two minutes later Dougan also scored after a rebound, this time when a Nicholson free-kick fell kindly after being parried by Herodotus in goal for the Wolves man to net easily.

Nicholson was then brought down in the area for a penalty just four minutes from time which Best converted.

MANCHESTER UNITED 2 TOTTENHAM HOTSPUR 1
DIVISION ONE 6 FEBRUARY 1971

LAW ASIDE, BEST and Bobby Charlton were United's strongest doubts. George had suffered a bruised foot in Cyprus. Aston's omission from the starting line-up created a vacancy on the left wing.

United's results certainly suggested Busby's return was having the desired effect and the 'new' George Best was certainly living up to his promise to behave. Confidence seemed to have spread throughout the team and was a huge factor in the upsurge. A clever ball from Alan Gowling created an opportunity for the Irishman who made an impudent run

before shooting past Jennings. Best then assisted in the goal which increased the lead after playing in Brian Kidd with a clever flick. A foul led to a penalty which Willie Morgan smashed in.

Martin Peters pulled one back for Spurs after beating Bobby Charlton for the ball and then pace. An indication of The Reds downturn was that this was the first home win registered in three months.

MANCHESTER UNITED 5 SOUTHAMPTON 1
DIVISION ONE 20 FEBRUARY 1971

JUST A FEW weeks earlier the absence of players such as Brian Kidd, Denis Law and Tony Dunne would have seen United struggle to get a result. But with their tails up The Reds finally dished out a hammering. Alan Gowling was the star hitting four goals, including three in eight minutes.

In the process he became the first United player to score more than three during the course of a game since David Sadler in November 1966. Morgan hit the opener after a smart pass from Best. Aston set up three of the four Gowling goals with a cross and two corners.

EVERTON 1 MANCHESTER UNITED 0
DIVISION ONE 23 FEBRUARY 1971

VICTORY OVER SOUTHAMPTON was a boost but champions Everton would prove a sterner test. United played just as well as they had against The Saints but the gulf in class between the two opponents was obvious.

Both teams were extremely attacking in their attitudes and only one goal decided the result when Tommy Wright stabbed

the ball over the line during a skirmish in the area after Alex Stepney had fumbled a cross. United claimed their keeper was being fouled but play was allowed to continue.

George Best was a constant threat, dribbling and weaving and Everton struggled to contain him as he and John Aston both hit the bar.

MANCHESTER UNITED 1 NEWCASTLE UNITED 0
DIVISION ONE 27 FEBRUARY 1971

ALAN GOWLING MISSED out, allowing Brian Kidd to come back into the reckoning. Gowling had recently scored a fistful of goals drawing him level on seven as the club's top scorer with George Best. The statistic revealed just how much United had struggled up front as a team and also the difficulties Best had in rekindling his old form. It was Kidd's effort that settled the destination of both points here.

Wilf McGuiness had earlier decided this day would be his last as a Manchester United employee and left the club he loved feeling humiliated at his treatment since his demotion from first team manager almost two months earlier. He told waiting reporters that he had been devoted to United for 18 years but now had to find a future in football away from Old Trafford.

WEST BROMWICH ALBION 4 MANCHESTER UNITED 3
DIVISION ONE 6 MARCH 1971

A LAST MINUTE GOAL consigned United to a second defeat in three games but there was no denying the fans packed into The Hawthorns had witnessed one of the most entertaining and unpredictable games of the season.

Best hit the first early on, sauntering on to a Bobby Charlton pass before netting. John Aston's header from Willie Morgan's cross registered the second United goal and Aston provided the centre for Brian Kidd. Oldham born Tony Brown's hat-trick proved the basis of Albion's victory.

MANCHESTER UNITED 2 NOTTINGHAM FOREST 0
DIVISION ONE 13 MARCH 1971

AFTER MISSING FIVE games with a broken nose, Denis Law returned but there were a number of doubts right up until the last minute. Most managed to prove their fitness with Kidd omitted to allow Law back.

It was a decision Kidd questioned but there could be no arguing with the decision when Law opened the scoring after 12 minutes. George Best headed in to make it 2-0 before half-time. At the back United had virtually nothing to worry about as Forest offered little threat.

STOKE CITY 1 MANCHESTER UNITED 2
DIVISION ONE 20 MARCH 1971

A CAUTIOUS GEORGE Best, always looking out for the benefit of the team, was the result of his recent troubles. according to reports. Yet the player's alter ego emerged at Stoke as he became embroiled in a flare-up which almost cost The Reds.

Two well-taken Best goals ensured United took both points. His first was a well taken lob and the second saw him beat Gordon Banks for pace with a shot from an acute angle after a mazy dribble through a crowded penalty area.

John Ritchie halved the deficit after the break but United still looked in control. However a row with the referee after that strike saw Best in danger of at least another appointment at the FA if not an early bath.

WEST HAM UNITED 2 MANCHESTER UNITED 1
DIVISION ONE 3 APRIL 1971

WEST HAM, FIGHTING for their First Division lives, pulled away from The Reds with two goals in the opening ten minutes from Geoff Hurst and Bryan 'Pop' Robson. Willie Morgan had a penalty saved for the first time in United colours, though it has to be noted that Bobby Ferguson's stop was little short of miraculous.

In the second period United finally dragged themselves back into the game. To that point it had been a disjointed performance. More determination was shown by the much-criticised midfield which in turn allowed creative elements to spark and chances emerged as a result.

It was a poacher's instinct which allowed Best to pull one back but the closest United got to another goal was Law hitting the woodwork.

MANCHESTER UNITED 1 DERBY COUNTY 2
DIVISION ONE 10 APRIL 1971

A SOMEWHAT OVERLOOKED but always prepared Nobby Stiles was brought back into the side to take over from David Sadler and, as long as he performed well, there was the promise of an extended chance as the first choice centre back was not expected to return for at least a month. The only other change saw Francis Burns deputising for John Fitzpatrick. The absence of these defenders, who had proved a mainstay for United, led to some uncertainty at times. One such lapse allowed John O'Hare in for a header. Otherwise it proved to be a quiet first half in which The Reds posed few threats.

A shot early in the second period from O'Hare doubled Derby's lead and in the quest to mount a comeback central midfield remained the weakest area. Law and Best had little to feed off meaning each dropped back at various times. When they did there was little movement up front or around them allowing County's defenders to swarm back.

MANCHESTER UNITED 1 WOLVES 0
DIVISION ONE 12 APRIL 1971

ALAN GOWLING, WHO had been named as a substitute for the match against Derby, came in from the start. Brian Kidd was withdrawn to the bench while an injury to John Aston provided an opportunity to make changes. Kidd, who came on after the break, had been talked out of a move the previous season but in recent weeks had revived a desire to leave club.

The Reds still looked shoddy at the back but Alex Stepney did well when others couldn't help him. The United midfield was markedly different from the one which turned out 48 hours earlier.

There were few thrills except for Paddy Crerand's interception which set up the goal. His pass for Gowling allowed the forward to advance to the area then dispatch a shot which fizzed past a helpless keeper.

Best and Morgan, who many teams would like to have in their ranks for that flash of inspiration when the team needed pulling out of a hole, whirled around their flanks creating little but with two precious points secured there could be few grumbles.

COVENTRY CITY 2 MANCHESTER UNITED 1
DIVISION ONE 13 APRIL 1971

PADDY CRERAND REMAINED a stoic presence as well as creative force and the glue which held The Reds together ensured the team was always in with a chance of snatching something at Highfield Road. He combined with Best for the opener and, buoyed by hitting the net, George began looking for the ball.

However, most times he was too keen to heap all the responsibility on himself

rather than seek out simple passes which required less of a flourish. If he had United may well have won the game.

Ernie Hunt put goal-shy Coventry into the lead on five minutes and hit another soon after half-time. United enjoyed plenty of possession but didn't threaten sufficiently to pull the side through.

CRYSTAL PALACE 3 MANCHESTER UNITED 5
DIVISION ONE 17 APRIL 1971

DENIS LAW AND David Sadler made welcome returns but the exclusion of Brian Kidd only strained his fraught relationship with the club further. Paddy Crerand made his 300th league appearance in his finest form for some years but mistakes at the back allowed

Palace to build a 2-0 lead.

Once again Best looked superb in the early stages of moves but at a certain point in almost every attack he ran out of both steam or ideas. That said there was little spark or desire evident in a number of his colleagues. This mitigated in his favour.

Two teammates who did look interested were Alan Gowling and Denis Law who fashioned a goal just before the interval. A spectacular scissor-kick just after the players reconvened was the finest goal of the afternoon. On this form it was only a matter of time before Law completed his first hat-trick in over two years.

As United finally found their groove George Best, on his first return to London since the infamous Chelsea game, notched twice. His final goal to make it 5-3 was the most exquisite chip.

MANCHESTER UNITED 0 LIVERPOOL 2
DIVISION ONE 19 APRIL 1971

MANY ASSOCIATED WITH the club in various capacities had their feet brought firmly back to earth as United followed up a high with a crushing low. This time a demoralising defeat at home to Liverpool provided the anguish.

Steve Heighway cracked in a shot midway through the first half and the same player's harrying of Paul Edwards caused a headed back pass to be over-hit on the hour. The ball flew high over Alex Stepney clipping the post on its way to goal.

Unfortunately on this occasion the attack could not bail out the defence. Best made runs but was well dealt with as were contributions from Willie Morgan, Denis Law and Alan Gowling. George had plenty of shots and a number of headers but most were from distances and angles which made life easy for Ray Clemence, although the keeper was still forced into a a number of excellent saves.

NORTHERN IRELAND 5 CYPRUS 0
EUROPEAN CHAMPIONSHIP QUALIFIER 21 APRIL 1971

FORMER MANCHESTER UNITED keeper Ray Wood was in charge of the Cypriot side and found he could offer no resistance to Best who capped a great display with a hat-trick in a complete trouncing at Windsor Park.

For some reason Wood's charges gave George as much space as he desired and paid the price. Dougan took just 90 seconds to head in Sammy Todd's cross but some poor finishing kept the score down until Best netted just before the break.

A brace within 10 minutes of the resumption rounded off the treble and saw Ireland take things slightly easier though Nicholson hit a fifth and final goal before the end.

MANCHESTER UNITED 3 IPSWICH TOWN 2
DIVISION ONE 24 APRIL 1971

MATT BUSBY'S FINAL game in charge of the side at Old Trafford created a frenzied desire to mark the event in the right manner. Brian Kidd returned in place of Willie Morgan while Steve James came in for Paul Edwards who was in a bad run of form and had seen his confidence dip as a result.

Kidd's persistence and trickery earned a penalty from which Best made it 1-0. The Ipswich defenders had no way to stop the forward other than to foul him.

Landmark moments seemed to litter this game including Bobby Charlton scoring his 200th league and FA Cup goal in the process of making it 2-1 after Kidd had centred. Kidd then added a third.

As an attacking unit United looked good but there were still obvious problems at the back as evidenced by the two goals conceded. Peter Morris had opened the scoring from 25 yards with Frank Clarke bringing the visitors to within a goal of late on.

BLACKPOOL 1 MANCHESTER UNITED 1
DIVISION ONE 1 MAY 1971

JIMMY ARMFIELD PLAYED his 626th and final game for The Seasiders on the last day of the league season. He had been out of the side for a while but returned for this special occasion after over two decades of service at Bloomfield Road where many believed he would one day return as manager. He had long standing links with Busby having been offered to The Reds in the wake of the Munich Disaster.

Though condemned to relegation - a fate which marked a sad end for a great player - Blackpool had plenty of spirit but fell behind when John Burridge dropped a straightforward catch and Denis Law knocked the ball in. Tony Green managed to level, beating Crerand in a battle for possession before sweeping the ball home.

Crerand and John Craven were sent off for persistent foul play which erupted into a mini-battle. Otherwise the game was played in a fine spirit with everyone in the ground paying their respects to the retiring right back who signed off by marking the finest winger of recent years, George Best.

MANCHESTER CITY 3 MANCHESTER UNITED 4
DIVISION ONE 5 MAY 1971

IF UNITED PROVED a fitting ending to Jimmy Armfield's career there could be no more fitting opposition for Matt Busby to end his 1159 game managerial career against than Manchester City. Not just because of the rivalry but the fact he had served the club for six years prior to World War Two playing over 200 games at wing half.

City's European commitments as European Cup Winners' Cup holders (their defence ended in the semi-finals by a slim defeat to Chelsea) meant the game had to played at the end of the season. Both sides seemed keen to draw a curtain on this campaign and look forward to the next. An end of term feel certainly spread across both defences.

The Holy Trinity provided Sir Matt with a 3-0 half-time lead. Freddie Hill pulled one back after the break then Francis Lee and Ian Mellor would have levelled had Best not headed in a fine goal. In the end it was 4-3 to United. The fixture hadn't seen seven goals since 1926. A number of presentations were made before and after the game plus heart felt speeches including one from Joe Mercer which brought a tear to many eyes. However, Sir Matt became one of the few people in the public eye to be featured on TV's *This is Your Life*. Eamonn Andrews sprung the surprise after the United boss believed he was to be presented with an award from the Dublin born personality.

NORTHERN IRELAND 0 ENGLAND 1
HOME INTERNATIONAL 15 MAY 1971

GEORGE NEVER LOOKED quite the same player for his country as he did at club level. The ability of the players surrounding him was a factor. The Province rarely produced players of the same talent as those brought to Old Trafford which meant results at that level were mixed. However, the chance to take on the English and other home nations each season was looked forward to with some relish.

Beating Gordon Banks, universally acclaimed as the finest keeper in the world, was no easy task, even for George Best, but in one of the most talked about incidents in international football he made an impudent attempt which unfortunately failed to count.

Banks, who had pulled off an amazing save from Pele during the previous summer's World Cup, calmly collected a cross and prepared to kick from his hands oblivious to the fact that Best was lurking just behind him. When he tossed the ball up to punt it upfield, George poked the ball away from the swinging leg and over the keeper's head. Calmly running round the other side George nodded before nodding home the bouncing ball.

The officials initially seemed bemused but with George taking the congratulations of his teammates, albeit

WATCH IT, GORDON
One of the most infamous incidents of all-time. Here George is poised to flick the ball over Gordon Banks and into an empty net. Disappointingly, George's impudence was disallowed.

chased by a furious Banks and irate England defenders protesting about the legitimacy of the goal, the referee decided that the move constituted dangerous play.

England won the game 1-0 but the moral victory was Northern Ireland's and even if he had kept a clean sheet, Banks had certainly been embarassed by the incident.

SCOTLAND 0 NORTHERN IRELAND 1
Home International 19 May 1971

A 14TH MINUTE OWN goal by John Grieg was the difference and gave Northern Ireland a first win in Glasgow since 1934 and a first victory in the British Championships since George Best's greatest ever international game almost four years earlier.

The Scottish defence had been put in

a whirl by the threat of Dougan and Best. A Pat Rice free-kick led to the goal. Grieg attempted to put the ball out but instead of knocking it behind the ball it bounced off his knee and past Bobby Clark.

Scotland should have done better but were well marshalled in both midfield and defence.

NORTHERN IRELAND 1 WALES 0
Home International 22 May 1971

WALES HAD HELD England to a draw at Wembley and claimed their first point at the famous venue as a result. However, The Dragons looked a shadow of that brave side in Belfast where they had not lost since 1959. Terry Yorath tried to limit George Best's effectiveness with some stiff challenges but did so at the expense of their front two - John Toshack and Ron Davies who were isolated and became more so as Northern Ireland controlled

the midfield.

Bryan Hamilton had the easy task of slotting the ball in for the only goal. There had actually been appeals for a penalty in the build-up and Wales looked at an unmoved referee rather than Dave Clements who made a simple pass to the scorer. The win helped Northern Ireland finish runners-up to England who won the title with five points.

1970-71

Though United had reached the League Cup semi-final, all the good work in getting to the last four had been undone by an embarrassing exit to Third Division Aston Villa. Results like this and reverses in the league meant it was inevitable, if regrettable, that Wilf McGuiness would be shown the door. Boxing Day was as good a point as any, even if it lacked the goodwill usually associated with the festive season.

The return of Matt Busby, who had managed George and his dalliances in the past, was not enough to induce Best into better behaviour or much better form. His excesses continued and he continued to miss training sessions but turning up late for his disciplinary hearing before the FA in London was the worst snub George managed all season.

There were, as usual, plus points such as scoring twice in his old manager's last game before control was handed over to Frank O'Farrell. Fittingly a 4-3 win over City on the final day plus a decent second half of the season masked a poor start to the campaign and allowed United to finish in mid-table rather than the lower half or even the relegation positions which looked likely after just five wins in the opening 22 games.

Sir Matt Busby resumed stewardship of the club but continued to look for a long term replacement. At one point there was talk of someone taking over during the season. Later it seemed he had convinced his old friend Jock Stein to succeed him after meeting the Celtic boss at a petrol station between Glasgow and the North West.

Stein had achieved it all on the other side of Hadrian's Wall and relished the challenge of proving himself in England. However, maybe conscious of not only working in the shadow cast by Matt Busby but also reporting to the man himself, he got cold feet and remained at Parkhead.

The entire first team was rocked by the ongoing off-field problems but none more than Best. He was seen more often on the front pages than the back as his playboy lifestyle dominated the tabloids. As a consequence his football suffered and the frustration with his team-mates and their frustration with his drinking and disciplinary problems only made matters worse. The resulting bans and fines pushed George into searching for solutions at the bottom of a bottle. The appointment of Frank O'Farrell at least provided some hope for the forthcoming season but getting the best out of George would prove the new manager's toughest task.

DATE	OPPONENT	VENUE	SCORE	ATTD	1	2	3	4	5	6	7	8	9	10	11
15 August	Leeds United	Old Trafford	0-1	59,365	Stepney	Edwards	Dunne	Crerand	Ure	Sadler	Fitzpatrick	Stiles	Charlton	Kidd	Best
19 August	Chelsea	Old Trafford	0-0	50,979	Stepney	Edwards	Dunne	Crerand	Ure	Sadler	Morgan	Fitzpatrick	Charlton	Stiles	Best
22 August	Arsenal	Highbury	0-4	54,117	Stepney	Stiles	Dunne	Crerand	Ure	Sadler	Morgan	Fitzpatrick	Charlton	Law	Best
25 August	Burnley	Turf Moor	2-0	29,385	Rimmer	Edwards	Dunne	Fitzpatrick	Ure	Sadler	Morgan	Law[2]	Charlton	Stiles	Best
29 August	West Ham United	Old Trafford	1-1	50,643	Rimmer	Edwards	Dunne	Fitzpatrick[1]	Ure	Sadler	Morgan	Law	Charlton	Stiles	Best
2 September	Everton	Old Trafford	2-0	51,346	Rimmer	Edwards	Dunne	Fitzpatrick	Ure	Sadler	Stiles	Law	Charlton[1]	Kidd	Best[1]
5 September	Liverpool	Anfield	1-1	52,542	Rimmer	Edwards	Dunne	Fitzpatrick	Ure	Sadler	Stiles	Law	Charlton	Kidd[1]	Best
12 September	Coventry City	Old Trafford	2-0	48,939	Rimmer	Edwards	Dunne	Fitzpatrick	Ure	Sadler	Stiles	Law	Charlton[1]	Kidd	Best[1]
19 September	Ipswich Town	Portman Road	0-4	27,776	Rimmer	Edwards	Dunne	Fitzpatrick	Ure	Sadler	Stiles	Law	Charlton	Gowling	Best
26 September	Blackpool	Old Trafford	1-1	46,647	Rimmer	Watson	Burns	Fitzpatrick	James	Sadler	Morgan	Gowling	Charlton	Kidd	Best[1]
3 October	Wolves	Molineux	2-3	38,629	Rimmer	Watson	Burns	Fitzpatrick	James	Sadler	Morgan	Gowling[1]	Charlton	Kidd[1]	Best
10 October	Crystal Palace	Old Trafford	0-1	42,979	Rimmer	Edwards	Dunne	Fitzpatrick	Ure	Stiles	Morgan	Best	Charlton[1]	Kidd	Aston
17 October	Leeds United	Elland Road	2-2	50,190	Rimmer	Edwards	Dunne	Fitzpatrick[1]	Ure	Stiles	Burns	Best	Charlton	Kidd	Aston
24 October	WBA	Old Trafford	2-1	43,278	Rimmer	Edwards	Dunne	Fitzpatrick	Ure	Burns	Law[1]	Best	Charlton	Kidd[1]	Aston
31 October	Newcastle United	St. James' Park	0-1	45,140	Rimmer	Edwards	Dunne	Fitzpatrick	James	Sadler	Burns	Best	Charlton	Kidd	Aston
7 November	StokeCity	Old Trafford	2-2	47,451	Rimmer	Edwards	Burns	Fitzpatrick	James	Sadler[1]	Law[1]	Best	Charlton	Kidd	Aston
14 November	Nottingham Forest	City Ground	2-1	36,364	Rimmer	Watson	Dunne	Fitzpatrick	James	Sadler	Law	Best	Charlton	Gowling[1]	Sartori[1]
21 November	Southampton	The Dell	0-1	30,202	Rimmer	Watson	Dunne	Fitzpatrick	James	Sadler	Law	Best	Charlton	Kidd	Aston
28 November	Huddersfield Town	Old Trafford	1-1	45,306	Rimmer	Watson	Dunne	Fitzpatrick	James	Sadler	Law	Best[1]	Charlton	Kidd	Aston
5 December	Tottenham H	White Hart Lane	2-2	55,693	Rimmer	Watson	Dunne	Fitzpatrick	James	Sadler	Law[1]	Best[1]	Charlton	Kidd	Aston
12 December	Manchester City	Old Trafford	1-4	52,636	Rimmer	Watson	Dunne	Fitzpatrick	James	Stiles	Law	Best	Charlton	Kidd[1]	Aston
19 December	Arsenal	Old Trafford	1-3	33,182	Rimmer	Fitzpatrick	Dunne	Crerand	James	Fitzpatrick	Morgan	Best[1]	Charlton	Kidd	Sartori[1]
26 December	Derby County	Baseball Ground	4-4	34,068	Rimmer	Fitzpatrick	Dunne	Crerand	Ure	Sadler	Morgan	Best[1]	Charlton	Kidd[1]	Law[2]
30 January	Huddersfield Town	Leeds Road	2-1	41,464	Stepney	Fitzpatrick	Burns	Crerand	Edwards	Sadler	Morgan[1]	Law[1]	Charlton	Kidd[1]	Aston
6 February	Tottenham H	Old Trafford	2-1	48,965	Stepney	Fitzpatrick	Burns	Crerand	Edwards	Sadler	Morgan[1]	Kidd	Charlton	Gowling	Best[1]
20 February	Southampton	Old Trafford	5-1	36,060	Stepney	Fitzpatrick	Burns	Crerand	Edwards	Sadler	Morgan[1]	Best	Charlton	Gowling[4]	Aston
23 February	Everton	GoodisonPark	0-1	52,544	Stepney	Fitzpatrick	Dunne	Crerand	Edwards	Sadler	Morgan	Best	Charlton	Gowling	Aston
27 February	Newcastle United	Old Trafford	1-0	41,902	Stepney	Fitzpatrick	Dunne	Crerand	Edwards	Sadler	Morgan	Best	Charlton	Gowling[1]	Aston
6 March	WBA	The Hawthorns	3-4	41,112	Stepney	Fitzpatrick	Dunne	Crerand	Edwards	Sadler	Morgan	Best[1]	Charlton	Kidd[1]	Aston[1]

Date	Opponent	Venue	Score	Att.											
13 March	Nottingham Forest	Old Trafford	2-0	40,473	Stepney	Fitzpatrick	Dunne	Crerand	Edwards	Sadler	Morgan	Best[1]	Charlton	Law[1]	Aston
20 March	Stoke City	Victoria Ground	2-1	40,005	Stepney	Fitzpatrick	Dunne	Crerand	Edwards	Sadler	Morgan	Best[2]	Charlton	Law	Aston
3 April	West Ham United	Upton Park	1-2	38,507	Stepney	Fitzpatrick	Dunne	Crerand	Edwards	Sadler	Morgan	Best[1]	Charlton	Law	Aston
10 April	Derby County	Old Trafford	1-2	45,691	Stepney	Dunne	Burns	Crerand	Edwards	Stiles	Morgan	Best	Charlton	Law[1]	Aston
12 April	Wolves	Old Trafford	1-0	41,886	Stepney	Dunne	Burns	Crerand	Edwards	Stiles	Best	Gowling[1]	Charlton	Law	Morgan
13 April	Coventry City	Highfield Road	1-2	33,818	Stepney	Dunne	Burns	Crerand	Edwards	Stiles	Best[1]	Gowling	Charlton	Kidd	Morgan
17 April	Crystal Palace	Selhurst Park	5-3	39,145	Stepney	Fitzpatrick	Dunne	Crerand	Edwards	Sadler	Best[2]	Gowling	Charlton	Law[3]	Morgan
19 April	Liverpool	Old Trafford	0-2	44,004	Stepney	Dunne	Burns	Crerand	Edwards	Sadler	Best	Gowling	Charlton	Law	Morgan
24 April	Ipswich Town	Old Trafford	3-2	33,566	Stepney	Dunne	Burns	Crerand	James	Sadler	Law	Gowling	Charlton[1]	Kidd[1]	Best[1]
1 May	Blackpool	Bloomfield Road	1-1	29,857	Stepney	Dunne	Burns	Crerand	James	Sadler	Law[1]	Gowling	Charlton	Kidd	Best
5 May	Manchester City	Maine Road	4-3	43,626	Stepney	O'Neill	Burns	Crerand	James	Sadler	Law[1]	Gowling	Charlton[1]	Kidd	Best[2]
FA Cup															
2 January	Middlesbrough	Old Trafford	0-0	47,824	Rimmer	Fitzpatrick	Dunne	Crerand	Ure	Sadler	Morgan	Best	Charlton	Kidd	Law
5 January	Middlesbrough	Ayresome Park	1-2	41,000	Rimmer	Fitzpatrick	Dunne	Crerand	Edwards	Sadler	Morgan	Best[1]	Charlton	Kidd	Law
League Cup															
9 September	Aldershot	Recreation Gd	3-1	18,509	Rimmer	Edwards	Dunne	Fitzpatrick	Ure	Sadler	Stiles	Law[1]	Charlton	Kidd[1]	Best[1]
7 October	Portsmouth	Old Trafford	1-0	32,068	Rimmer	Donald	Burns	Fitzpatrick	Ure	Sadler	Morgan	Gowling	Charlton[1]	Kidd	Best
28 October	Chelsea	Old Trafford	2-1	47,565	Rimmer	Edwards	Dunne	Fitzpatrick	James	Sadler	Aston	Best[1]	Charlton[1]	Kidd	Law
18 November	Crystal Palace	Old Trafford	4-2	48,961	Rimmer	Watson	Dunne	Fitzpatrick[1]	James	Sadler	Law	Best	Charlton[1]	Kidd[12]	Aston
16 December	Aston Villa	Old Trafford	1-1	48,889	Rimmer	Watson	Dunne	Fitzpatrick	James	Stiles	Sartori	Best	Charlton	Kidd[1]	Aston
23 December	Aston Villa	Villa Park	1-2	58,667	Rimmer	Fitzpatrick	Dunne	Crerand	Ure	Sadler	Morgan	Best	Charlton	Kidd[1]	Law
Watney Cup															
1 August	Reading	Elm Park	3-2	18,348	Stepney	Edwards[1]	Dunne	Crerand	Ure	Sadler	Morgan	Law	Charlton[2]	Kidd	Best
5 August	Hull City	Boothferry Park	1-1	34,007	Stepney	Edwards	Dunne	Crerand	Ure	Sadler	Morgan	Law[1]	Charlton	Kidd	Best
8 August	Derby County	Baseball Ground	1-4	32,049	Stepney	Edwards	Dunne	Crerand	Ure	Sadler	Morgan	Law	Charlton	Kidd	Best[1]

1971-72
BACK TO HIS BEST?

Frank O'Farrell took the reigns at Old Trafford in June 1971. The former Leicester City boss had been an outsider for the job but was regarded as a safe pair of hands. Keeping George Best on the straight and narrow was the main task in hand. A task that would test the Irishman's man-management skills to the fullest.

HALIFAX TOWN 2 MANCHESTER UNITED 1
WATNEY CUP 1ˢᵀ RD 31 JULY 1971

BACK IN THE spring George had been offered £2,250 to play in South Africa for East London over three weeks in the summer. He rejected these overtures and returned for pre-season training on schedule to work with the new manager and for the first time in his club career his boss was an outsider. Many pundits argued this would be a positive in the forthcoming season.

Spending most of their time since joining the Football League 50 years earlier in the lower echelons meant Halifax had never played Manchester United before being paired with them in the opening round of the Watney Cup but after this shock win the unfancied Shaymen could now boast a 100% record.

Buoyed by a 19,765 crowd the Third Division outfit beat a full strength United 2-1 with goals from Bill Atkins and Bob Wallace. Best replied for United but Willie Morgan missed a penalty which would at least have given United an extra half-hour to find a winner. Though Charlton and Crerand worked hard, United struggled to create chances.

Brian Kidd was among the five substitutes which could be named as the system used on the continent was adopted for the cup's second season which also dropped the offside rule as an experiment.

DERBY COUNTY 2 MANCHESTER UNITED 2
DIVISION ONE 14 AUGUST 1971

ALAN GOWLING WAS drafted into midfield at right half to plug the gap left by Paddy Crerand's suspension while Tommy O'Neil, who had made his debut at right back in the final game of the previous season, was called in to serve in the same role. Derby had mauled United the previous season but that pain eased when The Reds built a 2-0 lead through Law and Gowling who each converted corner kicks. There should have been more but Frank O'Farrell had to be satisfied with his midfield which had Bobby Charlton and Willie Morgan alongside Alan Gowling at its heart. The sharpness of George Best was also a boost.

Derby's vigorous approach after the interval earned them a controversial draw. Frank Wignall slammed into Alex Stepney knocking the ball out of his hands, giving Kevin Hector an easy chance. Wignall claimed a less contentious equaliser but there was a feeling that justice had not been done to the visitors.

CHELSEA 2 MANCHESTER UNITED 3
DIVISION ONE 18 AUGUST 1971

GEORGE WAS A doubt for the trip to Stamford Bridge with a bruised instep which caused pain when he kicked a ball. Yet United recovered from an early deficit to storm into a commanding lead against the odds after the Ulsterman was sent off. George seemed to swear at the referee during prolonged remonstrations over Chelsea's contentious opener - it was his first dismissal in a domestic game.

There was a lot of talk surrounding the match as in the same fixture last year George had gone AWOL leading to an in-house punishment. This evening he left the pitch in tears and possibly faced a three-month ban as the authorities had promised to get tough over the abuse of referees before the season began.

A verbal barrage official Norman Burtenshaw felt was aimed at him led to first a caution and then a sending off. It was a dark night for the game as 38 players were booked and another two dismissed across a mere dozen games in England and Scotland.

United's 3-2 victory was a triumph for the ten players which remained but it only heightened the shame George felt. Chelsea went into the break still ahead but within minutes of the start of the second half keeper John Phillips was tested by a barrage of shots. He resisted as much as possible but was powerless to stop Kidd's headed equaliser from Tony Dunne's cross. Despite the tension, Willie Morgan put recent penalty misses out of his mind to make it 2-1 from the spot after Kidd had been felled by Phillips. A text book Bobby Charlton rip-snorter provided a two goal cushion. Peter Osgood gave Chelsea the chance of claiming a point but The Reds' well drilled defence proved unshiftable.

On the same night Carlo Sartori was dismissed while playing for the reserves in a 1-0 defeat by Bolton Wanderers.

MANCHESTER UNITED 3 ARSENAL 1
DIVISION ONE 20 AUGUST 1971

UNITED WERE PUT in the unusual position of opening their home campaign at Anfield after the Football Association decreed that an incident where a knife had been thrown on to the pitch during last season's home match against Newcastle would cost United £7,000 in fines and a two-match ban on playing games within 25 miles Old Trafford.

Victory over double winners Arsenal was made to look ridiculously easy courtesy of Bobby Charlton's outstanding contribution. The midfielder showed not only his superb range of passing but great anticipation for the positions others would take once he got the ball.

Frank McClintock had opened the scoring after five minutes but United's best start for many seasons had increased confidence. Patient approach work paid off just after the break when a Charlton free-kick was lobbed to Gowling who had stolen a few yards behind the wall courtesy of clever positioning.

A finish as emphatic as any of the goals Charlton had scored throughout his career saw United go ahead from another set piece. Brian Kidd wrapped things up just before the end, combining to good effect with Denis Law.

Though he had also looked a threat for most of the afternoon, George's foot injury re-occurred forcing him off well before the final whistle.

MANCHESTER UNITED 3 WEST BROMWICH ALBION 2
DIVISION ONE 23 AUGUST 1971

THE FOOT INJURY made Best a doubt for the visit of West Bromwich Albion to the Victoria Ground, Stoke for United's second 'home' fixture. George made it through however, taking Denis Law's shirt while John Aston took over on the left. A seemingly settled and assured centre back pairing of David Sadler and Steve James was proving to be the foundation of United's winning start.

Amongst those seeking to make a difference up front, Best realised he was on trial for as long as his season would last before any ban was placed upon him. Lesser players may have suffered and seen their form nosedive but George was outstanding and contributed royally to a team performance which exuded quality.

With an iron grip in the centre bolstered by a trio of creative talents, he and Kidd more than fulfilled expectations as central strikers.

A simple finish from George opened the scoring from a Charlton corner and George took the ball from the subsequent re-start sending Alan Gowling clear to run on to the ball and plant a header past The Baggies' keeper.

Some poor defending allowed George to nip in and score The Reds only goal of the second half. Having all but won the game United then took their foot off the gas. Tony Brown got one back for Albion but it was far too late to signal a meaningful comeback.

WOLVES 1 MANCHESTER UNITED 1
DIVISION ONE 28 AUGUST 1971

DENIS LAW'S RETURN to fitness allowed George to revert to the flanks and, although he was suffering at the hands of one edict from the FA regarding conduct to officials, another instruction to referees was doing wonders for his performances. After many years of being cynically hacked to the ground, it was decided that those who committed such challenges would be harshly dealt with. It was supposed to afford flair players more protection than they had been used to as the offenders knew they could ultimately be dismissed without further warning.

Best hit United's only goal of the game on 15 minutes. There could have been far more as Wolves failed to cope with a tidal wave of United attacks but for some reason The Reds sat back on that slender lead and paid the price and they found it difficult to snap back into gear once Wolves had levelled.

David Wagstaffe, on the right for The Old Gold, was also revelling in the freedom he found and started running the game. Fortunately Alex Stepney was equal to everything except Bernard Shaw's 30-yard drive which the keeper seemed sure to reach until he was wrong footed by a large deflection.

EVERTON 1 MANCHESTER UNITED 0
DIVISION ONE 31 AUGUST 1971

WITH A WIN sufficient to take United top, no player wanted to miss this game especially George Best who suffered a minor knock at Molineux but had recovered by midweek to face Everton. Arsenal aside, this would be the strongest opposition faced to date and the Merseysiders' much vaunted midfield lived up to their billing commanding the central area. Not only could they hold their own in a tactical fight Everton could also switch quickly into attack. It was a lead United could not follow.

Best was patrolled well by Terry Darracott and as a result of the home team's dominance United's forwards struggled to make an impact.

David Johnson scored the sole goal when he anticipated a through-ball to sneak behind the defence just before the break. United posed more threat as the game wore on and could have equalised through either Law or Best. The latter's effort was one of real class and intuition which deserved more than to sail narrowly wide.

MANCHESTER UNITED 1 IPSWICH TOWN 0
DIVISION ONE 4 SEPTEMBER 1971

A BUMPER CROWD was attracted to United's first proper home game of the season. However, many of the XI which had thrived during the club's enforced exile looked jaded and though The Reds claimed both points they were lucky to do so. After a strong start, defensive lapses crept in and up front Kidd and Law struggled with injuries which ensured

Ipswich had far less to do than they might have expected prior to kick-off.

Despite yielding plenty of possession, Town were only beaten by a George Best corner which flew into the net despite attackers and defenders straining to reach it.

IPSWICH TOWN 1 MANCHESTER UNITED 3
LEAGUE CUP 2ND RD 7 SEPTEMBER 1971

UNITED AND IPSWICH renewed battle 72 hours later in the League Cup knowing that a similar type of game to the weekend could have a totally different ending at Portman Road. Best was switched to inside-left replacing Law while Aston was drafted on to the wing George had vacated. Brian Kidd played despite having stitches in his ankle.

Willie Morgan hit one but the hero of the night, remarkably given his impending disciplinary hearing, was Best who grabbed a brace - at least that was the referee's opinion. John Aston also had a superb night causing all manner of problems down the left and claimed he applied the finishng touches to one of the efforts after Best had a header pushed on to the bar. The ball came back to George who was still trying to regain his footing so flung a boot out to tap it in. He made a connection but not a clean one so Aston made sure.

CRYSTAL PALACE 1 MANCHESTER UNITED 3
DIVISION ONE 11 SEPTEMBER 1971

WITH AN FA HEARING due a couple of days after this match, Best refused to let the matter influence his game and turned in his finest performance for some time. Despite his heroics in the cup John Aston was dropped with Law back to fitness. An angelic George Best, now in top form, was still susceptible to the odd tantrum such as a petulant kick at the ball when Palace won a free-kick.

It was a relatively small incident in comparison to the subject of most hearings, but a moment of madness could have culminated in a backlash and marred a performance full of trickery in which he led The Eagles a merry dance. His diversions created space for Kidd and Law. It also allowed Kidd to equalise a Palace goal scored against the run of play. Law, who had a couple of efforts disallowed for offside, put United 2-1 ahead then rounded the scoring off ten minutes from the end as The Reds hit the opposition on the counter-attack.

Later that week George attended the hearing flanked by manager Frank O'Farrell and club colleague Willie Morgan, who would provide crucial evidence in mitigation of the charges. George arrived 20 minutes early for his hearing. As usual the press were huddled outside all the entrances and exits.

Most anticipated a six-week suspended ban should George be found guilty, with the threat of further charges to follow from subsequent games. Yet surprisingly Best was cleared when teammate Willie Morgan successfully argued that George's volley of expletives had been aimed at him. The FA, who had never been afraid to flex their muscle on football's wayward genius, cleared him of the offence ensuring he was able to avoid suspension and aid the club's best start to a season for some time.

The Football League seemed displeased and only issued a terse, non-committal statement on receiving the news. However, once referee Burtenshaw said his instructions to each side prior to the game could have been misleading and given due contemplation to the evidence Morgan provided, there was more than enough doubt cast on the charges and only the lesser indictment of dissent was upheld, for which a booking was viewed as sufficient punishment.

However, there remained a six week suspension still in place from last season that could have been invoked. In those circumstances George had to count himself lucky not to be in deeper water especially as Carlo Sartori's sending off for the second string on the same night led to a £75 fine and a brief ban.

MANCHESTER UNITED 4 WEST HAM UNITED 2
DIVISION ONE 18 SEPTEMBER 1971

A RAUCOUS RECEPTION greeted George on his first outing since the FA's verdict was delivered. Everyone at Old Trafford was delighted to see him run out in a red jersey - well almost everyone one. Doubtless the West Ham defenders had been hoping not to have to contend with the Irishman. He was in good form prior to his meeting with the game's authorities. With the matter now resolved in his favour it seemed likely his performances would improve.

Despite not playing at Old Trafford until the seventh game of the season, United had dropped very few points. It was some relief to all at Old Trafford and with West Ham only recording a first win by the fifth game of the season this was a fixture United were looking to win in order to underline their title credentials.

The Hammers' own Best - striker Clyde - was enjoying an equally good run having netted five times in as many games but it was George who prevailed and helped United climb to second. The team's improving form was bringing the best out of George and never more so than on this afternoon when he scored a classic hat-trick - goals scored with both feet and his head. The latter was utilised first when Best nodded in from a Bobby Charlton corner.

Corners, this time taken short, were the source of his other goals. Best collected the ball then took it past a number of players and shot with his left foot, the ball flying in despite George appearing to lose his balance in the process.

He repeated the same move for his hat-trick goal, this time taking the ball past Bobby Moore amongst others. The West Ham and England skipper was a man George admired and named as his toughest opponent but he was comfortably beaten and ended up on his backside while George hit a right footed drive past Bobby Ferguson.

Clyde Best pulled one back for West Ham and Trevor Brooking notched another for the visiting side. Bobby Charlton scored the only other goal for United after rampaging through the middle and, although the headlines belonged to George, plaudits were extended to the ten other players on duty as the flair and passion displayed contributed to a fine team performance.

LIVERPOOL 2 MANCHESTER UNITED 2
DIVISION ONE 25 SEPTEMBER 1971

FRANCIS BURNS HAD found himself pushed into a striker's role for the reserves, hitting five goals but on his recall to the senior side he returned to a more accustomed left back role in place of the injured Tony Dunne. Meanwhile Kevin Keegan was back after a short lay-off for Liverpool.

It seemed the heady heights of leading the chasing pack had made United dizzy as Liverpool went 2-0 up within 24 minutes through Bobby Graham and Brian Hall. United refused to cave in though and fought back to earn a creditable draw.

Best marked his 300th league outing with a delicious ball which curved through an otherwise solid looking defence to play in Denis Law.

He then set up Bobby Charlton with a neat pass allowing the England man to hit a drive past Tommy Lawrence giving the keeper no chance from the edge of the area.

Liverpool had penalty claims for hands against Steve James but the referee waved them away. It may have been a slice of fortune but United did not deserve to lose a point they had worked so hard for.

MANCHESTER UNITED 2 SHEFFIELD UNITED 0
DIVISION ONE 2 OCTOBER 1971

TONY DUNNE CAME back into the reckoning meaning Francis Burns was omitted. John Aston was due to contest a place on the bench with the versatile defender but the late withdrawal of Denis Law, who injured his thigh during a 5-a-side match in training, saw him slot in at left midfield. Best again deputised in the forward line. Frank O'Farrell was crowned Manager of the Month for September following The Reds' near faultless record and some fine displays. He was able to pit his wits against the only member of his peers with a better record than him over the course of the season so far - Sheffield United's John Harris.

The top of the table Blades were confident and looked to demonstrate their title credentials early on but United fought out a very entertaining match.

An extremely solid defence held the Yorkshire side at bay and the game looked certain to finish goalless until a moment of inspiration turned the game.

With a minute remaining George Best set off on a trademark weaving run. Taking possession wide on the left he headed diagonally across the pitch beating defenders at will. At one stage he looked like he was willing to lay the ball off but, using his team-mates to distract defenders, Best dawdled mid-pitch as he considered the next course of action.

Defenders were desperate not to commit themselves and this allowed Best time to meander his way toward goal. Danger seemed to have been averted as George drifted nearer the right touchline with Blades defenders happy to lead the Irishman into a dead end.

Most players would have looked to earn a corner at this point but Best was not most players - he feinted one way then accelerated again pulling a yard clear of the cover through quickness of thought before drilling an effort across goal and into the opposite corner.

An already shattered side headed back across The Pennines on the back of a 2-0 defeat having allowed Brian Kidd to release Alan Gowling to notch deep in injury time.

MANCHESTER UNITED 1 BURNLEY 1
League Cup 3ʀᴅ Rᴅ 6 October 1971

DESPITE HOPES THAT he might make it, Law remained injured so there were no changes. Burnley may have lost their First Division status five months previously but still had the ethos of a top flight team which helped them dominate the initial exchanges and grab the lead through Leighton James after half an hour.

Charlton equalised against the run of play just before half-time following a scramble in front of goal. Peter Mellor performed heroics to stop the ball going in with a double save from George Best's initial header but could only throw his palm out during the second block which created the chance.

Paul Fletcher hit a post on the resumption and with the exception of Best, who made runs which often defied football physics, The Clarets had little to worry about until the final throws of the game when Mellor performed miracles to keep his side level - he was beaten once but Bobby Charlton hit the bar.

A defeat would have been rough justice on a spirited Burnley side who deserved at least a replay.

HUDDERSFIELD TOWN 0 MANCHESTER UNITED 3
Division One 9 October 1971

A TIMELY RETURN to fitness saw Denis Law come back to face his first league club and end John Aston's two game run. A calf injury suffered by George may have led to an extended chance but the problem cleared up in time.

A well-contested game with few chances was played out until the hour mark when Best netted from a Willie Morgan run and cross which bore all the hallmarks of a set up from the scorer himself. Law and Bobby Charlton added the extras as Huddersfield imploded. The Terriers proved true to their name and adopted a vigorous approach to the game, although some very good team work saw United through. However, there were casualties including Best who was left limping having apparently aggravated his calf problem.

MANCHESTER UNITED 1 DERBY COUNTY 0
DIVISION ONE 16 OCTOBER 1971

WITH THE RARE luxury of seven days to recover, George was fit for the mouth watering clash with Derby County who were two points ahead of The Reds although with an inferior goal average which meant a narrow victory would take United top. The task was achieved in midfield as Charlton, Morgan and Gowling played to their recognised strengths that cast the veteran as playmaker.

It was only the quality of Derby's backline that ensured The Rams were level for 54 minutes before succumbing to a sumptuous strike from Best.

Derby mounted some raids towards the close as United became less adventurous as the whistle drew nearer.

BURNLEY 0 MANCHESTER UNITED 1
LEAGUE CUP 3RD RD REPLAY 18 OCTOBER 1971

AS DEFENCES REALISED they could only halt Best by foul rather than fair means the knocks came thick and fast. Despite nursing bruised thighs there was no question of the winger changing his game or opting for a rest even on a night when heavy rain lashed Turf Moor and slippy conditions ensued. Already suffering from a cold he picked up another painful knock to a leg but saw the match out.

A Bobby Charlton sizzler which bent past the keeper on 80 minutes decided the game although Burnley had a penalty shout before the goal when Leighton James claimed Charlton had tussled with him in the area but the referee saw nothing untoward.

NEWCASTLE UNITED 0 MANCHESTER UNITED 1
DIVISION ONE 23 OCTOBER 1971

DESPITE THE BLOWS there was no keeping George Best off a pitch unless he could possibly help it. He was the joint top scorer in the league and cup with 12 although another man with a round dozen, Manchester City's Franny Lee, had scored one more in the First Division.

Malcolm McDonald, a £180,000 buy from Luton Town in the summer, had only hit six and failed to add to that tally as Steve James and David Sadler held him on a tight leash. The Reds had not won at St James Park in five seasons and a tough test early in the game meant no one could be sure of that hoodoo being broken. John Tudor hit the bar with a header before United, through that exceptional midfield, took control.

Willie Morgan, always looking to create an opportunity, worked with Law to fashion a chance for Brian Kidd. Iam McFaul saved but could only parry to Best who made no mistake. Law set up Charlton for another late on but an offside flag was waved before the ball hit the net.

MANCHESTER UNITED 1 STOKE CITY 1
League Cup 4ᵗʰ Rd 27 October 1971

As a team United turned in their worst performance for some months but still managed to avoid defeat. This time Alex Stepney was the hero. His fine saves ensured Stoke were limited to just one goal - a 73ʳᵈ minute strike from John Ritchie. The Reds tried hard to rescue something with movement from Kidd, Law and Best providing midfield with plenty of options but it was only a glancing header from Alan Gowling which saved their blushes.

Ultimately Gordon Banks was not as busy as his opposite number. Ritchie felt he had won the match after converting Jimmy Greenhoff's cross but a linesman's flag saved United and allowed a second chance at the Victoria Ground.

MANCHESTER UNITED 0 LEEDS UNITED 1
Division One 30 October 1971

Tony Dunne returned against an injury hit Leeds who could only recall Eddie Gray from their lengthy list of casualties. Probably for the first time in years The Peacocks were distant second favourites, so they savoured inflicting a first home defeat on their old enemies - the first in nine games - courtesy of some quick thinking by Johnny Giles who took a free-kick before United had arranged themselves. Alex Stepney was caught cold by an equally smart assessment of the situation from Peter Lorimer who placed a low shot well away from the keeper.

The scorer was also involved in the other major talking point of the game. A George Best lob set up an attack which broke down on the edge of the area. It was a late afternoon, gloomy and autumnal. Seemingly from nowhere a United fan latched on to the loose ball cracking a shot which Gary Sprake instinctively dived low to keep out.

Lorimer, possibly feeling that he should have checked the run of the man in the bomber jacket with a scarf tied around his wrist, took out his frustration with a kick to the knees. It was a challenge which sent the youngster sprawling to the ground and would usually have had the referee pointing to the penalty spot but the officials waved play on while the pitch invader was quickly intercepted by the constabulary.

Leeds had been one of the few sides to compete with The Reds in midfield which starved forwards of the ball, although Best did hit the bar with his clearest chance.

MANCHESTER CITY 3 MANCHESTER UNITED 3
DIVISION ONE 6 NOVEMBER 1971

ANOTHER YOUNG MAN from Belfast made his bow for United and in such a high profile game 17 year-old Sammy McIlroy emerged with distinction. He had been plucked out of a reserve team fixture with City scheduled for the previous evening and drafted into the forward line as a replacement for Denis Law. There were obvious comparisons to Best and, just like George himself, he had not been told he would be starting until the day of the game and believed he had been brought in should someone else drop out.

McIlroy had been identified as a real prospect but now Frank O'Farrell had a chance to preview not only his talents but his temperament. With the exception of Old Trafford there was no bigger stage for a budding Red Devil than a 63,000 plus crowd at Maine Road.

City fielded their recent £60,000 capture from Newcastle United Wyn Davies in attack but it was the teenager who made a real mark. He even had the audacity to more or less take the ball off George Best's toes to score.

That goal opened the scoring and Brian Kidd doubled the advantage just minutes into the second half. However, the occasion drew real spirit out of City as Colin Bell and Franny Lee both found the net to level. Lee with a spot-kick.

Wyn Davies looked to have put City ahead but his effort was ruled out for offside. Many in the ground, and not just partisan Blues, thought the linesman had got it wrong. It appeared the mistake could have cost at least two points when a John Aston shot deflected off Alan Gowling's shins. Joe Corrigan seemed pretty certain of collecting the mis-hit shot until the intervention.

With time all but up and the fat lady metaphorically clearing her throat, City earned a corner. The centre was initially cleared but Mike Summerbee gambled on the outcome and found enough space to fire home.

STOKE CITY 0 MANCHESTER UNITED 0
LEAGUE CUP 4TH RD REPLAY 8 NOVEMBER 1971

McILROY WAS RETAINED with Francis Burns taking over from Tony Dunne at left back. Gordon Banks went into the game with a leg injury but The Reds couldn't capitalise. George Best had a less than convincing game and as the midfield laboured few players were able to thrust themselves into the limelight.

However, a far more dangerous looking Stoke were held out without much fuss.

MANCHESTER UNITED 3 TOTTENHAM HOTSPUR 1
DIVISION ONE 13 NOVEMBER 1971

DENIS LAW declared himself fit but Sammy McIlroy was still favoured as Brian Kidd, who limped out of the League Cup replay, was injured. John Aston, who had shown great form and done little wrong, was initially called in but, seemingly jinxed, was also laid up by a late injury so Carlo Sartori found himself on the bench.

The Lawman's return seemed to add a key ingredient to the game of so many colleagues and certainly stopped United's

toil up front as he hit two excellent goals.

He went close with a header before finding the target. Willie Morgan created both goals. Converting crosses is never an easy task but no striker could fail to be assisted by passes of such quality. McIlroy was able to take a bow on his home debut after netting to make the game safe. Spurs had not won away from White Hart Lane all season and never looked like breaking their duck.

STOKE CITY 2 MANCHESTER UNITED 1
LEAGUE CUP 4TH RD 2ND REPLAY 15 NOVEMBER 1971

LAW FOUND HIMSELF sidelined yet again as he struggled to maintain fitness. Kidd and Aston remained out so Sartori at inside left was the only change. After two above average performances United set about settling this marathon tie but frustratingly went out. However, over three games justice was probably done. It was just a pity this type of work hadn't been put in during the other two encounters.

George Best buzzed around after a quiet few weeks and gave The Reds the lead just before half time, anticipating Alan Gowling's through ball and sending a low shot past Banks. United continued

to dominate but didn't add to their tally with plenty of chances missed including a couple by the goalscorer while Sartori had one cleared off the line by Denis Smith.

A lack of attention near the left touchline allowed the ball to be whipped into the box for Peter Dobing to equalise and Stoke, revitalised by George Eastham's introduction from the bench, began to dominate. Ritchie and Terry Conroy drew fine saves but the former got the better of one exchange when he met a corner. Steve James, who had done such a good marshalling job to that point, was too slow to rise.

MANCHESTER UNITED 3 LEICESTER CITY 2
DIVISION ONE 20 NOVEMBER 1971

THERE WAS MIXED news for Frank O'Farrell who was able to welcome Denis Law and Brian Kidd back but was dealt a

a blow losing David Sadler to tonsillitis. It give Paul Edwards a first chance to establish himself since April. Sammy

McIlroy was demoted to the bench with Sartori omitted. Law hit his 200th goal despite struggling with an ankle problem which recurred during the warm-up. He played the entire first half but was only due to be given 10 minutes after the interval. During that time he hit another. Kidd had put The Reds ahead on two minutes smashing the ball into the back of the net with a shot that owed as much to timing as it did to power.

Law headed in the first courtesy of Charlton's ball into the area then followed up a Charlton shot which came back after a block close to the line.

United were defending well but there were clear signs that the back four and the keeper were unaccustomed to one another and Leicester were allowed a way back in, reducing their arrears to 3-2 through Alan Birchenall and Len Glover.

The last knockings saw The Foxes hit a post and denied a very good penalty shout as United dithered under pressure.

SOUTHAMPTON 2 MANCHESTER UNITED 5
DIVISION ONE 27 NOVEMBER 1971

LAW WAS DIAGNOSED with an Achilles tendon problem rather than the suspected ankle strain which allowed Sammy McIlroy a route back into the side. Sadler returned to bolster a defence that had looked shaky of late.

Yet it was a vintage performance from George Best, hitting his second hat-trick of the season, that stole the show. Some poor defending, or at least marking, was to blame as no team could afford to give Best the kind of space he was afforded here. Once again a good team performance was the foundation and fantastic distribution from the centre of the field a huge factor. On the ball Best was sublime. He could have notched at least one more but was forced off with 20 minutes remaining.

McIlroy hit a screamer with Brian Kidd also finding the net. Ron Davies and Jimmy Gabriel replied for the Saints. With United now three points ahead of Manchester City in second with just over half a season to go, hopes of claiming the title were high.

MANCHESTER UNITED 3 NOTTINGHAM FOREST 2
DIVISION ONE 4 DECEMBER 1971

TOMMY DOCHERTY, MANAGER of the Scottish national side, said he would not be picking Denis Law for the foreseeable future after leaving him out of his third squad. Injuries were a problem but now Docherty suggested form was another issue. He was still considered vital to The Reds' cause and even though he scored a goal acting as his deputy, Sammy McIlroy was moved to one side for Law's return. His international manager's claims seemed odd given that he had scored four goals in two games prior to missing the Southampton game.

Peter Cormack gave Forest an early lead whipping United into action. A header from Law and two superb efforts from Kidd put The Reds in exhibition mode and most of the game became a parade of their skills. Too many players, including Best, took it upon themselves to taunt the visitors when, regardless of the advantage, they should have been looking for more goals.

Forest had already shown they could find the net and closed the gap in the last quarter of the game through Martin O'Neill.

STOKE CITY 1 MANCHESTER UNITED 1
DIVISION ONE 11 DECEMBER 1971

A FOURTH MEETING with Stoke in little more than a month had built up some familiarity and the Staffordshire side used their experience to frustrate United again. The Potters were a very busy team who looked to maintain the pressure and contain far more skilful players than their own side was able to boast. They did so extremely well and took a grip on midfield. Drifting back didn't even assist the cause as even those with enough skill to breakthrough such as George Best found the central area too congested.

John Mahoney capitalised on fine work by John Ritchie to put The Potters ahead but Law equalised before the break. Best would probably have scored after finally wriggling his way through had it not been for a foul by John Marsh, who dumped the winger to the ground. Ritchie missed an open goal but defeat would have been rough justice on the United defence which held out well as pressure from Stoke grew.

IPSWICH TOWN 0 MANCHESTER UNITED 0
DIVISION ONE 18 DECEMBER 1971

AFTER A LENGTHY lay off, Tony Dunne was ready to return and face a tough Ipswich side who had not lost at Portman Road since September. Mick Hill ran through to score for the home side but was pulled back for offside. Though United were extremely tight at the back Jimmy Robertson kept Dunne busy and had a late penalty claim denied. The Reds rarely had to resort to such desperate measures.

The first United chance fell to Best but was hit too close to the keeper. Having heeded the lessons from the League Cup meeting the home side remained watchful at all times. Defenders surrounded anyone in possession with resources also centred around those within passing range but George never stopped trying to work his way through and at times was only just thwarted.

MANCHESTER UNITED 2 COVENTRY CITY 2
DIVISION ONE 27 DECEMBER 1972

COVENTRY FIELDED MANCHESTER City's reserve keeper Ron Healey who had been signed on loan and was called into early action by Brian Kidd. United were busy but seemed to run out of ideas allowing The Sky Blues to gain the upper hand and score through Quintin Young. Poor work in defence allowed Willie Carr an easy goal to make it 2-0.

Best was extremely quiet and offered little. Only 20 minutes remained when Law headed in from a Bobby Charlton centre before Steve James claimed a late share of the points. He had been tidy at the back following the goal though was carried off before the end with concussion.

WEST HAM UNITED 3 MANCHESTER UNITED 0
DIVISION ONE 1 JANUARY 1972

A SURPRISE 3-0 reverse at West Ham United marked not only United's heaviest defeat of the season but a worrying portent for O'Farrell's reign. Not only for the fact that The Reds had claimed just one point from their Christmas fixtures and three from the last eight available but the manner in which they went down here.

Bobby Moore was outstanding when called upon but did not have much to do until late. As earnestly as United attacked there was very little end product while The Hammers posed constant menace and scored through Bryan 'Pop' Robson, Clyde Best's deflected shot and a Geoff Hurst penalty given for handing against Alan Gowling.

George Best seemed mortified and publicly admitted he felt out of touch and worried about the contribution he was making to the team plus any effect his form may have having on others.

However, on the surface his comments seemed to make little sense. United had been well beaten at Upton Park but this appeared to be the type of blip any team could suffer and despite not playing at Old Trafford until the seventh game of the 1971-72 season United had lost just

once and had established a decent lead by the turn of the year suffering just two defeats.

At the same time Best had scored 17 goals. He had been helped by shrewd tactical decisions which assisted not only the team but Best in particular. For example, Alan Gowling had dropped back from attack to midfield partnering Willie Morgan who had been playing on the wing. It was a simple switch but helped bring George into the game more as both were not only good ball winners but exceptionally good distributors of possession.

That made Best's decision to absent himself from training over the course of an entire week around New Year extremely puzzling. Nobody officially knew his whereabouts after he failed to contact the club following the West Ham game and predictably he was dropped for the meeting with Wolves at Old Trafford on 8 January.

In-between times he was photographed with reigning Miss Great Britain Carolyn Moore at Tramp nightclub in London. The 19 year-old from Nantwich met George the previous month in his Blinkers club. The two were rumoured to be making wedding plans though both parties denied this and stayed in the Piccadilly Hotel until George's bolthole was discovered. He was said to be staying with friends. No one knew if this was in the capital or back in Manchester.

His manager said there were no thoughts of disciplinary action in the early stages of the incident just his player's welfare and getting him prepared for the cup match with Southampton midway through the month as he would be missing the game at Wolves which finished in a 3-1 defeat. A demand to present himself at Frank O'Farrell's office on Monday was issued.

When George did return he was handed a swift punishment in the shape of a two week £400 fine and told to move back to his old digs. Though Mrs Fullaway, a lady George felt genuine affection for, tried her utmost to tame him his fondness for other women won out.

There was seemingly a never ending queue of girls willing to take him into their hearts and they went hand-in-hand with the booze and a good night out.

SOUTHAMPTON 1 MANCHESTER UNITED 1
FA Cup 3ʀᴅ Rᴅ 15 January 1972

TONY DUNNE WAS welcomed back in the hope that his presence would stabilise a creaky defence. Tommy O'Neil made way with Sammy McIlroy axed to accommodate Best's return.

George was quiet for the most part but Bobby Charlton made the most out of a piece of his trickery by taking the ball after a dummy had sent the entire Southampton defence in the wrong direction. Brian Kidd struggled with double vision after an early clash of heads. If he had remained free of knocks he too may have made more of the very presentable chances created by Best and others.

The Reds turned in a good performance across the pitch to earn a replay and resisted the Saints well at the back, defying the threat of Ron Davies though he did set-up Jimmy Gabriel's equaliser, heading down Terry Paine's quick free kick.

MANCHESTER UNITED 4 SOUTHAMPTON 1
FA Cup 3ʀᴅ Rᴅ Replay 19 January 1972

KIDD'S BLOW TO the head led to Sammy McIlroy coming in as Old Trafford witnessed George Best's return to top form blasted Southampton out of the cup. His performance inspired United to a first win in six games which was also the last time George had scored.

Southampton took the lead through Mick Channon as both defences seemed nervy. United couldn't seem to apply a finishing touch to any of their moves until Best latched on to a pass from Charlton and danced through a number of defenders before shooting. It may have taken a deflection on the way in but the set up was nothing short of brilliant. Neither side could add another until extra-time when David Sadler found the net. A tidy finish by Best made it 3-1 with John Aston adding another to ice the cake.

During his celebrations George

delivered a damning verdict on someone or something which must have irked him in recent weeks by flicking V-signs with both hands.

MANCHESTER UNITED 0 CHELSEA 1
DIVISION ONE 22 JANUARY 1972

IN CONTRAST TO midweek, United seemed off the pace in midfield. George Best had individual highlights but they were too few and far between courtesy of his very clever handling by Chelsea who always had more than enough to combat any threat. Despite looking in poor form and continuing to suffer from an ankle problem which made his participation doubtful, Sammy McIlroy thought he

had scored but Law had strayed offside. Willie Morgan was the most persistent threat but had far too much to do just holding midfield together.

Peter Osgood tore through the middle of United's defence to score in the second half and seal a defeat which knocked The Reds off the top of Division One for the first time since November.

WEST BROMWICH ALBION 2 MANCHESTER UNITED 1
DIVISION ONE 29 JANUARY 1972

BRIAN KIDD SCORED early on but that seemed to affect United adversely. Despite much possession, too little of it was utilised up to any great effect. West Brom eventually overran midfield which gave an anxious back four no breathing

space and errors essentially led to both Albion goals.

Alex Stepney was well worked in his 200th league appearance and required to pull off a number of great saves just to keep The Reds in with a shot.

PRESTON NORTH END 0 MANCHESTER UNITED 2
FA CUP 4TH RD 5 FEBRUARY 1972

TONY DUNNE'S ABSENCE led to extensive alterations to the formation. Francis Burns switched to left back with Alan Gowling returning to the forward line from where he notched twice in the last five minutes to give United victory.

A poor first half was enlivened after the break as both Preston and United looked for an advantage. The North End defence was tested on a regular basis but Best was kept quiet by David Connor.

MANCHESTER UNITED 0 NEWCASTLE UNITED 2
DIVISION ONE 12 FEBRUARY 1972

THOUGH FIT, TONY Dunne found there was no quick way back into the side and there could be no question of asking Gowling to step aside after his heroics at Deepdale. Willie Morgan, who had been suffering from 'flu during the week, was cleared to play although he looked heavy legged and mis-kicked with the first opportunity of the game.

Unfortunately the same formation didn't work for a second time but it was not for the want of trying. Gowling hit the post and Best constantly threatened though only got through twice. The failings were in other areas particularly midfield which eventually weakened the potency of the strikers and left the defence wide open to an onslaught. Two goals were scored as a result when individual contributions at the back deserved more.

NORTHERN IRELAND 1 SPAIN 1
EUROPEAN NATIONS CUP 16 FEBRUARY 1972

FOLLOWING HEIGHTENED TENSIONS in the province, this 'home' tie was played at Hull City's Boothberry Park, the home ground of player/manger Terry Neill. Fortunately Neill had the presence of mind to call Sammy Morgan into his squad as a late replacement 48 hours prior to kick-off.

The Port Vale forward had looked to quit the game in favour of a career in teaching but decided to plough on and become a full-time professional. In that role he salvaged a point for his country with a 73rd minute strike. Morgan had almost opened the scoring with a header from George Best's devilish cross early on. Spain had taken the lead three minutes before the break when an error by Neill allowed Aguillar to centre and provide a simple headed chance for Rojo.

LEEDS UNITED 5 MANCHESTER UNITED 1
DIVISION ONE 19 FEBRUARY 1972

UNITED HADN'T WON at Elland Road since April 1965. However, The Reds were not just beaten here but totally humiliated after an amazing turnaround in the second half. Leeds had been dangerous in the first half but the game was scoreless until the interval.

Stepney was in fine form to keep Leeds at bay yet a Mick Jones hat-trick, together with Alan Clarke and Peter Lorimer efforts ended majestic moves during which The Tykes dominated possession.

There was a consolation for Francis Burns but the overall performances of many players was way below par. George Best cut a sad and distant figure who, for the most part, seemed happy to make up the numbers. A very gloomy sight in view of his troubles the previous month.

MANCHESTER UNITED 0 MIDDLESBROUGH 0
FA Cup 5ᵀᴴ Rd 26 February 1972

Nobby Stiles returned to Old Trafford for the first time since becoming Middlesbrough player/manager. His Boro team had already accounted for Manchester City in the third round and relied on a solid defence which the high-flying Blues had failed to breach. Stiles would have been encouraged by doubts over Willie Morgan and Denis Law although both played.

George Best looked brighter and seemed to enjoy the game and a fair bit of banter with the man who acted as his protector for many seasons. Best put an effort wide after vaulting a tackle from Stiles. Denis Law also went close. Gowling went closer still, hitting a post as The Reds had most of the play but other than these chances lacked punch.

A John Hickton header was well saved by Alex Stepney who scooped the ball away with one hand.

MIDDLESBROUGH 0 MANCHESTER UNITED 3
FA Cup 5ᵀᴴ Rd Replay 29 February 1972

United's performance had many wondering just why they had seemed to struggle scoring goals in recent weeks as the rampant Reds outclassed Boro 3-0 to win a place in the last eight of the FA Cup. Any win away from home could be categorised as a fine victory but this one was extremely impressive starting with the move which saw Denis Law upended in the area. Willie Morgan slotted the penalty away.

Middlesbrough looked beaten from that point on but The Reds only turned the screw after the interval when balls were worked quickly through midfield. George Best popped up to apply the finishing touch and Charlton completed the scoring just past the hour.

Martin Buchan, who had been signed in the week running up to the tie, watched from the stands and his presence may have led the defence, particularly the centre backs, to concentrate a little more than they may have been doing over recent weeks. It gave Frank O'Farrell the difficult job of deciding who to drop.

TOTTENHAM HOTSPUR 2 MANCHESTER UNITED 0
Division One 4 March 1972

The answer to that conundrum was Francis Burns, who made way with David Sadler taking his place in midfield. There was never any question of the £125,000 acquisition from Aberdeen not coming in at the first opportunity but he must have wondered about the size of the task facing him after this debut as, despite falling to a sixth successive league defeat, United played quite well.

Buchan's presence did assist other defenders although Sadler, who had been acting as a deep lying sweeper for three seasons, didn't seem too happy in his new role and United suffered as Spurs began to dominate this area before getting their goals within minutes of each other through

Steve Perryman and Martin Chivers. Once the Londoners went ahead there was no chance of United pulling things back. Best looked isolated but was not helped by problems behind him - even when he had the chance to influence matters he failed to find his usual rhythm.

MANCHESTER UNITED 0 EVERTON 0
DIVISION ONE 8 MARCH 1972

NEW ADDITIONS CONTINUED to arrive with the signing of Ian Storey-Moore for a record £200,000 fee. The player had actually been paraded by Derby manager Brian Clough at The Baseball Ground before negotiations with Nottingham Forest were concluded, meaning the deal fell through allowing United to nip in.

Without a league win since early December and having now moved to shore up the defence, Frank O'Farrell turned his attentions to a spluttering attack which at times seemed as good as anything else in the country but more often than not appeared toothless.

Big decisions were made with Charlton and Morgan dropped and Burns, Gowling and Sadler stepping into the breach.

A first point in eight league games was achieved by sterling defensive work brought together by Buchan who talked and cajoled his colleagues throughout. United were also very strong in the middle it was only in attack that they looked ill at ease although Best hit a post and saw a well executed lob beat a stranded keeper before being headed off the line by Tommy Wright.

Storey-Moore, watching on, seemed certain to gain a place in the side, it only remained to see where the axe would fall. Brian Kidd and Denis Law, who endured fairly torrid games, seemed to be most at risk.

MANCHESTER UNITED 2 HUDDERSFIELD TOWN 0
DIVISION ONE 11 MARCH 1972

AS EXPECTED STOREY-MOORE was selected and wore the number 11 shirt with George Best taking over in Law's stead. The new face provided a great boost to Best in link up play and it was his input which saw The Reds gel upfront and score more than one for the first time in the league since the end of December. Moore got one and made the other for Best who had failed to score in three months after a prolific run.

Bobby Charlton and Willie Morgan were back and, though initially as sluggish as they had been before they were dropped, they eventually managed to bring themselves back up to speed.

MANCHESTER UNITED 1 STOKE CITY 1
FA Cup 6ᵀᴴ Rd 18 March 1972

WITH STOREY-MOORE CUP-TIED Law came back. The forwards, who revelled in the previous weekend's game, seemed to suffer as despite creating chances and having most of the first half nobody could muster a decent finish. When they did Gordon Banks was in his usual excellent form.

Jimmy Greenhoff found the net for Stoke on the hour. It was a messy goal but looked like it could be the winner until Best struck five minutes from time. That effort would have sealed the game had an otherwise perfectly good effort from Bobby Charlton not been ruled out for obstruction when the scorer cried "leave it". It was unfortunate given the United skipper's experience but Stoke could also point to a close shout for a penalty.

STOKE CITY 2 MANCHESTER UNITED 1
FA Cup 6ᵀᴴ Rd Replay 22 March 1972

DAVID SADLER, WHO had been substituted for Alan Gowling at Old Trafford, failed to prove his fitness for the replay. Stoke went through courtesy of Gordon Banks and a string of outstanding saves throughout normal time and the additional 30 minute period required to break the deadlock. He needed to be in top form as against any other keeper The Reds would have been runaway winners.

The England international denied Charlton and Kidd at bay with saves almost on a par with any of the heroics he had performed throughout his illustrious career. He was beaten by a shot Best rifled hard and low but Dennis Smith levelled with just three minutes remaining after some lax work.

Thirteen minutes into extra-time Terry Conroy fielded a high ball, brought it down and crashed a shot into the net to end United's cup hopes.

MANCHESTER UNITED 4 CRYSTAL PALACE 0
Division One 25 March 1972

A BRUISED HIP suffered at Stoke ruled Willie Morgan out of any participation in a convincing United win as once again Ian Storey-Moore showed exactly what had been missing from the side during midweek and helped drive The Reds to a fine 4-0 win.

Gowling hit an early goal followed by Storey-Moore early in the second half. Law rounded off with a tap in after Bobby Charlton had hit his first league goal since October. Best looked far happier in this set-up with someone else searching out chances and taking the responsibility which had previously been heaped on his shoulders.

COVENTRY CITY 2 MANCHESTER UNITED 3
Division One 1 April 1972

COVENTRY WERE OUTCLASSED and three excellent long range goals from Storey-Moore, Best and Charlton won the game early on - or so it appeared. Bill Glazier had kept out a hatful of efforts from each of the scorers plus Law and others. Coventry could have pulled it back at 1-1 through Ernie Hunt but missed out and that proved to be the turning point though the home side still competed.

Roy Barry's deflected shot and a late Bobby Graham effort showed Coventry were not content to see time out which made for a tense finale.

MANCHESTER UNITED 0 LIVERPOOL 3
Division One 3 April 1972

No MATTER WHAT the result, the day was a poignant one for Bobby Charlton who equalled the club record of 563 league appearances set three years previously by Bill Foulkes and could reasonably expect to set his own mark the following day. Willie Morgan came back in for Brian Kidd with David Sadler vying for a place on the bench.

United's hopes of breathing life back into their season were frustrated at the hands of title-challenging Liverpool who soaked up a lot of pressure then caught United cold. Best headed just wide and Ray Clemence saved well from Alan Gowling. Willie Morgan hit the keeper square in the face but it still counted as a save even if a fortunate one.

Once the Anfield club eased into their stride the United forwards were kept quiet allowing right back Chris Lawler to make his way up field and ghost into the area to glance a header past Alex Stepney. John Toshack, who had been well patrolled by Steve James, made the most of the turmoil which followed getting in behind to net with a header within 90 seconds. The Reds had little left although they still made a game attempt to get some pride back.

Terry Young, who was given a 13 minute debut from the bench, looked sharp on occasions as Emlyn Hughes tied matters up close to the end.

SHEFFIELD UNITED 1 MANCHESTER UNITED 1
Division One 4 April 1972

JOHN CONNAUGHTON WAS promoted from the reserves as Alex Stepney's confidence had hit rock bottom after recent matches. With games on successive days it appeared as good a time as any to make a change. Whether it would be a permanent arrangement remained to be seen and very much depended on the debutant. Being beaten by a Geoff Salmons cross which went over his head and landed in the net was a bad start and he had to accept some responsibility for not his positioning and failure to get back once it became clear the flight may beat him.

In mitigation there was the matter of bright halogen bulbs which had recently been positioned above the stands shining in his eyes, a fact the keeper was quick to point out to those defenders who didn't

have their head in their hands.

Among them was United goalscorer David Sadler who realised that no matter what the reason, such poor fortune had probably cost a vital point.

LEICESTER CITY 2 MANCHESTER UNITED 0
DIVISION ONE 8 APRIL 1972

DAVID SADLER HAD been asked to play at a centre forward for the first time in many years but was back in his more familiar role deeper down the field. There was some bad blood with Frank O'Farrell's former club and Peter Shilton in particular, who he forced to stay at Filbert Street not long before he left.

The keeper was keen to inflict some embarrassment as a result and made an excellent save from Best. United kept

going as the midfield gave a display of perpetual motion playing balls through at a rapid rate but Shilts continued to excel.

The statistics suggested United deserved more but football is a very cruel game at times and Keith Weller made the most of some indecision to breeze through the middle on 13 minutes. Another error gave Alan Birchenall a chance to lash home late on.

MANCHESTER UNITED 1 MANCHESTER CITY 3
DIVISION ONE 12 APRIL 1972

THOUGH HE COULD not be blamed for either of the goals conceded at Leicester, there remained speculation about John Connaughton who many expected to be packed off to the reserves sooner rather than later. However, he was given a third chance here and made a trio of fine saves to keep the match goalless at half-time.

Denis Law was not so lucky and was demoted to the bench while Brian Kidd was given his chance after regaining fitness. City were strong candidates to win the championship while United, now safe from the drop, were aiming to finish as high as possible and bag a UEFA Cup place. The Reds were streets behind and the gulf that had emerged between the two sides over recent years showed.

Buchan scored his first goal for the club on the hour but Francis Lee pulled matters level within a minute courtesy of a flicked header from Willie Donachie's cross. Five minutes later Lee put City ahead following a sweet half-volley from Bell's header after a free-kick from Mike Summerbee. Colin Bell dispossessed the usually impeccable Buchan and found Rodney Marsh for the third.

Bobby Charlton seemed up for the fight to restore some pride but too many others looked lethargic. Best often felt the need to drift back and compensate for the lack of passes coming through but that left Kidd and Storey-Moore short of support.

MANCHESTER UNITED 3 SOUTHAMPTON 2
DIVISION ONE 15 APRIL 1972

FOCUS WAS SHIFTED to attack as Denis Law returned. Alex Stepney was also back as time and patience ran out for John Connaughton. Gowling was dropped for Terry Young while Bobby Charlton was ruled out through injury. The changes failed to disrupt United who played as smoothly as at anytime in the last few months. The attack was kept well supplied and their numbers bolstered by great support. A George Best penalty opened the scoring. A sizzling effort from Storey Moore followed soon after then another superb goal from Brian Kidd.

A couple of Ron Davies goals led to a tense finale with Mick Channon instrumental in each and a draw looked a real probability for a long spell.

ARSENAL 3 MANCHESTER UNITED 0
DIVISION ONE 25 APRIL 1972

A HEAVY COLD had ruled George out of the scoreless trip to Nottingham Forest but he had recovered sufficiently to bring The Reds back up to full strength at Highbury. However, the season couldn't seem to end quick enough for some. John Roberts was booked for a clattering challenge on Best though he had little need as George laboured enduring one of his worst ever games in a United shirt. Yet he wasn't alone as too little effort and character was shown.

The sole exception was Alex Stepney who was exceptional until finally beaten by Ray Kennedy midway through the first half. Peter Simpson came from the back to double the lead before the break.

MANCHESTER UNITED 3 STOKE CITY 0
DIVISION ONE 29 APRIL 1972

SOME REVENGE WAS gained over Stoke for knocking United out of both cups but it only served to underline a disappointing season. The Potters fielded a scratch side due to injuries, giving a number of reserves the benefit of playing at Old Trafford.

Storey-Moore, who was looking forward to his first full season and linking well with Bobby Charlton, hit a goal on 13 minutes. Denis Law, with his eyes on a recall for Scotland, also played well and set up Charlton then had a header handled which resulted in a late penalty which George Best dispatched to seal the win.

1971-72

The first half of United's first season under Frank O'Farrell proved to be a false dawn. Before Christmas the Irishman seemed to be the answer to United's managerial problems as Law, Best and Charlton re-discovered the form which had made United champions of Europe just three years previously as The Reds soared to the top of the league.

Best, in particular, seemed to relish O'Farrell's stewardship as his strike-rate returned to something similar to that under Busby. Dynamic and ever-threatening, the Ulsterman's pre-Christmas form was a reminder of why George was still rated as one of the world's greats. His stellar performances against West Ham, Sheffield United and Southampton showed that when he put it all together he was an unstoppable force in the First Division.

Yet around Christmas time George lost it almost as quickly as he'd found it. The turning point coincided with his absences from training in early January only to be pictured with Miss Great Britain at a celebrity nightclub. From then on United suffered a rapid decline in form as the flair and imagination Best had conjured in autumn turned into New Year listlessness - the team enduring a 10-match winless streak which turned a title challenge into a relegation battle.

By now it was clear that Best's condition dictated the team's ability to compete. That said Best still finished as United's top scorer with 26 goals including 18 in the league and missed just two games across all competitions. Only Brian Kidd and Bobby Charlton could match that consistency.

Yet despite the presence of one or two good players, Best was holding up a struggling side which only saved itself through such an excellent start. But even George, especially with demons snapping at his once fleet footed heels, couldn't continue carrying the side. The pressure was beginning to show and never more so than at the end of the season when instead of joining a club tour to Israel before heading to Northern Ireland for the home internationals, George took himself off to Marbella from where he entertained journalists and underlined his unprofessional approach to the game.

Just hours before his 26th birthday he admitted to downing a bottle of vodka a day and claimed to be a nervous wreck. Pictures of George in bars drinking large quantities of bottled beer were wired around the world -

with it went the last remnants of his serious footballing career. The press may have followed his every move and no doubt all the papers were taken at Old Trafford but if George wanted someone to fly out and reason with him so a comeback could be arranged, he was to be disappointed. At one stage he would have expected representatives of the club to have bent over backwards to persuade him but United held firm and let him stew for the remainder of his 'holiday' - it was a fortnight before he returned to Manchester.

As it was, Best had few options - either retirement or another club. In the end he reported for training with his tail firmly between between his legs. Though his condition was visibly worsened by the months he spent lazing around, Frank O'Farrell was happy to welcome him back and for his part George started training as hard as he had ever done to repair the damage drinking in the Spanish sun had done. In the meantime he had been dropped from his national side for the British championships and seemed unlikely to make it back into Terry Neill's plans any time soon.

As punishment United imposed a two-week suspension along with an instruction to move in with a solid influence, in this case assistant manager Paddy Crerand and family, although Best later admitted that didn't last much longer than one night. Rumours abounded that many senior players were appalled with the latitude George was given, and claims that Matt Busby and Louis Edwards took punishments out of the manager's hands was said to affect team harmony.

Whereas Matt Busby had preferred evolutionary change to his sides with players brought slowly through the ranks - initially through necessity and then choice - Frank O'Farrell was already on the back foot and forced to bring players in for huge fees.

There was no greater example of this than in early spring when huge sums of money were splashed to ensure United beat any remote possibility of the drop. Martin Buchan was bought from Aberdeen for £125,000 with Nottingham Forest's star forward Ian Storey-Moore costing almost double that sum. These signings at least stopped the rot and, in Buchan at least, United had signed a future captain and one of the stars of the decade.

O'Farrell's biggest test was yet to come however. Acquiescing with Busby and Edwards in giving Best licence for an extended leave of abscence was one thing, getting him back to peak performance would be another - results would determine whether either Irishman had a long term future at the club.

DATE	OPPONENT	VENUE	SCORE	ATT'D	1	2	3	4	5	6	7	8	9	10	11
14 August	Derby County	Baseball Ground	2-2	35,886	Stepney	O'Neill	Dunne	Gowling¹	James	Sadler	Morgan	Kidd	Charlton	Law¹	Best
18 August	Chelsea	Stamford Bridge	3-2	54,763	Stepney	Fitzpatrick	Dunne	Gowling	James	Sadler	Morgan¹	Kidd¹	Charlton¹	Law	Best
20 August	Arsenal *	Anfield	3-1	27,649	Stepney	O'Neill	Dunne	Gowling¹	James	Sadler	Morgan	Kidd¹	Charlton¹	Law	Best
23 August	WBA *	Victoria Ground	3-1	23,146	Stepney	O'Neill	Dunne	Gowling¹	James	Sadler	Morgan	Kidd	Charlton	Best²	Aston
28 August	Wolves	Molineux	1-1	46,471	Stepney	O'Neill	Dunne	Gowling	James	Sadler	Morgan	Kidd	Charlton	Law	Best¹
31 August	Everton	Goodison Park	0-1	52,151	Stepney	O'Neill	Dunne	Gowling	James	Sadler	Morgan	Kidd	Charlton	Law	Best
4 September	Ipswich Town	Old Trafford	1-0	45,656	Stepney	O'Neill	Dunne	Gowling	James	Sadler	Morgan	Kidd	Charlton	Law	Best¹
11 September	Crystal Palace	Selhurst Park	3-1	44,020	Stepney	O'Neill	Dunne	Gowling	James	Sadler	Morgan	Kidd¹	Charlton	Law²	Best¹
18 September	West Ham United	Old Trafford	4-2	55,339	Stepney	O'Neill	Dunne	Gowling	James	Sadler	Morgan	Kidd	Charlton¹	Law	Best³
25 September	Liverpool	Anfield	2-2	55,634	Stepney	O'Neill	Burns	Gowling	James	Sadler	Morgan	Kidd	Charlton¹	Law¹	Aston
2 October	Sheffield United	Old Trafford	2-0	51,735	Stepney	O'Neill	Dunne	Gowling¹	James	Sadler	Morgan	Kidd	Charlton	Best¹	Best¹
9 October	Huddersfield Town	Leeds Road	3-0	33,458	Stepney	O'Neill	Dunne	Gowling	James	Sadler	Morgan	Kidd	Charlton¹	Best¹	Best¹
16 October	Derby County	Old Trafford	1-0	53,247	Stepney	O'Neill	Dunne	Gowling	James	Sadler	Morgan	Kidd	Charlton	Law	Best¹
23 October	Newcastle United	St James' Park	1-0	52,411	Stepney	O'Neill	Dunne	Gowling	James	Sadler	Morgan	Kidd	Charlton	Law	Best¹
30 October	Leeds United	Old Trafford	0-1	53,960	Stepney	O'Neill	Dunne	Gowling	James	Sadler	Morgan	Kidd	Charlton	Law	Best
6 November	Manchester City	Maine Road	3-3	63,326	Stepney	O'Neill	Dunne	Gowling¹	James	Sadler	Morgan	Kidd¹	Charlton	McIlroy¹	Best
13 November	Tottenham H	Old Trafford	3-1	54,058	Stepney	O'Neill	Burns	Gowling	James	Sadler	Morgan	McIlroy¹	Charlton	Law²	Best
20 November	Leicester City	Old Trafford	3-2	48,757	Stepney	O'Neill	Burns	Gowling	James	Edwards	Morgan	Kidd¹	Charlton	Law²	Best
27 November	Southampton	The Dell	5-2	30,323	Stepney	O'Neill	Burns	Gowling	James	Sadler	Morgan	Kidd¹	Charlton	McIlroy¹	Best³
4 December	Nottingham Forest	Old Trafford	3-2	45,411	Stepney	O'Neill	Burns	Gowling	James	Sadler	Morgan	Kidd²	Charlton	Law¹	Best¹
11 December	Stoke City	Victoria Ground	1-1	33,857	Stepney	O'Neill	Burns	Gowling	James	Sadler	Morgan	Kidd	Charlton	Law¹	Best
18 December	Ipswich Town	Portman Road	0-0	29,229	Stepney	Dunne	Burns	Gowling	James	Sadler	Morgan	Kidd	Charlton	Law	Best
27 December	Coventry City	Old Trafford	2-2	52,117	Stepney	Dunne	Burns	Gowling	James¹	Sadler	Morgan	Kidd	Charlton	Law¹	Best
1 January	West Ham United	Upton Park	0-3	41,892	Stepney	Dunne	Burns	Gowling	Edwards	Sadler	Morgan	Kidd	Charlton	Law	Best
22 January	Chelsea	Old Trafford	0-1	55,927	Stepney	O'Neill	Burns	Gowling	Edwards	Sadler	Morgan	McIlroy	Charlton	Law	Best
29 January	WBA	The Hawthorns	1-2	47,012	Stepney	O'Neill	Dunne	Burns	James	Sadler	Morgan	Kidd¹	Charlton	Law	Best
12 February	Newcastle United	Old Trafford	0-2	44,983	Stepney	O'Neill	Burns	Gowling	James	Sadler	Morgan	Kidd	Charlton	Law	Best
19 February	Leeds United	Elland Road	1-5	45,399	Stepney	O'Neill	Dunne	Burns¹	James	Sadler	Morgan	Kidd	Charlton	Gowling	Best
4 March	Tottenham H	White Hart Lane	0-2	54,814	Stepney	O'Neill	Dunne	Buchan	James	Sadler	Burns	Gowling	Charlton	Law	Best
8 March	Everton	Old Trafford	0-0	38,415	Stepney	O'Neill	Dunne	Buchan	James	Sadler	Burns	Gowling	Kidd	Law	Best

Date	Opponent	Venue	Res.	Att.	1	2	3	4	5	6	7	8	9	10	11
11 March	Huddersfield Town	Old Trafford	2-0	53,581	Stepney	O'Neill	Dunne	Buchan	James	Sadler	Morgan	Kidd	Charlton	Best¹	S-Moore¹
25 March	Crystal Palace	Old Trafford	4-0	41,550	Stepney	O'Neill	Dunne	Buchan	James	Gowling¹	Best	Kidd	Charlton¹	Law¹	S-Moore¹
1 April	Coventry City	Highfield Road	3-2	37,901	Stepney	O'Neill	Dunne	Buchan	James	Gowling	Morgan	Best¹	Charlton¹	Law¹	S-Moore¹
3 April	Liverpool	Old Trafford	0-3	53,826	Stepney	O'Neill	Dunne	Buchan	James	Gowling	Morgan	Best	Charlton	Law	S-Moore
4 April	Sheffield United	Bramall Lane	1-1	45,045	Connaughton	O'Neill	Dunne	Buchan	Sadler	Sadler¹	Best	McIlroy	Charlton	Young	S-Moore
8 April	Leicester City	Filbert Street	0-2	35,970	Connaughton	O'Neill	Dunne	Buchan	Sadler	Morgan	Best	McIlroy	Charlton	Young	S-Moore
12 April	Manchester City	Old Trafford	1-3	56,362	Connaughton	O'Neill	Dunne	Buchan¹	James	Sadler	Best	Gowling	Charlton	Kidd	S-Moore
15 April	Southampton	Old Trafford	3-2	38,437	Stepney	O'Neill	Dunne	Buchan	James	Sadler	Best¹	Young	Kidd¹	Law¹	S-Moore¹
25 April	Arsenal	Highbury	0-3	43,125	Stepney	O'Neill	Dunne	Buchan	Sadler	Gowling	Best	Young	Charlton	Kidd	S-Moore
29 April	Stoke City	Old Trafford	3-0	34,959	Stepney	O'Neill		Buchan	James	Young	Best¹	McIlroy	Charlton¹	Law	S-Moore¹

* - Home games - Old Trafford was closed as punishment for a knife-throwing incident the previous season

FA Cup

Date	Opponent	Venue	Res.	Att.	1	2	3	4	5	6	7	8	9	10	11
15 January	Southampton	The Dell	1-1	30,190	Stepney	O'Neill	Burns	Gowling	Edwards	Sadler	Morgan	Kidd	Charlton¹	Law	Best
19 January	Southampton	Old Trafford	4-1	50,960	Stepney	O'Neill	Burns	Gowling	Edwards	Sadler¹	Morgan	McIlroy	Charlton	Law	Best²
5 February	Preston North End	Deepdale	2-0	27,025	Stepney	O'Neill	Burns	Gowling²	James	Sadler	Morgan	Kidd	Charlton	Law	Best
26 February	Middlesbrough	Old Trafford	0-0	53,850	Stepney	O'Neill	Dunne	Burns	James	Sadler	Morgan	Gowling	Charlton	Law	Best
29 February	Middlesbrough	Ayresome Park	3-0	39,683	Stepney	O'Neill	Dunne	Burns	James	Sadler	Morgan¹	Gowling	Charlton¹	Law	Best¹
18 March	Stoke City	Old Trafford	1-1	54,226	Stepney	O'Neill	Dunne	Buchan	James	Sadler	Morgan	Kidd	Charlton	Law	Best¹
22 March	Stoke City	Victoria Gd	1-2	49,192	Stepney	O'Neill	Dunne	Gowling	James	Buchan(M)	Morgan	Kidd	Charlton	Law	Best¹

League Cup

Date	Opponent	Venue	Res.	Att.	1	2	3	4	5	6	7	8	9	10	11
7 September	Ipswich Town	Portman Road	3-1	28,143	Stepney	O'Neill	Dunne	Gowling	James	Sadler	Morgan¹	Kidd	Charlton	Best²	Aston
6 October	Burnley	Old Trafford	1-1	44,600	Stepney	O'Neill	Dunne	Gowling	James	Sadler	Morgan	Kidd	Charlton¹	Best	Aston
18 October	Burnley	Turf Moor	1-0	27,511	Stepney	O'Neill	Dunne	Gowling¹	James	Sadler	Morgan	Kidd	Charlton¹	Law	Best
27 October	Stoke City	Old Trafford	1-1	47,062	Stepney	O'Neill	Burns	Gowling¹	James	Sadler	Morgan	Kidd	Charlton	Law	Best
8 November	Stoke City	Victoria Ground	0-0	40,805	Stepney	O'Neill	Burns	Gowling	James	Sadler	Morgan	Kidd	Charlton	Law	Best¹
15 November	Stoke City	Victoria Ground	1-2	42,249	Stepney	O'Neill	Burns	Gowling	James	Sadler	Morgan	McIlroy	Charlton	Law	Best

Watney Cup

Date	Opponent	Venue	Res.	Att.	1	2	3	4	5	6	7	8	9	10	11
31 July	Halifax Town	The Shay	1-2	13,765	Stepney	Fitzpatrick	Dunne	Crerand	James	Sadler	Morgan	Gowling	Charlton	Law	Best¹

1972-73

BLOW-OUT

MANCHESTER UNITED 1 IPSWICH TOWN 2
DIVISION ONE 12 AUGUST 1972

DESPITE PLAYING LITTLE part in pre-season friendlies due to his summer of excess, a club suspension, lack of match fitness and subsequent injuries, George was declared fit enough to play in the opening league game despite a fractured bone in his hand. The unfortunate Tony Young made way and most experiments with youth prior to the season ended as stalwarts returned.

Ipswich took the lead through Trevor Whymark who made the most of Steve James letting the ball bounce from an otherwise innocuous thump upfield. Good anticipation by the striker bought him the extra yard. Outstanding in midfield, Town pushed for more and got the better of exchanges with each of their opposite numbers. It was only during the second half that United established some form of foothold but then only individuals raised their game.

George had scored on each of the last three visits Ipswich made to Old Trafford but looked timid and protective of his hand which had only just been taken out of its cast giving his marker, Ian Collard, a relatively easy afternoon. Ian Storey-Moore started to produce his best form from the left making chances for Denis Law and Brian Kidd. The former scored United's only goal with two minutes on the clock, converting from a few yards out after keeper David Best found Storey-Moore's shot too hot to handle.

LIVERPOOL 2 MANCHESTER UNITED 0
DIVISION ONE 15 AUGUST 1972

ON THE OPENING day of the season Liverpool had hosted Manchester City and won with goals at either end of the game. It was a clinical display during which City had exhibited robust tactics. United would not provide the same type of approach but were beaten at Anfield with similar authority. Tony Young stepped in for the injured Law who had damaged an ankle but was expected to make a quick return as he was only just ruled out of this one.

Best was pushed into the centre with Young, who had made his debut at the same venue last term as a substitute, moving into midfield. It was a merciless opening for United as Liverpool ripped through the midfield and defence at will. John Toshack confirmed that dominance with a goal on 12 minutes. The Welsh forward had chased every ball and more often than not beaten defenders. Within ten minutes the scorer muscled past Martin Buchan to set up Steve Heighway who made it two.

United quickly massed everyone behind the ball until half time to limit the damage but things began to look up after the break though George was still a peripheral figure with just the odd run. On the positive side there were periods where United passed well and asked their hosts a few questions yet the game remained a shut out.

EVERTON 2 MANCHESTER UNITED 0
DIVISION ONE 19 AUGUST 1972

DENIS LAW BROKE down in training but John Fitzpatrick ended a miserable 18 months by making his comeback and led a dogged resistance in a midfield which had seemed so lightweight in the opening games. And, although United still lost, it was the type of performance which may have earned more against a less capable team. Better service for the forwards ensured Best turned in his most potent performance of the term.

United could have taken the lead but,

after riding out the, storm Everton edged ahead through John Connolly who sent the ball back past Alex Stepney after the keeper had sought to punch away but got no distance.

There was some disarray at the back but United held out until the 75th minute when a controversial penalty awarded against Tommy O'Neil saw Joe Royle secure both points for The Toffeemen.

MANCHESTER UNITED 1 LEICESTER CITY 1
DIVISION ONE 23 AUGUST 1972

A VERY POOR start continued as United failed to maintain any momentum and looked to be on the end of yet another hiding as Leicester gained the upper hand. David Nish, an inexhaustible full back who found his fair share of goals, opened the scoring. However, half time signalled a change in outlook and until at least the final quarter George Best seemed to have rediscovered his impudence and finally seemed ready to resume his career.

Peter Shilton was called upon more often than not by Sammy McIlroy who was bursting through at will but as ever Shilts was equal to almost everything but

an effort from Best.

Sandwiched between this match and United's next clash 72 hours later was a reserve team game. Bobby Charlton, who had missed the trip to Everton, was told that he would not be in the side for the visit of Arsenal either and should report for duty with the second string.

It was the first time he had been asked to make an outing in the Central League for a decade. He would return to the top flight soon but, bearing in mind the leniency shown towards Best, eyebrows were raised about the manager's standing in the dressing room.

MANCHESTER UNITED 0 ARSENAL 0
DIVISION ONE 26 AUGUST 1972

A GOALLESS DRAW at Arsenal was more than a creditable result in the club's present strife. The Reds could not hope to run before they started to walk and only

tentative steps could be expected following a shocking start to the season. Avoiding defeat and resisting a very strong side was another key stage in the team's recovery.

United had a very defensive outlook, so the end result was perhaps as good as could have been anticipated. Arsenal were unbeaten and had chances but were well policed by the back four.

At the business end Best linked between midfield and the strike pairing of Ian Storey-Moore and Sammy McIlroy allowing him to join in and bolster the numbers in attack at the right time. He hit a post and Storey-Moore flashed one just wide. It was a hard working display and a credit to Best given his summer's sojourn. He received rousing applause during the game and at the close.

MANCHESTER UNITED 0 CHELSEA 0
DIVISION ONE 30 AUGUST 1972

BOBBY CHARLTON DIDN'T expect to receive another chance in the first team for some time but a good game for the reserves did his chances no harm. Nor did an injury picked up by John Fitzpatrick in the game before last.

Tony Young was drafted in for the visit of Arsenal but having played just 24 hours earlier the almost 35 year-old club captain could not be called upon - for the first time in his career Bobby had a place on the bench.

A chance to come on presented itself when patience with Ian Storey-Moore wore thin. His performance here was woeful and the price tag seemed to weigh heavily on him. In other areas of the pitch United looked more solid than of late.Fitzpatrick added a strength to midfield and in defence a vice-like grip on Chelsea's talented forward line earned United a third successive home draw. On the negative side, the forwards drew yet another blank. However it wasn't for the want of trying.

The ineffective Storey-Moore apart, United created the better chances with Best in particular, a tireless force. George seemed to have decided that the club's plight was more needy than his own and that his star could only rise as the team's fortunes did, unfortunately his efforts were to no avail.

A John Fitzpatrick header from a Willie Morgan cross which clipped the foot of the post was as close as anyone got. Alex Stepney did well denying Peter Houseman and Steve Kember in particular.

WEST HAM UNITED 2 MANCHESTER UNITED 2
DIVISION ONE 2 SEPTEMBER 1972

A BRUISED CALF for Fitzpatrick gave Bobby Charlton an opportunity to end his four-match absence from the starting line-up. He had looked sharp during his 15 minutes against Chelsea and helped The Reds to earn their first away point and first away goals of the campaign at Upton Park.

Hopes were high once a Best shot fizzed past a stunned Peter Grotier who didn't seem to pick the ball up until it was too late but after that atrocious defending allowed West Ham back in.

Best, trying to be everywhere at once, chased and ran gamely putting his all into lost causes. It buoyed up those around him and caused a significant attacking improvement but George needed to be upfront as most of his colleagues in that area seemed unable to round off his moves. 'Pop' Robson levelled just before half time but The Hammers would have gone in ahead had it not been for Alex Stepney.

The break allowed a rallying of the troops and Bobby Charlton began to look more like the influence of old and, as colleagues followed his lead, the burden lifted from Best and Storey-Moore.

The latter was visibly overjoyed at ending a poor run where he seemed so anxious to score that he often fell over the ball. Robson hit back to level again at 2-2 and though there was some disappointment at the outcome there were plenty of positives to take into the midweek League Cup tie with Oxford United.

OXFORD UNITED 2 MANCHESTER UNITED 2
LEAGUE CUP 2ND RD 6 SEPTEMBER 1972

HARD LESSONS HAD been gleaned by many top flight sides in the League Cup over recent seasons and Second Division Oxford United provided a potential banana skin for a club without a win in the league.

On three minutes Bobby Charlton served notice to Oxford, and those who would seek to inherit his place in the team, by letting fly with a long range shot which cannoned off the keeper's chest for Law to convert. However, within a minute the ball was at the other end. United's defence played the percentages leaving only a shot from distance, yet Ken Skeen lashed it in from the edge of the area.

Poise seemed to ebb away at both ends with only good stops by Alex Stepney resisting The U's. Buchan inexplicably missed from six yards out when he should have buried a chance and it looked like that error and others would be rued when Roy Clayton scored 12 minutes from time. Hard work had been put in but yielded little reward as the strikers were stranded by Oxford's cute play in midfield.

Best did what he could as hopeful glances were shot in his direction and the expectation seemed to weigh heavily at times. However, it was a high 30 yard drive from Charlton which kept United's hopes alive. The shot was hit with such ferocity that many thought it had hit the post and bounced out when it actually rebounded back into play off the stanchion at the back of the net.

MANCHESTER UNITED 0 COVENTRY CITY 1
DIVISION ONE 9 SEPTEMBER 1972

THREE CHANGES IN personnel barely reflected the number of tactical alterations made including Martin Buchan being asked to cover at left-back for Tony Dunne. Bobby Charlton and John Fitzpatrick were paired together in midfield with good results. Best carried the ball selflessly and for most of the game there only seemed one possible outcome.

The match was identified as a key one as Coventry were expected to be relegation candidates but points continued to elude The Reds as, despite their limited resources, the visitors took their sole chance.

Denis Law sent a header and a shot just wide. Another Charlton rocket was saved by Glazier but on 55 minutes Willie Carr benefited from some indecision to net. The midfielder had almost an unlimited amount of time to pick his spot.

From that point on Coventry withdrew and very few chances were made. When they did come too many United players snatched at them rather than calculatedly sticking the ball away.

MANCHESTER UNITED 3 OXFORD UNITED 1
LEAGUE CUP 2ND RD REPLAY 12 SEPTEMBER 1972

TOMMY O'NEIL AND Sammy McIlroy were unfortunate casualties of defeat over the weekend as Willie Morgan and Tony Young got a route back into the side. A crowd of just over 21,000, the lowest at Old Trafford since anyone could remember, saw a very one sided affair in which Ian Storey-Moore repaid his manager's faith and bounced back into form. He scored one and won a penalty after a devilish run which was only be ended by a lunge from

an Oxford defender. Best converted to make it 3-1.

Between those two moments a Geoff Bray equaliser just before the break and a Best goal when George picked up the leftovers from a Storey-Moore shot completed the scoring. A number of players had their finest match of the season and gave a timely morale boost to flagging fortunes with the club's first victory of the season.

WOLVES 2 MANCHESTER UNITED 0
DIVISION ONE 16 SEPTEMBER 1972

REGARDLESS OF MIDWEEK events, there was a clear need to improve the forward line. A number of players could be accused of growing stale, which left the manager little option if others lost form or picked up injury. Nothing would be sacred in the pursuit of more alternatives including breaking a 41-year transfer embargo with Manchester City who were persuaded to part with Wyn Davies for £65,000 48 hours before this game.

There was no time to prepare Davies

for a debut but changes were made. Willie Morgan made way for Young. Denis Law also stood down to allow Sammy McIlroy in. A little tinkering at the back took place and Brian Kidd was on the bench.

If Frank O'Farrell needed any vindication of his transfer activity it was highlighted here as despite chances created by Best, Charlton and Young, none of the strikers could apply a finishing touch.

Things looked better at the back but Derek Dougan exploited a rare chink of light between Sadler and James to put Wolves ahead. John Richards netted before the end despite standing some

yards offside during the build up, to leave sad United bottom of the league.

MANCHESTER UNITED 3 DERBY COUNTY 0
DIVISION ONE 23 SEPTEMBER 1972

ANOTHER DIP INTO the transfer market was set to take place but the strongest target identified was Bournemouth's Ted MacDougall. He had started out at Anfield but failed to make the grade so moved to Fourth Division York City and had stayed in the lower divisions ever since. He was a prodigious scorer at that having once netted nine in an FA Cup tie against Margate.

Yet despite earning admiring glances from many bigger clubs, none were brave (or desperate) enough to offer the correct amount of cash for a man unproved at the top level. A fee close to £200,000 was mooted but seemed steep considering the cost of debutant striker Wyn Davies who helped inspire The Reds to a first league

win of the season at the tenth attempt against the champions.

The new man provided an added dimension as a genuine target man. He caused problems for County and Ian Storey-Moore benefitted. Moore hit a good opener and lent a hand in a move which Willie Morgan rounded off. Davies ended his contribution with a well-taken goal.

There was still work to get through at the back as Derby threatened to get back into it but 20 year-old right back Ian Donald looked more than comfortable on his debut. United were still bottom after such a poor opening little more could be expected but at least a corner had been turned. Or so it seemed.

SHEFFIELD UNITED 1 MANCHESTER UNITED 0
DIVISION ONE 30 SEPTEMBER 1972

MACDOUGALL HAD BEEN bought for the fee requested by Bournemouth three days before the game but did not play. at Bramhall Lane. Nevertheless United's wretched run continued as The Blades claimed the points with a late penalty against Wyn Davies who seemed to do nothing more than jump against John Flynn at a corner. Both players were keen to get something on the ball but neither seemed to put in a challenge which could be said to have impeded the other. Certainly Flynn made no penalty claims.

Alan Woodward didn't complain and kept a cool head to convert from the spot. Maybe he felt there was some justice in events as he had been unceremoniously dumped to the ground 15 minutes earlier but failed to gain anything from it.

The Blades were value for the points but it seemed rough for United to go down in such circumstances. Best worked hard but could not re-discover his cutting edge.

BRISTOL ROVERS 1 MANCHESTER UNITED 1
League Cup 3ʳᵈ Rd 3 October 1972

MANY WONDERED WHETHER United already had their names on the League Cup after yet another rabbit was pulled out of the hat late on to save them from embarrassment.

This time Willie Morgan netted in the nick of time after cutting in from the right. The Third Division outfit had been living on their nerves at times but Brian Kidd missed a sitter from a Storey-Moore cross. Moore, along with Best, were the greatest dangers for United. This incident and others demonstrated The Reds' need for a spearhead up front.

A tap-in had earlier provided Rovers with a 64th minute lead after Stepney had made a save but could do no more than parry a short range fee-kick awarded for obstruction.

WEST BROMWICH ALBION 2 MANCHESTER UNITED 2
Division One 7 October 1972

BOBBY CHARLTON WAS the man omitted to accommodate Ted MacDougall who thought he had got his United career off to a flying start with an early goal until he was pulled up for an offence. Unfortunately the defence conspired to gift Ally Brown two goals and The Reds were chasing a game they appeared to be in control of due to these moments of madness.

A George Best penalty pulled one back although Tony Brown missed one for Albion which provided hope. Moore, who had risen to the challenge of retaining his place despite the new talent coming in, drew United level during the second half.

United were among a number of clubs now rumoured to be in for Arsenal's John Roberts and the performance from the United rearguard suggested the centre-half would be a welcome addition.

MANCHESTER UNITED 1 BRISTOL ROVERS 2
League Cup 3ʳᵈ Rd replay 11 October 1972

BOBBY JONES, A 35 year-old forward who had spent all but a year of his 16 season league career at Bristol Rovers, was brought in for his first game of the campaign and in a very brave decision considering the rank of the opposition and venue, manager Don Megson threw his all into attack.

The move paid off as John Rudge found the net after 30 minutes. Sammy McIlroy, a substitute for Brian Kidd, grabbed an equaliser with a very well directed shot and United could have gone ahead had Best not fluffed a penalty.

There were other opportunities but just four minutes remained when Bruce Bannister won the game to compound a miserable start to the season.

MANCHESTER UNITED 1 BIRMINGHAM CITY 0
DIVISION ONE 14 OCTOBER 1972

WITH UNITED ABLE to field their two new cup-tied acquisitions again, Bobby Charlton and Brian Kidd made way with Charlton winning the battle for a place on the bench. Birmingham had signed John Roberts after The Reds pulled out of the bidding and he made his debut for the Midland side against United with a chance to show Old Trafford what they would be missing.

It may have been a narrow win but it was no less deserved and the points saw United finally pull off the bottom. Victory came through Ted MacDougall's first United goal when he headed in a Tony Dunne cross. Wyn Davies pulled cover away with a dummy run to the near post meaning the scorer was under no pressure.

David Sadler, playing in place of the injured Steve James, showed there was little need for Roberts as the United defence recorded their first cleansheet for four games.

BULGARIA 3 NORTHERN IRELAND 0
WORLD CUP QUALIFIER 18 OCTOBER 1972

THE LEVSKI STADIUM in the Bulgarian capital of Sofia was not a venue George Best would want to revisit in a hurry after this tie. He took some severe punishment throughout the game until his second international dismissal five minutes from time. He had already been booked for dissent when the German referee awarded a penalty which allowed the home side to open the scoring on 18 minutes before Kolev extended the lead.

The incident which led to his dismissal resulted in a second penalty when George felt aggrieved at being brought down by Stoyanov in his own area while assisting his defence. The two lashed out at each other on the ground but when George got up he kicked Bonev who went down but picked himself up easily enough to score from the spot a second time.

Northern Ireland were already long shots to qualify for the World Cup finals but with George likely to miss most if not all of the remaining games as punishment, their chances had effectively disappeared.

NEWCASTLE UNITED 2 MANCHESTER UNITED 1
DIVISION ONE 21 OCTOBER 1972

AN UNCHANGED SIDE was put out but United stuttered again with MacDougall and Davies falling prey to the gloom which had marred the early part of the season. George Best looked to be running on empty until Charlton's introduction after which he made some good darting runs to trouble The Magpies and set up a late goal for the skipper. Unfortunately The Reds were already 2-0 down after John Tudor and Terry Hibbitt had beaten Stepney.

MANCHESTER UNITED 1 TOTTENHAM HOTSPUR 4
DIVISION ONE 28 OCTOBER 1972

A POOR SHOWING in defence allowed the impressive Martin Peters to hit a treble before half-time. Sadler and Martin Buchan made life extraordinarily easy for the England striker while a decidedly lightweight midfield offered little in the way of protection.

Only a 30 minute period during which United finally imposed themselves saw Charlton and Best, who had looked helpless without adequate support, gain some reward as Charlton notched a consolation.

LEICESTER CITY 2 MANCHESTER UNITED 2
DIVISION ONE 4 NOVEMBER 1972

THE WORDS MANCHESTER UNITED and relegation had rarely been uttered in the same sentence since the war but a trip to Filbert Street to face fellow strugglers Leicester City was billed as a six-pointer. The match finished 2-2 though The Reds could so easily have won as two howlers by Alex Stepney, who complained about the floodlights after dropping two crosses, gifted the home side a couple of goals. Once they pegged it back Leicester could have made further capital out of the

keeper's discomfort but United tightened up and high balls were cut out at source.

United had knocked the ball around with an accuracy and pace which deserved more. The midfield had been slightly reshaped with Ian Storey-Moore at the apex doing a lot of work with Best who opened the scoring. George then made a smart pass to Morgan who crossed for Davies to head in. MacDougall hit the woodwork with another headed chance.

MANCHESTER UNITED 2 LIVERPOOL 0
DIVISION ONE 11 NOVEMBER 1972

AN ODD ASPECT of United's dire campaign was that they could put the skids under far better teams than themselves and that included this top against bottom clash at Old Trafford. Having accounted for champions Derby they now succeeded against their high flying rivals from down the East Lancs.

Good performances across the park and a little bit of luck gave The Reds renewed hope that they could avoid the drop. The luck came in the shape of Peter Cormack

missing a very presentable chance and a seemingly clear cut penalty for Stepney's clattering of Steve Heighway being waved away by the referee.

Liverpool had been in demanding midweek action with a trip to Athens in the UEFA Cup but this was still a strong side. United kept the visitors first choice backline busy with intelligent runs by players who buzzed around to provide options to the man in possession, a contrast to most of the season.

Ted MacDougall gained revenge against the club that had disguarded him as a trainee by scoring and creating another for Wyn Davies.

Bobby Charlton was magnificent not only in midfield but as an emergency left back for the final 21 minutes after Tony Dunne was forced off. Kevin Keegan, who had not only been scoring but creating goals, was kept quiet by Martin Buchan who looked untroubled throughout.

MANCHESTER CITY 3 MANCHESTER UNITED 0
DIVISION ONE 18 NOVEMBER 1972

THE BLUES CLAIMED this derby win by some distance thanks not only to their goalscorers but a defence determined to remain intact. Even when stretched, City seemed to have more desire than The Reds who shrank from the challenge. A physical approach intimidated many including George Best who was so ineffective that he could have walked from the pitch and his absence would not have been noticed. With United lacking any spark or will to win, depressed supporters could have been forgiven for thinking that they were watching relegation certainties.

Alex Stepney continued to experience handling problems and dropped the ball for Colin Bell to profit. Although United shut him out until late on he grabbed another and was only denied a hat-trick despite when a deflected shot past Stepney was given as an own goal.

MANCHESTER UNITED 2 SOUTHAMPTON 1
DIVISION ONE 25 NOVEMBER 1972

PAUL EDWARDS, WHO had been loaned to Oldham Athletic for two months earlier in the season, was on the verge of making his transfer permanent but was drafted into the United side to face Southampton as a replacement for David Sadler. He had shown good form at various levels for a few months and jumped over Steve James in the pecking order.

Ted MacDougall was a player in form claiming the first and creating the second for Davies. Each and every player did exactly what had been asked of them with fine performances in all departments. That is with one exception.

A visibly troubled George Best appeared in what proved to be his last first team game for almost a full year as United sought to save themselves from the drop without him.

1972-73

George turned heads wherever he went and a posse of journalists were detailed to follow his every move. The chance to snap him with either a drink in his hand or a girl on his arm was too great for the nation's tabloids. So when George decided to take in the atmosphere of a well-known London night spot there was little chance that it would escape anyone's attention at Old Trafford. Within days Best's antics off the pitch and his disinterested attitude on it led to the Irishman being put on the transfer list.

While it may be said that Best had brought what amounted to his sacking by the club on himself, it should also be noted that a combination of United's lack of form, poor team spirit and abysmal league position helped push him towards drowning his sorrows.

Since the start of the decade Best had carried a team of ageing legs and successive managers had ignored potential quality additions to the squad that may have made United competitive again. Charlton and Law were clearly not up to it any longer, but where were their replacements?

Having challenged for trophies from the moment he made his debut, United were now struggling to compete with the also-rans. Despite, or more likely because of, the weighty gaze of Matt Busby, United now faced the real prospect of relegation and Best, still one of the most talented players in the world, rightly wondered about the point of it all.

George couldn't adjust to mediocrity for either himself or the club he loved. Many lonely nights were spent in his state of the art home in Bramhall but none of these featured in the press who were more concerned with the attention he received in the company of females.

The problems encountered with Frank O'Farrell and the difficulty not only United but George Best had in filling the legacy left by Matt Busby could not be underestimated. Busby's careful handling of the player who he would publicly admonish for his indiscretions but behind the scenes treat with kid gloves may not have been fair to all but it had worked to the club's benefit. Now the same rules were fracturing team spirit and the only solution seemed to be to ostracising the Ulsterman for the good of the club.

George's special status particularly irked O'Farrell who was said to be ready to hand in his resignation because of it. In the end O'Farrell's placement of Best on the transfer list at a price of £350,000 led to offers from clubs as diverse as Chelsea, Bournemouth and New York Cosmos while Manchester City at one stage threatened to pull off the unthinkable and clad George in sky blue!

Just 10 days after the nightclub incident, club chairman Louis Edwards announced that Best would resume training with the club. Everyone took this as an indication that he was off the transfer list including O'Farrell who assumed he would not be able to cash in on the asset despite several promising enquiries. There were plenty of other suitors but the fee was a large one for a player who had proved so volatile. One fascinating prospect would have been Best signing for Brian Clough's Derby County who announced to the media that he was giving the idea serious thought.

However, O'Farrell was concerned this was an appeasement too far. Of course he had to keep picking Best, at least until the point he was listed, as United didn't have the luxury of players with similar quality to rely on. There was also a need to maintain any attacking flair.

On December 16th United slumped to a 5-0 defeat at Crystal Palace a team in deeper trouble at the beginning of the day but who leapfrogged over them. Within ten miutes of the final whistle O'Farrell was sacked along with assistant Malcolm Musgrove and Chief Scout John Aston Senior.

On the day the manager parted company with the club it was reiterated that the transfer listing remained in place. But a letter already lay unopened on the club secretary's desk from Best announcing his decision to retire and stating that his mind could not be changed.

Tommy Docherty was swiftly appointed manager. The Scot had enjoyed a distinguished playing career with Preston, Arsenal and Chelsea earning himself a great reputation as a manager after hanging up his boots. While in charge of Chelsea he got the side into the top flight, a cup final and guided them to League Cup success in 1965 but following his resignation in the autumn of 1967 he had taken a number of low profile jobs including a 29-day stint at Queens Park Rangers and a four month sojourn at FC Porto. He was later appointed assistant to Terry Neill at Hull City who also served as Northern Ireland boss in a part-time capacity. Docherty also got a chance at international level as caretaker manager of Scotland. Within two months he was offered the post permanently and accepted.

There was, it seemed, no greater honour for a man who had defied Preston's wishes and joined Scotland for the 1958 World Cup campaign and left Deepdale as a result. However, that was until he was offered the

United job - a challenge he just could not resist. His entire reign with The Tartan Army, including his temporary control, lasted just 10 games.

His relationship with Best would prove to be tempestuous but for now United settled into their relegation battle with gusto, signing Lou Macari, George Graham, Alex Forsyth and Jim Holton to give the United dressing room a steely Scottish flavour. The Reds eventually avoided the drop, losing only five league games under the new manager until the end of the season, finishing a comfortable seven points above the relegation places.

The end of the season proved emotional in more ways than one as Bobby Charlton finally called time on his career. Early in the 1972-73 season he had been dropped for the first time since he became a regular member of Matt Busby's great squad in the late 1950s and, realising that it was better to leave on his own terms, announced his decision to retire once the campaign closed and left to become manager of Preston. He had amassed 752 appearances by this stage and scored 247 goals.

His last match at Old Trafford against Sheffield United saw more than 57,000 fans bid a fond farewell. 3,000 more had attended his testimonial against Glasgow Celtic earlier in the season. George Best, who it was said had fallen out with the World Cup winner many years earlier, did not play in the benefit game but if that was the case he very publicly modified his opinion when invited to rejoin the side by Docherty, to begin a volatile relationship with the new United manager.

DATE	OPPONENT	VENUE	SCORE	ATT'D	1	2	3	4	5	6	7	8	9	10	11
12 August	Ipswich Town	Old Trafford	1-2	51,459	Stepney	O'Neill	Dunne	Morgan	James	Buchan	Best	Kidd	Charlton	Law[1]	S-Moore
15 August	Liverpool	Anfield	0-2	54,799	Stepney	O'Neill	Dunne	Young	James	Buchan	Morgan	Kidd	Charlton	Best	S-Moore
19 August	Everton	Goodison Park	0-2	52,948	Stepney	O'Neill	Dunne	Buchan	James	Sadler	Morgan	Fitzpatrick	Kidd	Best	S-Moore
23 August	Leicester City	Old Trafford	1-1	40,067	Stepney	O'Neill	Dunne	Buchan	James	Sadler	Morgan	Fitzpatrick	McIlroy	Best[1]	S-Moore
26 August	Arsenal	Old Trafford	0-0	48,108	Stepney	O'Neill	Dunne	Buchan	James	Sadler	Morgan	Young	McIlroy	Best	S-Moore
30 August	Chelsea	Old Trafford	0-0	44,482	Stepney	O'Neill	Dunne	Buchan	James	Sadler	Morgan	Fitzpatrick	Law	Best	S-Moore
2 September	West Ham United	Upton Park	2-2	31,939	Stepney	O'Neill	Dunne	Buchan	James	Sadler	Morgan	Law	Charlton	Best[1]	S-Moore[1]
9 September	Coventry City	Old Trafford	0-1	37,073	Stepney	O'Neill	Buchan	Fitzpatrick	James	Sadler	McIlroy	Law	Charlton	Best	S-Moore
16 September	Wolves	Molineux	0-2	34,049	Stepney	Buchan	Dunne	Fitzpatrick	James	Sadler	Young	McIlroy	Charlton	Best	S-Moore
23 September	Derby County	Old Trafford	3-0	48,255	Stepney	Donald	Dunne	Young	James	Buchan	Morgan[1]	Davies[1]	Charlton	Best	S-Moore[1]
30 September	Sheffield United	Bramall Lane	0-1	37,347	Stepney	Donald	Dunne	Young	James	Buchan	Morgan	Davies	Charlton	Best	S-Moore
7 October	WBA	The Hawthorns	2-2	32,909	Stepney	Donald	Dunne	Young	James	Buchan	Morgan	MacDougall	Davies	Best[1]	S-Moore[1]
14 October	Birmingham City	Old Trafford	1-0	52,104	Stepney	Watson	Dunne	Young	Sadler	Buchan	Morgan	MacDougall	Davies	Best	S-Moore
21 October	Newcastle United	St James' Park	1-2	38,170	Stepney	Watson	Dunne	Young	Sadler	Buchan	Morgan	MacDougall	Davies	Best	S-Moore
28 October	Tottenham H	Old Trafford	1-4	52,497	Stepney	Watson	Dunne	Law	Sadler	Buchan	Morgan	MacDougall	Davies	Best	Charlton[1]
4 November	Leicester City	Filbert Street	2-2	32,575	Stepney	Donald	Dunne	Morgan	Sadler	Buchan	Best[1]	MacDougall	Davies[1]	Charlton	S-Moore
11 November	Liverpool	Old Trafford	2-0	53,944	Stepney	O'Neill	Dunne	Morgan	Sadler	Buchan	Best	MacDougall[1]	Charlton	Davies[1]	S-Moore
18 November	Manchester City	Maine Road	0-3	52,050	Stepney	O'Neill	Dunne	Morgan	Sadler	Buchan	Best	MacDougall	Charlton	Davies	S-Moore
25 November	Southampton	Old Trafford	2-1	36,073	Stepney	O'Neill	Dunne	Morgan	Edwards	Buchan	Best	MacDougall[1]	Charlton	Davies[1]	S-Moore

League Cup

DATE	OPPONENT	VENUE	SCORE	ATT'D	1	2	3	4	5	6	7	8	9	10	11
6 September	Oxford United	Manor Ground	2-2	16,560	Stepney	O'Neill	Dunne	Buchan	James	Sadler	Morgan	Law[1]	Charlton[1]	Best	S-Moore
12 September	Oxford United	Old Trafford	3-1	21,486	Stepney	Fitzpatrick	Buchan	Young	James	Sadler	Morgan	Law	Charlton	Best[2]	S-Moore[1]
3 October	Bristol Rovers	Eastville	1-1	33,957	Stepney	Donald	Dunne	Young	James	Buchan	Morgan[1]	Kidd	Charlton	Best	S-Moore
11 October	Bristol Rovers	Old Trafford	1-2	29,349	Stepney	Watson	Dunne	Young	James	Buchan	Morgan	Kidd	Charlton	Best	S-Moore

1973-74
OBLIVION

Little more than a month after resuming training, George Best was back in the first team. He had played in testimonials for Eusebio in Lisbon and Denis Law against Ajax at Old Trafford. He had also turned out for the reserves in a Central League game with Aston Villa but it was a friendly in Dublin against Shamrock Rovers the previous Monday that convinced Tommy Docherty that George was ready to return.

There was no escaping the fact that he was not only rusty but out of peak condition. Even accounting for a lot of hard work on his fitness the Best touch was most definitely back. Such was the fervour about his return that Dalymount Park could have sold out many times over. A number of those that did gain admission mounted a good natured pitch invasion 10 minutes from time which forced an abandonment. George played from the start to that impromptu end.

Having guided the club to safety at the end of the previous season, Docherty's United were still struggling and a record of three wins in eleven games left them hovering above the drop zone.

MANCHESTER UNITED 1 BIRMINGHAM CITY 0
DIVISION ONE 20 OCTOBER 1973

KNOWING A PUBLIC statement about Best's participation against Birmingham would boost flagging attendances at Old Trafford and create an intimidating atmosphere for the opposition, Docherty wasted no time in declaring the player a certain starter.

But that was only half of his plan. To reduce the odds of what had to be considered a gamble and perhaps desperate to turn United's fortunes around The Doc discarded the cautious approach that had seen United stave off relegation and switched his emphasis to attack.

As a result Lou Macari was recalled despite a dispute with the manager which had resulted in him being transfer-listed. Trevor Anderson and Alex Forsyth were left out as a result of this tactical switch.

There were other unfamiliar names on the teamsheet for George's return. Among others who had never represented the same United side as Best were Brian Greenhoff, Jim Holton and former Arsenal forward George Graham who had joined for £120,000 the previous December. Despite offloading him to the Gunners during his time with Chelsea (after he broke a club curfew with a number of other players) Docherty made 'Stroller' his first signing five days after taking over at Old Trafford.

Best didn't believe he would taste the atmosphere of a top flight game at Old Trafford again at stages of his exile. Even though he yearned to return, he felt too much water had passed under the bridge and that a strict manager like Docherty would prefer to leave him out in the cold. It was therefore a pleasant surprise to be invited back. Prior to the game Best predicted he would score two goals though he did revise that bold forecast as his big day got nearer.

Alex Stepney proved the match winner though, and not for his saves. The keeper had recently taken over penalty responsibilities and his well hit spot-kick proved to be the only goal of the game.

Kidd and Morgan, pushing up with the recalled pair to form a four-pronged attack, giving the side a shape reminiscent of the one Matt Busby once used to build a team around George. Best was the key figure in this formation although he wasn't looking to beat defenders with searing pace any more instead relying on his quick feet and speed of thought, neither of which had lost anything. Defenders got sucked in and then had to watch as the ball was flicked to a colleague who had run into the space created.

Morgan and Kidd linked up with an anticipation which should only have been established over the years, it was as if George had never been away. Macari also seemed to enjoy playing a senior team game with Best for the first time. Before the end a well-deserved round of applause from everyone in the ground, including Birmingham fans, was heard as George made way for Mick Martin.

George could create a crowd if he washed his car but this wasn't just a shrewd attempt to increase gate receipts or create a buzz amongst the fans - Best had something to offer and hopefully he would help banish thoughts of relegation before the situation at the bottom got critical.

BURNLEY 0 MANCHESTER UNITED 0
DIVISION ONE 27 OCTOBER 1973

WITH JIM HOLTON suspended for a couple of games, a new face shared the pitch with George Best for the first time as 19 year-old Clive Griffiths was called into the squad replacing David Sadler who was on the bench. Willie Morgan played despite the death of his mother having attended her funeral back in Scotland the previous day.

Against high-flying Burnley every resource The Reds had was needed and The Clarets were made to look ordinary by United who remained energised by Best's return. George continued to prove he wasn't just playing on reputation but genuinely competing. A playmaker role seemed suited to Best's clever use of the ball allied to the willing running of others.

Despite changes at the back, United were strong enough to resist Leighton James who was enjoying one of his most productive ever seasons in front of goal.

Griffiths came through every test alongside Steve James. Sadler was later introduced, replacing Brian Kidd who had started to move gingerly.

MANCHESTER UNITED 2 CHELSEA 2
DIVISION ONE 3 NOVEMBER 1973

DAVID SADLER WOULD grace any team and had served United for a decade but his time at the club came to an end when he joined Bobby Charlton and a host of other familiar faces at Preston North End. The fee had been cut from the £60,000, which reflected his true market value, to £25,000 which accommodated both parties. There were no changes to the team on duty at Chelsea, which was a rarity in recent months and a mark of some consistency being achieved.

George renewed battle with old adversary Ron Harris but their paths only crossed infrequently. Even Ron couldn't just kick a player merely for holding the ball. He was more interested in those scuttling around the danger zone. As United continued to focus on attack he had plenty to do as Chelsea's rearguard faced a barrage of shots all of which failed to find the net. Sometimes plain inaccuracy was to blame. The recognised forwards had not scored since mid-

September and on this evidence it looked like the goal drought might continue.

Of the efforts which were not wasted but failed to earn a goal was a George Best drive which cannoned off the crossbar but didn't cross the line.

Chelsea took the lead after three minutes when Peter Houseman was given too much room and squared the ball for Tommy Baldwin to convert. The winger then crossed for Peter Osgood to head in powerfully.

At 2-0 down a few weeks ago United would have caved in and accepted their fate but now they persisted with their attacking strategy and deservedly notched late goals through Tony Young and Brian Greenhoff who combined to create each other's efforts within a minute.

Young's from the edge of the area was the most eye catching but Greenhoff's the most celebrated as it earned The Reds a vital point.

TOTTENHAM HOTSPUR 2 MANCHESTER UNITED 1
DIVISION ONE 10 NOVEMBER 1973

NEWSPAPERS WERE PRE-OCCUPIED by another Best no show on Saturday morning, though this time it was an appearance on BBC Television's Nationwide where he was due to be interviewed by Jimmy Hill.

Tommy Docherty later claimed that he had refused permission for the interview as it fell within 24 hours of a game. George rang to explain but that wasn't how things

were presented.

A narrow 2-1 defeat, rather than the type of pummelling that United had suffered on other recent away trips, was scant reward for their efforts which were undermined when Holton allowed Martin Peters to nip in for the opener on ten minutes without a challenge.

Best scored the first goal of his comeback, though it took a huge deflection off Brian Kidd to flick the ball on before it hit Knowles on the line as he tried to clear. The full back atoned by hitting in a free-kick before the break.

Despite being far better in all areas throughout the second half, United could not find a way back. Best provided many intelligent passes and regularly switched play to confuse Spurs. The home side often looked in trouble but managed to hold out.

PORTUGAL 1 NORTHERN IRELAND 1
WORLD CUP QUALIFIER 14 NOVEMBER 1973

BEST HAD PLAYED for United 24 hours before Northern Ireland were due to take on Portugal in the final game in Qualifying Group 6. He may have been tired but having missed four games after his dismissal in Bulgaria George had no intention of rejecting a call-up. During his absence Ireland had done moderately well with one win, two draws and a defeat.

The results were credible but ensured there was no prospect of reaching the finals in West Germany. Unless a huge win was registered Irish would stay in third place. Portugal would not be playing in the finals either which explained a paltry crowd in Lisbon. Liam O'Kane's goal ensured both teams ended their qualification campaigns with a draw.

NEWCASTLE UNITED 3 MANCHESTER UNITED 2
DIVISION ONE 17 NOVEMBER 1973

ON THE LAST occasion United had won at St James Park in October 1971, Best had scored the only goal of the game. The Reds showed a desire equal to that of the previous week here although unfortunately they suffered the same result despite Lou Macari and George Graham getting United into the lead by the break.

Further poor defending allowed George Hope and Tommy Cassidy to nick the game on the resumption.

MANCHESTER UNITED 0 NORWICH CITY 0
DIVISION ONE 24 NOVEMBER 1973

DEFEAT WOULD PUT The Reds back in the bottom three and see the day's opponents Norwich leap out. Docherty felt his team was up to the job so didn't make alterations but enjoyed almost as little luck as in the last few weeks. Kidd put a header on to the woodwork but he and Macari could and should have gobbled up far easier chances.

Best made space for Steve James to let fly with a rasping effort that Kevin Keelan was happy to tip out for a corner. He also had one cleared from under the bar as he sought to not only provide impetus in moves but round at least one opportunity off given the profligacy of his colleagues.

MANCHESTER UNITED 0   SOUTHAMPTON 0
DIVISION ONE 8 DECEMBER 1973

JIM HOLTON FAILED to recover from injury and Lou Macari was also out with Clive Griffiths and Alex Forsyth stepping in but Martin Buchan was unhappy at being moved to left back. Docherty showed that he was prepared to exert not only discipline but change a team he didn't feel was functioning correctly even if that meant dropping his skipper George Graham.

Willie Morgan took over as captain but failed to lead by example missing a good chance after two minutes. Trevor Anderson, on for Brian Kidd, delivered an equally poor finish.

George was still not looking to get on the scoresheet at this stage in his rehabilitation and was more than happy to plug away in a reserved role and assist The Reds to become a better side in the second half. Even when far from fit and reduced to a comparative walking pace he was still the most dangerous man on the park but needed some help.

MANCHESTER UNITED 2 COVENTRY CITY 3
DIVISION ONE 15 DECEMBER 1973

IN THE RUN up to the game Best publicly admitted he missed the guiding hand and influence of Bobby Charlton who was now playing for and managing Preston North End but played for Stoke in a testimonial for Gordon Banks against United.

The Reds' only consistency was a failure to find a winning formula. From week to week no one quite knew how they would play. Very few could claim they were regulars. In this ever-changing line-up, it wasn't a surprise that United struggled for form.

Yet, there was a positive effect up front as United attacked with more menace. Best and Morgan profited but a 3-2 defeat put down to defensive lapses meant the team now hovered dangerously above the relegation places by a single point.

Buchan put through his own goal and Steve James struggled with cracked ribs so was helpless to stop David Cross heading the winner.

LIVERPOOL 2 MANCHESTER UNITED 0
Division One 22 December 1973

THE SELECTION MERRY-GO-ROUND continued as George Graham was restored and Alex Forsyth dropped. Tony Young dropped from midfield to left back in order to accommodate this change. During the week George had opened his Slack Alice nightclub which may have been more of an indication of his future - although many believed it was where his problems lay. He was pushed into a central striking role for the visit to Anfield but failed to prosper as the system was not suited to his game and, in truth, he didn't try to adapt so was easily handled by Liverpool's back four.

A Kevin Keegan penalty before half time underlined Liverpool's superiority and Steve Heighway hit the second to put United in the drop zone. Tommy Docherty remained upbeat but realised the size of the task at hand.

MANCHESTER UNITED 1 SHEFFIELD UNITED 2
Division One 26 December 1973

THERE WAS NO improvement in results but this was a match United didn't deserve to lose. They had looked dangerous and likely to stick a goal in from the whistle but never more so than the last 20 minutes when play was camped in the Sheffield half.

The score was balanced at 1-1 and maybe a point should have been protected but with two for the taking no one could blame United for committing themselves before their own crowd. However, that proved to be their downfall as The Blades made a quick break during injury time and Alan Woodward scored.

Best and Morgan were good value up front. Lou Macari hit a 7th minute header but former United stopper John Connaughton had an inspired match. Tony Currie scored midway through the first half before the calamitous ending left United in the bottom three.

MANCHESTER UNITED 2 IPSWICH TOWN 0
DIVISION ONE 29 DECEMBER 1973

THERE WERE NO changes from the team which finished the game against Sheffield United as the XI were deemed worthy of another chance and recorded a first win in 10 games. If nothing else it gave hope of salvation and ensured the Old Trafford faithful could look forward to the approaching New Year with some hope.

Victory was only achieved in the final minutes through McIlroy and Macari.

Ipswich deserved a point for their obduracy alone, but as United could testify worth didn't always match reality.

Best was capable of good and bad within the same minute as an awe-inspiring piece of skill would be followed by a wasted final ball in what proved to be his last competitive game at Old Trafford.

QUEENS PARK RANGERS 3 MANCHESTER UNITED 0
DIVISION ONE 1 JANUARY 1974

UNITED WERE TOTALLY outclassed with too few players keen to pitch in. Without this United were only destined for one place - Division Two. It was only a number of great saves from Alex Stepney which kept United in with a shout. George was disappointing but far from the only offender.

Once former United striker Don Givens opened the scoring in the 19th minute, after bursting into the area and selling a dummy to Jim Holton, there was only going to be one conclusion to this

game and two Stan Bowles goals rounded matters off.

Few in the 32,339 crowd would have realised that this was Best's last game for the club as Tommy Docherty finally lost patience with his wayward star and dropped the Irishman before the cup-tie with Plymouth Argyle a week later.

In truth Best was a shadow of his former self and the brief optimism of his return against Birmingham in October had disappeared as United headed toward a probable relegation dogfight.

1973-74

For the first time since the war, Manchester United ended the season in the Second Division. Yet it was the manner of relegation, as much as the fact of it, that hurt all the more. That it was Manchester City and Denis Law, King of the Stretford End, who had been sold by Docherty at the start of the season and found a new lease of life at Maine Road, who scuppered Docherty's Reds was the cruellest cut of all.

Law's tearful realisation that he had sealed the fate of the club where he was still worshipped brought a swift substitution from the City management seconds before the Stretford End, sensing that this final embarassment was too much to take, invaded the pitch in an attempt to get the match abandoned. Needless to say the result stood and United had hit rock bottom. The fact that they would have been relegated regardless of the result is, of course, conveniently forgotten whenever the match is recalled.

Tommy Docherty's vain attempt to keep United up had failed. Law's departure, following a falling out with The Doc at the end of the previous season, might have seemed significant but the Scot was a fading force. His replacement, Lou Macari, scored just one league goal and new recruits McCalliog and Daly fared little better as United struggled to come to terms with a team shorn of superstars. As if to underline these failings, keeper Alex Stepney became joint top scorer during October and once Ian Storey-Moore was forced to retire through injury at Christmas, the writing was on the wall.

In truth Docherty's task was larger than initially imagined - perhaps only an outsider could properly gauge the depths United would have to plunge before returning to former glory. The casualty list included most of the 1968 European Cup winners. Even the younger, lesser lights of that side, Messrs Sadler, Aston and Kidd, had failed to take their chance at Old Trafford while the likes of Charlton, Crerand, Foulkes and Law had lingered at the club, some growing old in the first team, other retiring to influential coaching positions which, in hindsight, did United few favours and only prevented the team's evolution.

After the McGuinness and O'Farrell experiments, the influence of Matt Busby and Louis Edwards waned as board members recognised the full-scale of the crisis at the club. In early 1974 Docherty's broom finally swept the last of those cobwebs away as George Best made his final failed comeback in the first team. In the long-run the new manager was proved correct in his assessment of the extent of the re-building work required. If anything relegation allowed Docherty scope to re-build and, after strolling to the Second Division title, they returned to the top flight with a fast, free-flowing side good enough to take United to successive cup finals and back into Europe.

Docherty's role in the final stages of George Best's career remains a point of conjecture today. At 28 the Irishman should have been at his peak but years of partying had taken its toll and the old Best was now a distant memory, having had his last sustained run of form during the autumn of 1971. Still, Docherty was desperate enough to give George one last chance.

When Best returned to the fray in October he looked like a man capable of reviving past glories. The booze and high life had taken their toll on his waistline but he still had the skills to boost a poor United side and helped them achieve a first win in five matches against Birmingham City. Yet where the old George might have won games single-handedly, he was now capable only of occasional flashes of his old self. Once First Division defences figured this out, his influence waned.

When United took to the field against Plymouth Argyle in the 3rd round of the FA Cup without Best, the winger turned playboy knew his Old Trafford career was over. The events leading to his dismissal remain shrouded in mystery. All parties agree that George had played in the January 1st defeat at Queens Park Rangers but went on a bender and missed training. There had been an agreement that time could be made up later in the day but this time either Docherty's patience was at an end or George had overstepped the line once too often. Docherty claimed that Best turned up at Old Trafford late and in an 'advanced state of refreshment' accompanied by some girlfriends. Best denied he had been drinking, was alone and always turned up at the same time every home game. What is clear is that Docherty had made his mind up and decided to ditch his star player - the rest is conjecture.

The love affair between United and the Belfast Boy who had graced Old Trafford was over. Best knew it and hours after the game he sat alone in the same stands in which he had been idolised, tears streaming down his face as he took in the scene of so many triumphs one last time.

Back in 1963 he had watched the club lift the FA Cup at Wembley. He was just three days away from his seventeenth birthday and hours away from joining the professional ranks. It was the club's first success since Munich but it was a huge regret for the player that he never appeared at the showpiece occasion of English football.

Instead Best's sole Wembley appearance for United came five years later against Benfica. He had been the principle reason behind United's successful quest for the European Cup. Along the way the Irishman had lit up Europe with vintage performances yet, now he must have reflected on his own part in the club's decline. They had failed to compete in any season since that triumph and now languished at the foot of the First Division.

It has been claimed that by the end of his career Best owed United nothing (after all he made 470 appearances for the club scoring 179 goals, an amazing goals-to-games ratio for a winger). Yet by the same token by 1974 it was clear that United owed the Irishman nothing either, having given him more slack than a bungee-jumper. Best flouted club rules so often that the manager, whoever he was, rarely had control of the dressing room and team spirit became non-existent.

For fans the Best saga had become tiresome. The club were in decline, George was becoming an embarrasment while the likes of Derby(!), Leeds, Liverpool and Arsenal were picking up trophies and turning The Reds over on a regular basis. As if to underline the fans' disappointments United hadn't won a league derby since Busby's last game in 1971. To them Docherty's exciting brand of management pointed the way forward. Meanwhile Best's battle with the bottle was a sad reflection of the post-Busby era.

Best missed large swathes of his last two seasons struggling with his life. As a result United struggled, which most probably added to his woes, and the vicious circle was fixed. Jettisoning one of the finest talents British football had ever seen was the only way forward as United would eventually recover and Best would begin to his enjoy his football away from the pressures of the First Division.

Nobody could quite put their finger on where it had all gone wrong for Best and United. It seemed that Best's thoughts in the aftermath of the European Cup final were correct. Both had reached a peak in May 1968 but from then on a steady decline had sealed United's fate.

Yet the question remains did United fail George by not signing high quality additions or installing the right type of manager?

Or would Best have descended into an alcoholic haze in any case as the pressures associated with being football's first superstar took hold?

DATE	OPPONENT	VENUE	SCORE	ATT'D	1	2	3	4	5	6	7	8	9	10	11
20 October	Birmingham City	Old Trafford	1-0	48937	Stepney[1]	Buchan	Young	Greenhoff	Holton	James	Morgan	Kidd	Macari	Graham	Best
27 October	Burnley	Turf Moor	0-0	31,976	Stepney	Buchan	Young	Greenhoff	James	Griffiths	Morgan	Kidd	Macari	Graham	Best
3 November	Chelsea	Old Trafford	2-2	48,036	Stepney	Buchan	Young[1]	Greenhoff[1]	James	Griffiths	Morgan	Macari	Kidd	Graham	Best
10 November	Tottenham H	White Hart Lane	1-2	42,756	Stepney	Buchan	Young	Greenhoff	Holton	James	Morgan	Macari	Kidd	Graham	Best[1]
17 November	Newcastle United	St James' Park	2-3	41,768	Stepney	Buchan	Young	Greenhoff	Holton	James	Morgan	Macari[1]	Kidd	Graham[1]	Best
24 November	Norwich City	Old Trafford	0-0	36,338	Stepney	Buchan	Young	Greenhoff	Holton	James	Morgan	Macari	Kidd	Graham	Best
8 December	Southampton	Old Trafford	0-0	31,648	Stepney	Buchan	Forsyth	Greenhoff	James	Griffiths	Morgan	Young	Kidd	McIlroy	Best
15 December	Coventry City	Old Trafford	2-3	28,589	Stepney	Buchan	Forsyth	Greenhoff	James	Griffiths	Morgan[1]	Macari	McIlroy	Young	Best[1]
22 December	Liverpool	Anfield	0-2	40,420	Stepney	Buchan	Young	Greenhoff	Sidebottom	Griffiths	Morgan	Young	Kidd	Graham	Best
26 December	Sheffield United	Old Trafford	1-2	38,653	Stepney	Young	Griffiths	Greenhoff	Holton	Buchan	Morgan	Macari[1]	McIlroy	Graham	Best
29 December	Ipswich Town	Old Trafford	2-0	36,365	Stepney	Young	Griffiths	Greenhoff	Holton	Buchan	Morgan	Macari[1]	McIlroy[1]	Graham	Best
1 January	QPR	Loftus Road	0-3	32,339	Stepney	Young	Houston	Greenhoff	Holton	Buchan	Morgan	Macari	McIlroy	Graham	Best

FROM 1974 ONWARDS
THE CIRCUS ACT

Shortly after taking charge of Dunstable Town in the summer of 1974, former United apprentice Barry Fry asked George Best to turn out in the club's pre-season fixtures. The two had played together at junior level but their career paths diverged. At 28 Fry had drifted out of the Football League despite joining the Old Trafford ground staff and making an appearance for England schoolboys.

He had been made player/manager of the Southern League outfit who had finished bottom of the table in each of the last eight seasons. Just 37 people had turned up to his first game in charge towards the end of the previous season but after a meeting at George's Slack Alice nightclub, a deal to play in a handful of friendlies plus one or two competitive games was brokered. One of those matches included a Manchester United XI. A record 10,000 fans attended the game and mobbed Best after a 3-2 win. A few weeks earlier the cash strapped club had received a new set of nets paid for by George at a cost of £25. Jeff Astle was another big name signing.

Prior to this stint in Bedfordshire, Best had played five games in South Africa for the Jewish Guild of Johannesburg. It was never intended to be a long term arrangement but heavy drinking, gambling and too much womanising curtailed the deal before it was due to end.

Though George turned out once for Deportivo La Coruna it was November 1975 before his name reappeared on football's radar. He had been prevented from playing in the UK as United still held his registration. However, following his release, he was allowed to join Stockport County on a short but lucrative contract. The Edgeley Park club offered a one month deal and while it may have been Fourth Division football, George was happy for the chance to return to the English game. Chelsea were said to be keeping an eye on his progress but the prospect of bringing him to London with all the temptations it could offer was a risk that the powers that be at Stamford Bridge shied from.

Meanwhile the NASL was growing in America and contracts were offered to players who, while past their peak, would attract more fans to an emerging league. The competition had started in the 1960s but failed to get off the ground until big name European and South American talent arrived. Many had seen better days and were older than George but the opportunity proved a new lease of life for Best.

New York Cosmos were the most ambitious and successful club in the NASL and offered a very generous deal. The only drawback as far as the player was concerned was the suggested length. George was only interested in something which tied him up for no more than a single season and rejected Cosmos' advances. This allowed Los Angeles Aztecs to swoop and offer George acceptable terms.

While he had been waiting for the American season to start, a stint at Irish League side Cork Celtic was curtailed due to a lack enthusiasm. It has to be said that George had added almost two stones since his last game for United and was clearly in need of a prolonged period of training.

Aztec's owner John Chaffetz knew he had signed a player of some quality but was slightly concerned by the temperament displayed at various times during his career and confessed that he remained unsure whether George would arrive as scheduled in February 1976 to start training and meet his new teammates.

There were few signs of trouble once George arrived in LA looking fitter than he had in recent months. The swagger was also back and though there was obvious physical work to do, it became clear that he was ready to play again. He also enjoyed life on the Pacific coast where he could walk the streets enjoying a level of anonymity unavailable in Britain.

A press conference arranged at Los Angeles airport where he had walked off the plane with a t-shirt bearing the words: 'Who the hell's George?' gave an early demonstration of his mood to make a splash in the States. When asked by attending journalists about comparisons to Joe Namath, a gridiron star who was one of the most talented players in the game yet also enjoyed the high life, George declared that he was better than Namath at both soccer and American Football.

While he might have struggled at quarterback, Best certainly proved his worth as a footballer and after 23 games of the regular season had scored 15 goals. Just as important for the statistic focussed nature of American sport, George provided seven assists as The Aztecs finished third in the Pacific Conference's Southern Division. Best was the club's top scorer and the sixth most potent marksman across all leagues. He had missed just a single game and was nominated in the NASL All-Star Team.

Dallas Tornado were seeded to meet Los Angeles in the opening phase of the play-offs. George had prospered against the Texans with three goals in two games during the regular season though they had finished a place higher and underlined that superiority with a 2-0 win.

Best was a massive influence on his peers both on and off the field. Remarkably this extended to diet. At the first pre-match meal in mid-April almost everyone ordered a steak while George insisted on a bowl of cornflakes. Based on his performances most felt there had to be nutrients in the cereal they were missing out on and to a man they opted for cornflakes thereafter.

A summer with the Aztecs was followed by a season back in England with Fulham. The Cottagers had signed two other players who had been turning out in America - Bobby Moore, who played for San Antonio Thunder, and Rodney Marsh, someone who George had faced many times in Manchester derbies, from the Tampa Bay Rowdies.

Craven Cottage was no stranger to great players. Fulham had plenty during their history and back in March 1973 had hosted Pele's Santos. A number of English grounds were picked for a tour which proved highly popular with the public who crammed in to catch a glimpse. It was the only time the legendary forward played in London. Santos won the game 2-1 with Pele scoring a penalty.

George took just 71 seconds of his debut to register his opening goal. It proved to be the winner in a home game with Bristol Rovers. For the first time in many years he looked as if he was enjoying his football. Fulham also benefited and achieved a decent run of results.

There was also a remarkable strike in his second game - a League Cup 2nd Round replay at Peterborough which encapsulated the reason why he was brought back. In an otherwise turgid game George took possession close to half way. Forwards hared across the pitch in front of him expecting to be played in. However they, like everyone else in the ground, could only watch in awe as the ball was flicked from Best's left foot to his right before he sent a volley from 45 yards towards goal. It travelled at lightening speed and hit the net beating a stunned keeper who, like everyone else in a sporting London Road crowd, could only applaud not only the audacity but the sheer skill of Best's effort.

Despite Best, Marsh and Moore The Cottagers were a modest side and remained low in the table. But results just didn't matter to George as he rediscovered his love for the game.

On one occasion Best and Marsh mocked their reputation for never passing by tackling one another. During another game Marsh decided a cross along the edge of the penalty area was begging to be knocked in with a scissor kick. He mastered the difficult technique and gave the keeper no chance. Unfortunately Rodney was, or at least should have been, defending at the time. The ball had been played in by an opposition winger.

The bad boy still emerged on odd occasions as frustrations boiled over when his colleagues failed to meet a satisfactory standard. A sending off against Southampton was one such instance but Best failed to vent his spleen at colleagues or the opposition. Instead he argued with the referee. Sometimes those fits of temper came due to his own physical limitations.

Many seasons as the target of kicks, hacking, elbows and blatant punches along with George's less than ideal lifestyle had taken their toll and the legs were not as sprightly as they once were. While they were sufficient to meet the requirements in the USA, they nor the body were sometimes lithe enough to evade much of the rough treatment many in the second rung of the English game thought they were entitled to dish out to stars who had shined earlier in the decade and Best was regularly targetted.

His effectiveness was also limited by the London nightlife. George had never progressed beyond an FA Cup semi-final but like his esteemed colleagues hoped that as beaten finalists two years previously Fulham could give them one last shot of glory in the world's most prestigious cup competition.

The run they hoped to begin started with a home tie against Third Division Swindon Town who had progressed at the expense of non-league sides Bromley and Hitchen. Nine times out of ten The Cottagers would have fancied themselves to beat the Wiltshire club without too much fuss but George, Rodney and Bobby were out until 5am on the morning before the game - their pre-match routine leading to a 3-3 draw and affording another chance at The County Ground. However, when the teams reconvened Fulham looked no better than they had a few days earlier and crashed out 5-0. It was George's last appearance in the competition.

As if to complete his rehabilitation, 1976 saw George re-selected by his national side. Northern Ireland had struggled without him and had won just one game in the three years he had been out.

*   *   *

In the summer of 1977 George flew out to California to meet his obligations with the LA Aztecs. Criss-crossing the Atlantic seemed to suit him and did wonders for his health as for long periods he kicked the booze, though he often quipped that despite living just one block from Hermosa Beach he never got to the sand as there was a bar on the way.

It was in this season he played in one of Pele's last competitive games when The Aztecs met the New York Cosmos. Both had named the other as the world's greatest ever player and although the Brazilian was in his late 30s at the time, he remained a class apart from all but one other man on the pitch. Neither scored as The Aztecs cruised to a 4-1 win but Pele did make an outrageous foul challenge on Best. It was the type which could sometimes provoke an angry response but George just picked himself up and shook hands. As well as scoring 11 goals George made 18 assists that season which equalled the all time NASL record held by none other than Pele himself.

Bobby McAlinden, an old friend from Manchester who played inside left for City in the 1964 FA Youth Cup semi-final, was a player George insisted The Aztecs brought to the West Coast - so much so that he footed the travel bill. The two helped the club finish third in the Southern Division once more and they met San Jose Earthquakes in the divisional play-offs.

A narrow win qualified The Aztecs for a two legged play-off against Southern Division champions - Dallas Tornados. Defeat by that club 12 months earlier was avenged by resounding 3-1 and 5-1 victories but Seattle Sounders of the Western Division proved just too strong in the semi-finals.

An end to Best's Football League career came in November 1977 when he was suspended by Fulham for missing training. He didn't play again until the following April when he linked up with the LA Aztecs. There had been a number of changes to the make up of each league. The franchise system saw many clubs switch to cities many miles away from their original homes and another half dozen created from scratch. The Aztecs found themselves in the far trickier National Conference Western Division up against Vancouver Whitecaps, Portland Timbers and Seattle Sounders. Wins were at a premium with just nine recorded from 30 games. For the first time in their existence The Aztecs failed to make the play-offs.

By this time George had swapped California for Florida joining Fort Lauderdale Strikers in June 1978 who he helped go within one match of The Soccer Bowl - the equivalent of the American championship. It was a change that had to happen. In a dozen games for Los Angeles George had found the net just once and failed to add a single assist to his tally - a telling statistic for such a creative player.

In just nine games with The Strikers he netted four and laid on two successful strikes for a colleague. Emerging from the American Conference's Eastern Division, Fort Lauderdale accounted for the New England Tea Men and runaway leaders of the Central Division, Detroit Express.

Tampa Bay Rowdies had been outstanding against most sides during the regular season but had an even record against Fort Lauderdale. Best scored the final goal of a 3-2 win in the opening leg at Lockhart Stadium but a 3-1 defeat back in Tampa edged The Strikers out.

Two friendly ties in Austria for Detroit Express, one of the teams he had starred against in both the regular season and the play-offs, followed in September but there was little chance of a comeback in the UK as Fulham retained his registration and refused to release it without adequate compensation.

On 12 October 1978, a day after FIFA imposed a suspension until some form of solution could be found, George's 54 year old mother Anne was found dead. The cause was alcohol related although she had never touched a drop until 14 years previously.

Football-wise Best's future was sorted in time for a him to play for Fort Lauderdale in March 1979 but he made just 19 more appearances before he was disciplined by The Strikers for missing training and a host of club functions. On the field he looked average but still way above a level most others could achieve which allowed him to score twice and provide a very respectable 11 assists in just 17 games.

In November of the same year, and a month after United had refused him a testimonial, George joined Scottish First Division side Hibernian for a very lucrative £1,500 a match. Ambitious chairman Tom Hart knew he would lure large attendances but also expected the team to benefit in terms of results. Over two stints from 1979 to 1981 George, by now approaching his mid-30s, still possessed plenty of ability but was beginning to slow drastically. His battles with booze escalated while in Scotland forcing him out of a cup match on one occasion. He scored three times for Hibs in 25 appearances including one on his debut at St Mirren.

His time at Easter Road was punctuated with further spells in the United States including a return to California with San Jose Earthquakes for whom he scored one of his very finest goals. Taking the ball 25 yards out he evaded the challenge of one defender then threaded his way past another three and into the six yard box. The keeper came out to narrow the angle and put in a challenge but the ball was casually rolled past him.

Performances like this saw Best rumoured to be ready for a comeback with Northern Ireland who finally qualified for the World Cup finals in 1982. However, hopes were dashed when team boss Billy Bingham said that Best was "playing more like a cornflake than an earthquake".

San Jose were a fairly average side with few star names and finished a distant bottom of the Western Division in each of George's two seasons there. Best was the main stay of their side and scored eight times in 26 games in his first campaign then 13 from 30 outings in his second season which also turned out to be his last in the NASL. His assist ratio remained consistent.

The opinion of the national team manager wasn't shared by many in America who begged him to reconsider his decision to leave their shores. He had been voted into the 1981 All Star Second XI losing out to the three allowed selections of Teofilo Cubillas, Vladislav Bogicevic and Arno Steffenhagen in the midfield category but after seeing his World Cup dream finally shattered George seemed to lose his appetite for the game.

Player ratings had him in the league's all time top ten on a ranking system based on points awarded for goals scored and assists made with six campaigns and 139 games yielding 54 successful strikes on target with as many assists. One point was awarded for efforts in the latter category with two for finding the net and an overall total of 162. This sees George at 23rd in the all time list compiled between 1968 and the league's demise in 1984. Each of the 10 play off games do not count in this analysis but would have produced a further three goals and six assists for an extra 12 points.

George had been said to have signed for Middlesbrough in December 1981. Boro announced the deal after speculation which followed an appearance in Jim Platt's testimonial but George quickly scotched the rumours.

Bournemouth had also enquired about signing Best when he was first put up for transfer by United in December 1972. It took him almost 11 years to arrive at Dean Court where he made his Cherries debut in March 1983. Just months earlier there was an offer on the table from Manchester United to make a sensational return. Ron Atkinson had taken charge of the club and was serious about the proposed deal but George, realising he could no longer do the club he loved real justice, declined.

The agreement with Bournemouth was that he would only turn out in

THE LEGENDS CLASH
Pele and George finally met on a football field in this NASL clash during the Brazilian's last season in the US league. It wasn't all about skilful football however as Pele upended George during one encounter.

home games though he did make one of his five outings at Southend. Now 36, bankrupt and needing to support his two year-old son Calum he was glad of a wage. One of his games for Bournemouth included a game against Wigan Athletic managed for one game as a caretaker by former Old Trafford teammate Bobby Charlton.

His posting ended when the 1982-83 season closed as he accepted another well financed package in Australia with Brisbane Lions. That 'have boots will travel' lifestyle and living out of a suitcase existence lasted until the final game of his career in January 1984 for Tobermore United against Ballymena in the Irish Cup. It was the only time he played a competitive club game in his native Northern Ireland.

By the end of the year George was imprisoned for drink driving and assaulting a police officer. He also failed to answer bail, so a warrant for his arrest was issued and led to a three month sentence in Ford Open Prison where he spent Christmas.

A testimonial in August 1988 saw Best captain a host of current and former stars at Windsor Park against an international XI featuring Trevor Francis and Ossie Ardiles.

The George Best XI included Pat Jennings, German midfielder Paul Breitner plus Chris Hughton and Liam Brady from the Republic of Ireland. Former England skipper Emlyn Hughes was also on duty along with three great Dutch players George admired Rudi Krol, Johan Neeskens and Johnny Rep.

George had played in a huge number of testimonials since early in his career. Some estimates say more than 200 over the course of two decades. However, he had failed to be honoured with his own benefit game by Manchester United or the Irish FA who had turned a request down earlier that year only to relent after public pressure. A crowd of more than 30,000 turn out despite drizzling rain to raise £750,000 to pay tribute to Northern Ireland's greatest ever player.

The game was tied at 6-6 towards the end. George had already scored with a chip from outside the area and delighted the crowd by hitting a late winner from the penalty spot.

HOLLAND 2 NORTHERN IRELAND 2
World Cup Qualifier 13 October 1976

IRELAND'S BID TO reach the 1978 World Cup in Argentina could not have got off to a trickier start. Iceland were expected to be the whipping boys of Group Four but Belgium and Holland, who were runners-up at the 1974 tournament, would be far stiffer opposition. That made the first game in Rotterdam all important and after good spells in America and at Fulham Danny Blanchflower decided to draft George Best in to his first squad.

It was a controversial decision but proved to be the right one as with attack his only instruction, George was allowed to prove he was at least as good as Dutch masters Cruyff and Neeskens.

Chris McGrath of Spurs, who was said to be catching the eye of Manchester United, grabbed the first goal. As expected Holland were dangerous in attack and found the net twice but Derek Spence, on as a substitute for the scorer, grabbed a late, deserved leveller.

BELGIUM 2 NORTHERN IRELAND 0
World Cup Qualifier 10 November 1976

BELGIUM WERE CONTENT to pull men behind the ball for long spells but still won the game with a couple of goals. Defensive tactics aimed at stifling Best only worked in spells and couldn't stop an early lob falling an inch or so wide. Even at 2-0 down following goals by Roger van Gool and Raou Lambert, George kept trying to find a way through and linked well with Jimmy Nicholson who crossed for Trevor Anderson to head just over. Unfortunately there were few other clear chances.

WEST GERMANY 5 NORTHERN IRELAND 0
International Friendly 24 April 1977

REMARKABLY THIS WAS the first friendly international George Best had played since winning his second cap against Uruguay 13 years earlier, while the Germans were playing their first game without Franz Beckenbauer for a decade.

Best had never had the chance to come up against der Kaiser, even in the NASL as although Beckenbauer had signed for the New York Cosmos, he would not be making his debut until the new season started in a few week's time. After coming up against the greats of the Dutch game in their prime and doing well George was looking forward to testing his skills against one of the finest international players of his generation.

As he often did, Danny Blanchflower instructed his side to employ an open style. Germany struggled to cope for some time but eventually hauled themselves ahead when Rainer Bonhof punished Sammy Nelson for handling in the area. It was all one way traffic from then on and within 10 minutes Klaus Fischer and Gerd Muller had made it 3-0. Fishcer grabbed another before Heinz Flohe completed the rout.

NORTHERN IRELAND 2 ICELAND 0
WORLD CUP QUALIFIER 21 SEPTEMBER 1977

DESPITE COMING UP against another side who were already ruled out of qualification for Argentina in the summer, Iceland showed little interest in anything other than defending. The tie marked George Best's first match in Northern Ireland in six years, an absence accounted for by Best's 'lost weekend' at the end of his United career and the heightened tension during the Troubles that ruled out Windsor Park as a venue.

The only justification for their approach was that they were missing eight of their first choice side. The Manchester United pairing of Chris McGrath and Sammy McIlroy scored late goals but otherwise the game was worthy of few highlights.

NORTHERN IRELAND 0 HOLLAND 1
WORLD CUP QUALIFIER 12 OCTOBER 1977

THE PENULTIMATE GAME of the qualifying campaign brought the runaway group leaders Holland to Windsor Park needing a win to guarantee their place in the World Cup finals.

The game was only decided by a Willy van der Kerkhof effort 12 minutes from time. Cruyff was injured and limped off which proved a sad note on which George would end his international career.

The highlight for many was the sight of Best and Cruyff on the same pitch and although both were coming to the end of their careers, Best provided one last reminder of his audacity.

In the opening moments George received the ball on the left-hand side of the pitch and made his way toward Cruyff on the opposite flank. The Windsor Park crowd watched in astonishment as Best took the ball up to the Dutch master and nutmegged him before laying it off. Cruyff was gobsmacked and, as far as George was concerned, that was mission accomplished - he'd shown Johan who was boss.

Needless to say the Irish lapped up Best's antics on what proved to be his last appearance for the province. This was Cruyff's penultimate outing for his country as he ended his international career against Belgium just a fortnight later.

Of course Best never got to play on the biggest stage of all whereas Cruyff had dominated the 1974 World Cup but opted out of the 1978 tournament after the latest in a long running series of rows with the coach.

It wasn't known at the time but Blanchflower, realising a number of players had grown older and would not be around to make the next finals in Spain, decided he had to give others a chance for the final group game against Belgium.

DATE	OPPONENT	VENUE	SCORE	ATT'D	1	2	3	4	5	6	7	8	9	10	11
28 November	Swansea City	Edgeley Park	3-2	9,220	Hopkinson	Turner	Buckley	Lawther	Bradley	Fogarty	Best[1]	Seddon	Hollis	Massey	McNeill
12 December	Watford	Edgeley Park	2-2	4,755	Hopkinson	Smith	Buckley	Lawther[1]	Bradley	Fogarty	McNeill	Hollis	Coyne	Cross	Best[1]
26 December	Southport	Edgeley Park	1-0	6,321	Hopkinson	Smith	Buckley	Deere	Bradley	Fogarty	McNeill	Hollis[1]	Massey	Cross	Best

LOS ANGELES AZTECS - NASL 1976

DATE	OPPONENT	VENUE	SCORE	ATT'D	1	2	3	4	5	6	7	8	9	10	11
17 April	San Jose	Spartan Stadium	1-2	19,807	Horn	Kelley	Moraldo	Lopez(J)	Linton	Fagan	Mason[1]	McAlinden	Davies	Velazquez	Best
25 April	Rochester	El Camino College	1-0	7,236	Horn	Kelley	Moraldo	Marotti	Linton	Fagan	Mason	McAlinden	Davies	Velazquez	Best[1]
2 May	San Diego	El Camino College	2-0	7,495	Horn	Kelley	Moraldo[1]	Marotti	Linton	Fagan	Smith(P)	McAlinden	Davies	Velazquez	Best[1]
8 May	San Antonio	Alamo Stadium	2-3	5,520	Horn	Kelley	Moraldo	Marotti	Linton	Fagan	Smith(P)	McAlinden[2]	Davies	Velazquez	Best
9 May	Seattle	El Camino College	4-3	7,165	Horn	Kelley	Moraldo	Marotti	Linton	Fagan	Smith(P)	McAlinden	Davies[1]	Velazquez[2]	Best[1]
14 May	Philadelphia	Franklin Field	2-1	6,237	Horn	Kelley	Marotti	Lopez(J)	Linton	Fagan	Smith(P)	McAlinden	Davies[1]	Velazquez	Best
17 May	New York	Yankee Stadium	0-6	24,292	Horn	Kelley	Marotti	Lopez(J)	Linton	Fagan	Smith(P)	McAlinden	Davies	Lopez(M)	Best
2 June	Toronto	Toronto	0-2	6,580	Horn	Lopez(J)	Moraldo	Smith(P)	Linton	Fagan	Mason	Garber	Davies	Lopez(M)	Best
5 June	Portland	El Camino College	1-0	7,921	Horn	Marsh(J)	Moraldo	Smith(P)	Linton	Fagan	Mason	Garber	Davies	Velazquez	Best[4]
12 June	Vancouver	El Camino College	2-1	6,843	Horn	Marsh(J)	Moraldo	Smith(D)	Linton	Fagan	Mason	Garber	Davies[1]	Smith(P)	Best[1]
19 June	Tampa Bay	El Camino College	2-1	9,345	Horn	Marsh(J)	Moraldo	Smith(D)	Linton	Fagan	Mason	McAlinden	Davies	Smith(P)	Best[2]
20 June	Dallas	Ownby Stadium	3-6	13,421	Horn	Marsh(J)	Smith(D)	Garber	Linton	Fagan	Mason	McAlinden	Davies	Smith(P)	Best[1]
26 June	Minnesota	El Camino College	0-1	8,166	Horn	Marsh(J)	Moraldo	Smith(D)	Linton	Fagan	Mason	McAlinden	Davies	Cooke	Best
3 July	San Antonio	Alamo Stadium	1-2	8,313	Horn	Marsh(J)	Moraldo	Smith(D)	Linton	Lopez(M)	Sorgie	McAlinden[1]	Davies	Cooke	Best
5 July	Portland	Civic Stadium	2-1	19,375	Mishalow	Marsh(J)	Lopez(M)	Smith(D)	Linton	Mason[1]	Sorgie	McAlinden	Davies[1]	Cooke	Best
10 July	St Louis	El Camino College	2-1	9,910	Mishalow	Marsh(J)	Lopez(M)	Smith(D)	Linton	Mason[1]	Sorgie	McAlinden	Davies	Cooke	Best
16 July	San Diego	Aztec Bowl	2-1	6,700	Mishalow	Marsh(J)	Mason	Smith(D)	Garber	Fagan	Lopez(M)	McAlinden	Davies	Cooke	Best[1]
18 July	Boston	El Camino College	8-0	7,472	Mishalow	Marsh(J)	Mason(2)	Smith(D)	Linton	Fagan	Sorgie[1]	McAlinden	Davies	Cooke[2]	Best[3]
23 July	Vancouver	Empire Stadium	1-2	13,252	Mishalow	Marsh(J)	Mason	Smith(D)	Linton	Lopez(M)	Sorgie[1]	McAlinden	Davies	Cooke	Best
25 July	San Jose	El Camino College	0-1	9,204	Mishalow	Marsh(J)	Mason	Smith(D)	Linton	Fagan	Sorgie	McAlinden	Davies	Cooke	Best
31 July	Seattle	Kingdome	0-1	25,810	Mishalow	Marsh(J)	Mason	Moraldo	Linton	Fagan	Sorgie	McAlinden	Davies	Cooke	Best
10 August	Minnesota	Metropolitan Stadium	2-6	42,065	Mishalow	Marsh(J)[1]	Mason(1)	Smith(D)	Moraldo	Fagan	Sorgie	McAlinden	Davies[1]	Cooke	Best
14 August	Dallas	El Camino College	4-1	7,536	Mishalow	Moraldo	Mason	Smith(D)	Linton	Fagan	Sorgie[2]	McAlinden[2]	Davies	Cooke	Best[1]
Play-off															
18 August	Dallas	Ownby Stadium	0-2	9,413	Mishalow	Marsh(J)	Moraldo	Smith(D)	Linton	Fagan	Sorgie	McAlinden	Davies	Cooke	Best

THE COMPLETE GEORGE BEST

FULHAM - Football League Division Two 1976-77

DATE	OPPONENT	VENUE	SCORE	ATT'D	1	2	3	4	5	6	7	8	9	10	11
4 September	Bristol Rovers	Craven Cottage	1-0	21,177	Mellor	Cutbush	Strong	Slough¹	Howe	Moore	Best¹	Evanson	Busby	Marsh	Barrett
7 September	Peterborough Utd	London Road	2-1	16,476	Mellor	Cutbush	Strong	Slough¹	Howe	Moore	Best¹	Evanson	Busby	Marsh	Barrett
11 September	Wolves	Craven Cottage	0-0	25,794	Mellor	Cutbush	Strong	Slough	Howe	Moore	Best	Evanson	Busby	Marsh	Barrett
18 September	Luton Town	Kenilworth Road	2-0	19,929	Mellor	Cutbush	Strong	Slough	Howe	Moore	Best	Evanson	Mitchell	Marsh¹	Barrett¹
25 September	Hereford United	Craven Cottage	4-1	18,935	Mellor	Cutbush	Strong	Slough¹	Howe	Moore	Best	Evanson¹	Mitchell	Marsh²	Barrett
2 October	Southampton	The Dell	1-4	29,489	Mellor	Bullivant	Strong	Slough	Howe	Moore	Best	Evanson	Mitchell¹	Marsh	Barrett
16 October	Sheffield United	Bramall Lane	1-1	28,792	Mellor	Cutbush	Strong	Slough	Howe	Moore	Best	Evanson	Mitchell¹	Marsh	Barrett
23 October	Hull City	Craven Cottage	0-0	18,671	Mellor	Cutbush	Strong	Slough	Howe	Moore	Best	Evanson	Mitchell	Marsh	Bullivant
30 October	Bolton Wanderers	Burnden Park	1-2	25,251	Mellor	Lacy	Strong	Slough	Howe	Moore	Best¹	Evanson	Mitchell	Marsh	Bullivant
6 November	Cardiff City	Craven Cottage	1-2	12,366	Mellor	Slough	Strong	Lacy	Howe	Moore	Best¹	Evanson	Mitchell	Mahoney	Dowie(J)
13 November	Plymouth Argyle	Home Park	2-2	25,335	Mellor	James	Strong	Slough	Howe¹	Moore	Best	Evanson	Mitchell¹	Marsh	Bullivant
16 November	Carlisle United	Craven Cottage	2-0	9,215	Mellor	James	Strong	Slough	Howe	Moore	Best	Evanson	Mitchell	Marsh²	Barrett
20 November	Notts County	Craven Cottage	1-5	12,191	Mellor	James	Strong	Slough¹	Howe	Moore	Best	Evanson	Mitchell	Marsh	Bullivant
27 November	Blackpool	Bloomfield Road	2-3	16,781	Teale	Cutbush	Strong	Slough	Howe	Moore	Best	Evanson	Mitchell²	Maybank	Barrett
4 December	Oldham Athletic	Craven Cottage	5-0	14,326	Peyton	Cutbush	Strong	Slough	Howe	Moore	Best¹	Evanson	Mitchell²	Maybank²	Barrett
11 December	Orient	Brisbane Road	0-0	11,237	Peyton	Cutbush	Strong	Slough	Lacy	Moore	Best	Evanson	Mitchell	Maybank	Barrett
14 December	Blackburn Rovers	Craven Cottage	2-0	8,543	Peyton	Cutbush	Strong	Slough	Lacy	Moore	Best¹	Evanson	Mitchell	Maybank¹	Barrett
27 December	Chelsea	Stamford Bridge	0-2	55,003	Peyton	Howe	Strong	Slough	Lacy	Moore	Best	Greenaway	Mitchell	Evanson	Barrett
3 January	Bolton Wanderers	Craven Cottage	0-2	12,594	Digweed	Cutbush	Strong	Slough	Howe	Moore	Best	Evanson	Mitchell	Greenaway	Barrett¹
15 January	Burnley	Craven Cottage	2-2	8,815	Peyton	Cutbush	Strong	Slough¹	Howe	Moore	Best	Bullivant	Camp	Marsh	Barrett¹
22 January	Nottingham Forest	City Ground	0-3	24,718	Peyton	Strong	Jump	Slough	Lacy	Moore	Best	Evanson	Mitchell	Marsh	Bullivant
5 February	Charlton Athletic	Craven Cottage	1-1	14,958	Peyton	Strong	Jump	Slough	Lacy	Moore	Best	Evanson	Mitchell¹	Marsh	Bullivant
12 February	Bristol Rovers	Eastville Stadium	1-2	11,078	Peyton	Strong	Jump	Slough	Lacy	Moore	Best	Evanson	Mitchell¹	Margerrison	Bullivant
19 February	Wolves	Molineux	1-5	25,865	Peyton	Strong	Slough	Bullivant	Lacy	Moore	Best	Mitchell¹	Warboys	Marsh	Evanson
2 April	Hull City	Boothferry Park	0-1	61.58	Peyton	Evans	Strong	Storey	Lacy	Moore	Best	Maybank	Warboys	Slough	Mitchell
8 April	Chelsea	Craven Cottage	3-1	29,690	Peyton	Evans	Strong	Storey	Lacy	Moore	Best¹	Maybank	Warboys¹	Mitchell¹	Slough
9 April	Millwall	The Den	0-0	11,001	Peyton	Evans	Strong	Storey	Lacy	Moore	Best	Maybank	Warboys	Slough	Mitchell
11 April	Plymouth Argyle	Craven Cottage	2-0	11,710	Peyton	Evans	Strong	Storey	Lacy	Moore	Best	Maybank¹	Warboys	Slough	Mitchell
16 April	Notts County	Meadow Lane	0-0	14,847	Peyton	Evans	Strong	Storey	Lacy	Moore	Best	Bullivant	Warboys	Slough	Mitchell
23 April	Blackpool	Craven Cottage	0-0	10,956	Peyton	Evans	Strong	Storey	Lacy	Moore	Best	Maybank	Warboys	Slough	Mitchell

LOS ANGELES AZTECS - NASL 1977

DATE	OPPONENT	VENUE	SCORE	ATT'D	1	2	3	4	5	6	7	8	9	10	11
20 May	Portland	Civic Stadium	0-1	14,872	Rigby	Fagan	Davies	Beal	Mancini	Cohen	Cooke	David	Sibbald	Backos	Best
22 May	Vancouver	LA Coliseum	3-2	8,267	Rigby	Fagan	Davies	Beal	Mancini	McAlinden²	Cooke	David¹	Sibbald	Backos	Best
28 May	Seattle	Kingdome	2-1	22,730	Rigby	Mihailovich	Davies	Beal	Mancini	McAlinden	Cooke	David¹	Sibbald	Backos	Best¹
30 May	St Louis	LA Coliseum	3-2	10,651	Mishalow	Mihailovich	Davies¹	Beal	Mancini	McAlinden	Cooke	David¹	Sibbald	Backos	Best¹
5 June	Dallas	LA Coliseum	4-3	7,770	Rigby	Mihailovich	Davies¹	Beal¹	Mancini	McAlinden	Cooke	David¹	Sibbald	Backos	Best¹
12 June	Las Vegas	LA Coliseum	3-0	10,250	Rigby	Fagan	Davies	Beal	Mancini	McAlinden	Cooke	David¹	Sibbald	Backos¹	Best¹
19 June	Minnesota	Metropolitan Stadium	3-2	28,284	Rigby	Fagan	Davies¹	Beal	Mancini	Cohen	Cooke	David¹	Sibbald	Backos	Best¹
22 June	Rochester	Holleder Stadium	3-4	7,133	Rigby	Fagan	Davies¹	Beal	Mancini	McAlinden	Cooke	David²	Sibbald	Cohen	Best
26 June	New York	Giants Stadium	2-5	57,191	Rigby	Fagan	Davies	Beal	Mancini	McAlinden	Cooke	David¹	Sibbald	Cohen	Best¹
29 June	Connecticut	Yale Bowl	3-2	2,915	Rigby	McGrane	Mason	Beal	Mancini	McAlinden	Cooke¹	David²	Sibbald	Cohen	Best
2 July	New York	LA Coliseum	4-1	32,165	Rigby	McGrane	Davies	Beal¹	Mancini¹	McAlinden	Cooke	David¹	Sibbald	Cohen	Best
4 July	Toronto	LA Coliseum	0-2	8,543	Rigby	McGrane	Davies	Beal	Mancini	McAlinden	Cooke	David	Sibbald	Cohen	Best
9 July	Washington	Kennedy Stadium	4-2	11,168	Rigby	McGrane	Davies	Beal	Mancini¹	McAlinden	Cooke¹	David²	Sibbald	Cohen	Best
13 July	Tampa Bay	Tampa Stadium	1-4	16,135	Rigby	McGrane	Davies	Beal	Mancini	McAlinden	Cooke	David	Sibbald	Cohen	Best
17 July	Fort Lauderdale	LA Coliseum	1-3	6,616	Rigby	McGrane	Davies	Beal	Mancini	McAlinden	Cooke	David	Sibbald¹	Cohen	Best
22 July	Team Hawaii	Aloha Stadium	5-6	6,392	Rigby	McGrane	Davies¹	Beal	Mancini	Cohen	Cooke	David²	Sibbald	Backos¹	Best¹
27 July	Las Vegas	Las Vegas Stadium	3-2	8,136	Rigby	McGrane	Davies	Beal	Mancini	Cohen	Cooke	David¹	Sibbald	Backos¹	Best¹
30 July	San Jose	LA Coliseum	2-3	5,997	Rigby	McGrane	Davies	Beal	Mancini	Cohen	Cooke	David¹	Sibbald	Backos	Best¹
4 August	Vancouver	Empire Stadium	2-0	18,037	Mishalow	McGrane	Davies	Mihailovich	Mancini	McAlinden	Cooke	Cohen	Mason	Backos	Best¹
7 August	Seattle	LA Coliseum	2-4	5,105	Mishalow	McGrane	Davies	Mihailovich	Mancini	McAlinden	Cooke	Cohen	Sibbald	Backos	Best¹
Play-offs															
10 August	San Jose	LA Coliseum	2-1	4,038	Rigby	Rys	Davies	Beal	Mancini	McAlinden	Cooke	Cohen	Sibbald	Backos	Best¹
14 August	Dallas	LA Coliseum	3-1	5,295	Rigby	Mihailovich¹	Davies	Beal	Mancini	McAlinden	Cooke	Cohen²	Sibbald	Backos	Best¹
17 August	Dallas	Ownby Stadium	5-1	18,489	Rigby	Mihailovich	Davies	Beal	Mancini	McAlinden	Cooke¹	Cohen²	Sibbald	Backos¹	Best¹
21 August	Seattle	LA Coliseum	1-3	9,115	Rigby	Mihailovich	Davies	Beal	Mancini	McAlinden¹	Cooke	Cohen	Sibbald	Backos	Best
25 August	Seattle	Kingdome	0-1	56,256	Rigby	Mihailovich	Davies	Beal	Mancini	McAlinden	Cooke	Cohen	Sibbald	Backos	Best

THE COMPLETE GEORGE BEST

FULHAM - Football League Division Two 1977-78

DATE	OPPONENT	VENUE	SCORE	ATTD	1	2	3	4	5	6	7	8	9	10	11
3 September	Blackburn Rovers	Craven Cottage	0-0	10,095	Peyton	Evans	Strong	Storey	Lacy	Gale	Bullivant	Mitchell	Warboys	Maybank	Best
24 September	Cardiff City	Ninian Park	1-3	8,789	Peyton	Evans	Strong	Bullivant	Lacy	Gale	Margerrison	Evanson	Mitchell	Maybank	Best¹
1 October	Crystal Palace	Selhurst Park	3-2	28,094	Peyton	Evans	Strong	Howe	Lacy	Gale¹	Best¹	Margerrison	Mitchell	Maybank²	Evanson
4 October	Burnley	Craven Cottage	4-1	6,895	Peyton	Evans	Strong	Howe	Lacy	Gale	Best¹	Margerrison	Mitchell²	Mahoney¹	Evanson
8 October	Blackpool	Craven Cottage	1-1	9,190	Peyton	Evans	Strong	Margerrison	Lacy	Howe	Best	Mitchell	Maybank	Evanson	Bullivant
15 October	Luton Town	Kenilworth Road	0-1	12,736	Peyton	Evans	Strong	Howe	Lacy	Gale	Best	Mahoney	Mitchell	Evanson	Margerrison
22 October	Orient	Craven Cottage	1-2	9,196	Peyton	Evans	Strong	Howe	Lacy¹	Gale¹	Best	Evanson	Mitchell	Mahoney	Margerrison
29 October	Sheffield United	Bramall Lane	1-2	16,741	Peyton	Evans	Strong	Bullivant	Lacy	Gale¹	Best¹	Margerrison	Mitchell	Mahoney	Evanson
5 November	Sunderland	Craven Cottage	3-3	10,548	Peyton	Evans	Strong	Bullivant	Lacy	James	Best¹	Margerrison	Mitchell¹	Maybank¹	Evanson
12 November	Stoke City	Victoria Ground	0-2	14,156	Peyton	Evans	Strong	Bullivant	Lacy	Howe	Best	Margerrison	Mitchell	Maybank	Evanson

LOS ANGELES AZTECS - NASL 1978

DATE	OPPONENT	VENUE	SCORE	ATT'D	1	2	3	4	5	6	7	8	9	10	11
2 April	Houston	Rose Bowl	2-3	10,112	Rigby	Sibbald	Clarke	Davies	McGrane	Mifflin	Cooke	McAlinden	David	**Suhnholz**[2]	Best
9 April	New York	Rose Bowl	0-1	23,681	Rigby	Sibbald	Clarke	Davies	McGrane	Mifflin	Cooke	McAlinden	David	Suhnholz	Best
16 April	California	Anaheim Stadium	4-1	16,226	Rigby	Sibbald	Clarke	Davies	McGrane	Smuda	**Cooke**[1]	McAlinden	David	**Suhnholz**[2]	Best
22 April	Fort Lauderdale	Lockhart Stadium	0-2	7,778	Rigby	Sibbald	Clarke	Mihailovich	McGrane	Smuda	Cooke	McAlinden	Ybarra	Suhnholz	Best
30 April	Oakland	Rose Bowl	1-2	7,545	Rigby	Sibbald	Clarke	**Davies**[1]	McGrane	Smuda	Ybarra	McAlinden	Jones	Suhnholz	Best
7 May	Seattle	Rose Bowl	0-2	6,832	Rigby	Sibbald	Clarke	Davies	McGrane	Smuda	Cooke	McAlinden	Jones	Ybarra	Best
18 May	Tulsa	Skelly Stadium	1-0	6,021	Rigby	Sibbald	Clarke	Davies	McGrane	Smuda	Cooke	McAlinden	Jones	Hayes	Best
27 May	Colorado	Mile High Stadium	2-1	7,153	Rigby	Sibbald	Clarke	Davies	**McGrane**[1]	Smuda	Cooke	McAlinden	Jones	Hayes	Best
29 May	Portland	Rose Bowl	1-4	5,206	Rigby	Sibbald	Clarke	Davies	McGrane	Smith(T)	Cooke	McAlinden	Jones	Smuda	**Best**[1]
7 June	Portland	Civic Stadium	0-1	9,054	Rigby	Sibbald	Clarke	Davies	McGrane	Smuda	Cooke	McAlinden	Jones	Suhnholz	Best
17 June	California	Rose Bowl	2-1	15,231	Rigby	Sibbald	Clarke	Davies	McGrane	Smith(T)	Best	McAlinden	**Jones**[2]	Suhnholz	Hayes
20 June	Washington	Kennedy Stadium	0-4	9,621	Rigby	Sibbald	Clarke	Lennard	McGrane	Smith(T)	Best	Coyne	Jones	Suhnholz	Hayes

FORT LAUDERDALE STRIKERS - NASL 1978

DATE	OPPONENT	VENUE	SCORE	ATT'D	1	2	3	4	5	6	7	8	9	10	11
24 June	New York	Lockhart Stadium	5-3	13,569	Turner	Whelan	Whittle	Fowles	Ridley	**Hudson**[1]	**Irving**[2]	Leeper	Ronson	Callaghan	**Best**[2]
28 June	Memphis	Liberty Bowl	2-1	5,026	Turner	Whelan	Whittle	Fowles	Ridley	Hudson	**Irving**[1]	Leeper	Ronson	Callaghan	Best
1 July	San Jose	Spartan Stadium	1-0	15,214	Turner	Whelan	Whittle	Fowles	Ridley	Hudson	**Irving**[1]	Vaninger	Piper	Callaghan	Best
4 July	Toronto	Lockhart Stadium	4-0	15,362	Turner	Whelan	Whittle	Fowles	Ridley	Hudson	**Irving**[3]	Vaninger	Piper	Callaghan	Best
9 July	Houston	Astrodome	2-1	4,001	Turner	Whelan	Whittle	Fowles	Ridley	Hudson	**Irving**[2]	Vaninger	Ronson	Callaghan	Best
12 July	California	Anaheim Stadium	0-5	11,406	Turner	Whelan	Whittle	Fowles	Ridley	Hudson	Irving	Vaninger	Piper	Callaghan	Best
19 July	New England	Schaefer Stadium	2-0	20,740	Turner	Whelan	Whittle	Fowles	Ridley	Hudson	Irving	Piper	Nanchoff	Callaghan	Best
30 July	Detroit	Silverdome	2-4	21,972	Turner	Whelan	Whittle	Fowles	Aguirre	Piper	**Irving**[1]	Nanchoff	Ronson	Callaghan	**Best**[1]
4 August	Rochester	Lockhart Stadium	2-1	10,189	Turner	Whelan	**Whittle**[1]	Fowles	Ridley	Hudson	Irving	Vaninger	Ronson	Jones	Best

Play-offs

DATE	OPPONENT	VENUE	SCORE	ATT'D	1	2	3	4	5	6	7	8	9	10	11
9 August	New England	Schaefer Stadium	3-1	18,672	Turner	Whelan	Whittle	Piper	Ridley	Hudson	**Irving**[1]	Leeper	Nanchoff	Callaghan	**Best**[1]
13 August	Detroit	Lockhart Stadium	4-3	11,517	Turner	Whelan	**Whittle**[1]	Fowles	Ridley	Hudson	**Irving**[2]	Nanchoff	Ronson	Callaghan	Best
16 August	Detroit	Silverdome	0-1	32,319	Turner	Whelan	Whittle	Fowles	Ridley	Hudson	Irving	Vaninger	Ronson	Callaghan	Best
20 August	Tampa Bay	Lockhart Stadium	3-2	16,286	Turner	Whelan	**Whittle**[1]	Fowles	Ridley	Hudson	**Irving**[1]	Nanchoff	Jones	Callaghan	**Best**[1]
23 August	Tampa Bay	Tampa Stadium	1-3	37,249	Turner	Whelan	Whittle	Fowles	Ridley	Hudson	**Irving**[1]	Nanchoff	Jones	Callaghan	Best

FORT LAUDERDALE STRIKERS - NASL 1979

DATE	OPPONENT	VENUE	SCORE	ATT'D	1	2	3	4	5	6	7	8	9	10	11
31 March	New England	Lockhart Stadium	2-0	13,799	Mausser	Corish	Fogarty	Whelan	Whittle	Hudson	Park	Fowles	Jones	Cubillas[1]	Best
8 April	Toronto	Exhibition Stadium	2-1	18,552	Mausser	Corish	Fogarty	Whelan	Whittle	Hudson[1]	Park	Fowles	Jones	Cubillas[1]	Best
14 April	Washington	Lockhart Stadium	0-4	13,790	Salsamendi	Corish	Newman	Gaston	Whittle	Cougan	Demers	Chadwick	Fazee	Cubillas	Best
22 April	New York	Giants Stadium	2-3	72,342	Mausser	Corish	Fogarty	Whelan	Whittle[1]	Hudson[1]	Park	Fowles	Irving[1]	Cubillas	Best
28 April	Tampa Bay	Lockhart Stadium	1-2	16,668	Mausser	Fowles	Fogarty	Whelan	Whittle	Hudson	Park	Jones	Muller	Cubillas	Best
5 May	Philadelphia	Veterans Stadium	1-2	4,467	Mausser	Leeper	Fogarty	Whelan	Whittle	Hudson	Jones	Irving	Muller	Cubillas[1]	Best
12 May	Toronto	Lockhart Stadium	4-0	11,161	Mausser	Gemeri	Fogarty	Whelan	Whittle[1]	Hudson	Park[1]	Irving	Muller[1]	Cubillas[1]	Best
26 May	Memphis	Lockhart Stadium	3-1	13,052	Mausser	Gemeri	Fogarty	Whelan	Whittle	Hudson	Park	Irving[2]	Muller	Cubillas	Walker[1]
16 June	San Jose	Lockhart Stadium	3-1	11,104	Mausser	Gemeri	Stanley	Whelan	Whittle	Hudson[1]	Park	Irving[2]	Muller	Cubillas	Walker
20 June	Tulsa	Lockhart Stadium	3-2	10,289	Mausser	Newman(G)	Stanley	Whelan	Whittle	Hudson	Park[1]	Irving	Muller[1]	Cubillas[1]	Walker
23 June	Tampa Bay	Tampa Stadium	2-1	41,102	Mausser	Corish	Stanley	Whelan	Whittle	Hudson	Park	Gemeri	Muller[1]	Cubillas[1]	Walker
27 June	Detroit	Silverdome	2-8	17,229	Mausser	Corish	Stanley	Whelan	Whittle	Hudson[1]	Park	Gemeri	Muller[1]	Cubillas	Walker
4 July	Chicago	Lockhart Stadium	2-3	19,850	Mausser	Corish	Stanley	Whelan	Whittle	Hudson	Park	Walker	Muller[1]	Cubillas[1]	Ortiz-Velez
7 July	San Jose	Spartan Stadium	2-1	15,099	Mausser	Ralbovsky	Stanley	Whelan	Whittle	Hudson	Park	Irving	Muller	Cubillas[1]	Walker[1]
11 July	San Diego	San Diego Stadium	3-2	11,302	Mausser	Ralbovsky	Stanley	Whelan	Whittle	Park[1]	Walker	Irving	Muller[2]	Cubillas	Best
14 July	Rochester	Holleder Stadium	1-2	6,529	Mausser	Ralbovsky	Stanley	Whelan	Whittle	Park	Walker	Irving	Muller	Cubillas[1]	Best
18 July	New York	Lockhart Stadium	3-4	19,850	Mausser	Ralbovsky	Stanley	Whelan	Whittle[1]	Park	Walker	Irving	Muller[1]	Cubillas[1]	Best[1]
21 July	Portland	Civic Stadium	1-4	11,097	Mausser	Ralbovsky	Stanley	Whelan	Whittle	Park	Walker	Irving	Muller	Cubillas	Best[1]
25 July	California	Anaheim Stadium	6-3	8,765	Mausser	Ralbovsky	Stanley	Whelan	Whittle	Park	Jones	Irving	Muller[4]	Cubillas[1]	Walker[1]

HIBERNIAN - Scottish Premier League 1979-80

DATE	OPPONENT	VENUE	SCORE	ATTD	1	2	3	4	5	6	7	8	9	10	11
24 November	St Mirren	Love Street	1-2	13,670	McDonald	Brazil	Duncan	Rae	Paterson	McNamara	Callachan	MacLeod	Ward	Higgins	**Best**[1]
1 December	Partick Thistle	Easter Road	2-1	20,622	McArthur	Brazil	Duncan	Rae	Paterson	McNamara	Callachan	**MacLeod**[1]	Hutchinson	Higgins	Best
22 December	Rangers	Easter Road	2-1	18,740	McArthur	Brazil	Duncan	Rae	Paterson	McNamara	Callachan	MacLeod	**Higgins**[1]	**Campbell**[1]	Best
5 January	Kilmarnock	Rugby Park	1-3	6,000	McArthur	Brazil	Duncan	Rae	Paterson	McNamara	Callachan	MacLeod	Higgins	**Campbell**[1]	Best
12 January	Celtic	Easter Road	1-1	21,936	McArthur	Brazil	Lambie	Rae	Paterson	McNamara	Callachan	MacLeod	Higgins	Campbell	**Best**[1]
1 March	Rangers	Ibrox	0-1	30,000	McArthur	Brazil	Lambie	Cormack	Paterson	Rae	Callachan	MacLeod	Hutchinson	Duncan	Best
15 March	Dundee	Dens Park	0-3	8,065	McArthur	Brazil	Duncan	Paterson	Cormack	Rae	Tierney	MacLeod	Torrance	Campbell	Best
25 March	Dundee	Easter Road	2-0	5,000	McArthur	Brazil	Duncan	Tierney	Rae	McNamara	**Murray**[1]	Cormack	Torrance	Campbell	**Best**[1]
29 March	Celtic	Celtic Park	0-4	22,000	McArthur	Brazil	Duncan	Tierney	Rae	McNamara	Murray	Cormack	Torrance	Campbell	Best
2 April	Dundee United	Easter Road	0-2	5,000	McArthur	Brazil	Duncan	Rae	Paterson	Tierney	Murray	Campbell	Torrance	Cormack	Best
5 April	St Mirren	Love Street	0-2	4,000	McArthur	Brazil	Rae	Paterson	Stewart	Cormack	Campbell	MacLeod	Torrance	Tierney	Best
16 April	Aberdeen	Pittodrie	1-1	16,000	McArthur	McNamara	Duncan	Paterson	Stewart	**Rae**[1]	Callachan	Lambie	Torrance	Hutchinson	Best
19 April	Dundee United	Easter Road	0-2	4,921	McArthur	McNamara	Lambie	Paterson	Stewart	Rae	Callachan	Murray	MacLeod	Hutchinson	Best

Scottish FA Cup

DATE	OPPONENT	VENUE	SCORE	ATTD	1	2	3	4	5	6	7	8	9	10	11
26 January	Meadowbank Thistle	Tynecastle	1-0	8,415	McArthur	Brazil	Lambie	Paterson	Stewart	McNamara	**Callachan**[1]	MacLeod	Higgins	Campbell	Best
8 March	Berwick Rangers	Shielfield Park	0-0	7,228	McArthur	Brazil	Lambie	Paterson	Cormack	Rae	Callachan	MacLeod	Hutchinson	Higgins	Best
12 April	Celtic	Hampden Park	0-5	32,925	McArthur	Brazil	Duncan	McNamara	Stewart	Rae	Callachan	Torrance	Campbell	Paterson	Best

THE COMPLETE GEORGE BEST

SAN JOSE EARTHQUAKES - NASL 1980

DATE	OPPONENT	VENUE	SCORE	ATT'D	1	2	3	4	5	6	7	8	9	10	11
27 April	Edmonton	Commonwealth Stad.	2-4	14,783	Turner	Silva	Kadupski	Czuczman	Nikolic	Gersdorff	Bell	Maseko[2]	Mihailovich	Sautter	Best
30 April	San Diego	Spartan Stadium	2-3	10,233	Hewitt	Rutonsjski	Kadupski	Czuczman	Silva	Gersdorff[1]	Bell	Maseko	Mihailovich	Sautter[1]	Best
3 May	Seattle	Kingdome	0-4	19,360	Hewitt	Rutonsjski	Kadupski	Czuczman	Baptista	Gersdorff	Silva	Maseko	Mihailovich	Sautter	Best
10 May	New England	Spartan Stadium	0-1	12,213	Hewitt	Rutonsjski	Toomey	Czuczman	Lechermann	Sautter	Silva	Maseko	Mihailovich	David	Best
15 May	Edmonton	Spartan Stadium	1-0	10,763	Hewitt	Rutonsjski	Toomey	Czuczman	Kraay	Bell	Maseko	Sautter	Mihailovich	David[1]	Best
17 May	Houston	Spartan Stadium	3-0	13,118	Hewitt	Rutonsjski	Toomey	Czuczman	Kraay	Bell	Maseko	Sautter	Mihailovich	David[3]	Best
24 May	Portland	Civic Stadium	1-2	9,674	Hewitt	Rutonsjski	Toomey	Czuczman	Kraay	Hiddink	Maseko	Sautter	Mihailovich	David	Best
7 June	Vancouver	Spartan Stadium	2-0	15,636	Turner	Rutonsjski	Toomey	Czuczman	Nikolic	Pavlovic	Lechermann	Maseko	Mihailovich	Hiddink	Best
11 June	Detroit	Silverdome	1-0	7,186	Turner	Rutonsjski	Toomey	Czuczman	Nikolic	Pavlovic	Lechermann	Silveira	Mihailovich	David	Best[1]
14 June	Philadelphia	Spartan Stadium	2-1	15,163	Turner	Rutonsjski	Toomey	Czuczman	Nikolic	Licinar	Lechermann	Silveira	Mihailovich	David[1]	Best
17 June	Fort Lauderdale	Lockhart Stadium	0-4	12,295	Turner	Rutonsjski	Toomey	Czuczman	Nikolic	Maseko	Lechermann	Silveira	Mihailovich	David	Best[1]
22 June	Washington	Kennedy Stadium	4-5	14,322	Hewitt	Pavlovic	Toomey	Czuczman	Hiddink	Maseko	Lechermann	Silveira	Mihailovich	Licinar[1]	Best
26 June	Toronto	Exhibition Stadium	2-3	19,224	Hewitt	Rutonsjski	Toomey	Czuczman	Evans	Hiddink	Lechermann	Licinar[1]	Mihailovich	David[1]	Best[1]
29 June	California	Spartan Stadium	5-1	15,421	Turner	Rutonsjski	Toomey	Czuczman	Evans	Hiddink	Lechermann[2]	Maseko	Licinar	David[1]	Best
2 July	Dallas	Spartan Stadium	1-2	40,643	Turner	Rutonsjski	Toomey	Czuczman	Licinar	Hiddink	Lechermann	Maseko	Mihailovich	David	Best
5 July	New England	Schaefer Stadium	1-3	5,130	Turner	Rutonsjski	Toomey	Pavlovic	Nikolic	Kraay	Lechermann	Maseko	Sautter	David[1]	Best
9 July	Tampa Bay	Tampa Stadium	1-4	15,809	Hewitt	Rutonsjski	Toomey	Pavlovic	Nikolic	Kraay	Lechermann	Hunter	Ryan	David	Best
12 July	Atlanta	Fulton County Stad.	2-1	2,483	Turner	Rutonsjski	Hunter	Hiddink	Sautter	Kraay	Lechermann	Licinar	Mihailovich[1]	David[1]	Best
16 July	Tampa Bay	Spartan Stadium	0-3	16,397	Turner	Rutonsjski	Hunter	Czuczman	Nikolic	Kraay	Lechermann	Licinar	Mihailovich	David	Best
19 July	Vancouver	Empire Stadium	1-4	18,161	Hewitt	Rutonsjski	Hunter	Czuczman	Silveira	Pavlovic	Maseko	Licinar	Mihailovich	David[1]	Best
30 July	Memphis	Spartan Stadium	0-1	11,922	Hewitt	Pavlovic	Hunter	Czuczman	Silveira	Nikolic	Lechermann	Hiddink	Mihailovich	David	Best
9 August	Chicago	Chicago	1-4	10,063	Hewitt	Rutonsjski	Hunter	Czuczman	Nikolic	Hiddink	Silveira	Maseko	Mihailovich	David	Best[1]
12 August	Memphis	Liberty Bowl	0-1	7,653	Hewitt	Evans	Hunter	Czuczman	Nikolic	Pavlovic	Silveira	Maseko	Lechermann	Pavlovic	Best
16 August	Portland	Spartan Stadium	2-3	14,287	Hewitt	Rutonsjski	Hunter	Evans	Nikolic	Pavlovic	Silveira	Maseko	Lechermann	David	Best[2]
20 August	San Diego	San Diego Stadium	3-2	15,724	Hewitt	Rutonsjski	Hunter	Evans	Nikolic	Pavlovic	Silveira	Maseko[1]	Lechermann	Perez	Best[1]
23 August	Los Angeles	Spartan Stadium	1-2	16,419	Hewitt	Rutonsjski	Hunter	Evans	Nikolic	Pavlovic	Silveira	Maseko	Lechermann	Perez	Best[1]

SAN JOSE EARTHQUAKES - NASL 1981

DATE	OPPONENT	VENUE	SCORE	ATTD	1	2	3	4	5	6	7	8	9	10	11
29 March	New York	Spartan Stadium	0-3	20,671	Hewitt	Etherington	Rutonsjski	Powell	McAlister	Merrick	Lieinar	Harvath	Crescitelli	David	Best
5 April	Los Angeles	Coliseum	0-1	9,660	Hewitt	Etherington	Rutonsjski	Powell	McAlister	Silveira	Lieinar	Harvath	Crescitelli	David	Best
12 April	Jacksonville	Spartan Stadium	3-0	10,201	Hewitt	Etherington[1]	Rutonsjski	Powell	McAlister	Merrick	Silveira	Harvath	Perez	David[2]	Best[1]
19 April	San Diego	Spartan Stadium	2-1	8,198	Hewitt	Etherington	Rutonsjski	Powell	McAlister	Merrick	Silveira	Harvath	Perez	David	Best[1]
26 April	California	Spartan Stadium	0-1	11,635	Hewitt	Etherington	Rutonsjski	Powell	McAlister	Merrick	Lieinar	Harvath	Silveira	David	Best
2 May	San Diego	Jack Murphy Stad.	2-4	9,107	Hewitt	Etherington	Rutonsjski	Powell	McAlister	Merrick	Silveira	Harvath	Crescitelli[1]	David	Best[1]
6 May	Portland	Civic Stadium	0-3	4,669	Hewitt	Etherington	Hunter	Powell	McAlister	Merrick	Lieinar	Evans	Crescitelli	Silveira	Bst
10 May	Edmonton	Spartan Stadium	1-0	9,325	Hewitt	Etherington	Rutonsjski	Powell	McAlister	Merrick	Lieinar	Liveric	Crescitelli	David[1]	Best
15 May	California	Anaheim Stadium	2-1	25,230	Hewitt	Etherington	Rutonsjski	Powell	McAlister	Harvath[1]	Liveric	Liveric	Crescitelli	David	Best[1]
19 May	Atlanta	Fulton County Stad.	0-2	4,057	Hewitt	Etherington	Rutonsjski	Powell	McAlister	Silveira	Lieinar	Harvath	Liveric	David	Best
24 May	Calgary	McMahon Stadium	0-1	11,433	Hewitt	Etherington	Rutonsjski	Powell	McAlister	Lindsay	Hunter	Harvath	Liveric	David	Best
27 May	Los Angeles	Spartan Stadium	3-2	9,177	Stetter	Etherington	Rutonsjski	Harvath	Lindsay	Merrick	Hunter	Liveric[1]	David	Best	Hunter
31 May	Calgary	Spartan Stadium	4-3	10,627	Hewitt	Etherington	Rutonsjski	Powell	McAlister	Merrick	Lieinar	Lindsay[1]	Perez	David	Best[2]
7 June	Tampa Bay	Spartan Stadium	2-1	16,249	Stetter	Etherington	Rutonsjski	Powell	McAlister	Merrick	Liveric	Harvath[1]	Crescitelli[1]	Lindsay	Best
14 June	Edmonton	Commonwealth Stad.	2-6	9,110	Stetter	Etherington	Rutonsjski	Lindsay	McAlister	Merrick	Liveric[1]	Harvath	Crescitelli	Irving[1]	Best[1]
17 June	Atlanta	Spartan Stadium	3-1	10,648	Stetter	Etherington[1]	Rutonsjski	Powell	McAlister	Merrick	Liveric	Lindsay	Crescitelli[1]	Irving	Best[1]
20 June	Seattle	Kingdome	0-1	17,586	Stetter	Etherington	Rutonsjski	Powell	McAlister	Merrick	Liveric	Harvath	Crescitelli	Irving	Best
24 June	California	Anaheim Stadium	0-7	5,333	Stetter	Etherington	Rutonsjski	Powell	McAlister	Hukic	Liveric	Harvath	Crescitelli	Lindsay	Best
27 June	Los Angeles	Spartan Stadium	1-2	14,326	Parkes	Etherington	Rutonsjski	Powell	McAlister	Hukic	Liveric	Harvath	Crescitelli	Lindsay	Best[1]
1 July	Vancouver	Spartan Stadium	1-5	14,462	Parkes	Etherington	Rutonsjski	Powell	McAlister	Hukic	Liveric	Harvath	Perez	Irving	Best
4 July	Fort Lauderdale	Lockhart Stadium	1-4	18,512	Parkes	Etherington	Hunter	Powell	McAlister	Hukic	Silveira	Harvath	Liveric	Irving	Best
8 July	Tampa Bay	Tampa Stadium	2-4	13,236	Parkes	Etherington	Hunter	Cahill	McAlister	Hukic	Silveira	Harvath	Crescitelli	Irving	Best[1]
11 July	Jacksonville	Gator Bowl	3-4	7,891	Parkes	Etherington	Hunter	Cahill	McAlister	Hukic	Silveira	Harvath	Crescitelli	Irving	Best[1]
15 July	Montreal	Olympic Stadium	0-4	17,649	Parkes	Etherington	Hunter	Cahill	Schultz	Hukic	Silveira	Perez	Crescitelli	Irving	Best
22 July	Fort Lauderdale	Spartan Stadium	3-2	11,629	Parkes	Etherington	Rutonsjski	Cahill	McAlister	Hukic	Lieinar	Harvath	Crescitelli	Silveira	Best[2]
25 July	Los Angeles	Coliseum	0-3	4,467	Parkes	Etherington	Rutonsjski	Cahill	McAlister	Hunter	Lieinar	Harvath	Silveira	Irving	Best
1 August	Portland	Spartan Stadium	1-2	11,166	Parkes	Etherington	Silveira	Powell	McAlister	Hukic	Lieinar	Harvath	Crescitelli	Lindsay	Best[1]
5 August	San Diego	Jack Murphy Stad.	0-3	18,560	Parkes	Etherington	Rutonsjski	Powell	McAlister	Lindsay	Lieinar	Harvath	Crescitelli	Silveira	Best
15 August	San Diego	Spartan Stadium	2-3	14,345	Hewitt	Etherington	Rutonsjski	Powell	McAlister	Hukic	Lieinar	Harvath	Lindsay[1]	Silveira	Best[1]
19 August	Vancouver	Empire Stadium	1-3	27,986	Hewitt	Etherington	Rutonsjski	Powell	McAlister	Hunter	Perez	Perez	Crescitelli	Silveira	Best

HIBERNIAN - Scottish Premier League 1980-81

DATE	OPPONENT	VENUE	SCORE	ATT'D	1	2	3	4	5	6	7	8	9	10	11
9 September	Dundee	Dens Park	2-1	5,304	McArthur	Brown	Duncan	McNamara	Stewart	Callachan	Hamill	Rae¹	MacLeod¹	Jamieson	Best
20 September	Hamilton Academical	Douglas Park	1-1	5,197	McArthur	Brown	Duncan	McNamara	Paterson	Callachan	Jamieson	Rae	MacLeod	Connelly¹	Best
4 October	Dunfermline Athletic	East End Park	2-0	5,650	McArthur	Brown	Duncan	McNamara	Paterson	Callachan	Jamieson	Rae	MacLeod²	Connelly	Best
11 October	Falkirk	Easter Road	2-0	6,947	McArthur	Brown	Duncan	McNamara	Paterson	Callachan	Wilson	Rae	MacLeod¹	Connelly	Best

League Cup

DATE	OPPONENT	VENUE	SCORE	ATT'D	1	2	3	4	5	6	7	8	9	10	11
24 September	Clyde	Easter Road	2-1	3,773	McArthur	Brown	Duncan	McNamara	Paterson	Callachan	Jamieson²	Rae	MacLeod	Connelly	Best
8 October	Ayr United	Somerset Park	2-2	4,717	McArthur	Brown	Duncan	McNamara	Paterson	Callachan	Wilson¹	Rae	MacLeod¹	Connelly	Best

Bournemouth Football League Division Three 1982-83

DATE	OPPONENT	VENUE	SCORE	ATT'D	1	2	3	4	5	6	7	8	9	10	11
2 April	Newport County	Dean Court	0-1	9,121	Leigh	Heffernan	Sulley	Spackman	Brignull	Impey	Best	Beck	Lee	Nightingale	Dawtry
9 April	Chesterfield	Dean Court	2-1	5,227	Leigh	Heffernan	Sulley	Spackman	Brignull	Impey	Best	Beck¹	Morgan¹	Lee	Nightingale
16 April	Southend United	Roots Hall	0-0	4,608	Leigh	Heffernan	Sulley	Spackman	Brignull	Impey	Best	Beck	Morgan	Lee	Nightingale
23 April	Lincoln City	Dean Court	1-0	5,010	Leigh	Heffernan	Sulley	Spackman	Brignull	Impey	Best	Beck	Morgan	Lee	Nightingale
7 May	Wigan Athletic	Dean Court	2-2	4,523	Leigh	Heffernan	Sulley	Spackman	Brignull	Impey	Best	Shaw	Morgan	Lee	Nightingale¹

NORTHERN IRELAND 1964-1977

DATE	OPPONENT	VENUE	SCORE	ATT'D	1	2	3	4	5	6	7	8	9	10	11
15 April 1964	Wales	Ninian Park	2-3												
29 April 1964	Uruguay	Windsor Park	3-0												
3 October 1964	England	Windsor Park	3-4	58,000	Jennings	Magill	Elder	Harvey	Neill	McCullough	Best	Crossan	Wilson¹	McLaughlin²	Braithwaite
14 October 1964	Switzerland	Windsor Park	1-0	28,598	Jennings	Magill	Elder	Harvey	Neill	McCullough	Best	Crossan¹	Wilson	McLaughlin	Braithwaite
14 November 1964	Switzerland	Lausanne	1-2	22,162	Jennings	Magill	Elder	Harvey	Campbell	Parke	Best¹	Crossan	Irvine	McLaughlin	Braithwaite
25 November 1964	Scotland	Hampden Park	2-3	49,633	Jennings	Magill	Elder	Harvey	Neill	Parke	Best¹	Humphries	Irvine¹	Crossan	Braithwaite

Date	Opponent	Venue	Score	Att.	1	2	3	4	5	6	7	8	9	10	11
17 March 1965	Holland	Windsor Park	2-1	40.000	Briggs	Parke	Elder	Harvey	Neill¹	Nicholson	Humphries	Crossan¹	Irvine	Clements	Best
7 April 1965	Holland	Rotterdam	0-0	61.954	Jennings	Magill	Elder	Harvey	Neill	Parke	Best	Crossan	Irvine	Nicholson	Braithwaite
7 May 1965	Albania	Windsor Park	4-1	16.017	Jennings	Magill	Elder	Harvey	Neill	Parke	Humphries	Humphries	Irvine	Nicholson	**Best¹**
2 October 1965	Scotland	Windsor Park	3-2	50.000	Jennings	Magill	Elder	Harvey	Neill	Nicholson	Humphries¹	**Crossan³**	Irvine¹	**Dougan¹**	Best
10 November 1965	England	Wembley	1-2	70.000	Jennings	Magill	Elder	Harvey	Neill	Nicholson	McIlroy	Crossan¹	**Irvine¹**	Dougan	Best
24 November 1965	Albania	Tirana	1-1	16.381	Jennings	Magill	Elder	Harvey	Neill	Nicholson	McIlroy	Crossan	**Irvine¹**	Dougan	Best
22 October 1966	England	Windsor Park	0-2	48.600	Jennings	Parke	Elder	Todd	Harvey	McCullough	McIlroy	Crossan	Irvine	Dougan	Best
21 October 1967	Scotland	Windsor Park	1-0	55.000	Jennings	McKeag	Parke	Stewart	Neill	Campbell	Ferguson	Crossan	Dougan	Nicholson	Best
23 October 1968	Turkey	Windsor Park	4-1	38.363	Jennings	Craig	Harvey	Nicholson	Neill	**Clements¹**	Campbell	**McMordie¹**	**Dougan¹**	Irvine	**Best¹**
3 May 1969	England	Windsor Park	1-3	23.000	Jennings	Craig	Harvey	Todd	Neill	Clements	Campbell¹	Jackson	Dougan	Irvine	Best
6 May 1969	Scotland	Hampden Park	1-1	7.483	Jennings	Craig	Elder	Todd	Neill	Nicholson	Campbell¹	**McMordie¹**	Dougan	Jackson	Clements
10 May 1969	Wales	Windsor Park	0-0	12.500	Jennings	Craig	Elder	Todd	Neill	Nicholson	**McMordie¹**	McMordie	Dougan	Jackson	Clements
10 September 1969	USSR	Windsor Park	0-0	36.000	Jennings	Rice	Clements	Todd	Neill	Nicholson	Best	McMordie	Dougan	Clements	Best
18 April 1970	Scotland	Windsor Park	0-1	31.000	Jennings	Rice	Clements	Todd	Neill	Nicholson	Best	McMordie	Dougan	McMordie	Best
21 April 1970	England	Wembley	1-3	100.000	Jennings	Craig	Clements	O'Kane	Neill	Nicholson	Campbell	Lutton	Dougan	O'Doherty	Lutton
25 April 1970	Wales	Vetch Field	0-1	28.000	McFaul	Craig	Nelson	O'Kane	Neill	Nicholson	Campbell	McMordie	Dickson	McMordie	Clements
11 November 1970	Spain	Seville	0-3	26.215	McFaul	Craig	Nelson	Jackson	Neill	O'Kane	**Best¹**	Best	Dougan	Harkin	Clements
3 February 1971	Cyprus	Nicosia	3-0	9.119	Jennings	Craig	Clements	Hunter	Hunter	Todd	Campbell	Best	McMordie	Dougan	**Best¹**
21 April 1971	Cyprus	Windsor Park	5-0	19.153	Jennings	Craig	Nelson	Harvey	Hunter	Todd	Sloan	McMordie	**Dougan¹**	**Nicholson¹**	**Best³**
15 May 1971	England	Windsor Park	0-1	33.000	Jennings	Rice	Nelson	O'Kane	Hunter	Nicholson	Hamilton	McMordie	**Dougan¹**	**Nicholson¹**	Best
18 May 1971	Scotland	Hampden Park	1-0	31.643	Jennings	Rice	Nelson	O'Kane	Hunter	Nicholson	Hamilton	McMordie	Dougan	Clements	Best
22 May 1971	Wales	Windsor Park	1-0	20.000	Jennings	Rice	Nelson	O'Kane	Hunter	Nicholson	Hamilton	McMordie	Dougan	Clements	Best
22 September 1971	USSR	Moscow	0-1	51.186	McFaul	Craig	Hunter	Hunter	Neill	Hegan	**Hamilton¹**	Nicholson	O'Kane	Clements	Best
16 February 1971	Spain	Boothferry Park	1-1	19.925	Jennings	Rice	Nelson	Hunter	Neill	Clements	Clements	McMordie	**Morgan¹**	Dougan	Best
18 October 1972	Bulgaria	Sofia	0-3	60.000	Jennings	Rice	Nelson	Neill	Hunter	Clements	Hamilton	Hegan	Dougan	McIlroy	Best
14 September 1973	Portugal	Lisbon	1-1	3.000	Jennings	Rice	Craig	Lutton	Hunter	Clements	Hamilton	O'Neill	Morgan	McMordie	Best
13 October 1976	Holland	Rotterdam	2-2	56.000	Jennings	Nicholl	Rice	Jackson	O'Kane¹	Jackson	Jackson	McIlroy	**McGrath¹**	Anderson	Anderson
10 November 1976	Belgium	Liege	0-2	25.081	Jennings	Nicholl	Rice	Jackson	Hunter	Hamilton	Best	McIlroy	McGrath	McCreery	Anderson
27 April 1977	West Germany	Cologne	0-5	58.000	Jennings	Rice	Nelson	Jackson	Hunter	Hamilton	Best	McGrath	Armstrong	McCreery	Anderson
21 September 1977	Iceland	Windsor Park	2-0	15.000	Jennings	Rice	Nelson	Nicholl	Hunter	McCreery	**McGrath¹**	Best	**McIlroy¹**	O'Neill	Anderson
12 October 1977	Holland	Windsor Park	0-1	33.000	Jennings	Rice	Nelson	Nicholl	Hunter	O'Neill	McGrath	Best	McIlroy	McCreery	Anderson

THE END

The George Best story was always likely to end in tears. This time they were shed by friends, family and football fans throughout the world following the Irishman's sad demise in November 2005.

George's life seemed to have become a cautionary tale years before he actually died. But his passing led to an outpouring of emotion in British society that few figures have inspired. Comparisons with the death of Princess Diana were made at the time but somehow George's death touched ordinary people in a way Diana's failed to. The outpouring of grief that followed the former's death reached a mawkishness that many regarded with alarm, with George there wasn't so much anguish as celebration and pride that his talent had been allowed to flourish in English football.

For once the barriers between clubs didn't seem so vast as football supporters of all persuasions made a pilgramage to Sir Matt Busby Way to add to the ever-growing shrine to a man who was hailed the greatest British footballer of all time.

This isn't the place to debate George's standing in the pantheon of great footballers, however opposite is a statisical overview of his career.

Manchester United	League	FAC	LC	Europe	Other	Total
1963-64	17 (4)	7 (2)	-	2 (0)	-	26 (6)
1964-65	41 (10)	7 (2)	-	11 (2)	-	59 (14)
1965-66	31 (9)	5 (3)	-	6 (4)	1 (1)	43 (17)
1966-67	42 (10)	2 (0)	1 (0)	-	-	45 (10)
1967-68	41 (28)	2 (1)	-	9 (3)	1 (0)	53 (32)
1968-69	41 (19)	6 (1)	-	6 (2)	2 (0)	55 (22)
1969-70	37 (15)	8 (6)	8 (1)	-	-	52 (23)
1970-71	40 (18)	2 (1)	6 (2)	-	-	48 (22)
1971-72	40 (18)	7 (5)	6 (3)	-	-	53 (27)
1972-73	19 (4)	-	4 (2)	-	-	23 (6)
1973-74	12 (2)	-	-	-	-	12(2)
TOTAL (1963-74)	**360 (137)**	**46 (21)**	**25 (8)**	**34 (11)**	**4 (1)**	**470 (179)**

Stockport County	League	FAC	LC	Europe	Other	Total
1975-76	3 (2)	-	-	-	-	3 (2)
Fulham						
1976-77	31 (7)	-	-	-	-	31 (7)
1977-78	10 (3)	-	-	-	-	10 (3)

LA Aztecs	NASL	Play-Offs	Total
1976	23 (13)	1	24 (13)
1977	20 (11)	5 (2)	25 (13)
1978	12	-	12
TOTAL (1976-78)	**55 (24)**	**6 (2)**	**61 (26)**
FL Strikers			
1978	9 (3)	5 (2)	14 (5)
1979	11 (1)	-	11 (1)
TOTAL (1978-79)	**20 (4)**	**5 (2)**	**25 (6)**
San Jose Earthquakes			
1980	26 (8)	-	26 (8)
1981	30 (13)	-	30 (13)
TOTAL (1980-81)	**56 (21)**	**-**	**56 (21)**
TOTAL (1976-81)	**131 (49)**	**11 (4)**	**142 (53)**

AND NUMBER ONE WAS GEORGIE BEST...

In the days following George's death, there was a brief debate as to whether the club would retire his shirt number. The common consensus seemed to be that George's number 7 (worn subsequently by such luminaries as Bryan Robson, Eric Cantona, David Beckham and incumbent Cristiano Ronaldo) should be retired as a mark of respect.

There were a number of reasons why this American approach to revering past stars was resisted. For a start, it's never been done before and if we start retiring numbers there would be none left between 1 and 11 at a club like United. Secondly, Best was such an adaptable forward that he played all across the forward line, appearing in shirt numbers 7, 8, 9, 10 and 11 throughout his United career - so which would you choose?

Arguably the shirt number with which he was most associated was number 11 rather than number 7, following in the footsteps of the likes of Charlie Mitten, David Pegg, Albert Scanlon and Bobby Charlton. Indeed such was Best's success and unique ability, that the number 11 was often regarded as a poisoned chalice by a succession of wingers including fellow team-mate Willie Morgan. It could be claimed that no one had quite filled the Irishman's boots until Ryan Giggs emergence in the early 1990s.

Then again many of Best's finest moments also came when he was wearing the number 8 as an inside-left, I refer in particular to a famous goal scored against Chelsea where 'Chopper' Harris failed to poleaxe the Irishman as Best weaved his way through the gloaming to score a match-winning League Cup goal.

In any case, here is a comprehensive breakdown:

	7	8	9	10	11
1963-4	10	-	-	-	16 (6)
1964-5	-	-	-	1	58 (14)
1965-6	29 (13)	6 (3)	-	2 (1)	6
1966-7	32 (9)	1	-	-	12 (1)
1967-8	38 (26)	-	-	11 (6)	4
1968-9	11 (1)	2	1 (1)	-	41 (20)
1969-70	4 (1)	5	-	2	41 (21)
1970-71	4 (3)	26 (10)	-	-	28 (9)
1971-72	7 (2)	2 (1)	-	5 (6)	39 (18)
1972-73	5 (1)	-	-	18 (5)	-
1973-74	-	-	-	-	12 (2)
Total	139 (55)	41 (14)	1 (1)	38 (18)	257 (91)

COME ON, THEN
*A classic Best image, George beckons reluctant defenders to challenge him
during a game against Ispwich at Old Trafford in 1969.*

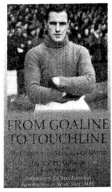

The Insider's Guide to
MANCHESTER UNITED

CANDID PROFILES OF EVERY RED DEVIL FROM ROWLEY TO ROONⁿ

BY JOHN DOHERTY WITH IVAN PONTING
FOREWORD BY PADDY CRERAND
ISBN: 1901746410 - £20 - Hardback
Over 300 photographs - 384 pp

CONTAINING THE LATE JOHN DOHERTY'S SUBJECTIVE views on each of the 348 men to the end of season 2004-05 who have played for the club at senior level since the war, The Insider's Guide To Manchester United is the definitive Manchester United players' guide. Documenting every player to have appeared for the Red Devils since the war, Doherty (an original Busby Babe and chairman of the United Former Players' committee) candidly reveals the strengths, weaknesses and his personal memories of United's finest.

THE INSIDER'S GUIDE TO MANCHESTER UNITED provides an in-depth look at both the significant and fleeting careers that have graced Manchester United. Alongside Ivan Ponting's comprehensive statistical analysis for each player, the entries will appear in debut order, offering an alternative chronology of the club while Doherty's comments will offer a former professional's view of the players involved.

COMPLETIST'S DELIGHT
THE FULL EMPIRE BACK LIST

ISBN	Title	Author	Price
1901746003	SF Barnes: His Life and Times	A Searle	£14.95
1901746011	Chasing Glory	R Grillo	£7.95
190174602X	Three Curries and a Shish Kebab	R Bott	£7.99
1901746038	Seasons to Remember	D Kirkley`	£6.95
1901746046	Cups For Cock-Ups+	A Shaw	£8.99
1901746054	Glory Denied	R Grillo	£8.95
1901746062	Standing the Test of Time	B Alley	£16.95
1901746070	The Encyclopaedia of Scottish Cricket	D Potter	£9.99
1901746089	The Silent Cry	J MacPhee	£7.99
1901746097	The Amazing Sports Quiz Book	F Brockett	£6.99
1901746100	I'm Not God, I'm Just a Referee	R Entwistle	£7.99
1901746119	The League Cricket Annual Review 2000	ed. S. Fish	£6.99
1901746143	Roger Byrne - Captain of the Busby Babes	I McCartney	£16.95
1901746151	The IT Manager's Handbook	D Miller	£24.99
190174616X	Blue Tomorrow	M Meehan	£9.99
1901746178	Atkinson for England	G James	£5.99
1901746186	Think Cricket	C Bazalgette	£6.00
1901746194	The League Cricket Annual Review 2001	ed. S. Fish	£7.99
1901746208	Jock McAvoy - Fighting Legend *	B Hughes	£9.95
1901746216	The Tommy Taylor Story*	B Hughes	£8.99
1901746224	Willie Pep*+	B Hughes	£9.95
1901746232	For King & Country*+	B Hughes	£8.95
1901746240	Three In A Row	P Windridge	£7.99
1901746259	Viollet - Life of a legendary goalscorer+PB	R Cavanagh	£16.95
1901746267	Starmaker	B Hughes	£16.95
1901746283	Morrissey's Manchester	P Gatenby	£5.99
1901746305	The IT Manager's Handbook (e-book)	D Miller	£17.99
1901746313	Sir Alex, United & Me	A Pacino	£8.99
1901746321	Bobby Murdoch, Different Class	D Potter	£10.99
190174633X	Goodison Maestros	D Hayes	£5.99
1901746348	Anfield Maestros	D Hayes	£5.99
1901746364	Out of the Void	B Yates	£9.99
1901746356	The King - Denis Law, hero of the...	B Hughes	£17.95
1901746372	The Two Faces of Lee Harvey Oswald	G B Fleming	£8.99
1901746380	My Blue Heaven	D Friend	£10.99
1901746399	Viollet - life of a legendary goalscorer	B Hughes	£11.99
1901746402	Quiz Setting Made Easy	J Dawson	£7.99
1901746410	The Insider's Guide to Manchester United	J Doherty	£20
1901746437	Catch a Falling Star	N Young	£17.95
1901746453	Birth of the Babes	T Whelan	£12.95
190174647X	Back from the Brink	J Blundell	£10.95
1901746488	The Real Jason Robinson	D Swanton	£17.95
1901746496	This Simple Game	K Barnes	£14.95
1901746518	The Complete George Best	D Phillips	£10.95
1901746526	From Goalline to Touch line	J Crompton	£16.95
1901746534	Sully	A Sullivan	£8.95

* Originally published by Collyhurst & Moston Lads Club

+ Out of print PB Superceded by Paperback edition

To order any of these books email: enquiries@empire-uk.com or call 0161 972 3319